BRITISH GOVERNMENT
AND ADMINISTRATION

S. B. CHRIMES

BRITISH GOVERNMENT AND ADMINISTRATION

STUDIES PRESENTED TO
S. B. CHRIMES

Edited by
H. Hearder and H. R. Loyn

CARDIFF
UNIVERSITY OF WALES PRESS
1974

© *University of Wales Press, 1974*

ISBN 0 7083 0538 5

*Printed in Great Britain
at the University Press, Oxford
by Vivian Ridler
Printer to the University*

Contents

Contents

Preface

THIS book, which has direct bearing on the actions of British government and administration, has been written by some of Professor Chrimes's colleagues and friends to mark the occasion of his retirement from the Chair of History at Cardiff. Professor Chrimes was a student at King's College, London, and later at Trinity College, Cambridge. He won the Alexander Medal of the Royal Historical Society in 1934, and held the posts of Lecturer and Reader in Constitutional History at the University of Glasgow from 1936 to 1953. He was a temporary principal at the Ministry of Labour and National Service, 1940–5. He has held the Chair of History, and Headship of Department, at Cardiff for the past twenty-one years. For the whole of this period Professor Chrimes has also been Acting Head of the Department of Welsh History, and some of these essays deal directly with the history of Wales. The book has a unity of its own, for the Studies concern themes relevant to Professor Chrimes's personal interest in the exercise of government, and the only sadness is that the plan has inevitably excluded many other colleagues and friends from contributing to the volume. On their behalf as well as on our own we wish to offer this book as a tribute to a scholar who has enlightened and enlivened generations of students by his writings and by his skill as a teacher. Although Professor Chrimes has taught widely in constitutional history, his reputation as a scholar rests above all on his authoritative and perceptive contribution to fifteenth- and early sixteenth-century British history, culminating in his fine biography of Henry VII. Integrity, massive common sense, and a strong awareness of reality are the qualities which pervade his writing, and which he communicated to all with whom he had dealings from the most senior colleague to the humblest first-year student. We congratulate him on a memorable and distinguished term of office, and present this book in gratitude for his friendship and scholarship and with our good wishes for his present and future work.

We wish, as editors, to thank all other contributors for their co-operation, and also for their patience in accepting the degree of standardization which we have had to impose in the matter of footnotes, format, and general arrangement. We also wish to thank Miss Patricia Warren for her help, generously given, to the typing and general secretarial arrangement of the volume.

All contributors are grateful to the officers of the University of Wales Press for the care and attention to detail which they have shown in the production of this book, and we wish especially to thank Dr. R. Brinley Jones for his active and constructive support at all stages of this venture.

H. HEARDER
H. R. LOYN

List of Abbreviations used in this volume

We do not include obvious contractions

B.I.H.R.	*Bulletin of the Institute of Historical Research*
B.M.(Add. Ch.)	British Museum: Additional Charters
C.C.R.	*Calendar of Close Rolls*
C.F.R.	*Calendar of Fine Rolls*
C.J.	*Commons Journals*
C.P.R.	*Calendar of Patent Rolls*
C.T.B.	*Calendar of Treasury Books*
D.K.R.	*Deputy Keeper's Report*
Econ.H.R.	*Economic History Review*
E.H.R.	*English Historical Review*
F.O.	Foreign Office
Hist. MSS. Comm.	Historical Manuscripts Commission
H.O.	Home Office
Lib. El.	*Liber Eliensis*
L.J.	*Lords Journals*
N.L.W.	National Library of Wales
O.U.P.	Oxford University Press
Parl. Pap.	*Parliamentary Papers*
P.C.C.	Prerogative Court of Canterbury
P.P.C.	*Proceedings and Ordinances of the Privy Council of England*
P.R.O.	Public Record Office
RA	Royal Archives
Rot. Parl.	*Rotuli Parliamentorum*
Scottish H.R.	*Scottish Historical Review*
Trans. Cym. Soc.	*Transactions of the Cymmrodorion Society*
W.H.R.	*Welsh History Review*

The Hundred in England in the Tenth and Early Eleventh Centuries

H. R. LOYN

I
N a volume which has as its main theme the effect of government on the inner workings of society it is altogether appropriate that some attention should be paid to the early history of the hundred. For many centuries the hundred court represented the practical limit of judicial knowledge for the bulk of the population. To the peasant in Devon, in Shropshire, more so still north of the Welland and Trent, the king's court had already become remote by 1066. Even the shire court was a special institution with a selective attendance, a big social event in the lives of the community, and often associated with a synod, formal or informal, when the bishop and his clergy descended on the shire town. The period from the death of Alfred in 899 to the Norman Conquest was the time when the full importance of the hundred was firmly established. From then continuously until the fourteenth century with only spasmodic moments of doubt and hesitation its institutional life flourished. Only in the later Middle Ages did the hundred lose its influence to new forms and procedures.

We face an initial problem because of the inbuilt ambiguity of the term 'hundred'. By the middle of the tenth century it had come to mean at least two separate and yet closely connected things. It was a territorial division, a part of a shire, and as such in constant use to describe a basic administrative unit in the community: only in parts of the Danelaw was the Scandinavian term 'wapentake' used in its place. The hundred was also a court, presided over under normal circumstances by a hundred-man, who could also be a king's reeve, and as a court it appears in the records independently of the territorial neighbourhood it served. A similar dual function was enjoyed at a higher level by the term 'shire', and the use of Latin, accentuated after the Norman Conquest, often brought further complexity into the proceedings with the result that it is not always clear whether the drafter of a document meant the territorial unit or a court when he referred to a *comitatus* or a *scir* or a *centenarium* or a *hundret*.

Further problems again arise when we consider the question of the nature of the geographical unit we know as the hundred. To call a hundred a subdivision of a shire is accurate but not immensely helpful when we appreciate the extraordinary diversity in size, ranging from the minute hundreds of Sussex and Kent (special areas it is true) through the modest-sized hundreds such as Hamfordshoe in Northamptonshire with its 26 square miles or so, to the hundred of Holt in Norfolk, extending over some 65 square miles. These territorial areas themselves were flexible, more inclined to change and to suffer distortion than most territorial divisions of this nature. The reasons for this diversity are historical. Whatever the ultimate origin in the Germanic and Celtic (but not the Roman) past, the hundred as a regular administrative unit owed its continuous history in England to Wessex, and it is precisely in the West Saxon lands that we meet the greatest diversities in shape and size. Within greater Wessex the ancient kingdoms of Sussex and Kent form a special case again, and there hundreds could be extremely small, embracing no more than two or three villages. The situation is analogous to that of the larger unit, the shire, another West Saxon creation and imposition. By the side of the variety and lack of consistency of the West Saxon shires and hundreds, the relative uniformity of the units in midland England testifies to their artificiality. Tenth-century England was in this respect—though not in all— Wessex writ large.

The elements of artificiality in the midland shires with their round number of hides of assessment, grouped around a central stronghold which (Danish or English) gave its name to the shire, are well known. Dependence on fortress towns remained so much a feature of the midland territories that some historians ascribe the achievement of full uniformity in the shiring pattern to the reign of Ethelred rather than that of Edward the Elder. This seems unnecessary. In all matters essential to the existence of a shire, including the institution of a regular court at the shire town, the Midlands had followed the West Saxon example by the end of the reign of Edgar. A similar tidiness, pointing to West Saxon imposition in the first half of the tenth century, can also be discerned at the hundredal level. In many of the midland shires the hundreds continued to be assessed at about one hundred hides for purposes of taxation as late as the reign of William I, and constant references to double hundreds (of 200 hides) and half hundreds (of fifty hides) indicate that the division was still thought of in these terms. The term *scir* itself, of course, still continued in use to describe a sphere of office, and as such gave rise to a proliferation of smaller 'shires', notably in the north of England, extending into Scotland itself.

Assessment to taxation in the midland shires is a pointer to the authoritarian nature of the new kingdom of England. It is also a significant characteristic of the institution of the hundred: a hundred was initially to be assessed at a hundred hides. This does not mean that tax was the prime reason of being of the hundred. Questions of origins are so often complex and can rarely be resolved by simple answers. Institutions called hundreds were not peculiar to England nor indeed to the Germanic world. On the Continent the existence of the hundred in the area covered by the Carolingian empire has led to hard discussion of nature and origin. The tendency now is to attribute origin in recognizable continuous institutional shape to Carolingian enterprise. The contrast then between the native Frankish lands where the hundreds exhibited an astonishing variety in shape and size, and the imperial lands among the Alemani and Suabians with their greater regularity makes a curious parallel on a bigger scale and a century earlier to that between tenth-century Wessex and Mercia. Only in Carolingian days did the *centenarius* take on clear judicial functions. This is not to deny some institutional life at the hundredal level in earlier centuries. Where there was complex tenure by individual and by kindred, a land-tax, hidage, or a system of assessment, there was certain to be occasional dispute that demanded local knowledge and local courts. It is one of the unsolved and possibly insoluble problems of European and English history to determine at what precise moment in time the tribunal at which such disputes were settled, the *mallus*, or folk-court, or popular court, came to take on the attributes we recognize in our traditional hundred courts.

In the English context it is likely that this process took place during the first half of the tenth century. There is no specific reference to such assemblies in the laws of Alfred nor in the associated laws of Ine, important negative evidence when it is considered that the Alfredian law code was intended as a thorough statement of law at a particularly critical moment in the growth of the English state. The most we find are references to charges brought in public meetings before a king's reeve (Alf. 22)[1] and to traders establishing their identity and number at such public meetings so that they could be brought to account if anything went wrong with their ventures (Alf. 34). Penalties were decreed for disturbances made at such public meetings in the presence of the ealdorman or his deputy (Alf. 38). For those who see the main line of descent in our administrative units as an extension of the authority of royal reeves at royal manors over public tribunals these are important statements, but they are not immediately recognizable as apposite to the development of the tenth-century hundred. Declarations of law made by Alfred's son, Edward the Elder, are more forthcoming. Edward was faced with a massive task of reorganization after his succession extension of West Saxon lordship over West Mercia and the Danish armies of the east. Late in his reign he issued two important and associated pieces of legislation that we know as *I Edward* and *II Edward*. The first code was published in the form of ordinances or general instructions to the king's servants (his reeves), who were to see that justice according to the principles of folkright was not lacking to anyone because of faults of procedure and lack of true witness. The second code was the more formal pronouncement of the two. It was made at Exeter with the advice of the witan, and represented a determined effort to establish good peace, based on Alfred's doom-book, throughout Edward's kingdom. Theft was the principal concern, especially cattle-theft. Royal reeves were the key agents in an attempted tightening up of royal supervision of folklaw, and the fine for disobedience to the king the principal instrument. The decrees were to apply to the lands lying to the east (East Anglia) and to the north (Northumbria) as well as to the English heartlands. The final statement (II Ed. 8) made at this assembly at Exeter was of great moment

---

[1] References to legal clauses are given in standard abbreviated form to the name of the king and the numbering of the clauses as given in F. Liebermann, *Die Gesetze der Angelsachsen*, i, Hallé, 1903: editions by F. L. Attenborough and A. J. Robertson (Cambridge, 1922 and 1925) and the translations by D. Whitelock, *English Historical Documents*, vol. i, London, 1955, 357–439, have also been consulted.

in the history of local administration in England, especially so in the light of the expressed far-ranging nature of the decrees;

> Each reeve was to hold a meeting (*gemot*) every four weeks, and to see to it that every man was worthy of his folk-right, and that each law-suit should have a day appointed for hearing and settlement (*ende 7 andagan hwænne hit forðcume*).

The reeve was to see to this under pain of penalty of fine for disobedience. The clause represents a conscientious attempt to put the iron of royal discipline into the fabric of popular courts.

It will be noticed, however, that these courts were not referred to as hundred courts. Interpretation of their function depends greatly on the weight we attach to the phrase 'worthy of his folk-right'. It could be that Edward was ordering his reeves, his officers in charge of royal estates, to make sure that all freemen on the royal estates were lawworthy and responsible for their actions, as freemen should be, at the full courts of the shire or *regio*. The nature of the document II Edward, a solemn declaration in the witan at Exeter, the precedent of Alfred's reign, and the concern of the contents with the establishment of a general peace speak against this view. It would be multiplying entities beyond what is reasonable to suggest that Edward was ordering his chief estate-managers to hold monthly courts to ensure that his tenants were fit to perform their proper legal function in a network of undefined popular courts. The simplest explanation is probably the most accurate, that is to say that Edward the Elder, faced with the specific problem of cattle-theft, and the more general problem of establishing a general peace over an area of diversified tradition and experience, ordered his chosen servants to regularize district meetings in convenient territorial divisions to ensure (in the terms of his father's (King Alfred's) will) that each man could obtain his folkright (*þæt folcriht arehton*). Emphasis on the need for proper procedures—the monthly meeting, the allotment of precise days for the hearing and settlement of disputes, and insistence on law-worthiness on the part of the suitors—points firmly in this direction. Evidence for the permanent regularization of courts in districts known as hundreds (or wapentakes in the Danish areas) if not for the creation of our historic hundred courts, *eo nomine*, is stronger for Edward the Elder than has always been allowed.

Certainly his successors, notably Athelstan, continued to legislate as if the presence of permanent courts in the localities was one of the basic facts in English institutional life. From Athelstan's Grately decrees alone (II Ath.) it can be seen that Athelstan relied heavily on his reeves, operating in public courts. In a section of these decrees, dealing primarily with boroughs (II Ath. 12. 20), importance was attributed to the witness of reeves in a public court (*folc-gemot*), and arrangements for the summons of such meetings were safeguarded by the levying of fines for failing to attend a *gemot* three times (II Ath. 20), and by the decree that notice of meeting was to be given seven days before it was to take place (II Ath. 20). The king's peace was to be proclaimed in a *gemot* (II Ath. 20. 3), and the importance of such meetings was implied throughout the code by the emphasis on the value of oaths, ordeal, and the process of vouching to warranty, all of which demanded the active use of some such tribunal. The key men again were reeves and they were to be subject to the fine for disobedience if they failed to carry out the king's ordinances zealously, with the bishop of the diocese empowered to exact the fine. It is true, indeed, that these references to courts are in one sense distressingly vague, but certainly the impression is given that they concern an area somewhat less than a shire. At Exeter again (can it be that the peaceful south-west was the most suitable place for reflection or mayhem and violence?) Athelstan decreed further measures against theft (V Ath.) which bring us a little nearer the historic hundred court. The reeve was specially empowered to nominate trustworthy witnesses within his district (V Ath. 1. 5: *manung*) in a context which implied a relatively small territorial area. The climax of Athelstan's peace-keeping efforts concerned, however, his efforts to establish effective peace in London and the district around London, and it is with these efforts that we must now concern ourselves.

Athelstan's ordinance of the bishops and reeves of the London district (VI Ath.) was an extraordinary document, prepared to deal with an extraordinary situation. The bishops and reeves of the London district had formed a peace-guild to implement and supplement the tremendous national efforts made by the king and witan at Grately, at Exeter, at Faversham, and at Thunderfield. There is a sense of urgency about the proceedings which may well suggest archiepiscopal or episcopal initiative. The first ten decrees described the organization of the peace-guild and the detailed actions expected of it in its efforts to suppress theft. The eleventh clause consists of a royal exhortation and command to keep the peace with a characteristic threat of deprivation of office for any reeve neglecting his duty. Clause 12 was a postscript, added after the king had spoken to his councillors at Whittlebury. It casts a humane light on the king who rejected the harshness of the death-penalty suggested for all those over 12 years of age, raised the age in question to 15, and ordered that no one should lose his life for a theft of property worth less than twelve pence. Two clauses throw special light on the antecedents of the hundred court. The third clause decreed that freemen shall be banded together into groups of ten (our first specific reference to tithings) with a senior in charge of each group, that each group of ten tithings shall again be banded together into a hundred, and that each head of a tithing together with one hundredman shall be banded together into a company of eleven men who were to have charge of the quite complicated accounting system of the hundred, as it is now called. These are not, of course, our territorial hundreds. It was indeed expressly ordered in connection with the arrangements for chasing cattle-thieves that a man was to be provided from *two* tithings in areas where the population was large and only *one* tithing where the population was sparse. But the busyness of the reeve in the whole organization and the constant references to territorial divisions within which men band themselves together to set out on the trail of thieves (VI Ath. 1. 84, for example) indicate the reality, and also in the London district the complexity, of institutional development below the shire level. The other clause that throws possible light on hundredal growth is the decree (VI Ath. 8. 1) that we (presumably the archbishop or bishop), the hundred men, and those who had charge of the tithing were to meet once a month to review progress (if time can be found for such meetings in a busy life) and to dine together. Personal groupings of chosen men, with the reeves acting as active agents, were to supplement the ordinary peace-keeping institutions of the community.

The agitation which prompted Athelstan's restless seeking after peace continued throughout the decades which followed his death. At some time during these decades, possibly in the very earliest years of Edgar's reign but equally possibly in the early forties during the reign of Edmund, there was issued an ordinance which is universally recognized as fundamental to our understanding of the legal history of the English hundred, the so-called Hundred Ordinance, found in manuscript in association with two other short texts, *Blaseras* (Incendiaries) and *Forfang* (Legal Seizure), both of which deal with details of legal procedure, *Blaseras* with the ordeal, *Forfang* with an attempt to standardize penalties whether the offences involved activity in one shire or more. The Ordinance itself laid down that the hundred should meet every four weeks, and that each man should do justice to other men there. A reference back to the organization into hundreds and tithings in pursuit of thieves is reminiscent of the arrangements made by the Londoners during Athelstan's reign, though our law code referred specifically to justice done on a thief, as Edmund decreed it. Most of the substance of the ordinance is further strongly reminiscent of the London decrees; the value of the stolen property was to be given to the owner on recovery, and the rest of the offender's property was to be divided into two parts, half for the hundred and half for the lord. If slaves were involved in the property, they were to pass to the lord. Any proved opposition to the hundred was to be punished by a series of financial penalties which reflect the delicate balance between corporate responsibility on the part of the hundred and effective physical power which was so often in the hands of a personal lord, an ealdorman or thegn. For the first offence a fine of 30*d.* was to be paid to the hundred. On a second occasion 30*d.* was to pass to the hundred and 30*d.* to the lord. The penalty was raised to half a pound (120*d.*, presumably again in proportion of 60*d.* to the hundred and 60*d.* to the lord) for the third offence, and after that the offender stood to forfeit all that he owned and to be outlawed. Emphasis was placed on the active authority of the hundred-man and of the tithingmen: without the participation of at least one among them the process of vouching to warranty (*team*) was incomplete. The hundred-man was to be directly responsible for following the trail of a thief, and neglect was to be punished by a fine of thirty shillings to the king. Simple compensation was to be exacted from any guarantor if an accused fled from justice, but if the guarantor abetted the escape (and so laid himself open to the charge of *flymena fyrmth*) he was to clear himself according to the custom of the district. The Ordinances finished with a clause reminiscent of Edward the Elder's decree on popular courts (II Edw. 8). It was stated that in the hundred as in any other court, common law should be enjoined in every suit (*þæt man folcriht getæce æt ælcere spæce*), and that a day should be appointed when that can be carried out (*7 andagie, hwænne man þæt gelæste*).

For all its occasional ambiguities and doubtful statements the Hundred Ordinance represented an important stage in the evolution of permanent institutions of government in England. The ordinance was royal, and represented in basic constitutional terms an assertion on the part of the king of the means by which good order could be maintained in the localities with special concern for the prevention of the evils of cattle-rustling and cattle-raiding. The direct responsibility of the hundred-man to help the posse from a neighbouring hundred on the penalty of a 30*s.* fine to the king and the invocation of the penalty of outlawry for noncompliance in the activities of the hundred (unless the king permitted him to stay in the land) illumine the direct contacts between the king and the hundred. Self-help, if not self-government, at the king's command stands revealed in this tenth-century ordinance.

Legislative activity during the later Anglo-Saxon period built on and reinforced the Hundred Ordinance. King Edgar systematized legal procedures as much as possible. His ideal arrangement of courts (III Edg. 5) was a tripartite division into hundred courts, which were to be attended as previously decreed, borough courts, to be held three times a year, and shire courts, to be held twice a year when the bishop of the diocese and the ealdorman were to be present to declare both ecclesiastical and secular law. A firm insight into the courts in practice is given in Edgar's declaration of law made at *Wihtbordesstan* in 962–3 (IV Edg.), occasioned by a severe outbreak of plague in 962, a declaration which may have owed much to the direct influence of Archbishop Dunstan. Specific measures were taken to safeguard legitimate trade. Panels of witnesses were established throughout the kingdom, thirty-six in each borough, twelve in each small borough, twelve in each hundred, unless more were wanted. They were to consist of lawworthy men who were to bear witness to all transaction, buying and selling, in borough and in wapentake. Men intending to buy or sell were to make their intention publicly known. If an unexpected purchase were made (and cattle were clearly in mind) the buyer was to announce his purchase on his return, and—if it were livestock—to bring it to the common pasture only with the witness of the village (*tunscip*). If he failed to make public his purchase and to gain such witness the villagers were to inform the hundred-man and, provided that this were done, they were then exempt from further penalty. The cattle were to be declared forfeit, the lord of the estate to have half and the hundred the other half. The hundred-man clearly had extensive reserves of legal and executive authority. If the villagers failed to inform him, the herdsmen were to be flogged and the suspect purchaser still had to declare from where he had bought the cattle. The hundred-man was then empowered to investigate. If the purchase were valid no further action was to be taken: the purchaser had incurred forfeiture because of his folly in failing to inform his neighbours and the hundred-man, but that was that. If it were not, he was to be regarded as a thief and to lose both life and property. The lord of the estate was to keep the stolen cattle or the value of the stolen cattle until the lawful owner put forward his claim successfully. Undoubtedly hints of rudimentary shrieval activity are to be found in this piece of legislation. The hundred-man was treated as an active and vigorous royal agent. Knowledge of this particular set of regulations was to be widely discriminated and the three great earls, Oslac of Northumbria with all his army, Ælfhere, earl of Mercia, and Æthelwine of East Anglia, were expressly commanded to give their full support.

The regularity and frequency of the hundredal meetings, coupled with their involvement in practical business that concerned theft and provision of good witness led to a natural extension of function. Under Ethelred a new emphasis is to be noted in legal enactments. The hundred was recognized as the natural place to find oath-helpers, compurgators. A lord wishing to vindicate his man who has acquired a bad reputation could choose two thegns from the hundred to swear to his good name: in case of a straight accusation his man could elect either to go to the simple ordeal or to proceed to an oath supported by compurgators within three hundreds. These regulations with minor variations are repeated in the *Laws of Cnut*.

Archbishop Wulfstan of York is now universally recognized as the principal begetter of the so-called *Laws of Cnut*. He had gained experience as a drafter of laws in the days of Ethelred, and in the stressful politics of that unhappy king's reign had also won a tremendous reputation as a powerful homilist and as a political theorist. His *Institutes of Polity* are far and away the most polished analysis of the rights and duties of all manner of men to be found in the Anglo-Saxon tongue. The *Laws of Cnut* is his masterpiece, a succinct and on the whole logical statement of Anglo-Saxon law, and as such recognized as authoritative even after the Conquest. When the Anglo-Norman lawbooks refer to the good laws of King Edward Confessor it is in practice more often than not the *Laws of Cnut* that they have in mind. A concentrated set of clauses referred directly to the hundred (II Cnut, 16 ff.; especially 19, 20, 22, and 30). The right to distrain property was rejected until justice had been demanded three times in the hundred. Even after that, an appeal was to be made to the shire court for the appointment of a fourth hearing and full legal support insisted on before the mechanics of distraint were set in motion. The hundred was to be a common and indispensable element in every freeman's life. If he wished to enjoy his rights to wergeld and if he wished his oath to be valid he must be brought into a tithing and a hundred once he had passed the age of twelve. It was in the hundred that he gave public demonstration of his *borh*, his protector, and this was true whether he had a household of his own or was another man's retainer. A trustworthy man could exculpate himself within his hundred while a man of bad reputation needed the support of oaths within three hundreds. The hundred was still an active riding body and failure to attend the court three times was followed by sending a posse to bring the offender along by force. The hundred court had the right to establish procedure and to dismiss a countercharge if brought by an accused or by an accused's lord: there was to be no easy evasion of a legitimate accusation. Perhaps most significant of all it was laid down that if a man was regarded with suspicion by the hundred and frequently accused, three men together had merely to make a formal accusation against him, presumably in the hundred court, and he would have to face the three-fold ordeal. We have something not unlike a rudimentary jury of presentment facing us here.

It is fair to conclude therefore that by the end of the Anglo-Saxon period the king, the Church, and his legal advisers expected to find much of the routine business conducted in a hundred court. The *Laws of Edgar* presented a solid statement on surety and men of poor reputation which is taken over at times word for word in the *Laws of Cnut*. But there is one vital difference. Clause 17 of the Cnut code states that no one was to appeal to the king unless he had formerly failed to obtain justice within the hundred, that everyone was to attend his own hundred court, and other hundreds, too, when required to do so by law, under pain of fines. By the eleventh century the hundred court represented the institution through the actions of which most inhabitants of England were made aware of law: and that law was increasingly associated with the power of the king.

A regular sequence of offences may therefore be established in the legislation relating to the hundred or allied courts throughout the tenth century to the reign of Cnut: cattle-theft, theft in general, all matters concerning trade, the process of vouching to warranty, the establishment of a legal *borh* or protector and with it assurance of good standing in a community, the testing of good reputation, and the presentment of offenders. The discipline of a hundred court ran parallel to the discipline of the growing borough courts, and parallel, too, to the discipline of lords over their men. In the relative simplicity of late Anglo-Saxon society concentration on offence naturally involved the whole community, and men of various lords and men of different orders found themselves affected by hundredal authority. It is no wonder that in the immediate post-Conquest period decisive steps were taken to withdraw from the hundred court causes that belonged to episcopal law and the clerical order, nor that great concern was felt, not significantly stilled until Henry I's time, at the number of hundreds which had passed into private hands.

The subtlety of the situation is indeed lost if we do not appreciate that private jurisdiction was contemporaneously achieving closer definition, and growing along lines parallel to and at times overlapping with the recognized jurisdiction of a hundred court. Our common terminology provides a valuable clue to the process. Charters from the last century of Anglo-Saxon England indicate that the most frequently specified juridicial rights were sake and soke, toll and *team*, and *infangenetheof*. A grant of sake and soke could in many areas and under many conditions be synony-mous with the grant of rights over a hundred court. These rights would involve full financial perquisites, the right to appoint or approve the hundred-men, and the duty as lord of the hundred to ensure that the hundred acted properly in matters such as the raising of a general hue and cry. A grant of toll would imply rights of protection over trade and traders in return for which toll would be paid. *Team* meant the right to supervise the business of vouching to warranty, a key element in our general hundredal legislation. *Infangenetheof*, or the right to hang a thief caught within the sphere of jurisdiction and to take the profits, is reminiscent of the police function of the hundred. It was rare for higher rights of justice than these to be granted out of the royal cognizance although it was recognized that payments for violation of the royal *mund*, for attack on men in their own houses (*hamsocn*), for assault (*forstal*), and for neglect of military service (*fyrdwite*), could be granted out as a special honour at least in Wessex and in the Danelaw (II Cnut, 12).

Our most clearcut evidence concerning the overlapping nature of hundredal and private jurisdiction comes from the eastern counties of England, particularly from the great Fenland abbeys of Ely, Peterborough, and Bury St. Edmunds. It is doubtful if historians have even yet given full weight to the influence of the great Benedictine revival in the second half of the tenth century in England as a means of ensuring continuity in law and administration during a century of almost unparalleled political turbulence in English affairs. Evidence from the abbey of Ely is especially illuminating. After the death of King Edgar in 975 great dispute arose over the endowments of the monasteries and the *Liber Eliensis* has preserved much material directly relevant to the wealth and authority of the abbey of Ely in the critical last quarter of the tenth century. Some elements of the administrative structure of the eastern shires emerge with startling clarity. The ealdormen were great men whose control of physical force was often decisive in bringing matters to judgement and in enforcing judgement. Prominent among them were Æthelwine, ealdorman of East Anglia, 962–92, the same Æthelwine who appeared by name in the code of Edgar's laws referred to above (IV Edg.), ealdorman over East Anglia and also at times over Cambridgeshire and Northamptonshire, and Brihtnoth of Essex, who was an ealdorman as early as 956 and met a hero's death at the battle of Maldon, 991. The archives of Brihtnoth's family were kept at Ely, proving a fruitful source for the *Liber Eliensis* itself. The ealdormen or their deputies presided over the shire court, over groups of hundred courts, or occasionally when special reason demanded it over a single hundred. In connection with a plea concerning lands at Wickford (*Lib. El.*, p. 91),[2] Æthelwine held court *cum toto hundreto* below the cemetery at the north door of the monastery at Ely, and there concluded a dispute that involved lands claimed by a certain *Sumerlede* and the abbot of Ely. Below the ealdormen in rank were numerous noblemen, *meliores*, *proceres*, some in these eastern counties specifically entitled *comites* or *eorls*, who were capable of acting on behalf of the ealdormen and so ultimately of the king, or of exercising jurisdiction themselves over a hundred or a group of hundreds. The *eorls* were to all appearance products of the situation early in the tenth century when the Danish armies of the east submitted to Edward the Elder and came to terms with him. Earl Scule, for example, who subscribed to charters among the *duces*, 931 × 5 and 946 × 9, held at one stage the manor of Sudbourne (*Lib. El.*, p. 111): to Sudbourne was later attached the great liberty of Ely in

[2] References are to *Liber Eliensis*, ed. E. O. Blake, Royal Historical Society, 1962.

Suffolk, the five and a half hundreds (described as six in *Lib. El.*, p. 114) of Wicklow. Of even greater interest is Wulfstan of Dalham (*Lib. El.*, xiii etc.). He was a *sequi-pedus*, maybe a high-reeve, a man of substance and energy, who presided at meetings in Cambridge in the ealdorman's absence and who had the power to summon two or three hundreds jointly to hear a plea. As for the hundreds themselves the out-standing impression left is one of ubiquity and flexibility. The hundred was the normal place by the reign of Ethelred for any land transaction to be attested. The phrase *coram totius hundreti testimonio* constantly recurs in the *Liber Eliensis* and there is no reason not to take this phrase literally: witness was provided naturally and properly at the hundred court. The hundred at this stage was unmistakably and completely territorial: litigation concerning land was to be held before the hundred, or group of hundreds, or shire in which the disputed territory lay. Hundreds were treated as if they were mature territorial institutions. Records going back well to the beginning of the tenth century were adduced in the hundred court. Testimony was offered concerning the ownership of lands in the late 910s or 920s when the Danish armies submitted to the West Saxon king. An impression is also given of great flexibility. Meetings of two or three hundreds jointly to treat of litigious matter were common-place. Dispute arose, for example, over the transmission of an estate at Kelling in Norfolk (*Lib. El.*, xiii and p. 116). Bishop Æthelwold is said to have bought it from Edric the Dane for £20, Edric receiving £5 from the bishop *coram hundreto* and the remaining £15 from the bishop's reeve *coram tribus hundretis in quibus Cillinge jacet*. At Wansford in Northamptonshire no fewer than eight hundreds were gathered together, and the eight hundreds *in australi parte Grantebrygge* were assembled to testify to the accuracy of what had been said concerning the purchase of two hides at Swaffham (*Lib. El.*, pp. 85 and 109). Evidence was frequently given *civium et hun-dretanorum* at Ely and at Cambridge. The impermanence of the territorial bounds of some hundreds must give no cause for surprise. Joint meetings could lead to frequent reshufflings. Such meetings also suggest the possibility of the existence of territorial division larger than the hundred at some earlier stage, spheres of jurisdiction of a Danish army, ship-sokes of 300 hides, or simply primitive *regiones* or divisions of such *regiones*.

The bustling activity of the hundred is also in evidence in other records of the great ecclesiastical houses. From Peterborough, for example, there has survived a list of gifts made by Bishop Æthelwold to the abbey.[3] After an account of paraphernalia, ranging from gospel-books, candlesticks, chalices, and maniples to altar-cloths, and a catalogue of books and estates, a description is given of the tithes that belong to Peterborough. From the two hundreds that owe suit (secæð) at Norman Cross, 350 acres of seed and 23 acres of clean wheat were due. From the two hundreds out on the headland on which Peterborough stood tithes were to come from six *tuns* at the rate of eight thraves for each plough. From the twenty-four *tuns* (presumably in the double hundred of Nassaborough) further renders were to be made. The document ended

---

[3] A. J. Robertson, *Anglo-Saxon Charters*, Cambridge, 2nd edn., 1956, xxxix. 72–5.

with a reference to the sureties who acted when first payment was made in a trans-action in the course of which ealdorman Æthelwine and Ealdulf (the abbot of Peterborough wrongly described here as a bishop) gave a 'last penny' on behalf of Peterborough. It is interesting to find the hundreds in casual use as a means of identi-fying the location of the *tuns* with the further implication that public knowledge of the detailed amounts of tithes and other dues would be possessed by the hundred court. Peterborough has also preserved a formal list of sureties which again underlines the importance of the hundred.[4] One entry in this list provides a significant clue to one aspect of hundredal development and growth in the tenth century. The monks of Peterborough were anxious to establish their good title to their landed possessions. Their title to an estate at *Leobrantestune* depended upon earl Ælfric's lawful ownership and we are told that he bought the estate at a meeting of the whole army (*on ealles heres gemote*) at Northampton when the whole army stood as surety (*boruhhand*) that the estate was unencumbered. Elsewhere the Peterborough sureties are more prosaic, named individuals, some identified by their personal names or their status or their kindred (their father's name), or by their place of residence (Thurwold of Helpston or Clac of Castor). Often and powerfully the hundreds are brought into the picture. Sureties stood with the witness of three hundreds pertaining to Oundle, or 'with two hundreds in addition', or again at Oundle this time with the witness of eight hundreds or 'in addition 8 hundreds pertaining to Oundle'.[5] The general picture is confirmed of the hundred as an active institution at which detailed infor-mation concerning payment would be publicized among those most fitted to know, and where suitable witness and testimony could be received.

The evidence from Ely and Peterborough therefore substantiates and fills out the legal edicts. The law tells us of hundredal institutions, stemming from historic Wessex and extended throughout the lands subject to the newly wide-ranging English kings. From an early period when police functions and safeguards against theft were paramount the hundreds developed under the impetus of peace and peaceful trading into the maids-of-all-work of English administration. Heavy concentration in the Ely charters on the function of the hundred to provide good witness is revealing. No institution could possibly meet as frequently as the hundred —once a month—without a regular routine job to perform. Some of the inadequacy of abstract general discussion of early hundredal organization has arisen precisely through failure to take social reality into account. Men do not assemble once a month without purpose. If, as seems likely, courts were held before the tenth century in territorial areas smaller than a shire it does not follow that these courts were held with the routine regularity of the late tenth-century hundred. It was much more likely that they were summoned, probably to fixed places, to moot-stows, at more natural and irregular intervals connected with the rhythms of an agrarian people to decide matters concerned with military service, boundary disputes, taxation, and allocation of hidage, but not to provide witness to trading transactions. The royal

---

[4] A. J. Robertson, op. cit., xl. 74–83.   [5] Ibid. 78. 32, 82. 4 and 17.

reeve at the royal *tun* would provide such service. The need for a hundred as a routine regular institution was a product of the greater England of Edward the Elder and his successors: territorial organization brought with it respect for the discipline of the calendar rather than the seasons.

Provision of witness and vouching to warranty guaranteed continuity to the life of the hundred. The police function remained important and was itself increasingly connected with the need for accurate testimony to legitimate ownership of land, cattle, and chattels. The legal progression we have traced from control of hue and cry through vouching to warranty to general legal competence within a compact territorial area has a historical logic to it, though it must of course be recognized that the decrees published at any given moment may reflect the particular concerns of the lawyers at that moment: the early hundred may possibly have had wider competence than the chance of survival in the evidence would allow us to see.

Yet on the whole the idea of a developing institution seems more in tune with the nature of tenth-century society. One huge problem and complication still remains. It is well known that the tenth century was a time when principles of secular lord-ship were in the ascendant throughout western Europe. In England and in Ottonian Germany the monarchy succeeded in controlling the secular lords to a considerable extent, but they had no permanent body of dependent bureaucrats they could rely on to act as their agents. Their best servants were the reeves of royal manors and it is no accident that hundreds were frequently attached to royal manors or ancient demesne, even if the hundreds themselves were separate from the demesne. Miss Cam has shown that the association of manors and hundreds, a widespread phenomenon in the thirteenth century, could be traced back continuously to the eleventh and beyond. She summarizes the regional situation as 'pretty general in all the counties south of the Thames, being most strongly marked in the south-west and least perceptible in Sussex; . . . sharply marked on the western borders and in East Anglia, well established in Essex and Northamptonshire, and hardly discernible in the typical Danelaw counties, and in Cambridgeshire, Huntingdonshire, Hertfordshire, Bedfordshire, Bucking-hamshire, and Middlesex'.[6] In Cheshire and in Hereford the hundredal manors were naturally comital not royal. The kings had also to look to the Church for help. In England the monastic revival during the reign of Edgar represented an outstanding manifestation of fruitful co-operation between Church and State. Massive endow-ments were granted to the new and newly reformed abbeys. In return they were called on to play a prominent part in the maintenance of peace and good order. Not only the king but the king's closest and most powerful servants were involved in the transactions we have touched on earlier in our discussion. Earl Æthelwine himself was a great patron of Ramsey abbey; and he was one of the men who had been expressly ordered to supervise the effective carrying out of Edgar's decrees. The result was an extensive granting of franchisal rights, notably in the eastern counties. It was

---

[6] *Liberties and Communities in Medieval England*, Cambridge, 1944, 83: this article on 'Manerium cum Hundredo' appeared first in *E.H.R.*, 1932, and is fundamental to all modern investigation of the hundred.

not against the spirit of the royal ordinances that the principal law-keeping institutions, the hundreds, should pass under the supervision of the new and vigorous abbots. By 1066 Ely already exerted control over the two home hundreds of Ely and the five and a half hundreds of Wicklow in Suffolk. Bury St. Edmunds held eight and a half of the twenty-four hundreds of Suffolk, and came to exercise rights equivalent to those of a sheriff over them. Peterborough, Ramsey, and Thorney also exercised their authority over hundreds in Northamptonshire and Huntingdonshire, Peterborough over the eight hundreds which were attached to Oundle. The jurisdiction of the bishop of Worcester over the great triple hundred of Oswaldslow was probably pre-hundredal in origin: no fewer than seven of the twelve extremely complex hundreds of Worcestershire were in ecclesiastical hands (Worcester itself, Evesham, Pershore, and Westminster) by the time of Domesday Book, a clear indication of similar processes at work in English England. Such franchises were safe and helpful to the king when held by great ecclesiastical lords.

In the more troubled early eleventh century hundreds fell increasingly into lay hands. Hundredors, reeves in charge of a hundred, became key figures. Private jurisdiction tended to be regarded as hundredal jurisdiction, even when there was little justification for such confusion. After the Conquest the special setting apart of the principal royal officers tended to exaggerate rather than diminish the process. There were at least 130 hundreds in private hands by the end of the reign of William the Conqueror.[7] Even in areas such as the land between the Ribble and the Mersey where, in 1086, the six hundreds were in royal hands and indeed took their names from the king's capital manors, feudalization and possibly the building of castles by subtenants of great feudal lords hint at the dangers of a dominical mastery of local administration under a smooth royal façade. The Church itself grew anxious and while the great abbeys and bishoprics continued to enjoy their own franchises Archbishop Lanfranc and King William successfully withdrew pleas which should properly go to a bishop's court from the hundreds.[8] It was only too easy for a powerful local landowner or his reeve, resident at a convenient *aula*, to dominate a hundred court, and tensions persisted between manors and hundreds, between dominical presence and royal rights. The executive strength of early Norman government, exercised at local level by powerful sheriffs, alone helped to preserve the integrity of the hundred court. The sheriff had the duty of visiting each hundred in the shire twice a year to make sure that the tithings were full. This duty was also a profitable right, and the customary tithing-pennies paid at the so-called sheriff's *tourn* was a further powerful factor that helped to keep the hundred court in being. In time the

[7] F. E. Harmer, *Anglo-Saxon Writs*, Manchester, 1952, 127, n. 1: there is important discussion of Abingdon's relationship to the Hundred of Hormer (125–30) and also of the only surviving writ expressly directed to a hundred court (Queen Edith to the hundred at Wedmore), 274–7: writ no. 72, 285–6.

[8] C. Morris, 'William I and the Church Courts', *E.H.R.*, 1967, 449–63 gives the best insight into this problem. On territorial matters some of Lanfranc's claims against Odo of Bayeux were to be determined in the hundreds, F. R. H. Du Boulay, *The Lordship of Canterbury*, London, 1964, 39. I owe this last reference to my colleague Dr. David Bates.

increased efficiency of the shire courts and of royal justices diminished the functional importance of the hundred but this was a matter for slow attrition in the future. Right through to the reign of Edward I the hundred remained a vital link in the chain of institutions which articulated the government of England, and provided an essential means by which the will of the central government was transmitted into every corner of the kingdom.

The Justiciarship in England
1258–1265

C. H. KNOWLES

THE revival of the justiciarship during the period of baronial reform and rebellion, 1258–65, was the fulfilment of a generation of intermittent agitation by the English baronage. The restored office was essential to the implementation of the reform programme, and it also allowed its holders to exert a powerful influence on the future of the baronial government established in 1258. Successive changes of justiciar as well as in the character of the office marked stages in the increasingly violent struggle for control of the royal government. Only the overwhelming defeat of the Montfortians in 1265 finally consigned the controversial office to oblivion.

Despite its importance, the history of the justiciarship during these momentous years has attracted less attention than it deserves. The first and only detailed studies of the office, now more than forty years old, are confined to the years before 1263 and form part of much broader investigations of the rebellion against Henry III.[1] More striking evidence of neglect is the period's complete omission from the only general history of the justiciarship so far published.[2] This peters out in 1234 and inexplicably makes no reference to the revival of the office a generation later. In the absence of any comprehensive treatment, this brief essay, the first separate account of the subject, may serve to sketch some of the main features of the history of the office in its last critical phase.[3]

The reign of Henry III witnessed the transformation of the justiciarship from an office functioning to strengthen royal authority into one intended to fulfil baronial aspirations. Though historians continue to dispute whether the jucticiarship came into being under Henry I, or as late as the reign of Henry II, they agree that it was established to superintend the royal administrative machine, to remedy failures of justice, and to meet the need for a vice-regal authority in England when the monarch

---

[1] The indispensable works are E. F. Jacob, *Studies in the Period of Baronial Reform and Rebellion, 1258–1267*, Oxford Studies in Social and Legal History, vol. viii, Oxford, 1925, and R. F. Treharne, *The Baronial Plan of Reform, 1258–1263*, Manchester, 1932, reprinted 1971. The most detailed list of the justiciars will be found in Sir Maurice Powicke and E. B. Fryde (eds.), *Handbook of British Chronology*, 2nd edn., London, 1961, 70–1.

[2] F. J. West, *The Justiciarship in England 1066–1232*, Cambridge, 1966.

[3] I am grateful to Mr. Malcolm Hogg, who is working on the justiciarship in this period, for his comments on the draft of this essay.

was visiting his continental lands. Though occasionally overshadowed by other royal officials, the justiciar was always one of the most powerful men in the kingdom.

Yet in the late twelfth and early thirteenth centuries, two factors are usually identified as working against the office's continued existence. The loss of the Norman and Angevin dominions lessened the need for a powerful official to represent the king during long absences from England. The increasing complexity of royal government, and especially its growing departmentalism, made the justiciarship an obstacle to efficient rule and direct royal control of affairs.

Nevertheless, the potentialities of the office remained enormous. During the long minority of Henry III, far from proving obsolete, the justiciarship, in the person of Hubert de Burgh, reached a new peak of power and authority. When Henry came of age it was inevitable that, with his high regard for kingship, he should seek an early opportunity to dispense with an office whose powers detracted from his own and whose justification was in any case past. He rid himself of Burgh in 1232 and substituted Stephen of Seagrave whose powers were exclusively judicial. In 1234 Seagrave in turn was dismissed and the office lapsed. In this way an office created by the Crown for its own purposes was suppressed once it seemed an obstacle to untrammelled royal rule.

The idea of the justiciarship was kept alive by the king's critics amongst the baronage who saw it as a means of furthering their collective interests. The revival of the justiciarship was demanded at least three times between 1244 and 1258. Evidence is scanty, but enough to indicate the baronial conception of the office. It is clear that the barons accepted the traditionally wide-ranging character of the justiciar's responsibilities. In the Paper Constitution of 1244 they readily allowed that because the justiciar 'ought to be at the king's side' he might be one of the four conservators of liberty with wide administrative, judicial, and financial powers, which they wished to add to the king's council.

What the barons were primarily concerned to ensure was that the holders of the office should be acceptable to themselves. The misgovernment of Henry III, about which they increasingly complained, was often attributed to the way royal officials were entirely under the king's control. Henry's influence might be curbed by filling the justiciarship with a non-professional magnate of higher social and political status than the ordinary run of royal official, but the barons did not insist on it. They were aware that a magnate, unfamiliar with his duties, would be dependent on the loyal co-operation of the very officials they feared and distrusted. So the demand for the revival of the justiciarship falls into line with the simultaneous pressure for a chancellor and treasurer acceptable to the barons. Whether these offices were filled by lay magnates or experienced royal officials was less important than that the holders should be trustworthy men chosen by the barons and in some undefined way responsible to them rather than to the king.

For two decades Henry successfully opposed these recurrent demands. But after his ill-judged involvement in the Sicilian business, his difficulties mounted and his capacity to resist was fatally undermined. To forestall new pressure for a justiciar, he combined the leadership of the two central courts. In 1256, Henry of Bath, already senior justice of the court *coram rege*, became chief justice of the Bench.[4] This manœuvre failed because Bath's reputation was tainted with corruption and his long career as a royal official deprived him of independent standing. Moreover, piecemeal changes could not head off the mounting crisis. By 1258 the king's opponents were content with nothing less than a reconstruction of royal government under their collective control.

The re-establishment of the office of justiciar was a central feature of the new form of government set up in the Provisions of Oxford. Yet the new justiciarship was markedly different from that envisaged in earlier baronial demands, let alone the office as it had existed before 1232. Now that the magnates were taking over the government, rather than merely seeking a guaranteed part in it, there was no need to assign an important administrative role to the justiciarship. At the same time, the barons were aware of their special obligation to satisfy the clamour for judicial action against royal officials and others guilty of tyranny and extortion. The traditional association of the office with justice could be harnessed to achieve this end. Together these factors probably determined both the special character of the new office and the identity of its first holder.

The Provisions of Oxford and associated documents make it abundantly clear that the justiciar was envisaged as the chief judicial officer of the Crown. His dual functions were to preside over the court *coram rege* and to undertake a series of eyres to correct wrongs brought to light by the special county commissioners appointed by the new baronial government. The justiciarship was to be the means by which grievances should be redressed and oppressions removed, using for that purpose the full judicial authority of the Crown.

The other striking feature of the new justiciarship was the attention devoted to ensuring its independence of the Crown while keeping it firmly under the control of the baronial government. The justiciar's immense salary of 1,000 marks a year was not so much intended to be commensurate with his responsibilities as to free him from undesirable pressures, especially those of the king. At the same time, the new ruling Council of Fifteen was given full authority over the justiciar who took an oath of loyalty to it. And to prevent the justiciar acquiring too much personal influence, it was laid down that he was to hold office for one year only and then was to account for his activities in the presence of his successor.

The barons' wish to prevent the justiciarship again falling under Henry's control is also reflected in their choice of the first holder of the office. The man best fitted to the task would be someone of high standing capable of overriding privilege and inspiring trust, and yet not so powerful as to escape their control. Hugh Bigod fulfilled these requirements. In spite of chroniclers' assertions to the contrary, there is no

---

[4] C. F. A. Meekings, *List of Rolls and Writs of the Court Coram Rege Henry III* (bound for the Literary Research Room, Public Record Office, 1957), 12.

evidence that he was particularly well acquainted with judicial matters. On the other hand, he had been at the centre of affairs for several years, and along with his brother, the earl of Norfolk, had helped plot the conspiracy which had forced Henry to submit to baronial rule. Equally important, he seems to have enjoyed the trust of his colleagues and even, at this difficult time, the king. Significantly, Bigod's appointment as justiciar was the first important decision of the barons after drawing up the Provisions.

During the first few months after the baronial seizure of power, the basic character of the justiciarship remained unchanged. Within a week of his appointment Bigod had set to work. Secure in the exceptional status of his office, he used his authority to override liberties and privileges and to extend the use of the simple and effective process of the *querela* or informal complaint. The public impact of his work was considerable even though he was careful to refer to the Council of Fifteen all cases touching the king and the interests of the magnates.

As late as the summer of 1259 the justiciar was still attending to his judicial duties, but his office had already undergone a complete transformation in powers and responsibilities. Gradually Bigod had undertaken more and more duties which extended his influence to all spheres of government activity. The climax came in the winter of 1259–60, during Henry's prolonged absence in France, when the justiciar was assigned much the same vice-regal powers as those enjoyed by his predecessors. How far Bigod's personal ambition contributed to these developments is impossible to say, but they can hardly have occurred against his will. Nevertheless, the basis of a more powerful and politically orientated justiciarship had been present from the beginning.

The Provisions of Oxford had contributed by conferring a formal precedence on the justiciarship. The justiciar's oath preceded that of the chancellor, provisions about his office occur before those concerning the treasurer and other officials, and his superior status was acknowledged by the reference to 'the chief justiciar and all other persons'. The financial provision for the justiciar underlined his exalted rank. His annual salary was two and a half times that assigned to the chancellor (who was expected to pay his clerks out of his stipend) and ten times that paid to the treasurer. Moreover, in line with previous practice, the custody of the Tower of London, the chief royal fortress in the country, was assigned to the justiciar *ex officio*. The fact was that the justiciarship was the most important office created by the baronial government. It had been set up in defiance of the king to redeem the barons' promise to redress all grievances. In so far as it was by the justiciar's work that they would be judged, the office was of vital political importance from the beginning.

Bigod's close relationship with the Council of Fifteen, even more than the initial status of his office, proved the main foundation of the justiciarship's growing importance. Formally he was not included in its membership, but in practice he took part in all its important deliberations. His participation in the original conspiracy against the king would have ensured this. Convenience also dictated his presence.

Along with the other two officers of state, it facilitated the day-to-day work of the council. More especially, from mid July 1258 onwards 'the barons held conference daily, sometimes at the New Temple, sometimes elsewhere, concerning the improvement of the usages and customs of England'. In working out the details of the judicial and administrative changes later incorporated in the Provisions of Westminster, the justiciar's experience was especially relevant and valuable. Despite his judicial commitments, he kept in close touch with the council, making frequent trips to Westminster between eyres, and always being present at parliaments. This record is all the more impressive in view of the irregular attendance of some other members of the council.

From the autumn of 1258 evidence mounts of the justiciar's increasing involvement in political and administrative matters, while the breaks in his judicial activities become more frequent. Bigod played a part in the attack on the Poitevins, and in supervising the disposal of their funds after their flight. His authorizations of writs became more numerous and his responsibilities were extended to include custody of several important castles. The most arresting evidence of the justiciar's importance is provided by his role in the Exchequer, where the quickening of activity reflected the barons' deepened interest in the king's finances. Like previous justiciars he was called upon to act as its president, and in this capacity transacted a wide variety of financial and judicial business. No doubt his task was eased by the co-operation of Exchequer officials appointed by his brother as hereditary marshal of England.[5] Other officials, including the treasurer Philip Lovel, were removed at Bigod's insistence in October 1258. John Crakehall, Lovel's successor, was a nonentity, which only served still further to enhance Bigod's authority.

In urging the removal of Lovel, Bigod probably acted in an official rather than a personal capacity, but this in itself is testimony to the justiciar's standing. As spokesman for the council in August 1259, Bigod again experienced an enhancement of his power. Acting on its behalf, the justiciar censured Richard de Grey, another council member, for allowing a messenger bearing a controversial papal bull into the country. The constableship of Dover Castle, taken from Grey, was conferred on the justiciar, who in addition to his other duties was now put in control of the main entry to England.

When the barons drew up the administrative 'establishments' of the Provisions of Westminster in October 1259 they implicitly accepted the changed character of the justiciarship, and thrust greater responsibilities on it even as they whittled down its routine judicial duties. First and foremost the 'establishments' set a limit to the justiciar's judicial duties. By the autumn of 1259 it was apparent that the scheme for the redress of grievances set in motion the previous year had broken down. The sheer weight of cases would have overtaxed the energies of even the most vigorous justiciar. In fact, Bigod had been obliged to give increasing attention to his ever

---

[5] e.g. Master Roger Gosbeck, marshal of the Exchequer, appointed in 1250 (E368/26, m. 1d) and still in office a decade later (Treharne, op. cit. 211, n. 9).

.tiplying duties. To go on single-handed would have been to drag out the judicial proceedings interminably. So the justiciar's eyre was replaced by a special eyre of seven circuits allotted the twin tasks of proclaiming the legislative clauses of the Provisions of Westminster and carrying out the still unfulfilled pledge to redress all grievances. Special arrangements permitted the justiciar to play a part without interfering with his other responsibilities. He was assigned to the circuit nearest to London, and he was allowed, if he wished, to appoint a deputy.

Other clauses of the 'establishments' make it clear that the justiciar was now regarded as the head of the executive charged with the responsibility of performing a wide variety of administrative and political tasks. With the intention of paying off the king's debts and providing for the cost of his household, he was given supervisory powers over certain fields of royal revenue and expenditure. Together with other commissioners, he was empowered to sell wardships falling in to the Crown, to decide on which payments Queen's gold could be exacted, and to estimate total receipts from tallages since the king's accession. Amongst the other administrative commissions were those empowering the justiciar to ensure that keepers of royal castles received adequate allowances, and directing him, in conjunction with the treasurer, to appoint officials to report what reforms were necessary in the Exchequer and the Exchequer of the Jews. Another measure commanded the justiciar, together with members of the council, to select barons to sit with the justices at the Bench, in the Exchequer, and in each circuit of the special eyre.

Arrangements concerning the king's forthcoming visit to France to ratify the Treaty of Paris provide the most impressive evidence of the justiciar's new-found authority. He was to be regent during the king's absence, advised by members of the council specially assigned for that purpose. While the king was abroad between November 1259 and April 1260 not only did new duties devolve on the justiciar but a great impetus was given to existing developments. Throughout that period all letters patent and close issued in England were attested by him, and frequently letters issued by the king for execution in England were addressed to him alone.

During the winter of 1259–60 Bigod reached the peak of his influence. To the formal authority as regent conferred on him in the administrative 'establishments' was added a decisive role in political affairs made possible by the division of the council. For in the hope of maintaining control over both the king while abroad and the government of England during his absence, some council members had accompanied Henry to France whilst others remained in England to advise the justiciar. This division of its membership, which undermined the cohesion of the council, not only enabled the king to recover the initiative in affairs, but gave a new weight to the political views of the justiciar.

Yet precisely because his influence was based on an exceptional combination of circumstances, it was essentially transitory. Once Henry returned to England, the justiciar lost his vice-regal status and reverted to being an ordinary member of a council now seemingly tottering on the edge of dissolution. Moreover, the period of his regency had fatally compromised Bigod in the eyes of the king's more extreme opponents.

His growing influence after June 1258 had owed much to the measure of confidence all elements had in him. It was testimony to this that when the barons conferred new powers on the justiciarship in the Provisions of Westminster, they brushed aside their earlier decision that no holder was to retain office for two consecutive years, and ordered Bigod to remain in office until the next parliament. But as Bigod reached the climax of his personal influence, it was thrown increasingly behind the king against the more extreme barons. In face of the opposition of Simon de Montfort, he used his authority as regent to secure the king's immediate wishes: the postponement of the regular Candlemas parliament required by the Provisions of Oxford, and the dispatch of large funds to Henry in France. As the political situation worsened, he further incurred Montfort's wrath by advising the king to bring foreign troops on his return.

Henry's confidence in Bigod's sympathetic outlook had been apparent even in 1258 when the king was allowed to choose him as one of the electors of the Council of Fifteen. Thereafter the justiciar's outlook may have been influenced by his friendly relations with the earl of Gloucester,[6] who was simultaneously reaching a closer understanding with the king. As the earl's quarrel with the Lord Edward and Montfort deepened, so Bigod and Gloucester were drawn deeper into the king's confidence. After Henry's return to England in April 1260 the justiciar continued to authorize writs but he was increasingly isolated from many of his former colleagues. As the council's control slackened, so the king's personal direction of the government progressively increased.

When the king's opponents temporarily reasserted themselves in October 1260 they carried out a thorough-going reconstruction of the government. Its most arresting feature, the supplanting of Bigod, brought an end to the most constructive period in the history of the restored justiciarship. Thereafter, though there was no major diminution in their responsibilities, the gathering crisis prevented succeeding justiciars from effectively carrying out all their duties. Furthermore, the standing of the office markedly declined. The best indication of this is the personal status of the next two justiciars, the last before the office was finally abolished in 1265. Both Despenser and Basset were barons of the second rank. The choice of them to fill the office suggests that with the changed character of attempts to fulfil the pledge to redress all grievances, a justiciar of exceptionally high standing was no longer necessary. It may also indicate that, from their different points of view, neither the king nor his baronial opponents wished again to run the risk of creating an officer of too great power and independence. Certainly, after 1260 the justiciars were men of committed allegiance who alternated in office as the political situation swayed first one way and then the other.

The career of Hugh Despenser, who replaced Bigod in October 1260, provides

[6] Hist. MSS. Comm., *Middleton*, 67–9.

some good evidence of these changes. Sprung from a family of royal administrators, he had played an increasingly important part in affairs as one of the barons of middle rank given charge of royal castles in 1258 and as a member of the parliamentary committee of twelve. As an associate of Montfort since at least 1258, his political reliability was presumably beyond question. Chosen justiciar by an inner group of five councillors,[7] he assumed the wide responsibilities of his predecessor, and was specially active on eyre in Sussex in the winter of 1260–1. He also presided in the court *coram rege* where he was for a time without a professional colleague.[8] But the baronial reaction was short-lived. The council was unable to present a united front, some of its members transferred their loyalties to the king, and Henry regained his authority. During the spring of 1261 the pressure on the justiciar mounted as his salary went unpaid, his actions were criticized, and his powers were curtailed. Eventually, in June 1261, despite his protests, he was dismissed from office.

Henry's repudiation of the council was not followed by the immediate suppression of the justiciarship. Although he was determined to rule as he wished, free of the restrictions—such as the justiciarship—imposed by the Provisions of Oxford, the king evidently saw advantages in keeping the office for the time being. The revival of the justiciarship had aroused expectations Henry would have been short-sighted to ignore until his authority was better established. His choice as justiciar fell on Philip Basset, Despenser's own father-in-law, and the brother of a distinguished royal servant and a former bishop of London. Basset's public career had begun as early as 1245 when he acted as proctor of the baronage at Lyons. Like Despenser he had been a member of the parliamentary committee of twelve set up in 1258, in which year he also joined the ruling Council of Fifteen. He moved closer to the king in 1259 when, as one of the councillors of middle rank assigned to advise the regent, he supported the justiciar against the more extreme magnates. After April 1260 he joined the inner circle of royal advisers who planned or acquiesced in the overthrow of the Provisions of Oxford. So it was as a powerful and experienced administrator, deep in the confidence of the king, that Basset took office as justiciar in June 1261.

The king made no attempt to limit the broad scope of the justiciar's duties. He even increased Basset's burden of responsibility by appointing him sheriff of two pairs of counties (Oxford and Berks., and Dorset and Somerset), and choosing him as one of the six arbitrators to decide the proper method of electing sheriffs. The justiciar's opportunity for political initiative, on the other hand, was tightly controlled, despite the fact the king was out of the country for the second half of 1261. Basset was recognized as the head of the administration responsible for attesting writs issued during the king's absence, but in all except matters of administrative routine he deferred to the king who kept firm control by a steady stream of instructions, usually addressed to the justiciar and the chancellor jointly.

The political crisis of July 1263, which re-established the form of government set

---

[7] E. F. Jacob, 'The Complaints of Henry III against the Baronial Council in 1261', *E.H.R.*, 1926, 565, no. 4.   [8] Ibid. 566, no. 10.

up under the Provisions, led to the dismissal of Basset and the reappointment of Despenser. He resumed control of an office which was outwardly unchanged. He took charge of the Tower, attested writs, supervised financial matters and was assigned the official salary of 1,000 marks yearly. During the king's brief absence in France in the autumn, he was effectively head of the administration, dealing, in conjunction with the chancellor or on his own, with a wide variety of business. All this could not obscure the fact that government was disintegrating and England drifting towards civil war. By the late summer of 1263 there was no treasurer or resident barons of the Exchequer, and the disturbed conditions prevented Despenser from resuming his judicial activities. It was only a matter of time before the king regained his independence and struck at his opponents.

In October 1263 he was free once again to fill the government with his own supporters. The justiciar was not amongst those formally dismissed during this reorganization. Despenser continued to use the title as the opposing sides manœuvred for advantage, and it was as justiciar that, on 13 December 1263, with other Montfortians, he agreed to Louis IX's arbitration 'on all provisions, ordinances, statutes, and obligations of Oxford'. By affecting to ignore the existence of the justiciarship, Henry now gave notice of his unalterable intention to overthrow all the restrictions on his authority contained in the hated Provisions of Oxford.

The battle of Lewes, not the Mise of Amiens, decided the immediate fate of the justiciarship. After Montfort's victory, the justiciarship recovered its former status and functions without need for formal reinstatement. It was intended that the justiciar should play a central part in dealing with the general disorder which had accompanied the outbreak of civil war. On 30 June 1264 the sheriffs were ordered to apprehend the culprits and detain them until further orders from the king or the justiciar. If any resisted, they were to be reported and the king or justiciar would do justice to them.[9] Four months later ambitious plans were announced to deal with offences against the Church. The justiciar was to have a staff of at least one hundred knights or serjeants to distrain offenders at the request of three bishops who were to settle reasonable compensation for offences.[10]

The variety of administrative tasks undertaken by the justiciar again indicate that he was the recognized head of the executive. He authenticated writs, superintended financial matters, was given custody of castles, and acted as spokesman for the baronial government. In addition, after Lewes, he was a member of Montfort's informal council, and though not formally included in the Council of Nine set up in June 1264 he took part in its deliberations.

Even more than Basset, however, his duties were shaped by the serious political situation. With the hostile king virtually a prisoner in the hands of the rebels, the overriding problem of government was not the revival of the reform plans of 1258 but the perpetuation of Montfort's personal sway.

During the summer and autumn of 1264 the Montfortian government faced two

[9] *C.P.R., 1258–66*, 362.   [10] Ibid. 375.

difficulties. It had, as the first priority, to defend the kingdom against the threats of invasion by loyalists who had fled abroad. Meantime it had to explore every possibility of a negotiated settlement which would ensure continued Montfortian domination, and win the consent, reluctant or otherwise, of the king and his followers. In both these fields, the justiciar was assigned an important role.

The possibility of invasion was especially threatening in the summer of 1264 when it fell to the justiciar to co-ordinate the defences of the country. Under his direction, levies from all over England were assembled at London and ships at Sandwich were provisioned to repel an attack. The justiciar had specific responsibility for the defence of the coastline of Norfolk, Suffolk, and Essex. In those counties, troops were gathered at convenient points and instructed what to do by the justiciar or one of his subordinates.[11]

As the danger eased, the justiciar was allotted an important share in the increasingly desperate search for a negotiated settlement with the king's supporters. The Mise of Lewes, agreed to immediately after the battle, had stipulated a new French arbitration on the matters in dispute. When Louis IX rejected Montfort's requests, the threatened 'shorter way of peace' was followed. Yet by August 1264, when it was decided that the *Ordinatio* of two months earlier setting up the Council of Nine should remain in force for the remainder of Henry's reign and for an unspecified time into that of his successor, a lasting settlement was no nearer. Montfort again resorted to negotiations, choosing the justiciar as one of his representatives in nearly all his schemes of arbitration.[12] Every design foundered on the intransigence of the king and his supporters.

The Montfortians were now an embattled faction fighting for survival. Throughout the spring and summer of 1265 the justiciar was constantly with the king, except for those increasingly rare occasions when he was away on other business. He was present, with other members of the council, in February 1265 at Westminster when John de Chishull, the chancellor, surrendered the great seal and it was committed to Master Thomas de Cantilupe, nephew of the Montfortian bishop of Worcester. The careful attention to the formalities of the transfer could not disguise the fact that government was again breaking down. There were no Trinity sessions of the court *coram rege* and on 23 April the rolls were sent to Nicholas de Turri, a justice of the Bench, who with an associate was ordered to hear and determine the cases as far as possible.[13] In May the justiciar took part in abortive negotiations with the earl of Gloucester who had already thrown in his lot with the loyalists. As the Montfortian sphere of control dwindled to the area around Hereford, the justiciar was reduced to busying himself with trivial judicial business. The justiciarship had become an intolerable affront to the king; it died with Despenser at the battle of Evesham on 4 August 1265.

[11] Ibid. 351, 353, 360–1, 362.
[12] Ibid. 347–8, 369, 370, 371; N. Denholm-Young, *Collected Papers*, Cardiff, 1969, 162.
[13] *Close Rolls, 1264–68*, 112.

The justiciarship, in spite of its achievements during the period of baronial reform and rebellion, failed to re-establish itself as part of the governmental system. Part of the explanation lies in the fact that the initial task assigned to it—the speedy redress of all grievances—was beyond the capacity of any one official, however important, to perform. Far more damaging to its prospects, the development of the office was increasingly determined by the need for someone who could answer to the baronial council for the whole organization of government. As a result, though few of the magnates had personal knowledge of the old justiciarship, the restored office evolved into something approximating to it: the king's *alter ego* who would not only redress wrongs, but also supervise the administration and act as the king's deputy when he was overseas. This was precisely the omnicompetent office which Henry had deliberately allowed to lapse thirty years before. Its revival as an instrument of baronial policy finally ensured that it could never again find a place in royal government.

The Collectors of the Customs in the Reign of Richard II

ANTHONY STEEL[*]

THIS paper is an attempt to supplement for the rest of the country an earlier article of mine entitled 'The Collectors of the Customs at Newcastle-upon-Tyne in the Reign of Richard II'. That article appeared as long ago as 1957 in a volume of essays presented to Sir Hilary Jenkinson.[1] Very little work has been done on the subject since then, but at any rate the conviction which I expressed on that occasion that there was a great change in the type of person appointed collector of the customs in Newcastle from about 1392 onwards has not been challenged, though the question whether this was simply a local peculiarity or was reproduced in the remaining twelve English ports of that period has not been answered. On the other hand a very interesting article on 'The Collectors of Customs in London under Richard II' has been published by Miss Olive Coleman of the London School of Economics,[2] and, although her approach was slightly different, Miss Coleman does not disagree substantially with my suggestion that what was done at Newcastle in 1392 was also done elsewhere. Miss Coleman, moreover, having subsequently read the typescript of this further article of mine, has been good enough to send me certain comments on it. Professor William Rees has also sent me a few notes garnered from his great experience, and I propose to use the observations of these two historians—of course, with their permission—as an introduction to my own findings. This also seems to be the point at which I ought to acknowledge my great debt to Miss Ruth Bird's *The Turbulent London of Richard II*[3] in compiling my section on London.

Professor Rees points out that as early as 1389 there was a powerful attack on exchequer procedures in the parliament of that year. This attack was entirely directed at 'the great and outrageous farms, profits etc. charged on the sheriffs in the exchequer and the ancient increases in the counties as appears in the great roll of the exchequer'. It had nothing to do with the customs, but it may well have been a prelude to a further parliamentary attempt to galvanize the exchequer into reform during the next two or three years. At this point Miss Coleman takes up the story by

---

[*] It was with great regret that we heard of Dr. Steel's death on October 3rd., 1973, shortly after he had returned the proofs of this paper.

[1] *Studies Presented to Sir Hilary Jenkinson*, ed. J. C. Davies, O.U.P., 1957.
[2] *Studies in London History*, ed. A. E. J. Hollaender and W. Kellaway, London, 1969, 181–94.
[3] Ruth Bird, *The Turbulent London of Richard II*, London, 1949.

pointing out that 'the receipts from the wool custom in 1390–91 were about the lowest of the reign. It was in fact a bad year for exports—a situation which parliament had largely brought upon itself by prohibiting exports by native wool merchants', who were charged at a lower rate than aliens. These regulations 'obviously misfired'. 'They seem', writes Miss Coleman, 'to have been quietly dropped during the course of the year since some native exports are recorded in most ports. Both exports and revenue were, however, seriously down', and it looks as if this led parliament on to blame the administration of the customs. At any rate Miss Coleman tells me there was a Commons petition in 1390 (*Rot. Parl.* iii. 381) that customers should not be allowed to own any ships or 'meddle with the freight of ships'. This part of the petition was granted in the consequent statute (14 Ric. II, c. 10); but this statute also incorporated a purely royal stipulation that no customs collector should hold office for life (as many had done hitherto), but only at the king's pleasure. It will be seen in the body of this paper that these two clauses in the statute were put into at least partial operation, not only in Newcastle upon Tyne but in all the other English ports, during the next few years. This explains why we find almost everywhere from 1392 a strong tendency to get rid of the well-established burgess collectors, who were all too frequently also traders, and even buccaneers, in their own right, and replace as many as possible of them by respectable country gentlemen living in the vicinity of the ports or, more commonly, by professional clerks, that is, civil servants.

At this point Professor Rees takes up the story again. He suggests that

the changes in 1391–2 may have been part of a wider re-shuffle and seem to be linked with the break with Calais in the Westminster parliament of November 1391 as the sole staple port for staple products. Merchants, alien and native, were now allowed to use several staples, as they had been earlier in the century, and these included at least one home staple— at Westminster. None the less, by as early as 1397 merchants of the staple were pleading that all merchandises have recourse to the staple of Calais and to no other, and the Calais monopoly does seem to have been firmly re-established by the time of Henry IV, if not earlier.

I am myself inclined to doubt whether this flurry over the staple had any real connection with the changes in the recruitment and tenure of customs collectors which were going on at much the same time, but the fact that it took place at all and was even continued for some years underlines the general dissatisfaction with contemporary conditions in the changing wool-trade, including the alarming fall in the revenue derived from it, which was the special concern of the exchequer. However, I must now proceed to the partial implementation of the changes in custom administration asked for by parliament in 1390 and granted, in a slightly modified form, by the Crown, as they stand revealed in the great chancery calendars of the Patent, Close, and Fine Rolls, which are the source of this paper. The ports in question are those of Boston, Bristol, Ipswich, Kingston upon Hull, London, Lynn, Sandwich, Southampton, and Great Yarmouth, together with the lesser ports of Chichester, Exeter, and Melcombe, all of which had their own collectors of customs. I have constructed rather over 150 short biographies of these collectors, ignoring those who were not active after 1385 or were not, at the very least, collectors of tunnage (on wine) and poundage (on goods avoirdupois), the big fish I have really been looking for being of course the collectors of the more lucrative customs on wool and hides. For want of any better order I shall take the ports alphabetically, excluding the special case of London, which is given a rather longer section to itself at the end. It will be remembered that the critical year is 1392, and that what I am trying to prove is that a change of customs administration took place almost universally about that date. This in turn must be set against the background of the troubles of 1386–9 and 1397–9. There was civil war in 1387, culminating in the brief ascendancy of a baronial group known as the appellants in 1388, after they had got rid of the royalist leaders in the merciless parliament. Richard resumed his personal power in the summer of 1389, but exercized it with some moderation for nearly eight years. Then in the last three years of his reign he attempted a kind of counter-revolution which misfired and ended with his deposition in 1399 and the accession of Henry IV.

From 1385 to 1391 Boston customs were dominated by Sir Robert Sutton, a wealthy wool-merchant and citizen of Lincoln, where he had held the office of mayor. He seems to have been an excellent example of the old-fashioned type of customs-collector—namely a substantial burgess, reasonably useful to the Crown, but, being himself a wool-merchant, perhaps over-inclined to line his own nest. It is significant that, though far from being disgraced, and indeed quite active in other spheres up to 1398, he is not employed in the customs service after 1391, and in 1392 takes out a general pardon for personal infringement of the regulations of the wool trade. Sutton's chief colleague in the customs for his last four years was Philip Gernon, a minor Bostonian of much lower social standing, who is briefly associated with an obscure clerk in 1391 and disappears from the service after 1392, except for a year or two in office with John Thorp (1396–7), a very professional king's clerk from Southampton. A more prominent associate of Sutton and Gernon in the customs was John Belle, originally of Leake in Lincolnshire, who has strong curialist connections at the start but ends up as a Boston alderman in 1398. He survives a little longer than the other two as a collector of tunnage and poundage but is not in office between 1394 and 1398, and then only with the said John Thorp. Another, but much more obscure, clerk called William Bele was Gernon's colleague, as already mentioned, for a short time in the early 1390s, all of which suggests that, although there is certainly no dramatic happening in Boston about the year 1392, from that time onwards powerful merchants there, as elsewhere, did tend to be replaced by, or associated with, clerks.

My next port, Bristol—though *sui generis* in many respects—conforms rather more closely to the expected pattern. Alone among the great ports, Bristol's main interest lay much less in wool and hides than in wine. Her outports ranged from Chepstow to Bridgwater, and at one time even included Exeter, while her customs collectors and controllers were responsible for the prevention of smuggling on both shores of the Severn Sea. She was also a great centre for licensed privateering and the headquarters of the king's admiral in the west. Her merchant princes were rich and powerful and, led by Thomas Beaupyne—or Bewepeny—a small group of them dominated the customs from 1382 to 1390. But the last of this type—Thomas Knap, merchant, shipowner, and mayor in 1391—does not figure in the service after 1392. Instead we have a humble clerk, Richard des Armes; an obscure official called John Hertham; and finally a notorious king's esquire, Richard Mawardyn, who was destined to be one of the most active of the Ricardian sheriffs. John Stephenys, the rather undistinguished mayor of 1394, was allowed to act occasionally, but only in association with one or other of these professional royal servants.

Passing over the relatively minor ports of Chichester and Exeter for the time being, we come back to the east coast at Ipswich. Here the customs service is dominated by two names from 1377 to 1392—those of Geoffrey Sterlyng and Robert Waleys. There are in fact two Geoffrey Sterlyngs—probably father and son—who cover the first fifteen years of the reign. They appear to have been rather minor burgesses, though the elder represented the borough in parliament in 1386 and the younger was elected a bailiff of Ipswich towards the end of the century. Waleys, on the other hand, though certainly a merchant and a burgess, was rather more colourful and was freely used by the Crown for military and other purposes. His connection with the customs ends, however, in 1389. The only other customs-collector worth a mention before 1392 is John Sewale of Coggeshale, a substantial country gentleman of Essex, and at one time sheriff of that county: it is also just possible to identify him with a citizen and fishmonger of the same name in London. Sewale was consistently loyal to whatever government was in power, but possessed no private interests north of Essex. He is the sort of man one would have expected to find in the customs service of a neighbouring port in the 1390s, as at Newcastle upon Tyne, rather than in the late 1380s; and indeed Sewale might well have been cast for such a role, had he not died in 1391. Almost immediately after his death there is a marked change in the Ipswich customs service. Professional king's clerks are imported from Southampton and Newcastle upon Tyne and combined with burgesses of the second or lower rank. One of these nonentities was a man of seventy, and although another was of rather more substantial standing the reign closes with a flurry of at least three king's servants of positively menial quality.

Further up the coast at Kingston upon Hull the picture is much the same, except for the fact that both burgesses and clerks are of notably higher standing. Three burgesses who at one time or another reached the rank of mayor were active in the Hull customs before 1392, and another, Walter Frost, had the rare distinction of being employed on a wide range of duties not only under the Crown but also in the revolutionary years of 1387 and 1388 under the appellants. Then comes the big change, as usual. Frost, who died in 1391, does not seem to have been disgraced, but of his burgess successors one was a senior citizen of York, much trusted by the Crown, while the other two—one of them of mayoral standing—were closely associated with an unusually powerful group of king's clerks. Easily the most important of these was a leading chancery clerk, Robert de Garton, whose long civil-service career is very fully documented and of quite exceptional interest; I pass it over with regret.

Setting aside the complexities of London for the moment, I shall now turn to Lynn, where the picture is comparatively simple. Once again the reign opens with a long period of service (1378–90) by a rather uninteresting burgess, one Thomas Drewe, who also served briefly at Great Yarmouth. He was, however, undoubtedly a burgess of Lynn, though not a very distinguished one, and in 1388 was joined there by another Drewe, named John—also a Lynn burgess, and, presumably, a relative— who went on until 1392. Then comes the usual run of clerks—this time men of no great standing but invariably associated with John Brandon, the one remaining burgess collector at Lynn during the reign. Brandon was a more colourful figure than the Drewes: he was clearly a merchant shipowner of importance, who traded with Norway from an early date and put his maritime expertise in many different capacities at the disposal of the Crown. Yet in spite of his services in national (not merely local) relations with the Prussians and the Hanseatic League he was not en- tirely trusted by the exchequer: for example he was in trouble over supposedly illegal sales of wine in 1393 and was never allowed to act in the customs, as we have seen, without a clerk at his elbow.

Melcombe I must postpone for the time being as of relatively small importance, and this brings me to the flourishing port of Sandwich, which had successfully reduced its neighbours, Queenburgh and Dover, to the rank of subordinate outports, though they had both been independent early in the reign. We start with the usual run of burgesses, such as John Roper, who was evidently a leading citizen of Canterbury from 1377 to 1396 and was much used on military commissions at times, though not in the customs after 1391. Then we have Thomas Elys, an important and fairly wealthy burgess of Sandwich itself and at one time mayor of the borough. Much used by the Crown in various capacities, he seems to have been politically uncommitted, in spite of royalist leanings. He happened to die in the winter of 1391–2 at the very time when changes were taking place in the staffing of the customs: as with Sewale at Ipswich, it is interesting, but useless, to speculate on the part he might have played in them had he lived. Another burgess collector, John Godard, lived on into the late nineties, but there are difficulties of identification in his case, since there may possibly have been two, or even three, John Godards in the area at that date. However this may be, the John Godard in the customs service between 1391 and 1393, and again in 1397, was closely associated with a royal clerk in the first phase and with a curialist layman in the second. The same difficulties arise in connection with another layman, Roger Wyggemore, collecting in 1390–1, but he was almost certainly a king's esquire. Then we have a minor burgess of Sandwich, Hugh atte Well; another man from Canter- bury, William Preston; and finally John Strete, a prominent burgess of Dover, who became mayor there in 1396; but none of these were in the Sandwich customs after 1392. From that date their mainstay was a well-known king's clerk (as he subsequently became), Richard Clifford, accompanied and followed by a number of obscure nonentities, probably all creatures of the Crown. Clifford has the rare distinction of serving in two adjacent ports simultaneously, since his middle years at Sandwich almost certainly coincided with similar service in London, under which head I shall have more to say about him. Perhaps he used a deputy at Sandwich for those years, as the distance from London is about sixty-six miles.

My next port, Southampton, offers the largest volume of evidence after London. It included Portsmouth and the whole Isle of Wight, and at one time stretched as far west as Melcombe. Customs-collectors were unusually powerful—even in the civil-servant phase, which set in here, as elsewhere, in and after 1392. We begin with a somewhat rascally ex-mayor, William Bacon—apparently a bastard from Bristol, who traded in wine (illegally at times), farmed the tunnage and poundage of South-ampton from 1382, until dismissed for making an excessive profit, and was none the less prominent as an ordinary customs-collector and in public works until 1388. He died a tenant-in-chief in or about 1397, and it was only then that his illegitimacy was discovered, or at least proved, by the Crown. Bacon's chief associate, and superior in most respects, John Polymond, is one of the most heavily documented characters in the whole of this inquiry. He was an immensely active merchant, shipowner, and privateer, who was twice mayor of Southampton but also did a lot of work for the Crown, most of which redounded to his own advantage. Although he took his turn very frequently in the collection of the customs for over twenty-five years, he was precisely the sort of man the exchequer did not want to employ after 1392, when his services in that particular capacity were terminated. Polymond was always much concerned with trading from Portugal, apparently in wine, but seems to have been on very poor terms with his Portuguese trading rivals, some of whom, in spite of their allied status, he actually attacked at sea. Early in his career he had to take out pardons for forestalling, profiteering, and trading with the enemy in Normandy, but, in spite of this dubious record, he was made a 'principal receiver' of tunnage and poundage in 1382, together with Thomas Beaupyne of Bristol, for the whole south and west, though this was only for a short term of years. As such, one of his first steps was to farm these valuable taxes out for a ridiculously small sum (less than £200 per annum) to his disreputable friend, William Bacon, with the consequences already noted above. In short, Polymond was a municipal tycoon and buccaneer—of some service to the Crown in many ways (I forbear to mention most of them) but usually at great advantage to himself.

Another Southampton burgess of Polymond's complexion and generation, but much less prominent, was one Nicholas Langestok, who had served as mayor some time before 1380. A conviction for forestalling and an indictment for conspiracy to defraud may possibly have caused the long gap in his public career between 1380 and 1389, but he was back for a brief period in the customs service in 1390–1. At least three well-known London citizens—William Venour, Thomas de Newton, and Gilbert Maghfeld—held office in the Southampton customs in the middle eighties; but of these only Venour deserves any special notice, which he will receive when I come to deal with London.

The only respectable ex-mayor of Southampton to serve as a collector seems to have been Philip Cake, who had been commissioned to inquire into customs irregularities when mayor in 1386, and became a collector himself in 1390–1. He is associated in this office with John Bitterlegh—a little-known burgess of Salisbury, who had, however, represented that borough in parliament in February 1388. After this the inevitable change to clerks and king's esquires is ushered in with the appearance of the obscure clerk, John Lawrence, who holds office until 1395. Obscure or not, he was evidently intended to control his first associate, John Flete—the last of the fore-stalling merchants of Southampton and a younger friend of Polymond and Bacon: he became mayor in 1397. The remaining collectors up to 1399 are all civil servants and, though not of high standing, they are none the less an interesting lot. The first is a clerk, John Newport, who has obvious connections with the powerful group of curialist officials consisting of his namesake, the king's esquire; his possible relative, Andrew Newport—a royal tool *par excellence* in Cambridgeshire and elsewhere; and the Ricardian treasurer of Calais, Roger Walden—himself a future archbishop of Canterbury and treasurer of England. John Newport is associated with, and succeeded by, a rather obscure king's esquire, Thomas Midelton, after whom we find the name of Roger Walden's brother, John, who was also a king's esquire; William Audeley, a local esquire in the county of Southampton; and finally Henry Somer, a highly professional civil servant of humble origin. After the revolution of 1399 Somer prospered exceedingly as the Lancastrian chancellor of the exchequer—at that time an office only of the middle rank—and was able to lend over £1,353 to Henry IV on his own account: he is therefore an excellent example of that continuity of adminis-tration through the revolution of 1399 especially noted by Tout.

This brings us to Great Yarmouth, the last of the more important ports outside London. Here there are no outstanding or particularly colourful figures, but the pattern is the same. Once again the customs are dominated up to 1391 by a succession of worthy, but rather uninspiring, burgesses, such as John Elys, Alexander Fastolf —member of a famous Norfolk family—and Ralph de Ramesey, who had been a bailiff of the borough in 1386. Setting aside the brief intervention in 1390–1 of Thomas Drewe from Lynn, we now come to the usual clerk, a rather obscure one. His name was Thomas de Grymesby, and he served continuously in the Yarmouth customs from 1391 to 1397. He was associated all this time with a very respectable burgess called Hugh atte Fenne—so respectable in fact that when Grymesby retired atte Fenne was allowed to act in 1398 with another equally respectable, and notably pious, burgess, William Oxeney, much given to good works.

Turning to the minor ports, we shall find nothing much to detain us in Chichester or Melcombe, but Exeter is a different matter. The Chichester customs are dominated up to 1390 by two singularly colourless figures, Richard atte Halle and Stephen Holt. They were probably both burgesses, but, in spite of numerous references to their activities as collectors of the customs, there is really no evidence at all about their back-grounds. They are succeeded in the nineties by half a dozen even more shadowy figures, about whom practically nothing is known. It is therefore impossible to say for certain whether appointments at Chichester repeated the pattern at other ports, but if there is no positive evidence in favour of the proposition there is equally nothing against it.

Much the same is true of Melcombe, which in all but name was practically an outport of Exeter. Several of its leading customs-collectors were Exeter or Dart-mouth men, and the only natives of the place at all prominent in the customs were Henry Frompton and John Chichester, who served together from 1377 to 1388. Very little is known about either of them, but Frompton at least was a merchant. What is interesting is that even in Melcombe we get the change-over to a clerk, William Holyme, in 1392–4. Holyme was probably in the royal service, judging from his benefices, but he seems to have been rather a humble individual, who was actually threatened with violence during an inquiry into customs evasion in his area during his term of office. He worked with a certain Thomas Canway, 'of Poole', and the two of them were succeeded by four shadowy figures in succession, of whom almost nothing is known. None the less Melcombe shows slightly more signs than Chichester of conforming to the general pattern, which is certainly sustained in its dominant neighbour, Exeter.

Here we are principally concerned with the burgess trio, Richard Bozoun, John Hauley, and Thomas Asshenden, though Bozoun was the only one of these to hold office in the customs for any length of time, and also the only one from Exeter: the other two were Dartmouth men. All three were obviously independent merchant shipowners, and Bozoun and Hauley at least were men of substance and standing in the south-west. All three again served in the Melcombe customs at various times as well as at Exeter, and all three, but especially Hauley, were not far removed from being part-time, but full-blooded, pirates. Bozoun at one time farmed the Exeter customs (on goods other than wool), while Hauley had a short spell as farmer of the tunnage and poundage at Melcombe. Asshenden seems to have been the most respectable of the three, but the other two were constantly in trouble with the Crown. There could be no better examples of the buccaneer burgess type which the exchequer was so anxious to exclude from customs service, and in fact none of them did serve after 1391–2. There followed at Exeter, as elsewhere, the usual succession of clerks and esquires—first, a very obscure clerk, Robert Morton, about whom nothing is known; then a Dartmouth esquire, William Damyot, possibly a hanger-on of Hauley's; then a clerk, William Selby, specially assigned to inquire into customs evasion and report to the exchequer; then an old king's esquire, Henry Rithere, previously active as a royal agent in the Channel Islands. It may seem from this summary that there could have been a set-back towards corruption under Damyot, but after 1392 he is in fact associated only with the exchequer agent, Selby. Exeter therefore conforms to the general pattern of appointments outside London, to which we must now turn.

The history of the customs administration in London during Richard II's reign is rather different from that of other ports, owing to the city's size and wealth, its own internal rivalries, and the part it played in national affairs.[4] As regards the internal struggle, the municipal politics of London were influenced for half a generation by the conflict which took place between the so-called 'reformer', John of Northampton, and the grocer Nicholas Brembre between 1382 and 1384. In essence this was an attempt to break the power of the great London capitalists—mainly victuallers—and to replace their narrow oligarchy by a somewhat wider one in which the non-victualling misteries could play an effective part. The struggle was fought out with great bitterness and divided leading Londoners for years, although John of Northampton and his friends, after early successes, were finally discredited and driven from the city in 1384. None the less, the goldsmith Adam Bamme found it necessary to make a proclamation during his second mayoralty as late as 1396-7, to the effect that no one should speak or give his opinion as to either Brembre or John of Northampton, because this led to dissension, even at that date. This quarrel between the factions of Brembre and his rival was further complicated by the fact that Brembre, having succeeded John of Northampton as mayor, rapidly developed into an ardent royalist. He was knighted, became something of a country gentleman in Middlesex, and put himself and his great wealth at Richard's disposal. All this led directly to his impeachment and execution during the period of appellant, or baronial, ascendancy in 1388. Yet the city as a whole, including many of Brembre's friends, was inclined to sympathize with, if not actively support, the appellants against the king; so here was a cross-current of considerable significance in the history of London. It provides the most plausible explanation of the extraordinary incident of 1392, when the city and its liberties were suddenly taken into the king's hand 'for lack of governance'; the mayor, sheriffs, and aldermen dismissed and replaced by nominated officials; and a corporate fine of three thousand marks (£2,000) imposed upon the out-going officers and aldermen. Yet within a very few months the fine was remitted and London's liberties restored again. Could the 'lack of governance' have had anything to do with maladministration of the immensely important London customs, which had so far been entirely in the hands of wealthy citizens? I find this difficult to believe in view of the turbulent condition and general hostility of London under Richard II, which in itself might well have justified a sharp political lesson or demonstration—yet abuse of the customs may perhaps have played a small part.

If we turn to those Londoners specially prominent in customs administration, we find Brembre himself, usually in conjunction with a mercer, John Organ, completely dominant up to his disgrace in 1387. The critical years 1387-90 are covered by a fishmonger, Nicholas Exton, and another grocer (wrongly described by me as a draper in my paper of 1957), William Venour. Exton was a leading London citizen

---

[4] For this section I am much indebted to Miss Ruth Bird's *Turbulent London of Richard II*, but I have not attempted to incorporate any material from Miss Coleman's article (loc. cit.) which runs on lines more or less parallel to my own.

before the reign began and in 1376 had represented Middlesex in the Good Parliament. He was a member of the capitalist party and, as such, one of the bitterest enemies of the reformer, John of Northampton, who returned his hostility with interest. But up to 1386 he was overshadowed by the early leaders of the London capitalists, Walworth, Philipot, and Brembre, and it was only in that year, when he succeeded Brembre as mayor and proceeded to a double term of office, that he became a figure of national importance. It fell to Exton in fact to guide London through the perils of the appellant revolution, during which a contemporary chronicler (the continuator of Knighton) represents him as willing to support Richard but unable to do so, owing to the attitude of the Londoners. He even asked permission to resign from the mayoralty, but the king refused, whereupon Exton wisely admitted the appellants to the city and obtained a personal clearance from them, as well as a precautionary pardon from the Crown for all treasons and felonies that might ever be alleged against him. He also joined the widow of another London citizen in lending the appellants £1,000, besides collecting a rather small contribution from the London customs towards the £20,000 voted them for their services by parliament. All this seems to have saved him from the fate of Brembre but still did not endear him to the Londoners, who never forgave him for his partiality to Richard. Thus in October 1388 he had to obtain from the appellants a notification prohibiting the citizens from defaming him for alleged disloyalty to the city—which was a little hard in view of the numerous royal pardons he had obtained between 1384 and 1387 for lesser London citizens involved as 'principal insurgents' in the Peasants' Revolt. We need not pursue Exton's career beyond 1390, apart from mentioning the fact that, in spite of his royalist proclivities, he was one of those aldermen temporarily disgraced in 1392. He died the following year.

Exton's contemporary and colleague, William Venour, was probably even richer, and certainly more withdrawn from politics. Though a citizen of London, he served first in the customs at Southampton, and only between 1388 and 1390 in London, where he was elected mayor in 1389. Although nominally a grocer, he seems to have owed much of his wealth to his practice of buying Welsh wool of somewhat inferior quality through agents at Carmarthen or Bristol; transporting it in his own ships to Southampton; and eventually selling it free of customs in Calais, on the ground that it had already paid customs—apparently at a lower rate—in Wales. This he did from as early as 1365 to the day of his death in 1396 or 1397. However, this was by no means his only commercial activity, and from one source or another he acquired enough money to lend very substantial sums to the Crown, with a 10 per cent hedge on the appellants. In 1392 he was again acting as a customs collector in London, but only in association with the future king's clerk, Richard Clifford. This appointment is dated only a few days after the general pardon and remission of fine granted to Venour himself, as a recent mayor, and other city officials and aldermen, after the city had been temporarily taken into the king's hand a month or two before. But this blanket restoration of liberties evidently did not entirely satisfy the cautious Venour—

or else he was genuinely in some special trouble of his own—for as much as two years later the pardon and remission of the fine had to be specifically repeated in his case, at the prayer of the queen and of the citizens of London. By that time he had already had another general pardon for all treasons, felonies, and so forth, and of the consequential outlawries and forfeitures which might arise. Though he remained an active trader for some years, we hear no more of him in connection with any public office or event, from which it is sufficiently obvious that, like all the Londoners already mentioned, he belonged to the tycoon merchant group disapproved of by the exchequer.

Another of these merchant princes, John Hadley, who was twice mayor of London, held office in the customs for a short time from 1391, but his career is so similar to those of Exton and Venour—of whom he was a close contemporary—that it is not worth recapitulating. In any case he was associated with the professional Richard Clifford, whose appointment during service at Sandwich—a collectorship which, as we have seen, he did not resign—marks the turn of the tide in London. Unfortunately, there were two Richard Cliffords in the clerical civil service at this time, both of whom became king's clerks, which makes identification rather a problem. However, it is pretty clear that the customs-collector was much the junior of the two, and he can in fact be fairly easily distinguished from his better-known namesake, who became in turn keeper of the great wardrobe (1390) and keeper of the privy seal (1397). The younger Richard Clifford never rose to these heights, although he achieved the grade of king's clerk in 1397, but it is evident that ten years before that date he was regarded as a trustworthy and competent civil servant. He does not seem to have served in the London customs after 1392—though he went on into 1394 in Sandwich—and it is remarkable that in spite of the change of policy suggested by his appointment only one other clerk—the completely obscure Henry Cokham—appears there before the revolution, and that only in connection with tunnage and poundage and the petty custom. On the other hand we do have one out-and-out royalist hireling, the layman Andrew Newport, serving in 1397.

Apart from these exceptions London customs-collectors through the nineties continued to be merchants, but merchants of a rather different type. For a short time in 1391 we get the first of the goldsmiths in the person of the Crown jeweller, John Punchon, who died in 1393. Although one of the aldermen disgraced in 1392, Punchon does not seem to have taken any part in city politics, and at the same time from the nature of his profession must have stood very close to the king. The goldsmiths always give the impression of being set apart from other misteries, and from this date onwards, right down to the time of Charles II, gradually came to be more and more employed as agents and financiers by the Crown. Thus Punchon's brief appearance in the customs is followed by that of another goldsmith, Adam Bamme, who served in 1392 and was at least reappointed in 1396, though this may have been vacated on his second election as mayor: incidentally, he was one of the few mayors of London to die in office, which he did in 1397. Essentially a craftsman, though not

warden of his gild after 1377. Bamme, together with a man called Twyford, was
among the most notable goldsmiths of Richard II's reign. In the early days he had
supported John of Northampton, but had changed sides, formed a marriage connection with Hadley, and the Brembre family, sat as alderman continuously from 1385
to 1388, and even represented London in the Merciless Parliament. During the appellant revolution he again proved a turncoat, siding first with one party, then with the
other; but this did not prevent him being elected mayor of London (in succession to
Venour) in 1390. The curious thing is that, although his name appeared on the king's
black list in 1392, this did not prevent him becoming a nominated alderman during
the short period when the city was in the king's hand. The extent of exchequer
confidence in Bamme is illustrated by the fact that he was also made a London
customs-collector in that year, and further reappointed—though he may not have
served—in 1396, both times with London citizens as colleagues. This may have been
due to his nearness to the king, the narrowness of his specialized profession, and the
equivocal part he had played in both London and national politics. But from this
time on, as I have said, for nearly three centuries it was almost enough to be a London
goldsmith to win the confidence and financial trust of the Crown.

This leaves, for London, only John Wodecok, who acted with the royal agent,
Andrew Newport, from 1397, and with another partner—according to the receipt
rolls—in 1400. Wodecok was a mercer, and subsequently lent a good deal of money
to Henry IV, but he was apparently trusted by Richard II's government and certainly
well known in London from at least 1387. His associates before the revolution
included another later (and much more vigorous) supporter of the Lancastrians in the
famous 'Dick' Whittington, but also the Ricardians, Hadley and Venour. There is,
however, some doubt about all these attributions relating to the same man, since in
April 1399 we get a sudden, unexplained reference to a John Wodecok, 'the elder',
though I do not think this is of any great significance.

This completes my survey of the medieval English ports under Richard II, and I
think it can be generally agreed that they all more or less follow the pattern set in
Newcastle upon Tyne, with the possible exception of London—and even London is
not so very different after all. It is pretty obvious that round about 1391 to 1392 the
exchequer became so dissatisfied with leakages in the collection of the customs—
particularly as the rate had been slightly increased in 1390—that they decided either
to get rid of merchant princes entirely in favour of clerks and special agents or at least
to place them under strict supervision. The result was perhaps not so much a great increase in yield as an improvement in stability: thus there is a notable decline in the
practice of assignment—that is, of anticipating customs revenue by drafts drawn on
the collectors—from the spring of 1393, and this lasts over three years. During that
time a much greater volume of hard cash coming from the customs poured into the
exchequer than had ever been the case before, and all the signs point to a considerable
reduction in fiddling and evasion. This was presumably the result of an official
decision, but how can we identify the officials who made it? There is no evidence

that the king himself had anything to do with it, and I doubt if we can find any trace of the discussions which must have taken place in the exchequer—let alone the names of the persons who took part in them—without searching the most formidable records of all, the so-called memoranda 'rolls' kept in duplicate from term to term by the king's and lord treasurer's remembrancers. These are not 'rolls' at all but vast files of parchment in innumerable leaves two or three feet long and some eighteen inches wide, all fastened together at the top and covered with closely written Latin notes in a minute hand, full of technical abbreviations. Their sheer bulk and complexity place them among the most forbidding of records, and they have seldom been consulted—and never more than dipped into—by historians. They cover the day-to-day problems and decisions of the exchequer, from the detail of routine administration to matters of high policy. There is no clue through this labyrinth, and it would take a team of highly skilled specialized research-workers several years to do for even a short run of them what has long since been done for the chancery enrolments—namely, calendar them in English. Until this is done—if it ever is done—I must confess defeat. But at least it is nice to know that the treatment meted out to Newcastle upon Tyne in 1392–3 was not a local aberration but part of a national pattern, and to feel that one may have added a footnote to a footnote of history.

The English Campaign in Scotland, 1400

A. L. BROWN

THE English invasion of Scotland in August 1400, the last to be led by an English king in person, was utterly futile. A large army took part, but it achieved nothing and withdrew after little more than a fortnight. Contemporary writers had little to say about the campaign and there is indeed little of interest in it. But there are two questions well worth investigating. First, why was it mounted at all; and second, how was it organized? The first tells something about the outlook of Henry IV who had usurped the English throne in September 1399. The second, because it is comparatively well-documented, is an interesting case-study of an aspect of the English government at work.

The immediate history of the campaign goes back to the beginning of Henry's reign. In the last ten years of Richard II's reign, following the agreement with France at Leulingham in 1389, there had been a series of truces between England and Scotland. The latest had been agreed at a meeting of commissaries at Haddenstank, near Kelso, on 14 May 1399 to last for a year from the following Michaelmas. In the circumstances of the usurpation it was clearly in Henry's interest to continue this truce, and even before he became king on 30 September he wrote to Robert III asking him to send some of his council to confirm it.[1] It was equally in Robert's interest to try to gain advantage from Henry's weakness, and when he (in practice probably his son David, duke of Rothesay, who was lieutenant of the kingdom) replied on 6 October it was merely to delay. Individual Scots meanwhile were disturbing the marches; Wark castle on the English side of the Tweed was destroyed; but no other major incident is known and it is, therefore, surprising that Henry reacted so very strongly. On 10 November the earl of Northumberland, Constable of England, by command of the king, reminded the lords temporal in parliament that it had been explained to them earlier that the king intended to make war on the Scots, and that some had then said that this course should only be taken by the advice and instigation of Northumberland and the earl of Westmorland, the Marshal of England. The two earls now excused themselves and begged the king to make his own will known, and Henry himself spoke 'in full parliament'. He declared that God had sent him to the realm and made him king for its salvation, and that he intended to undertake this campaign personally. The lords were questioned individually and consented to the plan. The king then thanked them in emotional terms.

---

[1] The letter is known only from Robert's reply printed in *Royal and Historical Letters during the Reign of Henry IV*, ed. F. C. Hingeston, Rolls Series, 1860–1965, i. 4–6. I am grateful to my wife for her helpful criticism of this paper.

What this oddly worded account seems to convey is that the campaign was the king's own scheme, that it meant a lot to him, and that it had met with criticism, perhaps because it was thought unlikely to succeed, perhaps because it would interfere with the preserves of the marcher lords. The Commons were more forthright; they petitioned Henry not to go himself to the marches.[2] What both lords and Commons favoured was probably what they had petitioned for on 31 October, strong provision for the border, not a campaign, something like the ordinance for the marches made after the campaign of 1400.[3]

What provoked Henry's belligerent attitude? It is tempting to say that it was a letter from Robert III dated at Linlithgow on 2 November.[4] In this he did not offer to confirm the truce as Henry had asked, but instead offered to send commissaries and deputies to Haddenstank on a date to be arranged to treat about a truce or a more comprehensive settlement, and to remedy past breaches of the truce. In the meantime he suggested that the wardens should meet for a pacification. It was a politic but not unreasonable reply except that it was addressed to Henry not as king but as duke of Lancaster, earl of Derby, and Steward of England. This was probably the style Henry had used in his September letter, but Robert must have known that Henry was now king, and it is difficult not to believe that it was a deliberate riposte to the English king's refusal to address the king of Scots as king; for years English royal documents had used words such as 'consanguineus noster' or 'adversarius noster' instead of 'rex Scottorum' much to the dislike of the Scots. Robert's emphasis in the letter that Haddenstank was a traditional meeting-place also seems to have caused offence because it touched on the delicate question of where the border lay. Meetings of representatives should take place near the border, but the problem was whether this should take account of areas in Scotland occupied in Edward III's reign but now largely recovered by the Scots. After long debate Richard II had surrendered the point in the 1390s; now Henry IV was taking it up again because Haddenstank was on the old border line. He instructed his negotiators to press for meeting-places well inside Scotland.[5] It was on matters like these, the independence of Scotland and its territorial integrity, that the Scots hoped to gain advantages from Henry; they wanted a peace on the basis of the Treaty of Edinburgh–Northampton of 1328. Robert's letter could have reached Henry by 10 November, but Henry had declared his intention earlier, and it was probably the general attitude of the Scots and their success against Richard II which had provoked him. They had ceased to pay David II's ransom in 1377 when £16,000 was still due; they had continued to recover parts of southern Scotland occupied during Edward III's reign; and they had forced the

---

[2] *Rot. Parl.* iii. 427–8; ibid. 434.

[3] *Anglo-Norman Letters and Petitions*, ed. M. Dominica Legge (Anglo-Norman Text Society, 1941), 25; *P.P.C.*, ed. N. H. Nicolas (1834–7), i. 119 and 124–6.   [4] Hingeston, 8–10.

[5] *P.P.C.* ii. 41. On this and other points I am greatly indebted to an unpublished thesis by Miss Edna Hamer (Sister Dominic Savio), 'Anglo-Scottish Relations in the Reigns of Robert II and Robert III', Glasgow, 1971. See R. L. Storey 'The Wardens of the Marches of England towards Scotland, 1377–1489', *E.H.R.*, 1957; J. A. Tuck, 'Richard II and the Border Magnates', *Northern History*, 1969.

English to take new measures to contain them—lieutenancies on the border for John of Gaunt, a campaign into Scotland in 1385, and the costly system of paid wardens of the marches. The Scots had all in all been distinctly successful, and Henry must have been well aware of this. The emotional words of 10 November suggest a man anxious to give a firm lead where this had previously been lacking.

Henry had probably never intended a winter campaign and, as his behaviour during the invasion shows, he was not vindictive towards the Scots. The belligerent words were, therefore, followed by negotiations or rather manœuvres preliminary to negotiations in which he must have felt the Scots were profoundly irritating. He replied sometime in December to Robert's letter of 2 November, telling him that he had ordered his wardens of the marches to send their deputies to Kelso on 5 January to arrange a meeting-place for commissaries, and on 10 December he prematurely commissioned three deputies and special commissaries, about the same time sending a spy, Thomas de la Hawe, to report on Scottish war preparations to the council. Robert received the letter only on 4 January, too late to do anything about the Kelso meeting even if he had wanted to do so, and when he eventually replied on 14 March he merely repeated his proposal for a meeting at Haddenstank.[6] This rebuff no doubt confirmed Henry's view that a campaign was the only way to deal with the Scots, and no more letter or payments to messengers with letters are known for some time. Negotiations, however, began with George Dunbar, the Scottish earl of March, who in February, after a quarrel with the duke of Rothesay, decided to renounce his allegiance and do homage to Henry, and with Donald of the Isles who could be a threat to the Scots in the west. The next direct move was a commission of 24 May to three envoys to offer Robert III the opportunity to renew the truce with England as the French had just done.[7] Nothing seems to have come of this and the army was summoned to assemble at York on 24 June.

At this point the Scots decided to open negotiations, clearly to try to halt the campaign. On 26 June at York three English commissaries were appointed to treat for a peace or a truce; the Scottish commissaries, an archdeacon and an esquire, had probably already arrived, and perhaps they had come without prior arrangement for they had to have safe conducts on 2 July to *return home*. They were still at York on the 8th when the keeper of the Hanaper was ordered to give them their safe conducts free, and on the same day another commission was issued to the English negotiators.[8] In the circumstances, an army assembling and the truce between England and France renewed, the Scots might have been expected to be accommodating, but they were

---

[6] Henry and Robert's letters are in Hingeston, 11–14 and 25–7; the commission in *Rotuli Scotiae* (1814–19), ii. 152–3; and the payment to the spy in Exchequer, Exchequer of Receipt, Issue Rolls, E403/564, 17 Dec. 1399.

[7] Ibid. 23–5, etc. An esquire was sent with letters and a safe conduct for Donald and his brother John to come to England. E403/567, 31 May. *Foedera*, ed. T. Rymer, 1704–35, viii. 146; also ibid. 144.

[8] *C.P.R., 1399–1401*, 352–3. In *Foedera*, viii. 150 the safe conduct to the Scots of 22 June is misdated 22 July. The full text (Chancery, Patent Rolls, c 66/388) grants safe conduct to the two commissaries for ten weeks to go to Scotland and return with twenty-five people in their company.

not. They were offering peace on the basis of the Treaty of Edinburgh–Northampton of 1328 by which Edward III had recognized the sovereignty of Scotland. This seems to have taken Henry by surprise because on 4 July he ordered the council at Westminster to search for 'remembrances et evidences' of this and other truces and peaces between the two countries and send them to him in haste. Considerable preparation was in fact made for negotiation.[9] But the Scottish commissaries are not known to have returned as they had intended and the campaign went ahead. The research done seems, however, to have had an important effect on Henry for he now began to stress a demand for homage from the Scots. On 6 and 7 August he addressed letters to King Robert and to the Scottish magnates calling on them to do homage to him at Edinburgh on 23 August on the basis of precedents going back to Locrine, son of Brutus, and he sent three knights and three esquires to proclaim this in public places in Scotland.[10] Henry cannot have been completely ignorant before this of English claims to sovereignty over Scotland, but homage is not mentioned in the earlier documents, for example in Henry's speech in parliament, and it is likely that what he had envisaged was a punitive expedition, at best leading to a decisive battle with the Scots, at least a major *chevauchée* which would end border disturbances and lead to a satisfactory peace or truce. No doubt he was encouraged in this by the defection of the earl of March, which must have raised the possibility of holding lands in southern Scotland. Now homage became the theme of the campaign which indeed became a war of words. The army crossed into Scotland on 14 August and rapidly advanced by Haddington to Leith, the Scots offering no resistance.[11] The duke of Rothesay holding Edinburgh castle sent letters to Henry, pointedly addressed merely to 'our adversary of England', offering to fight him with 300 or 200 or 100 nobles to avoid shedding Christian blood, and from Leith on the 21st Henry replied by again demanding homage.[12] All that he achieved was some kind of meeting at the cross between Edinburgh and Leith between messengers or commissaries, including Adam Forster, esquire, one of the Scots commissaries at York, at which the Scots spoke softly and

---

[9] *P.P.C.* i. 123. On 15 and 17 July charters and muniments, a small quaternion of memoranda (taken from Liber A) and a bag with divers chronicles were issued from the treasury to John Norbury, the treasurer, to take to the king on the expedition against the Scots, 'divina gracia devicendos' as the clerk wrote hopefully! *The Ancient Kalendars and Inventories of the Treasury*, ed. F. Palgrave, 1836, ii. 62–3. Later Henry Somer, an exchequer clerk much concerned with the financial side of the expedition, was paid a regard of £20 for bringing 8,000 marks to Newcastle and 'circa transcripturam diversorum rotulorum et evidencium tangencium homagium nuper factum per reges Scocie certis regibus Anglie et alios tractatus inter ipsos nuper reges ad diversas vices habitos pro avisamento et inspeccione in eisdem per dominum nostrum regem et consilium suum in Marchia Scocie existencium'. E403/567, 25 Sept. This is probably a payment for writing Glasgow University Library MS. Gen. 1053 (formerly BE 10-y. 3), a collection which could fit this description. See E. L. G. Stones, 'The Records of the "Great Cause" of 1291–92', *Scottish H.R.*, 1956.

[10] *Foedera*, viii. 155–7. See E. L. G. Stones, 'The Appeal to History in Anglo-Scottish Relations between 1291 and 1401', *Archives*, 1969–70.

[11] *Johannis de Fordun Scotichronicon*, ed. W. Goodall, Edinburgh, 1759, ii. 430, gives the date of entry and Adam of Usk, *Chronicon*, ed. E. M. Thompson, London, 1904, 47, the date of the return, and both dates are quite probable. [12] *Foedera*, viii. 157.

promised to consider Henry's claim.[13] There was little fighting and probably little booty; supplies were apparently running short; and Henry had to be content with this promise and return ingloriously over the border on 29 August.

All these dealings suggest that Henry was somewhat naïve. He had over-reacted to a situation which does not seem suddenly to have become more serious, though he certainly considered it serious. He behaved like an honourable but inexperienced man, conscious of his kingly dignity and duty, anxious to be firm but reasonable, to succeed where Richard II had failed and with the old-fashioned belief that a campaign could bring decisive results. The Scots had made him look foolish, and this is particularly striking when one considers the size of the army he led into Scotland and the effort and money it cost to organize the campaign.

There is a considerable amount of documentary evidence about the mounting of the campaign though it is primarily in financial records such as warrants for payments, the payments themselves, and the accounts of men who paid or provisioned the army and the accompanying ships. Most important are the account for £6,582. 15s. 8d. paid out in August by John Curson, treasurer of wars for the expedition, in wages for 1,771 men-at-arms and 11,314 archers, and a roll subsidiary to this which shows this sum made up of 199 payments to 212 named leaders who mustered contingents ranging from a single archer to the 1,200 men with the earl of Westmorland and the 1,476 in a Household brigade. A file of twenty-eight sealed certificates on whose authority Curson made payments gives the names of a further 650 men, mostly archers, in some of the contingents. There is also a number of accounts for transport and provisions, including those of three provisioners, John Stapulton, Piers Crulle, and Robert Cliderowe, which give the names of the captains to whom they issued stores;[14] and many other record sources provide further information. The great lacuna is the absence of any detailed Household accounts, for it handled a lot of money this year and clearly played a considerable part in the expedition. These administrative records contain a great many facts, but the difficulty, as always in this sort of study, is to make them yield a coherent picture of events they were not written to record.

These sources show that the army was one of the largest ever assembled in medieval England. Curson's account shows 13,085 fighting men at the muster. Crulle issued supplies at Leith for 11,188 men, but this was not necessarily the whole army near Edinburgh, nor in all Scotland. Indeed the fact that Crulle's account mentions 135 captains, including the earls of Arundel and Suffolk and Lords Lovel and Zouche, whose names are not recorded by Curson, might be held to suggest that the army had

---

[13] The meeting is mentioned in instructions given to English negotiators later in 1400. *P.P.C.* i. 169. Two years later Forster had the misfortune to be captured and in parliament Henry accused him of deceiving him 'par pluseurs blanches paroles et bealx promesses' to leave Scotland. *Rot. Parl.* iii. 487.

[14] Curson's account and the roll are Exchequer, L.T.R., Foreign Accounts, E364/34, Rot. D and Exchequer K.R., Various Accounts, E101/43/3. The certificates (E101/43/4), which vary considerably in form, relate to a block of payments towards the end of the account, and are clearly only part of a large file. The provisiones' accounts are E101/42/32 (Stapulton) and 35 (Crulle) and E364/34, Rot. F (Cliderowe).

increased since the muster. This may have been true of some contingents. William, lord Willoughby, for example, mustered 29 men-at-arms and 163 archers, but later accounted in the exchequer, the only commander known to have had this privilege, for wages for himself, 3 knights, 27 men-at-arms, and 179 archers for 25 days' service between 6 and 31 August, the days they left and returned to Newcastle.[15] If the figures are correct, the extra men could be late-comers, but they could be men from other contingents amalgamated with Willoughby's own. Reorganization seems to be the likely reason for the wide divergences between the accounts of Curson and Crulle. The earl of Northumberland for example mustered 7 men-at-arms and 160 archers but had provisions for 345 and 500. He could have recruited more men or taken some from the border garrisons, but the most likely explanation is simply that men from other contingents were placed under his command. Reorganization must have been necessary to make an army out of the miscellany of contingents almost half of whom mustered less than ten men, and it is surely an indication of this process that most of Crulle's issues were made to 100 or multiples of 100 men, often under a number of captains; in other words, to 'centuries' made-up of a number of contingents. Reorganization would also explain why there are variations in the men named in the two types of account. Curson's account conceals the names of knights and esquires in the contingents, particularly in the large Household contingent, men who became the commanders of fighting units. On the other hand, some men who led contingents to the muster were lost to sight as their contingents were amalgamated into larger units. These units in turn must have been grouped into strategic divisions, 'battles', advance and rear guards, or other formations but there is no record of this.

The most accurate figure for the size of the field army must be that in Curson's account based on the musters, just over 13,000 men; others may have come late, but no doubt some fell out. To this must be added the soldiers and sailors on the ships, perhaps some town contingents,[16] and the servants, the clerks, and so on. Between 15,000 and 20,000 men were on campaign. This is probably slightly smaller than the armies led into Scotland in 1314, 1335, and 1385, but larger than the armies taken to the continent in the later Middle Ages save for the huge army at Crécy–Calais in 1345.[17] There can be no doubt that this was a major enterprise, intended to achieve a significant result.

How then was this army raised? Not by feudal service, not by commissions of

---

[15] E364/34, Rot. E.

[16] Flour and herring were issued as a reward to two esquires who brought 120 men from the city of London by order of the Council 'en eide et refresshement de nous et de nostre host', but this could have been shipboard service. Exchequer, Exchequer of Receipt, Writs and Warrants for Issues, E404/15, no. 485. The banner of St. John of Beverley presumably with some of the townsmen was present (E101/42/32), and so was the banner of St. Cuthbert of Durham carried Dom by William Claxton, an ex-prior of Coldingham rejected by the Scots. E101/42/35. See A. L. Brown, 'The Priory of Coldingham in the Late Fourteenth Century', *Innes Review*, 1972.

[17] See J. H. Ramsay, 'The Strength of English Armies in the Middle Ages', *E.H.R.*, 1914; A. E. Prince, 'The Strength of English Armies in the Reign of Edward III', ibid., 1931; and N. B. Lewis, 'The Last Medieval Summons of the English Feudal Levy, 13 June 1385', ibid., 1958.

array, not by indenture, but by summoning all those who had a personal bond with the king. About the beginning of June messengers were sent out with privy-seal letters (many letters, for they were paid £7 for their wages and expenses) 'dominis, baronibus, militibus, scutiferis, et aliis personis de retinencia regis' in all counties ordering them to go with the king to resist the malice of the Scots and to assemble at York on the 24th.[18] Letters-close dated 9 June were sent under the great seal to all sheriffs and to the chancellor of the palatinate of Lancaster to proclaim that 'omnes et singuli milites, armigeri at valetti' who had fees, wages, or annuities from the king or from Edward III, the Black Prince, John of Gaunt, or Richard II which the king had confirmed were to come armed to York or wherever the king was on 24 June to go to Scotland under pain of losing their grants.[19] The first summons had to be repeated, at least in the south, for in July signet letters were sent to the archbishop of Canterbury and the sheriffs of ten southern counties to proclaim that knights, esquires, and other persons of the king's retinue were to hasten to Newcastle to join the expedition.[20] A force of sixty men-at-arms and 500 archers was called out to Newcastle on 12 July by signet letter to the sheriff of Chester dated 25 June.[21] This letter mentioned that the method had already been explained to him and no doubt a good deal of verbal arranging and pressing went on, particularly in the north and in the duchy of Lancaster from which many men came. The results are impressive, particularly when one remembers how recently Henry had become king.

The magnates, many of whom had been present in parliament and great council when the campaign had been discussed during the previous ten months, responded well as they normally did for campaigns. For them it was a matter of honour to serve. The king's eldest sons, Henry and Thomas, boys of twelve and eleven, were present, and so were seven of the eleven dukes and earls then of age. The exceptions were York and Warwick, discredited, elderly men whose heirs brought contingents, Devon who was probably blind, and Worcester who had probably been ordered to remain at the council at Westminster, and certainly attended a meeting there on 21 August. Almost half of the barons summoned to parliament in September 1400, seventeen of the thirty-five, also served. In terms of men, Westmorland's contingent of 1,200 was by far the largest, though a thousand of these were archers. On average earls (excluding Westmorland) brought 192 men, barons 77; and the total led by the princes, earls, and barons, as far as we know, was 578 men-at-arms and 2,594 archers. This is a smaller proportion of the army than in other expeditions in the later Middle Ages, but the explanation is not that the magnates held back but that an unusually heavy demand was made on lesser men.[22]

[18] E403/567, 4 June. Lord Willoughby is said to have been summoned by a privy-seal letter (E364/34, Rot. E says a signet letter, but this is probably a mistake) to come to York with all his retinue and to assemble it in the two days after 24 June. E404/16, no. 378.

[19] *Foedera*, viii. 146. [20] E403/567, 13 July.

[21] Chester, Chester Recognisance Rolls, 2/74, Rot. 9.

[22] The contingents brought by the magnates (with the numbers of men-at-arms and archers for which Curson paid them), Prince Henry (17+99), Prince Thomas (14+62), and the earls of Arundel, North-

These lesser men, the knights and esquires, are too large and disparate a group to consider fully in a short paper; indeed all that can be done is to give some impressions. For a start one must admit that there is a great gap in the evidence. Almost 400 of their names are known, but others are just numbers in other men's contingents. It would be particularly interesting for example to know the names of the 244 men-at-arms mustered by the treasurer and controller of the Household, Thomas Tutbury and Robert Litton. Presumably the backbone of this brigade was made up of Household officials, knights, and esquires of the Hall and Chamber, and others close to the king, and it is significant that none of the men later described as Chamber Knights was paid by Curson though five, Richard Arundel, John Dalyngrigge, Ralph Rocheford, Thomas Swynford, and Payn Tiptoft, had provisions from Crulle, and that none of the five knights and esquires sent with Curson to read the letters demanding homage from the Scots was paid by him. The Household chamberlain, Sir Thomas Erpingham, also had provisions but no payment, but it is not clear whether he and others like him were independent of this brigade. Men formally retained by the king probably also formed part of this brigade, though many came independently and were paid by Curson. More than one in three of these are recorded on the expedition, and as the true figure must be higher still, it seems reasonable to conclude that the summons to the king's retainers was successful.[23] The summons to those holding grants or annuities seems to have been much less successful, though the king must have anticipated this. His intention was probably to bring out the more warlike and willing, though there is evidence in the form of letters of exemption and of annuities refused for failing to serve to show that the summons was taken seriously.[24]

Two areas of the country deserve particular mention. In view of Chester's loyalty to Richard II and the rebellion there at the beginning of 1400 it may seem surprising to find John Mascy of Podyngton mustering fifty-six men-at-arms and 488 Cheshire archers in answer to a summons dated 25 June directed to him as sheriff. A list survives

---

umberland (7+160), Rutland (78+200), Somerset (39+160), Stafford (38+88), Suffolk, Westmorland (200+1,000), Charleton of Powys (27+136), Clynton, Scrope of Masham (3+14), Roos (26+100), Fitzhugh (20+80), Ferrers of Groby (10+32), Morley (7+23), Cromwell, Darcy (9+32), Fitzwalter (4+16), Willoughby (29+163), Lovel, Grey of Codnor (13+57), Grey of Ruthin (18+100), Bardolf (14+50), Scales (5+17), and Zouche. See also M. R. Powicke, 'Lancastrian Captains', in *Essays in Medieval History Presented to Bertie Wilkinson* ed. T. A. Sandquist and M. R. Powicke, Toronto, 1969, and J. R. Lander, 'The Hundred Years War and Edward IV's 1475 campaign in France', in *Tudor Men and Statesmen: Studies in English Law and Government*, ed. A. J. Slavin, Baton Rouge, 1972.

[23] I have discussed these retainers in a paper in *Fifteenth-century England 1399–1509*, ed. S. B. Chrimes, C. D. Ross, and R. A. Griffiths, Manchester, 1972, and I must retract a statement in it (p. 19) that only one in six retainers served in Scotland. This was based on Curson's account, but the evidence of the provisioners' accounts and other sources doubles the figure.

[24] For example members of Queen Isabel's Household who had fees and annuities had a patent of exemption (*C.P.R.*, *1399–1401*, 323) and there are five signet letters excusing individuals from service, a warning letter sent to a man inclined to disobey the summons and a letter of thanks for the substitute he sent in Ancient Correspondence (S.C. 1), vol. xliii. On 11 Oct. 1400 the council decided that only those who swore that they had been on the expedition were to have writs for payment of their annuities. Exchequer, T. R., Council and Privy Seal, E28/8.

of the knights and esquires and of the seven hundreds from which the archers came, and this was clearly a force ordered from the principality in the same way as forces had been raised for Edward III's campaigns and officered by the same men or the same families as had served then or in Richard II's Cheshire guard.[25] The Cheshire rebellion of January 1400 was outweighed by the value of the archers. And the outstanding example of personal loyalty is the response of the men of the king's own duchy of Lancaster, at least those in the north and Midlands and in the county of Lancaster. More than half of the stewards, bailiffs, receivers, and constables in the 'North Parts' are known to have served in Scotland, and some of the largest contingents came with them. The Chief Steward, Sir Richard Hoghton, mustered 310 men and his brother, Sir Henry, 300; Sir Robert Waterton, Steward of the Honour of Pontefract, and one of the first to join Henry IV in 1399, mustered 336; Sir Thomas Tunstall brought 225, Sir Thomas Radcliffe, 220; and so down through many smaller contingents. The total strength was at least 3,500 men, all but about 200 of them archers, and this is probably a conservative estimate. A good number of the same men had helped Henry to the throne in 1399 and they turned out again and again in the troubles of the first half of the reign.[26]

The writs of summons do therefore indicate quite accurately the character of the army. It was largely an army of the king's retainers leading out their men. It is striking what a small proportion of the county establishment, the sheriffs, the justices of the peace, the members of parliament, and so on, are known to have served. Southerners served; London sent some men; but it was very much an army from the north and the duchy. And it was an unusual army. The common method of contracting for troops by indenture was apparently not used. The men were paid, but the method of payment was also unusual. Only Lord Willoughby's contingent as far as we know was paid at daily rates according to status, 4s. for himself, 2s. for his knights, 1s. for his men-at-arms, and 6d. for his archers *per diem* for twenty-five days, counting from the day he left Newcastle until he returned. Curson paid 20s. for each man-at-arms and 10s. for each archer, though not all leaders were paid in full by him, and some certainly received further payments from other sources. At contemporary rates this was wages for twenty days' service, paid in advance, but it was a once-and-for-all payment unrelated to days of service. All this is so unusual that it requires explanation, and this must lie in Henry's financial circumstances. In February 1400, desperately short of money, Henry had appealed to the lords in a great council for help to meet the threats from the Scots (which he stressed) and to defend Calais and the seas, and the lay lords, or some of them, had promised not money but service for three months with specified troops at their own expense.[27] This is surely the background to the

[25] E101/42/29.

[26] The names of the officers are listed in R. Somerville, *History of the Duchy of Lancaster*, London, 1953. For example the names of many Lancastrians who brought out men to help Henry win the throne in 1399 and who were summoned to come out on a campaign in Wales in 1405 are to be found in the Duchy of Lancaster, Miscellaneous Books, D.L. 42/15, ff. 68ʳ–69ʳ and 16, f. 128ʳ. A similar summons had probably gone out in 1400.

[27] *P.P.C.* i. 102–6.

willingness of the lords to serve on these less favourable terms and why there was a general summons to the king's retainers and fee'd men. It was an attempt to mount an honourable expedition economically.

The character of the army also offers an explanation of the long delay between the assembly date at York on 24 June and the advance into Scotland in mid August. This must have been intentional for the preparations were not complete before August; the king's tents for example did not leave London until 17 July. Henry probably summoned the men early to allow for the delay there would be in assembling and ordering such an army, though the delay cannot have been good for morale or for the food supplies. There seems to have been a gradual build-up to an invasion always planned for August. For example, the men of the Cinque Ports were ordered by letters dated 12 June to bring the ships they owed to Newcastle upon Tyne on 9 August to sail with the king's fleet against the Scots.[28] The king himself reached York on 22 June with a skeleton administration, a section of chancery with the golden great seal and the signet office, while the three great officers remained at Westminster with the majority of the council to further the campaign from there and deal with other business. The king moved forward to Newcastle by 25 July, a day or two after the keeper of the privy seal and perhaps the treasurer and other officials left Westminster to join him, leaving chancellor Scarle and a few councillors 'on duty' there. At Newcastle on 3 August the treasurer handed over the bulk of the money Curson received to pay the troops,[29] and the army moved out on 6 and 7 August and advanced slowly to the Border, crossing into Scotland on the 14th.

The provision of food proceeded less smoothly. Almost all the evidence about this dates from July, and it seems likely that the king had hoped that normal Household methods would be sufficient to supply the army, and when this proved optimistic he was forced to take extra measures which were probably inadequate. A major drive certainly seems to have begun on 4 July when he wrote from York to the council at Westminster that he was not yet at all (*de tout*) provided with wine, flour, corn, and oats for the Household and the army.[30] He ordered the council to have privy-seal letters issued to the mayor and officers of London, the Cinque Ports, and east-coast towns from Orwell in Essex to Scarborough to send supplies by sea to Newcastle, Holy Island, and Berwick with promise of repayment from the local customs; and the treasurer was told to give the best security he could for this. This round-about method was used presumably because the privy seal was more authoritative than the signet particularly for guaranteeing repayment, though the king used the signet to send hastening letters to the ports from York and Newcastle. Privy-seal letters dated 12 July and letters from the treasurer were duly sent out,[31] and a number of

---

[28] *C.C.R., 1399–1402* (1927), 158. [29] E101/42/28. [30] *P.P.C.* i. 122–3.
[31] E403/567, 25 Sept. Four messengers received £4 for delivering the signet letters. *P.P.C.* i. 123–4. The only response that is recorded was twelve tuns of beer and other supplies delivered to Richard Cliderowe and John Feriby, governors of the king's supplies (see below). The beer had not been paid for in 1406. E404/22, no. 201.

small armed convoys did sail up the east coast during July and August, but the evidence is again too fragmentary to justify more than impressions of the operation.

The main centres of provisioning were the Thames and the Humber. At least three convoys set out from the Thames. John Stapulton took 100 tons of flour and ten tons of salt by sea from London to Newcastle and Edinburgh.[32] He bought the flour from three London merchants with money issued from the exchequer in the name of Thomas Tutbury, treasurer of the Household, and the salt came from the king's store (*stauro*) in the Tower. He loaded them on the *Marie* of Gosport, the *George* of Orwell, the *Margaret* of London, and an unnamed fourth ship, and sailed from London on 20 July with a guard of four men-at-arms and eight valets. At Newcastle some of the food was issued to the army, some was sold to pay the cost of transport, and, probably on the return, some was landed and taken to York for the king's use; more was then issued at Leith. The issues, all carefully detailed in his account, were made on the authority of the treasurer, John Norbury, and the whole operation cost 500 marks for the flour and £56. 13s. 2½d. for the transport—including £2 paid on the king's verbal order to fishermen fishing in the sea at Leith! Two other convoys sailed out of London, though we know much less about them. John Michel, a serjeant-at-arms, was in charge of unspecified supplies provided by the council, probably in London, and he and four others had forty men-at-arms and eighty archers as well as sixty seamen in the *Christopher* which presumably protected other ships.[33] The other convoy was a small fleet of the king's own ships, the *Trinity of the Tower*, the *Grace Dieu of the Tower*, the barges *Nicholas of the Tower* and the *Holy Ghost*, and the ballinger *Anne of the Tower*. They were made ready by the clerk of ships, John Chamberlain, and early in July commissions were issued to take 244 seamen to man them. A few days later Chamberlain drew wages for two months' service for the crews of all but the *Grace Dieu*. Some at least of the seamen were given arms from the Privy Wardrobe in the Tower, and an esquire, Richard Cliderowe, commanded 117 men-at-arms and 134 archers in the *Trinity* and the *Nicholas*. His commission was to pass and work with ships, barges, ballingers, and crayers taking food loaded in London to the king and the army in Scotland and to take soldiers to protect it. He was in effect an admiral who mustered his men before Chamberlain, made an indenture of service with him, and served with some of his men from 25 July until 29 September and with others until 23 November. Apart from a privateering fleet of six ships out of Lynn operating against Scots and Frieslanders, Cliderowe's was the only naval force protecting the supply ships.[34]

[32] E364/35, Rot. I is his enrolled account, E101/42/32 is the particulars. He seems to have been a former retainer of Gaunt who had experience as a deputy of the Chief Butler and in minor customs posts. He was probably the John Stapulton paid by the Chief Butler for taking wine to Scotland and this is why he was given the task of shipping the food. E403/567, 13 July. Three years later, described as a king's esquire, he was still due money for the work. *C.P.R., 1401–1405,* 248.

[33] E403/567, 14 Aug. and E404/15, nos. 481 and 485. The last mentions flour and herring in Michel's custody.

[34] The evidence for the preparations is E101/42/39, *C.P.R., 1399–1401,* 217, and E403/567, 13 July—

The information about provisioning on the Humber shows a different operation. Richard Cliderowe, esquire, of Newcastle upon Tyne accounted for £40. 7d. spent by order of the council in taking to Scotland wine, flour, corn, oats, peas and beans, stockfish, flatfish, cheese, sides of bacon, and some bows and bow cords delivered to him by John Thorp and William Rounde, customs collectors in Boston and Kingston upon Hull respectively.[35] They may have bought the supplies directly or they have received them from the townsmen in answer to the king's letter. Cliderowe had a small fleet and twenty men-at-arms and forty archers paid from 6 August until 2 September to protect it while he sailed to Newcastle and Leith and back. Cliderowe was also engaged in shipping other cargoes from the Humber, working with John Feriby and the same customs collectors. Cliderowe's task was the shipment and issue of provisions, though it was Feriby who had authority by a commission dated at York on 6 July to arrest the necessary ships. Feriby also collected provisions. Two of his men went round Holderness and the Wolds as far north as Scarborough buying food from individuals and constables while two more men remained at Kingston upon Hull, the centre of the operation, to receive it. Royal officials brought in more. For example, Thomas Dudley, valet of the bakery in the Household, handed over 61 tons of flour from Thornton in Lincolnshire to Cliderowe and Round by command and supervision of Feriby, 'commissarius in partibus Humbrie'.[36]

It is impossible to 'marry' the quantities of supplies mentioned in the various accounts and to give an over-all figure of the amount shipped. For example the most informative account from a military viewpoint is Crulle's but we don't know where his supplies came from, though his own connections were with Boston. And virtually nothing is known about the work done from the Household. It seems likely, however, because there are no exchequer accounts for them, that the initial arrangements were directed from the Household and were seen to be failing early in July. Food was probably short in any case because of bad weather.[37] The army was assembling, and so there began a rescue operation under the direction of the council and the treasurer. Money was provided from the exchequer and the customs collectors; an *ad hoc* group of men was set to work; food was bought from merchants or purveyed in the countryside; and it was checked and shipped north under guard. It was an impressive operation for which the treasurer, John Norbury, seems to deserve the credit, but it was probably too late to find food in sufficient quantity to sustain a long campaign. It is an indication of the difficulties that the Cinque Ports were told to be sure that twenty ships were at Newcastle on 4 August or earlier if possible, loaded

£188 paid to three masters, three constables, and 198 seamen; for the arms E364/35, Rot. G; for Cliderowe's command *Rotuli Scotiae*, ii. 153, E364/34, Rot. D, and E404/16, no. 397—his wage bill was £820. 7s.; and for the Lynn fleet, C.P.R., *1399–1401*, 291.

[35] E364/34, Rot. F and E101/42/30, 31 and 34. Cliderowe was a Newcastle man who served as deputy of the Chief Butler and customs collector in Newcastle and near-by ports and escheator in Northumberland.

[36] C.P.R., *1399–1401*, 355. Feriby, who may have been an official in the Household, was commissioned at York. E101/42/33 and 31.

[37] J. H. Wylie, *History of England under Henry the Fourth*, London, 1884–98, i. 135–6.

with food for their crews and the army, apparently in lieu of their quota of fifty-seven ships which had been summoned in June. Even more striking were the orders that went out dated 22 August from Westminster to sixteen ports from Southampton to Liverpool and to towns in Ireland to hasten support by the west coast for the army in Scotland.[38] This must represent instructions from the king of about a week earlier, from Berwick perhaps. This suggests that east-coast supplies were inadequate, though the king thanked the men of the Cinque Ports and the northern ports for their help, and that the king at that stage was contemplating a campaign through to the west coast. It seems to confirm the suggestion in an English and a Scottish chronicle that the campaign had to be abandoned for lack of supplies.[39]

Much more is known about the king's own 'supply' departments simply because they accounted in the exchequer and their accounts survive. A great deal of technical detail can be found for example about the work of the clerk of the king's ships. The king's pavilions and tents were made ready and shipped from London on 17 July by the serjeant in charge, John Drayton, and twenty-two tradesmen.[40] They were put ashore at Newcastle and went on with the army, eventually reaching London again by sea on 29 September. Horses, carts, and fodder must have been ready for them at Newcastle, presumably obtained by Household purveyors in the normal way, though individual commissions were issued to men to take what was necessary to carry materials from the Great Wardrobe and the king's jewels, significantly perhaps issued late in the day.[41] The king's horses came from the stud kept by the Master of the Great Horses, Robert Waterton, who was himself with the expedition, though no horse list survives for the campaign. Wine for the king's use was shipped north by order of the Chief Butler and more was bought locally. The soldiers came with their own arms but additional supplies were bought for them in the localities, and a great quantity came from the Privy Wardrobe in the Tower under its keeper, John Norbury, the treasurer of England. Bows, arrows, cross-bow bolts, lances, axes, shields, armour and head pieces, cannon and all their supplies, and other war materials were bought or made ready by his technicians, and then shipped to Newcastle and Leith.[42] The transport of these materials and foodstuffs meant a considerable exercise which must have greatly disturbed east-coast trade that summer. The method employed was probably the common one of commissioning a serjeant-at-arms to seize merchant-ships for the king's use,[43] and at least twenty-eight ships are mentioned by name in

[38] *C.C.R., 1399–1402*, 170–1. This letter dated 24 July confirmed an earlier privy-seal letter and demanded a statement of what food was being sent; ibid. 168–9.

[39] *Eulogium Historiarum*, ed. F. S. Haydon, Rolls Series, 1858–63, iii. 387; *Liber Pluscardensis*, ed. F. J. H. Skene, Edinburgh, 1877, i. 341.

[40] E364/35, Rot. D. Some of the tradesmen were still unpaid eighteen months later and some had been imprisoned for debt as a result. E404/16, no. 732 and 17, no. 386.

[41] *C.P.R., 1399–1401*, 347 and 355.

[42] E364/35, Rot. G. Arms and artillery, probably from Richard II's last expedition, were brought from Ireland to London and on to Scotland, and the *Marie* of Lynn was hired to ship military supplies. E403/567, 13 July.

[43] John Elyngeham was commissioned in January to seize ships in the ports from the Thames north-

the records as carrying supplies over and above the five king's ships, the Lynn fleet mentioned earlier, and the ships from the Cinque Ports. Traditional methods probably made this a straightforward though not a popular operation.

The last organizational problem I must mention was perhaps the most difficult of all, how to raise money to pay for the campaign. It was an economical campaign in terms of soldiers' wages, but it must have cost in excess of £10,000; the wages of the sailors on the merchant ships alone must have been more than £500. And Henry was very short of money for parliament in 1399 had done no more than renew the customs. At the great council in February the bishops had promised to advance a tenth and an appeal had been sent to abbots and priors to help, specifically mentioning the coming campaign in Scotland. The yield was not great, however, and as the army began to assemble, again far too late one would think, a large-scale drive to raise loans was begun. On 23 June eight serjeants-at-arms were sent round the counties with privy-seal letters to bishops, abbots, priors, and secular men to lend £100 each for the campaign, and they were engaged on the work until September.[44] A good many loans were made, mainly of smallish sums, but the immediate need, cash to pay the soldiers, was met by direct negotiation.[45] Six groups of foreign merchants in London made short-term loans totalling 2,000 marks; London lent 2,000 marks and gifted another 1,000 marks, and Mayor Knolles himself lent 200 marks. Other towns lent smaller sums, notably York 1,000 marks and Bristol and Newcastle 500 marks each. The judges and clerks at Westminster were persuaded to help with many individual loans and 1,000 marks collectively from the chancellor and the chancery clerks. William of Wykeham lent £500, Sir Hugh Waterton 500 marks, in September Treasurer Norbury himself lent the large sum of £1,038. 13s. 4d., and many more examples could be quoted. It was these loans which made the expedition possible. The merchant and civil-service loans in London undoubtedly provided the 8,000 marks which Henry Somer, an exchequer clerk, took north with Norbury and delivered to paymaster Curson at Newcastle on 3 August in three bound chests specially purchased and under guard in John Godeman's iron-bound cart.[46] The large lenders were mostly repaid quite quickly, but most of the others had to wait until at least the third year of the reign before they were repaid.

wards probably to meet a threat from France. *C.P.R., 1399–1401*, 267. No commission to do the same for the Scottish campaign survives but he received money for sailors' wages from the Kingston upon Hull, Lynn, and Boston customs in May and June and these may have been for the campaign. E403/567, 3 and 15 May and 21 June.

[44] E403/567, 13 July; E364/34, Rot. E and 35, Rot. H. Examples of the letters are to be found in E28/8.

[45] The following remarks are based on evidence from the Receipt and Issue rolls, the Warrants for Issues and the Chancery rolls. A. Steel, *The Receipt of the Exchequer 1377–1485*, Cambridge, 1954, found that the 'genuine' loans for the whole Easter term totalled £11,257. It should also be remembered that the king was not the only one who borrowed; a number of captains had to have 'subs' from the treasurer to meet their expenses and the earl of Somerset had to borrow 1,000 marks from Richard Whittington for his costs. E404/20, no. 134.

[46] E403/567, 13 July and 25 Sept. Godeman received ten marks for his costs and his horses and cart were bought on Norbury's advice for £46 to carry some of the king's goods into Scotland. Somer had £22 for his own expenses and those of the guards and an extra £20 regard.

One wonders what those who had lent money thought of the way their money had been spent. The organization of the campaign, as I have tried to show, was a complicated matter which is a tribute to the comparative sophistication of later medieval government. But in every other way the campaign was a disastrous failure. For a start it seems to have been unnecessary. Preparations were made too late and it is doubtful if there were sufficient resources in any case; and the objectives of the enterprise were not clear. Henry IV deserves no credit from it. It would probably be wrong to suppose that these lessons were learned, but in fact this campaign marked the end of an era in Anglo-Scottish relations. The four previous English kings had all campaigned in Scotland, but Henry IV never came to the march again, nor did his son, and his grandson came only as a refugee sixty years later. The claim to sovereignty was made again in negotiation and indeed was not abandoned until Elizabeth's reign, but only once in the last year of Henry VIII's reign was it more than a mere formality. At Durham, a few days after leaving Scotland, Henry made an ordinance for the marches which merely specified the numbers in the garrisons and the arrangements for paying them. Thereafter, border problems were to be left to the wardens, Henry Percy, Prince John, about whom Professor Chrimes has written, and their successors.[47]

[47] S. B. Chrimes, 'Some Letters of John of Lancaster', *Speculum*, xiv, 1939.

Government and the Welsh Community: the North-east Borderland in the Fifteenth Century

J. GWYNFOR JONES

TUDOR apologists in Wales such as Sir John Wynn of Gwydir were never at a loss when openly denouncing the deficiencies in fifteenth-century Welsh society both in the principality and the march. The memory of the amorphous block of territory which, to all intents and purposes, formed enclaves of private jurisdiction, had created a distinct impression upon him and, among his many anecdotes, he assiduously related the difficulties which his forebear Ieuan ap Robert had experienced in the pursuance of felons into the notorious Chirkland and Oswestry. The callous murder of the parson of Llanfrothen perpetrated by the unscrupulous wife of Hywel ap Rhys, his ancestor's deadly enemy, had so inspired the historian of Gwydir that, regardless of the imprecision and ambiguities of his narrative, brief but vital shreds of evidence emerge depicting the condition of disturbed areas in Gwynedd laid waste by revolt, war, and pestilence. Wynn, a man outspoken in his own affairs and (among his other pursuits) in his pronouncements on Lancastrian society in his native north Wales, compiled a disjointed and confused chronicle of events, and his caustic remarks unhesitatingly attributed all the misgivings of early fifteenth-century society to the ferocity and destructiveness of the Glyndŵr revolt: 'for it was Owen Glyndoores policie', he wryly remarked, 'to bring all thinges to wast, that the Englishe should find not strength nor restinge place in the Countrey'.[1] This comment, none the less, contained an element of truth, and a similar observation made on the century in general by another less eccentric Tudor commentator, George Owen of Henllys, Pembrokeshire, confirmed in substance what his contemporary had recorded: 'theare grewe about ye tyme', he asserted, 'deadly hatred betweene them and the English nation insomuch that the name of a Welshman was odyous to ye Englishmen, and the name of Englishman woefull to the Welshman'.[2]

If the revolt, as is generally agreed, did not initiate racial animosity, it most certainly heightened and prolonged it. The sporadic disturbances of the late

---

[1] *History of the Gwydir Family*, ed. J. Ballinger, Cardiff, 1927, 39–43, 53.
[2] George Owen, *The Description of Penbrokshire*, ed. H. Owen, London, 1906, iii. 37.

thirteenth and fourteenth centuries had created anti-English feeling. Rhys ap Maredudd, the staunchest of Crown supporters, had felt himself hemmed in by English administration in Ystrad Tywi in 1287 and, within a decade of the settlement of 1284, there were sufficient grounds of resentment on a large scale to encourage Madog ap Llywelyn, with widespread support in Wales, to lead a threatening revolt against English rule. On the other hand progressive clansmen from the mid-fourteenth century onwards, in an effort to augment their clan properties, were determined to consolidate themselves by estate building and usually by office-holding mainly on a local level. But they also felt inhibited when denied the right to exercise the full privileges of English land law. Disabilities with regard to marriage laws also prohibited Welshmen from granting dower in land as was the custom in England, and Englishmen who ignored this regulation and who granted their daughters (upon their marriages to Welshmen) a *maritagium*, were liable to severe punishment on the grounds that Welshmen were not allowed to hold land by English tenure. Furthermore, the imposition of an *amobr* fine on Welsh tenants alone in the event of a daughter's marriage or in the event of her unchastity served to exacerbate racial feelings. In 1398, when a royal charter was granted the commonalty of Hope, a clause stipulated that burgesses were to plead or be impleaded before an English jury even in a Welsh court.[3] Such prohibitions, regardless of the effects of social distress and war, had not endeared some of the emerging families to the Crown's policy either before or after the Glyndŵr revolt. Vaticination became more marked a feature in the works of bards like Iolo Goch and later Guto'r Glyn, bringing to the fore a new and intense spirit of national political consciousness which had not been unknown in the more constructive political schemes of Glyndŵr. The gentry were realists and probably paid little serious attention to the reverberations of the bards, but, even so, many felt a sense of insecurity which the Lancastrian statutes of 1401–2 certainly did not remove.

Hatred was hardened especially in the vicinity of garrison boroughs like Caernarvon, Beaumaris, and Conway and in the north-east borderland, traditionally an area of racial disaffection. The powerful Tudor group, Glyndŵr's staunch band of supporters in Gwynedd, had surreptitiously captured Conway castle on Good Friday, 1401. Conversely, Ieuan ap Maredudd, the anglophil squire of Y Gesailgyfarch, taking opposite sides to his hardy brother Robert (who was 'out with Owen Glyndoor') met his death defending Caernarvon castle, the redoubtable leader burning his houses of Cefn-y-Fan and Y Gesailgyfarch. Wynn graphically described how his body, to avoid ambush, 'was brought by sea (for the passages by land were shutt upp by owens forces) to Penmorva his p'ishe churche, to be buryed'.[4] Glyndŵr's cause divided kindred as well as intensified hatred between English and Welsh.

To generalize about the conflict is to avoid examining some of the intriguing problems of the history of Wales at a time, after the Henrician legislation of 1401–2, when divided loyalties ushered in a century of discord and resentment between the privileged and unprivileged even among the Welsh themselves. One interesting

[3] P.R.O. (*D.K.R.*), London, 1875, xxxvi. 248.   [4] Ballinger, op. cit. 2–12.

feature of social animosity between the races was the prohibition of intermarriage in special circumstances between parties when either one or other was or had been a partisan of Glyndŵr. Howell T. Evans in his standard study of the dynastic wars has created some confusion in the minds of historians when referring to legislation which forbade complete intermarriage between English and Welsh.[5] Was this, in fact, the case and, if so, what steps were taken either to maintain or evade such a stringent measure? The degree of social intercourse and also of conflicting attitudes common to both races in the fifteenth century repays further study if only to show more clearly what action certain English communities took (inspired, no doubt, by the agents of government) to discourage any dealings with the native population.

Henry of Lancaster's second parliament in its session on 20 January 1401 was harassed, among other imminent dynastic problems, by the revolt in Wales, the 'misgovernance and the riote' (as it was nervously described by Lord Grey), which had begun in the borough of Ruthin in September 1400. Serious disaffection existed throughout the country among the suppressed bondmen who survived, many of them grovelling in their pestilence-stricken tenements and inspired to action by a group of squires who, with military and administrative experience behind them, became a vital force in the long revolt which ensued. To subdue unrest in the west Henry IV initiated severe measures, and the ordinances decreed by Edward I in 1295 after the serious revolt of Madog ap Llywelyn which forbade to Welshmen, among other disabilities, the privileges of the English in the garrison boroughs of north Wales, were extended to include boroughs in England.[6] Impediments were placed on persons wholly Welsh, and offences committed by them against their English neighbours, especially border cattle raids, were to be harshly punished. Among other restrictions imposed, no Welshmen were to purchase lands in England or in any English borough in Wales and border strongholds such as Chester, Shrewsbury, and Hereford, by law, were closed to them and the same restriction applied to the garrison towns of the principality, notably Conway, Caernarvon, Beaumaris, and Harlech, and the borough of Flint, all of which, since their creation after the settlement of 1284, had been almost exclusively English in their composition.

Parliament was dissolved on 10 March 1401 although some of the marcher lords, still feeling uneasy with regard to the safety of their own boroughs, were firmly dissatisfied with the limitations imposed by the penal exactions. On 18 March further ordinances were enacted, having originally been agreed upon at Coldharbour and confirmed by royal Council on 22 March at Blackfriars.[7] These ordinances, applicable in royal and marcher boroughs alike, represented an even more stringent attitude towards the native community. Among other restrictions imposed upon the Welsh was the requirement to pay murage for the maintenance of walls and gates of the towns and castles of north Wales and to contribute towards the garrisoning of those

[5] H. T. Evans, *Wales and the Wars of the Roses*, Cambridge, 1915, 19–20.
[6] *Rot. Parl.* iii. 472, 476; *The Statutes of Wales*, ed. I. Bowen, London, 1908.
[7] *Foedera*, ed. T. Rymer, 1704–35, viii. 184–5; *C.P.R., 1399–1401*, 469–70.

castles for a period of at least three years. No Welshmen were to 'congregate' without the assent of the chief officers of the lordships and, repeating what had already been enacted, for three years Englishmen in Wales could not be indicted, accused, or attacked by the Welsh or be convicted by their inquest. Insurrections by Welshmen were to be suppressed, any damage done to the king's subjects was to be compensated for, and the bards were to be prevented from propagating sedition. These ordinances, severe though they were, became even more stringent judging by the version which appeared in the *Record of Caernarvon* where the relevant portions of the statute are reproduced along with the ordinances decided upon at Coldharbour.[8] A significant addition is appended to the ordinances as a result of discussions supposedly held in Prince Henry's council at Chester on 14 June 1401 which is assumed to have reconfirmed and supplemented the earlier proceedings at Coldharbour and Blackfriars. Henry of Monmouth had been granted the lands of the principality in October 1399, and the Council established in his name was delegated the authority which elsewhere remained in the King's Council.[9] It seemed, therefore, that the power and authority acquired by Henry in Wales was more than ample to cope with the serious situation which arose, and the establishment, once again, of Chester as an administrative and military centre against the Welsh no doubt exacerbated racial animosity and hardened the citizens' feelings against them. The additional clauses which appear in the *Record* seemed to have heightened the stringency of the original ordinances and provided that no Englishman or woman should marry or 'consort' with any Welshman or woman; that no Englishman or woman should send their children to be fostered among the Welsh; that no Welshman should enter a town or fortified castle with arms but should leave them with the porters or keepers on pain of forfeiture and imprisonment; and that English burgesses should not allow any man of mixed blood from the Welsh community to be freed among themselves in their towns on pain of forfeiture of their liberties and chattels. These interesting clauses which clearly prohibit intermarriage and social communication were agreed upon primarily at the instigation of marcher lords and royal officers on a co-operative basis providing one example of an attempt at co-ordination between marcher and royal government in times of crisis early in the fifteenth century.

The background to these ordinances of mid June 1401 was predominantly tense and uneasy. The government of the northern principality had been delegated to Prince Henry and a Council whose leading member was Henry Percy, eldest son of the earl of Northumberland who had been created Constable of Chester, Flint, Conway, and Caernarvon castles and appointed Sheriff of Flintshire in October 1399 and who was consequently in a very strong position to investigate and suppress any signs of unrest.[10] In May 1401 Henry IV received reports that Owain Glyndŵr, having swung his offensive to central and south-west Wales, had deliberated to set

---

[8] *The Record of Caernarvon*, ed. H. Ellis, London, 1838, 239–40.
[9] *C.P.R., 1399–1401*, 114.   [10] Ibid. 28, 158.

upon English settlements with substantial support and to fall heavily on those who owed allegiance to the Crown in the western principality. His appeal was by then widespread and his prestige and influence had grown remarkably. Although Henry had taken precautions to guard the coasts of Wales and to strengthen border garrisons, he departed on 14 June for Wallingford clearly thinking that the crisis had passed with the successes of Henry Percy and John Charlton in mid Wales in late May. The campaign at Cader Idris in Merioneth at approximately the same time led to the critical moment when Percy (who had led the expedition at his own expense) complained of insufficient financial aid, and later departed thus giving the Welsh further incentive to take the offensive leading to widespread attacks in Montgomery and Denbigh and in the regions of the north-eastern boroughs. In mid June 1401 Glyndŵr's forces reappeared in the original areas of disaffection which, for centuries, had been a continual buffer between Welsh and English aggression. The communities of Flint, Rhuddlan, Holt, Hawarden, and Welshpool had already experienced the severity of their onslaughts in the critical initial stages of the revolt and the insurgents once again unsuccessfully set upon Pool castle and the borough, and strengthened the allegiance of the rural population in Glyndŵr's cause. The siege of Conway castle, which probably did not end until late June 1401, and rebel turmoils in the northern march forced Prince Henry at his Chester headquarters to provide further measures designed to suppress any Welsh movement or any association with the English. It is probable that these additional ordinances were again ratified in conjunction with the lords of the march and had particular relevance to Chester and neighbouring boroughs which were threatened by a new wave of revolt.

During the fourteenth century there had in general been a gradual increase in the Welsh population of the marcher boroughs and so long as sufficient security for good behaviour had been made available, they had also been allowed to settle in purely English boroughs long before the revolt. The castellated boroughs of the principality were, to all intents and purposes, closed to them and the Welsh population of smaller boroughs like Bala and Harlech (unlike the preponderantly Welsh communities of Pwllheli and Nefyn) was not in any way remarkable in that period. Although intermarriage and the acquisition of borough property had become generally common in marcher boroughs the Crown probably viewed the attack on Welshpool as being mainly instigated by the native inhabitants so that the young prince's course of action, along with the lords of the march, became increasingly obvious. To what extent the ordinances of mid June were implemented there remains no way of ascertaining. The contemporary chronicler Adam of Usk had heard disturbing rumours concerning prohibition of intermarriage as early as the dissolution of parliament on 10 March: 'quo tamen die, modicum ante presens, audivi plurima aspera contra Wallenses ordinanda agitari, scilicet, de non contrahendo matrimonium cum Anglicis, nec de adquirendo aut inhabitando in Anglia, et alia plura gravia'.[11] Whether such severe forebodings, however, were substantiated in that year is not

[11] Adam of Usk, *Chronicon*, ed. E. M. Thompson, London, 1904, 60.

known, but the tense situation was exacerbated by growing apprehension at West-minster and, in 1402, the second and more permanent set of Lancastrian statutes was enacted reinforcing that of 1401.[12] When a close comparison is made with the ordinances of March of the previous year it is found that each clause is reinforced, but there is no clause in 1402, however, which corresponds to the complete prohi-bition of intermarriage as enacted in the additional clauses of June. Clause 34 of the 1402 statutes provided that 'no Englishman married to any Welshwoman of the amity or alliance of Owain ap Glendour ... or to any other Welshwoman ... or that in time to come marrieth himself to any Welshwoman, be put in any office in Wales or in the Marches of the same'. The situation regarding intermarriage was thus defined more clearly and, allowing for the penalty inflicted on English administrators, presupposed the continuation of matrimonial associations.

The situation in the north-east borderland, however, was not clear-cut. The burgesses of Welshpool in 1406 were practically all Welsh although in the charter extending the privileges of the burgesses granted by Edward Charlton, Lord Powys, in that year it was maintained that 'no Welshman ought to be taken within the said liberty except those who now stand faithful to our said lord the King', a necessary precaution after the violence which the borough had experienced in the early stages of the revolt.[13] Ruthin also remained Welsh after 1400 and intermarriage was common enough among families like the Thelwalls and Salisburys which became more Welsh than English. Furthermore, Oswestry, ravaged in the early weeks of the revolt, remained a predominantly Welsh town possessing strong commercial and racial links with Wales, and its praises were sung by two major Welsh bards of the mid century, Guto'r Glyn and Lewis Glyn Cothi, both of whom had experienced its generous hospitality and, later, it was admired by Tudur Aled.[14] Guto'r Glyn, complimenting the town, showed no signs of ill feeling and stressed his close family attachment to it and his respect for its lord the earl of Arundel whom he regarded as the best earl in England. Lewis Glyn Cothi, likewise, when praising Maredudd ap Morus, a promi-nent official of Oswestry, made laudatory observations on the borough itself, stressing its superiority over all other fortified towns.[15]

The city of Chester, however, known for its turbulence and upheaval, took severe steps to curtail and even suppress Welsh activity within its walls because its officials feared devastation at the hands of Glyndŵr. Relations between the Welsh princes and the justiciars of Chester had not been remarkably amicable in the reign of Llywelyn ap Gruffudd and it was within striking distance of the city that the revolt of his brother David had broken out on Palm Sunday 1282. The Glyndŵr rising was feared by its

[12] Bowen, op. cit. 33–6.

[13] 'Welshpool: Material for the History of the Parish and Borough', *Montgomeryshire Collections*, vii, 1874, 345–8.

[14] *Gwaith Guto'r Glyn*, ed. I. Williams and J. Ll. Williams, Cardiff, 1939, 183–5; *Gwaith Lewis Glyn Cothi*, ed. Gwallter Mechain and Ioan Tegid, Oxford, 1837, 378; *Gwaith Tudur Aled*, ed. T. G. Jones, Cardiff, 1926, ii. 261.

[15] *Gwaith Lewis Glyn Cothi*, 383.

burgesses, for the early years of the revolt had exhausted the Crown's resources and, furthermore, had interfered with the trade of Chester. The commercial trading in the north Wales boroughs had been almost exclusively controlled by the Chester merchants until the mid-fifteenth century and regular visits were made to Ireland and Gascony with Welsh and English wares. Owing to its nearness to north Wales and the continual threat of devastation precautions had to be taken to prevent the rebels from being assisted, directly or otherwise, by the transport of victuals purchased at Chester and sold again to them.[16] Precautions were also taken to stem all commercial relations with the Welsh and sureties were given for the good conduct of individual Welshmen. The resentful citizens, no doubt, attended the execution of Rhys ap Tudur ap Goronwy with a sigh of relief and with jubilation in 1410 after the unsuccessful rebel advance into Shropshire. Although Chester was never attacked by the insurgents, the irreparable damage done to the city's commercial prosperity by the revolt can be gauged by the letters patent granted by Henry VI in November 1456 to the inhabitants releasing them of the payment of £50 fee-farm for a period of fifty years 'in consideration of the poverty of the mayor, sheriffs and citizens of Chester'.[17]

Much of the evidence which points unmistakably to the severe attitude taken by the inhabitants of Chester towards the Welsh appears in the bardic compositions of the period. The classical bards of the fifteenth century symbolized the ancient traditions and prophetic aspirations, revived in Geoffrey of Monmouth's *Historia Regum Britanniae* (1136), of the greatness of the old British race. The reappearance of these vaticinations was given a moral boost by the Glyndŵr revolt and reached its climax with the accession of Henry Tudor to the throne in 1485. The central theme was the quest for a national political leader in the ancient British context who would 'deliver' the nation from the 'bondage' of English rule. Such propaganda led to the dissemination of anti-English poetry in the traditional strict metres and, in the bardic compositions of Guto'r Glyn, such aspirations acquired a specifically realistic meaning. The vituperative spirit aroused by this type of poetry was directed mainly against the English boroughs in Wales and odes castigating Flint and the city of Chester have survived. The frontier city and its inhabitants became objects of scorn and contempt for Lewis Glyn Cothi, and his alleged experiences seemed to have been sufficient testimony for the existence of a by-law in that city when he complained that the authorities had secured his expulsion, supposedly, for marrying a citizen's widow without their consent.[18] The by-law apparently stipulated that no citizen's widow should marry a Welshman but there seems to be no evidence in the Chester corporation records of such a regulation. The only reference relating to the political events of 1401 is a fragment of an order referring to the prohibition of the sale of food, goods, and arms to the rebels and a few presentments of offenders.[19] In 1402 one Thomas of Chester went surety for two Welshmen of Wrexham that they would not dispose of the beer they had bought in the City to the rebels and, in February the following year, the

---

[16] *D.K.R.* xxxv, 111 et seq.　　　　　　　　　　　　[17] *C.P.R.*, 1452–61, 331–2.

[18] *Gwaith Lewis Glyn Cothi*, 114, 376, 385.　　[19] Chester Record Office, MB/2/f/1[r] and 1[v].

Steward of Denbigh undertook to see that five merchants from the town would not sell Welshmen the grain brought by them from Chester.[20] The surviving ecclesiastical records supply no relevant evidence either, and papal registers for the period make no suggestion that such a by-law ever existed. Another contemporary bard Dafydd Llwyd o Fathafarn, in an ode which relentlessly attacked the boroughs, seemed to suggest that if the English burgesses were ejected their womenfolk and property would be readily available for Welshmen.[21] His theme emphatically underlined the basic grievance of Welshmen against burghal communities, namely the existence of privilege and the inequality which could only be destroyed by evicting the English and forcing them to serve the Welsh.

Guto'r Glyn, on the other hand, patiently prayed at the foot of the famous cross of Chester for relief of his physical encumbrances without any apparent interruption from irate burgesses and, seemingly, without any feeling of resentment.[22] Yet, even in the religious world, Welsh clerics were not allowed to go underided as Iolo Goch's odes to the Franciscan friar of Chester relate in response to the criticism that he had levelled against Hywel ap Madog, a Welsh cleric, for associating with a mistress. Iolo fiercely denounced the friar as a hypocrite who probably expected to find a sour Englishwoman to attract his attention.[23] Lewis Glyn Cothi, none the less, positively aggressive and revengeful, believed that he had suffered a raw deal. He had been robbed of his property and, in retaliation, had decided to avenge himself by the sword. In his *awdl* to the citizens he continued in a similarly vindictive mood denouncing this act of inexcusable vandalism, pouring his wrath upon the inhabitants, and relentlessly attacking the officers of the city.[24]

This incident and the subsequent bardic reverberations may be dated *c.* 1465 by which time the Lancastrian statutes against the Welsh had been reinforced in the boroughs of the northern principality. Welsh families had crept slowly into these garrison boroughs, especially Beaumaris, to the point that resentful burgesses petitioned the King's Council in 1442 for a renewal and firm application of Henry IV's penal statutes, and in 1444 the Commons ruled that every piece of legislation previously enacted against the Welsh was to be strictly observed.[25] They resented the denization for which Welshmen sued to 'the utter destruction of all Englishmen in the seid Townes' in the northern principality and it was recommended that 'no maner Welsh man of hole blode ne half blode on the fader side . . . be made Denisen or English' and they were not to hold offices in Wales on pain of 200 marks fine. It may have been that the authorities of Chester had also undertaken to strengthen their anti-Welsh policy. Decisive action against the Welsh of Chester, however, dates from as early as 1403 when the Prince of Wales took precautionary measures to ensure that

[20] *D.K.R.*, xxxv, 4, 13.

[21] D. J. Bowen, 'Y Gymdeithas Gymreig yn Niwedd yr Oesoedd Canol fel yr Adlewyrchir Hi yn y Farddoniaeth Uchelwrol' (unpublished M.A. dissertation, University of Wales, 1952), 144.

[22] *Gwaith Guto'r Glyn*, 283–4.

[23] *Cywyddau Iolo Goch ac Eraill*, ed. H. Lewis, T. Roberts, I. Williams, Cardiff, 1937, 64–9.

[24] *Gwaith Lewis Glyn Cothi*, 378, 385–7.   [25] *Rot. Parl.* v, 10.

all Welshmen and those with Welsh sympathies were expelled from the city.[26] They were not allowed to enter before sunrise or to remain within its walls after sunset under pain of decapitation. No meetings of three or more Welshmen were to be held and no weapons were to be carried except knives for cutting meat, a regulation which clearly echoed the earlier restriction of June 1401. The risk of cohabitation had already been reduced by keeping close vigilance on Welsh dealings with the city, and the legacy of hatred continued. Before 1536 only two Welshmen were considered suitable to be created freemen and only one sheriff, with some Welsh blood in his veins, appeared among the officials.[27] As early as 1406 one Ithel ap Gruffudd ap Goronwy and his companion were arrested for passing over the walls, and John de Hope, the mayor in 1427, was suspected of being 'wholly Welsh', and the escheator was directed to determine whether or not he had purchased lands in Chester contrary to the laws of Henry IV.[28] Market regulations were violated by Welshmen in 1450 and 1456, and the inhabitants of the city were later prevented from attending obstreperous Welsh weddings in the surrounding countryside. Two proverbs, still current in Welsh, serve to illustrate the despicable image which Chester had impressed upon the minds of many Welshmen—'Mae mwy nag un bwa yng Nghaer' [There is more than one bow at Chester], and 'Codi cyn cŵn Caer' [To rise before the watchdogs of Chester], both of which convey to our own day the awe which had instilled some unease into the Welsh of the north-east who, at the least provocation, aroused the wrath of the men of Chester.

Resentment and distrust became so common that Englishwomen were known to shun social contact with any Welshman lest they be regarded as whores as is perfectly illustrated in a short bilingual ode written by Tudur Penllyn describing a conversation between an Englishwoman and a Welshman (presumably the bard) whose advances she successfully resisted retorting sharply:

> I am not Wels, thow Welsmon,
> Ffor byde the, lete me alone. . . .
> 'Tis harm to be thy parmwr,
> Howld hain j shal be Kalde hwr.

Such a reply probably explains an aspect of the general attitude taken towards the Welsh and, in this case, the inviolability of Englishwomen in privileged communities, and throws into high relief the situation as it must have appeared to both groups of people in the vicinity of boroughs like Flint or Chester where daily contact was unavoidable. An ode again attributed to Tudur Penllyn (although Lewis Glyn Cothi has also been regarded by some scholars as the author) represented a bitter satire on the town of Flint portraying it as a typically English borough which the bard visited on a Sunday and at a time when a marriage feast was being celebrated.

[26] *D.K.R.* xxxvi. 3, 102.
[27] *Chester Freeman Rolls*, ed. J. H. E. Bennet, Birkenhead, 1906, i (1392–1700), 5, 7.
[28] *D.K.R.* xxxvi. 102.

The bard attempted to compose an *awdl* to commemorate the happy occasion, but was treated with scorn and derision by the guests who were unable to appreciate his bardic craft and to understand his medium of expression, and who preferably called for the services of William the piper.[29] The despondent bard, after his departure from the borough, had occasion to satirize the appearance and performance of the swarthy, fat, and lame piper who entertained his guests with glaring eyes and unmusical sounds. His description of the comical and pathetic attempts on the piper's part to play his instrument melodiously is demonstrative of the bardic craft at its best. He denounced the 'single-toned goat' who, in his opinion, could do no better than shout but who was well rewarded for his feeble efforts while the bard departed without reward. His feeling of deep resentment against the alien community was emphasized in bitter concluding couplets which reflected not only his intense hatred at being treated so unworthily but also the attitude of Flint burgesses towards Welshmen in their town.

Men of power also reacted similarly against the citizens of Chester as, for example, did Rheinallt ap Gruffudd of Y Tŵr in Ystrad Alun near Mold, one of the six Lancastrian captains who defended Harlech castle for Henry VI in 1461 and also in 1464 alongside his kinsman Dafydd ab Ieuan ab Einion, his mother's cousin. He was in continual feud against the men of Chester and, during the tensions of the dynastic wars in 1465, he is reputed to have captured and put to death Robert Byrne (a linen draper and mayor of the city in 1462) after an affray had occurred at Mold fair involving Chester men. Rheinallt was a patron of Tudur Penllyn who vividly recalled in his commemorative *awdl* the victory which he had achieved at that time after the massacre of the English of Chester. He descended from noble Welsh lineage in Iâl and, on his mother's side, had connections with the stock of Rhirid Flaidd and with the Vaughan family of Cors-y-Gedol. Tudur's *awdl*, in part, echoed some of the prophetic aspirations which had become so popular in his day and age.[30] He expected that the image of Christ in Mold parish church would participate actively in the assistance of Rheinallt against the 'twisted dogs' of Chester, and he referred to 'Siors', 'Wilcin', 'Hugyn o'r Grin', and 'Wilcoc o Stoc' as his victims. His wrath knew no bounds and he hoped that a deluge would flood the whole shire. Hywel Cilan also commemorated this event, with less ardour perhaps but still with pride in Rheinallt's achievements.[31] Tudur Penllyn also addressed his patron in an ode sung on behalf of a kinsman, Gruffydd Fychan of Cors-y-Gedol, attributing to Rheinallt all the qualities of a worthy gentleman. His power and reputation, the bard maintained, were well known before he had reached manhood and his wealth lay in his landed possessions. His death (*c.* 1465–6) was elegized by Ieuan ap Tudur Penllyn who described the grief felt by the people of Ystrad Alun and, in vivid contrast, the relief felt by the citizens of Chester. His policy had been to exclude Englishmen from holding any office within his landed jurisdiction and his bard prayed that it should remain so after

[29] *Gwaith Tudur Penllyn ac Ieuan ap Tudur Penllyn*, ed. T. Roberts, Cardiff, 51–3.
[30] Ibid. 19–22, 111–12.
[31] *Gwaith Hywel Cilan*, ed. I. Jones, Cardiff, 1963, 14.

his death. The ode illustrated inborn racial hatred in the north-east borderland areas half a century or so after the last embers of the Glyndŵr revolt had died out.[32]

Social intercourse between both races within individual families, however, reveals a marked inconsistency but, in the main, the breaking down of social barriers assumes greater prominence in the north-east in the course of the century among families of repute. The laws of Henry IV, it is true, hung like the sword of Damocles over the heads of ambitious men like Gwilym Fychan, son of Gwilym ap Gruffudd of Penrhyn who had found it necessary to petition Parliament in 1439 and 1442 to be made English. He requested denization pleading that he was English on his mother's side (Janet, daughter of Sir William Stanley of Hooton, and widow of Robert Paris, Chamberlain of Chester and North Wales in 1399) and that his father had been a firm ally of the Crown. His father, Gwilym ap Gruffydd, by his second marriage, had associated himself with a family which had achieved considerable influence in the fifteenth century and in this period of flux and hostility he probably agreed that most of his property should fall to his children by Janet and not to his son by his first wife, Morfudd, daughter of Goronwy Tudur of Penmynydd. The result was the establishment of the famous Gruffudd family of Penrhyn, a family typical of the rising gentry of the mid-fifteenth century. His son Gwilym Fychan was exempted from the penal enactments in 1440 on condition that he did not marry a Welshwoman and, in 1443, he was allowed to hold office.[33] True to his word he did marry an Englishwoman, Alice, daughter and heiress of Sir Richard Dalton of Apthorp, Northamptonshire and yet his praises were sung by many bards and, among them, Guto'r Glyn although he did not approve of Welshmen's desire for denization.[34] Rhys Goch Eryri even went as far as to enlist his noble Welsh forebears in order to undermine his pride in the part-English blood which ran through his veins.[35] His second wife, however, was Gwenllian, daughter of Iorwerth ap Dafydd ab Ednyfed Chwith, which indicates later relaxation in the laws, but the main family continued in the line of William Gruffudd, his son by his first marriage who became Chamberlain of north Wales (1483–90) and who also maintained close relations through marriage with Thomas 1st earl of Derby. Gwilym ap Gruffudd's daughter Elin by Janet Stanley married William Bulkeley of Cheadle, constable of Beaumaris castle in 1440, who was exempted from the reinforced penal laws of that year and who probably became the first of the Bulkeleys to settle in Anglesey.[36]

Aggressive gentry families of this calibre, both English and Welsh, were prepared to ignore restrictions whenever they could in an attempt to aggrandize themselves and prosper through influential matrimonial connections with either English or Welsh heiresses, predominantly in border areas. Siancyn Conway (1415–45), the grandson of Richard Conway, lord of Prestatyn, was the first of his family to marry a Welshwoman, namely Marsli, daughter of Maredudd ap Hywel ap Dafydd of

---

[32] *Gwaith Tudur Penllyn*, 54–6, 88–90.
[33] *Rot. Parl.* v. 14, 45; *C.P.R.*, *1436–41*, 416; ibid. *1441–6*, 164.
[35] *Cywyddau Iolo Goch ac Eraill*, 307–9.
[34] *Gwaith Guto'r Glyn*, 222.
[36] *Rot. Parl.* v. 104.

Cefn-y-Fan, Eifionydd, a forebear of the Wynns of Gwydir from which sprang the Conway family of Botryddan, Flintshire. Richard Langford, who was constable of Ruthin castle (1447), married the heiress of Hywel ap Gruffudd ap Morgan of Hope, and his grandson John Langford married the daughter of William ap Dafydd of Trefalun, Gresford. Tudur Penllyn praised Elizabeth, wife of Thomas Salesbury and daughter of Jenkin Don of Utkinton, Cheshire, because of her noble stock,[37] and Sir William Norris of Speake married Agnes, daughter of Maredudd ap Tudur ap Goronwy, a sister to Owain Tudur who greatly influenced posterity through his marriage to Catherine of Valois, widow of Henry V. Maredudd ap Hywel ap Morus of Oswestry was entrusted with the custody of the borough and was married to an Englishwoman. Similarly Nicholas ap Gruffudd Rhys, one of the yeomen of the Crown to Henry VI, attained a position of eminence in that borough and probably married Cicely Salter who came of an old-established Oswestry family. John Puleston (of Shropshire stock), the father of the staunch Lancastrian supporter Roger Puleston, married Angharad, daughter of Gruffudd Hanmer and granddaughter of Tudur ap Goronwy of Anglesey, and his father Robert Puleston of Emral in Maelor Saesneg (who was Glyndŵr's brother-in-law) forfeited all his lands in Cheshire, Flintshire, and Shropshire because of his participation in the revolt.[38] Many of these individuals had associated themselves with local administrative offices, a passport to influence and power. The historian of Gwydir referred to continuous efforts exerted by avaricious local magnates to gain office to the point of rivalry and cited the disputes between John ap Maredudd and William Gruffudd II of Penrhyn and especially between the Kyffin and Trefor of Bryncunallt families in Chirk and Oswestry where the 'two sects or Kinreds contended for the sov'antye of the countrey, and weare at contynuall strife one with another' protecting and maintaining outlaws 'as verie precious juells'.[39] They identified themselves with border families accumulating a considerable collective experience in public affairs. Was it not Guto'r Glyn, addressing William Gruffudd (Fychan) of Penrhyn (son and heir of Gwilym ap Gruffudd), who referred to his promotion in status which he attributed, in part, to his acquisition of lands at the expense of less fortunate kinsmen and, in part, to his father's ancestry and fortuitous marriage to Janet Stanley?[40]

The prohibition of intermarriage in the additional clauses of June 1401 must not be exaggerated. The cause of Glyndŵr, by mid century, had lost its appeal with the passage of two generations and with the emergence of other conflicts and loyalties which involved Welshmen. The clause in the Statute of 1402 meant practically nothing with the passing of the first generation after the revolt. Prohibition was restricted to the garrison boroughs—still jealous of their rights as the petitions of the 1440s indicate—and even then no guarantee could be given of an effective and fully main-

---

[37] *Y Bywgraffiadur Cymreig 1941–50*, London, 1970, 74; Ballinger, op. cit. 18; *Y Bywgraffiadur Cymreig hyd 1940*, London, 1953, 506–7; *Gwaith Tudur Penllyn*, 12–13.

[38] *Gwaith Lewis Glyn Cothi*, 382, 389–90; *Y Bywgraffiadur Cymreig 1941–50*, 148.

[39] Ballinger, op. cit. 41. [40] *Gwaith Guto'r Glyn*, 56.

tained policy of exclusion. The Boldes and the Hollands of Conway and the Spicers of Caernarvon intermarried happily with Welsh families and, in the north-east, the Hanmers, Thelwalls, and Salesburys cohabited naturally with the Welsh many of whom in Ruthin, for example, were rewarded with the minor offices of raglots, ringilds, and town bailiffs. The Lancastrian penal statutes were designed to warn the rising Welsh families of the disadvantages of disloyalty to a new dynasty. Their reinforcement in 1402 added greater weight to earlier less permanent promulgations. Disorder had to be suppressed by introducing drastic methods which aimed, but not entirely successfully, at stemming Welsh spheres of influence in burghal areas. The results of such a policy seemed more fruitful in the purely English boroughs of the principality and in the north-east, principally at Flint and Chester where racial feelings ran consistently high. The ordinances of June 1401 may well have represented panic measures to threaten the Welsh especially in Chester in the vicinity of which the Prince of Wales's Council knew a strong Welsh community to exist. The rural areas remained Welsh and the available evidence proves that relations between the races normally were not so strained. In 1402-3 eight Welshmen (one being bailiff of Hopedale) were entrusted to defend the territory against Glyndŵr. Welshmen were appointed as keepers of the peace in the lordship of Maelor. Safe conducts were granted and several named officials were appointed as collectors of subsidies in Flint-shire,[41] all of which suggest that a loyal band of Welsh officialdom existed at local level in north-east Wales prepared to maintain government and administration against tremendous odds even to the point of entering into truces or agreements of neutrality with the rebel forces. Evidence suggests strongly that Ruthin and its lordship prospered despite the upheavals. The Welsh character of the borough no more than that of Oswestry and Welshpool could never be uprooted because associations were far too strong, and even the exclusiveness of Chester could only be maintained through constant observation and ruthlessness. In certain instances the shoe pinched painfully especially when a prospering burgess of thorough Welsh stock like David Holbache found himself hemmed in between the Scylla of Glyndŵr's violent raids and the Charybdis of the anti-Welsh laws. He was a dutiful steward of the town and lordship of Oswestry and deputy steward of Bromfield and Yale. He petitioned parliament in 1406 that he had endured ravages on his lands and had lost many of his rents in Chirk as a result of rebel attack.[42] He feared the onslaughts of Glyndŵr on the one hand and bemoaned his denial of full rights of English citizenship because of his Welsh ancestry on the other. His plea was accepted and he gained privileges contrary to the spirit and action of the men of Chester. His success enabled him to become Member of Parliament for Shropshire four times between 1406 and 1414 and for the borough of Shrewsbury in 1413 and 1417 and also enabled him, no doubt, to endow the grammar school in the town with greater confidence and to secure the pardon of Adam of Usk in 1411.[43] Holbache's predicament early on in the revolt formed but yet another

[41] *D.K.R.*, op. cit. 163, 211, 337. [42] *Rot. Parl.* iii. 590, 600-1; *C.P.R.*, *1405-8*, 245, 298.
[43] Ibid. *1408-13*, 283.

aspect of many divergent loyalties which created the tangled pattern of Anglo-Welsh relations in the fifteenth century. Owen ap Maredudd and Sir Gruffudd Fychan, burgesses of Welshpool in 1406, were deemed worthy of bardic praise as was Hugh Say, constable of the borough in 1411 and 1417–20.[44] Thomas Salesbury of Llywenni (son of Thomas Salesbury Hen) was created constable of Denbigh in 1466, became leasee of Flint mills in 1482, and also became steward of Flint in 1482–5 and 1485–9. Ellis Wettenhall (a descendant of an old Cheshire family of Nantwich), like so many others in border communities, followed the established trend of inter-marriage and married the daughter of Gruffudd ab Ieuan ap Maredudd of Hope where he settled. Geoffrey Kyffin, son of Morus ab Ieuan Gethin who was granted a pardon in 1445, filled the office of constable of Oswestry.[45] There are many other examples in the north-east of individuals who followed the progressive trend during the century when the memory of the Glyndŵr revolt, for realistic, forward-looking families, had become, to all intents and purposes, remote and unimportant.

Guto'r Glyn had made his protest half a century or so later against the actions of men like Holbache, and Ieuan Deulwyn urged his patron to avoid the unpopularity of office.[46] Such sentiments and opinions voiced by the bards, however, were not unanimously accepted even within their own order judging by the preference expressed by Hywel Swrdwal for Welsh rather than English officers of administration in the country.[47] But influential Welshmen, in the north-east, were contented to cohabit happily with the English and to accept readily what offices were available to them if and when the opportunity arose. On the other hand the antipathetic feelings usually associated with the retaliatory policy of the authorities of Chester probably provides about the best yardstick to measure the degree of racial discord that persisted and to gauge what element of racial tension remained in the northern border lands up until and after the accession of Henry Tudor.

[44] *Cywyddau Iolo Goch ac Eraill*, 203–4, 318–19.
[45] *Gwaith Tudur Penllyn*, 12–13, 45–6; *Gwaith Guto'r Glyn*, 186–8, 268–9, 359.
[46] *Casgliad o Waith Ieuan Deulwyn*, ed. I. Williams, Bangor, 1909, 61.
[47] *Gwaith Barddonol Howel Swrdwal a'i Fab Ieuan*, ed. J. C. Morrice, Bangor, 1908, 13–14.

Patronage, Politics, and the Principality of Wales, 1413–1461

R. A. GRIFFITHS

I N the pre-democratic age, patronage—of offices, pensions, and property—was
the surest support of power. Kings, governments, bishops, nobles, and gentlemen employed it to reward good service and ensure future loyalty; aristocrat
and yeoman alike sought it to attain personal wealth, political power, or social
position. Throughout western Europe the prerogative of patronage was inseparably
united with the obligation to govern. The circumspect exercise of patronage would
ensure orderly government in the state and provide sufficient opportunity to obviate
tensions in society. Dangers and resentments would occur if patronage were im-
prudent or ineffectual, as those could testify who witnessed the disasters of King
John's reign in England or the conflicts in France while Charles VI was insane.
Lancastrian England and Wales amply illustrate the potentialities and pitfalls of
patronage.

Within the limits imposed on him by wisdom, advice, and importuning, the king
dispensed the greatest patronage. This power was implicitly reserved by Henry IV
when he asserted that he was 'in as great a royal liberty' as his predecessors. It was
inherited by Henry V in 1413, and when Henry VI began his personal rule, he
announced in November 1437 that this same power was his 'for to do and dispose for
hem as hym good semeth'. It remained intact when the king was too young or too ill
to exercise it personally, and then arrangements were made for others to do so for
him.[1]

Throughout England, Wales, and territories overseas, the Lancastrian kings
disposed of hundreds of offices, considerable quantities of cash augmented by tallies
and bills of assignment on future revenue, and a replenishable stock of demesnes,
escheats, forfeitures, and wardships. In England this patronage was often shared with,
and therefore limited by, several of their subjects; in Welsh marcher lordships that
were not their own, these kings had few rights at all. But in the palatinates of Chester
and Lancaster, in the duchy of Cornwall, and the principality of Wales, the Lancastrians were exclusive, direct lords. There, their patronage was rarely curtailed, and

[1] *Select Documents of English Constitutional History, 1307–1485*, ed. S. B. Chrimes and A. L. Brown,
London, 1961, 199, 235, 251–2, 275–6, 299–302. I am grateful to Dr. C. D. Ross for his valuable comments
on an earlier draft of this article.

hence the impact of their appointments and grants on government, society, and the practice of kingship can be clearly observed.

In the principality shires of Wales (Anglesey, Caernarvon, and Merioneth in the north, Cardigan and Carmarthen in the south), the king had an extensive repertoire of offices, rights, and resources by means of which the principality was governed. To keep gifts and government in perspective was the art of kingship. The greater offices conferred influence and political or military power, although their obligations were real and often heavy enough. The justiciars of north and south Wales were the king's vicegerents; limited patronage was delegated to them, for they could appoint lesser officers in the commotes of each shire and lease Crown lands.[2] Especially did they enjoy personal patronage in nominating lieutenants or deputies to act in their absence—friends, associates, or retainers whom they could trust. John and Henry Wogan, Pembrokeshire esquires of Edward, duke of York, deputized for the duke as justiciar of south Wales (1407–16); and Sir Thomas Stanley, controller of the king's Household, was made deputy-justiciar by William, earl of Suffolk, who was steward of the Household and, in 1440, justiciar of north Wales. The justiciar's responsibilities were onerous, especially at times of political turmoil. Sir Thomas Stanley was said to have resigned from the northern justiciarship in October 1450 because he was 'occupied in divers business whereby he has no leisure to exercise his office';[3] whereas lack of confidence in William, Lord Abergavenny, the justiciar who faced Glyndŵr's threat to south Wales, led to his dismissal in August 1401.

Principality finance was managed at Caernarvon and Carmarthen by two chamberlains, who also kept the king's great seals of north and south Wales, the very instrument of patronage; when leases were sealed, and fees and wages authorized, their advice was naturally sought. Most chamberlains employed a deputy, to whom they extended their own patronage. Sir Geoffrey Radclyff had an entrée to north Wales's government through the good offices of his kinsman, Sir John Radclyff (chamberlain in 1434–7),[4] whilst William Burghill, who was employed by Sir Edward Stradling in south Wales in 1430–5, had worked with Sir Edward some years earlier. A chamberlain's opportunities for enrichment were even greater. Thomas Barneby, chamberlain of north Wales (1406–14) during the Glyndŵr revolt, feathered his nest by embezzlement and extortion; the reckoning was correspondingly severe, for

---

[2] For a full discussion of this and other aspects of principality government mentioned in this article, see W. H. Waters, *The Edwardian Settlement of North Wales in its Administrative and Legal Aspects, 1284–1343*, Cardiff, 1935; R. A. Griffiths, *The Principality of Wales in the Later Middle Ages*, i: *South Wales, 1277–1536*, Cardiff, 1972.

[3] *C.P.R. 1446–52*, 403. Full references to officers of the principality in south Wales mentioned in this article, together with biographical details, are to be found in Griffiths, *Principality of Wales*. Appointments to office in north Wales are recorded in *C.P.R.*, unless otherwise stated.

[4] P.R.O. (Special Collections, Ministers' Accounts (henceforward Min. Acc.), 1216/4 m. 9.

Barneby was sacked in March 1414 after Henry V had inquired into the activities of royal officers in north Wales.

Military power was concentrated in a small group of castle-constables, whose duty was to protect the castles at Beaumaris, Conway, Caernarvon, and Harlech, Aberystwyth, Cardigan, and Carmarthen. After the rebellion, they commanded enlarged garrisons which put at their disposal a small, but permanent, core of fighting men maintained at the royal expense.[5] These constables, too, employed trustworthy lieutenants, although the shock of Glyndŵr's rising led to subsequent injunctions that they themselves should be resident, or at least visit their castles regularly.[6] John Stanley installed his relative, Rowland Stanley, in Caernarvon castle in 1437–8;[7] another deputy-constable, Gruffydd Dwnn at Carmarthen in 1431–2, was not only a colleague of the constable, Sir John Scudamore, in the administration of Kidwelly, but also his son-in-law.

Despite the similarities between north and south Wales at the apex of government, there were considerable differences at the secondary level. The statute of Rhuddlan had outlined the sheriff's judicial, executive, and financial responsibilities in the three northern shires, but the slow evolution of royal administration in the south dispersed these responsibilities among a sheriff, a steward, and two bailiffs itinerant in Carmarthenshire and Cardiganshire. Hence, the northern sheriffs were more prominent than any one of the southern officers; but in both areas unfulfilled obligations could jeopardize a career, as James Butler, earl of Ormond, and his deputy-sheriff in Carmarthenshire discovered in 1442–3, when they were imprisoned for allowing a detainee to escape.

These major offices combined obligations which were at times heavy, and a discretionary patronage that enabled friends, relatives, or servants to enjoy some of the perquisites and reciprocate their patron's favour. Another significant attraction of office-holding was the annual fee; Sir John Radclyff was specifically appointed chamberlain of north Wales in February 1434 so that the Crown could help discharge its enormous debt to him of more than £7,000.[8] If a friend could be found to deputize, or if obligations could be discharged lightly, these Welsh offices would be worthwhile catches.

On a smaller scale, commote offices were granted as gifts or farmed for an annual sum to men who made what they could from the customary fees; such offices had few—if any—duties attached to them. There were a surprising number in the principality, partly because Edward I retained certain Welsh elements of local government while at the same time creating new offices on the English pattern. His

---

[5] P.R.O. Min. Acc. 1288/2; 1223/8 m. 5; B.M. (Add. Ch.) 26597 m. 3.

[6] *P.P.C.*, ed. N. H. Nicolas (7 vols., Record Commission, 1834–7), v. 3 (1436); vi. 60 (1447), 302–4 (1460); P.R.O. Exchequer, T.R. Council and Privy Seal, 78/ 237 and 238 (27 February 1436, misdated to 1449).

[7] B.M., Add. Ch. 26597 m. 5.

[8] *P.P.C.* iv. 199–200; *C.P.R., 1429–36*, 269–70, 338. Radclyff was also allowed to keep the north Wales revenue until the debt was discharged.

conquest, therefore, had a legacy of over-administration which eventually made several offices well-nigh superfluous and irrelevant to current needs; there was no reason to cavil when they were held by deputy. The customary fees that ensured their survival provided patronage for the king and a modest profit for those whom he patronized. In south Wales, the archaic office of *rhaglaw* or constable had a monetary

FEES OF MAJOR OFFICERS[9]

Office	Annual fee £ s. d.			Other payments £ s. d.		
Justiciar, north	66	13	4			
south	40			66 13 4–133	6	8*
Chamberlain, north	20					
south	20					
Constable, Carmarthen	20					
Cardigan	40					
Aberystwyth	town's income			91	5	0†
Beaumaris	40			127	15	0
Conway	40			109	10	0
Caernarvon	40			167	5	10
Harlech	26	13	4	146	0	0
Sheriff, Anglesey	20					
Caernarvon	20					
Merioneth	20					

　* A 'regard' payable after the Glyndŵr revolt at a variable rate: Griffiths, *Principality of Wales*, p. 33.
　† This and the following four sums were maximum payments to support castle-garrisons under the Lancastrians: Min. Acc. 1223/5 m. 8; 1216/7 m. 4, 5, 6, 7; 1216/8 m. 4, 5.

value that ensured its continuance. The constableships of Caeo and Mallaen (Carms.) had once reimbursed a farmer who paid £12 per annum for them, though by 1451 £6 was a more realistic figure.[10] This was the order of profit anticipated by William Catton, Henry IV's servant who acquired both offices for life in September 1408. The *rhaglaw* and woodward in north Wales had a similar history, and in the fifteenth century their offices were granted to royal servants, most of whom remained strangers to Snowdonia: two grooms of Henry VI's larder, John Martin and William Bangore, shared the *rhaglaw*'s office in Ystummaner (Caerns.) from February 1433 with a reasonable expectation of 42*s.* a year; William Randolf, another royal servant, received the woodwardship of Is Conwy, Uwch Conwy, and Eifionydd (Caerns.) for life in 1438 in the hope that it would realize £8 per annum. The *amobr* fine paid throughout Wales when a woman lost her virginity in marriage (or less happy

　[9] P.R.O. Min. Acc. 1216/7 m. 3–8; 1223/8 m. 3–5.　　　　[10] Ibid. 1168/7 m. 5.

circumstances) was still imposed in the fifteenth century. In south Wales, *amobr* fines were extended at £7. 6s. 8d. per annum when their farmer, John Wodehouse, Henry V's dependable servant, died in 1431; but they were a wasting asset, for by 1450 their value was thought to have slumped to £3. 10s. 0d.[11] Offices such as these were desirable perquisites for yeomen, gentlemen, and esquires, to whom a few pounds from several of them could make the difference between poverty and comfort. None was a juicy plum, but several plucked together could content a royal servant, despite complaints of extortion and difficulties of collection which some officers experienced in post-Glyndŵr Wales.[12]

The remaining local offices still had essential functions in the fifteenth century, though their fees were modest at best. They were therefore pre-eminently the preserve of Welshmen, whose local standing was enhanced by becoming, for example, bailiff itinerant of Carmarthen. But those who served as commote beadle or reeve in south Wales and as *rhingyll* in the north did so reluctantly, for the small fees were poor compensation for the duties assigned them; hence, they occasionally had to be nominated to office by the justiciar or chamberlain—even offered a wage later in the fifteenth century. Such officers hardly thought of themselves as benefiting from royal patronage, but more likely as tenants discharging a tiresome obligation.

The Crown had few substantial demesnes to dispose of in Wales. Gerardston, near Cardigan, was one, and the hamlets of Maenorsilian, Talsarn, and Trefilan (Cards.) another. Rhys ap Thomas ap Dafydd, a king's esquire, secured both, Gerardston to the value of £6, and the three hamlets were farmed for £7. 0s. 4d. annually. Yet they need not have been jealously fought over, for Gerardston was never worth more than £5 and the hamlets' farm was soon lowered to £6. 3s. 4d. The decay of Dinefwr and Dryslwyn castles (Carms.) put these royal estates, too, on the market: John Perrot, a Pembrokeshire esquire, acquired Dinefwr for twenty years in 1433 for a £5 farm, and John Wodehouse was granted Dryslwyn in 1409 for £10 per annum. The manor of Aber (Caerns.) was similarly available, and in 1437 John Fray, a baron of the Exchequer, acquired it for life believing it to be worth 40 marks, although his predecessor had complained that its income never reached that level. Escheats and wardships were equally modest in a principality that had few large landowners and where Welsh inheritance customs retained their vitality and, indeed, were confirmed by Henry V even for former rebels and their sons![13] As the Glyndŵr revolt receded into the past, forfeitures, too, occurred less frequently. Here, the patronage nexus had less scope. Nevertheless, the Clements' Cardiganshire estates, as an example, were worth bestowing on Edmund Beaufort and Gruffydd ap Nicholas in 1437 at £40 per annum during the heir's minority.

---

[11] Ibid. 1161/5 m. 2; 1167/5 m. 3d; 1168/7 m. 4; 1162/7m. 4d; *C.P.R., 1429–36*, 253 (for north Wales).

[12] P.R.O. Exchequer, T.R. Council and Privy Seal, 47/40; 68/47; 73/2; 78/53. Leases of mills and woods, advowry fines in north Wales, and the income from the ferries between Anglesey and the mainland, were also part of the royal patronage: *C.P.R., 1422–9*, 48; ibid. *1436–41*, 63, 117; P.R.O. Min. Acc. 1305/5 m. 1.

[13] *Rot. Parl.* (6 vols., 1767), iv. 90–1; *C.P.R., 1413–16*, 380, 405; ibid *1436–41*, 50, 69.

Finally, the king had substantial sums of cash at his disposal once the expenses of Welsh government had been met. In 1433 the treasurer of England estimated them at £470. 5s. 4½d. in south Wales (in addition to £212. 13s. 4d. already spent on annuities) and £590. 18s. 4d. in the north. This was no wild—if a pessimistic—guess: at the end of the year 1435–6, £664. 6s. 11½d. (in addition to £376. 7s. 2½d. paid to annuitants) remained in south Wales and for the eighteen months up to Michaelmas 1438 £912 in the north. During Henry VI's minority a good deal of this cash was expended on annuities, sometimes in Wales itself, like the 5 marks from Bala which Thomas Sandeway, Prince Henry's servant, received for life in 1411. The payment of other annuities at Westminster was anticipated by bills of assignment when the chamberlains were thought to have money available. Richard Beauchamp, earl of Warwick, had assignments on south Wales worth £837. 7s. 3½d. in the summer of 1437 alone, though by April 1440 only £140 had been honoured.[14]

These grants of offices, lands, and cash brought the principality within the Court-centred scheme of patronage. Just and efficient government might be eroded if this patronage were dominated by courtly motives. The limitations on Lancastrian patronage were hardly likely to maintain a balance between the desire to reward and the obligation to govern. The grant of Merioneth to Henry V's widow between 1422 and 1437 merely restricted the extent of her son's patronage. The conferment of the entire principality on Prince Edward in 1457 placed all offices, estates, and pensions at the disposal of his Council. More fundamental were the limitations imposed by the Glyndŵr revolt, whose legacy of suspicion led to the careful control of patronage in the English interest. Responding to the Commons' petition, parliament in 1401–2 ordained that no Welshman should be appointed to office in Wales in his own right or as a deputy; even when the king exempted bishops and 'bons et loialx liges', this statute (extended to include Englishmen married to a relative of Glyndŵr or an active rebel, and upheld in 1410) was a major restriction on royal patronage. Sir Ralph Botiller was reminded in 1436 that his deputies as constable of Conway castle should be Englishmen.[15] More striking is the way in which Edmund Beaufort used this legislation to victimize Sir John Scudamore, the husband of Glyndŵr's daughter Alice; after a generation of loyal service in south Wales and elsewhere, in 1433 he was deprived of office for reasons far removed from the legislators' purpose.

The Crown's disposal of property was also curtailed by statute. After 1401 no Welshman should purchase land in the English boroughs in Wales or have burgages and liberties there; in the following year this was even applied to English burgesses who had married Welsh. It was presumably under this enactment that Madog ap Llygaid duon ('the black-eyed') was deprived in 1407 of ten acres given him in the franchise of Beaumaris. Parliament's concern for security produced the further declaration that castles, defensible buildings, and walled towns should be in non-

[14] *C.P.R., 1422–9*, 49; *P.P.C.* v. 32–3; P.R.O. Exchequer, E.R. Receipt Roll, 752.
[15] *Rot. Parl.* iii. 457, 509, 624; *Statutes of the Realm* (henceforward *S.R.*) (11 vols., Record Commission, 1810–28), ii. 141; *C.P.R., 1399–1401*, 469; *P.P.C.* i. 148–50; *C.P.R., 1429–36*, 590.

Welsh hands (bishops and lords only being excepted).[16] These statutory restraints on patronage profoundly affected for a time relations between government and governed, the opportunities open to Welshmen, and the effectiveness of local government in fifteenth-century Wales. Their severity was tempered in practice by a blind eye or by letters of denizenship, but their existence made the discharge of the king's responsibilities as patron even more complex than they already were.

Bribes and *douceurs*, inducements and importunings—all played a part in fifteenth-century patronage. By their nature they were commonly offered on the backstairs or by word of mouth, and are rarely documented. Men frequently and openly petitioned the king (or the king and Council) for a specific reward for services rendered, as did John Claiton, a page of Henry VI's cellar, in 1445. Some requests did not elicit quite the response the petitioner anticipated, which may explain why John Hampton was appointed sheriff of Merioneth in 1433 'until he be provided with some other office not requiring personal residence'.[17] But more sinister was the intrusion of a person confident of royal patronage into a life-grant enjoyed preferably by an older man, whose expected early demise would put the office or gift at the survivor's disposal. This was probably why Roger Norreys was associated with Rhys ap Thomas ap Dafydd, an active figure from about 1390, in the stewardships of Cardiganshire and Cantrefmawr in 1438; but patron and client had not bargained with Rhys himself, who was still alive at 'a great age' in 1446. Other grants in survivorship were willingly approved by the incumbent—even perhaps made at his suggestion. In December 1443 the earl of Suffolk took the unusual step of formally associating with him Sir Thomas Stanley, his colleague in the king's Household, as justiciar of north Wales and Chester. It was a device that also made possible the continuance of an office in the same family: John Stanley, the king's esquire, surrendered the constableship of Caernarvon castle in 1441 so that he and his son could be installed in survivorship. One can only speculate at the pressure which James Grisacre, yeoman of the Chamber, brought to bear on two other Household servants in 1435 for them to surrender offices in Ardudwy (Merioneth) which he promptly occupied. Equally concealed are Sir John Bolde's thoughts as he gave his consent to the surrender of the constableship of Conway castle in 1436 so that Sir Ralph Botiller could have it. Such pressures may have been most compelling in the king's Household itself, for it is striking that Suffolk, Henry VI's favourite and justiciar of north Wales, was steward of the Household when several Household servants secured Crown patronage in Wales by successful petition or mutual agreement. Confusion may have been one corollary, for John Water, a Chamber groom, acquired several minor Caernarvonshire offices in 1438 'provided always that the said offices are not already granted'.[18] Another was the needless dissipation of the Crown's financial resources, which was later corrected by

---

[16] *Rot. Parl.* iii. 476, 508–9; *S.R.* ii. 129, 140–1; P.R.O. Min. Acc. 1152/9 m. 8; *C.C.R., 1399–1402*, 328.

[17] P.R.O. Exchequer, T.R., Council and Privy Seal, 75/52; *C.P.R., 1429–36*, 266.

[18] Ibid., *1436–41*, 194. For the Council's concern for this and similar inefficiencies by about 1444, see Chrimes and Brown, op. cit., 277–9.

the insertion in patents of a clause that enabled a higher bidder to secure the grant. As offices, lands, and pensions were disposed of by such leverage hundreds of miles away at Westminster or Eltham, considerations of ability, experience, and merit were in danger of being shouldered aside.

Henry V's policy in Wales was statesmanlike and his patronage carefully considered. His father interfered incessantly during the early years of the Glyndŵr revolt, but by 1405 young Henry was making his own appointments and saw no need to change them in 1413. Continuity of government under Henry as prince and king was natural. The military crisis still cast its shadow over the highest offices: Edward, duke of York, justiciar of south Wales since 1407, and Gilbert, Lord Talbot, northern justiciar since September 1406, were successful soldier-magnates with estates in or near Wales. But by 1416 the king was laying greater stress on order and reconciliation, and in the south he turned to the Devon lawyer, Robert Hill, to deal with the post-war tangle of accusations, dispossessions, and treasons. In June 1421 he was replaced by one of Henry's most dependable administrators, John Merbury, a self-made Herefordshire esquire who was deputy-justiciar in 1411–13 and chamberlain from 1400. The financial recovery achieved by Merbury and William Botiller, his successor as chamberlain in 1421, owed much to their experience and lack of preoccupation elsewhere. Thomas Walton, a young Cambridge don who was prebendary of St. John's, Chester, from 1410, became chamberlain of north Wales in 1414 and restored the north's finances with equal effect. These men displayed that intense loyalty, efficiency, and dedication that Henry V could inspire. If Henry made a mistake, it was in appointing the resourceful but unprincipled clerk, Thomas Barneby, who was Walton's predecessor, but the speed with which the investigation of his corruption led to dismissal in March 1414 underlines Henry's concern for responsible government.[19] Justiciars and chamberlains such as these attracted equally capable deputies. Three notable lawyers were commissioned—Sir William Hankeford (1413) and John Russell (1413, 1416–17) in the south, Hugh Huls in the north (1413)—but especially were they assisted by loyal, experienced administrators from Wales or the border shires. Men like Sir John St. John from Herefordshire, Thomas Walter of Carmarthen, and Merbury himself acted for Duke Edward, while Thomas Walter and Henry Slack (who doubtless knew Merbury as a fellow Herefordshire gentleman) served as deputy-chamberlain in the south; the Cheshireman, Richard Bolde, was deputy-justiciar of north Wales in 1422. If the king was careful to abide by the legislation of 1401–2, he was wise enough to enlist men who were knowledgeable of Wales and Welshmen.[20]

[19] R. A. Griffiths, 'Wales and the Marches', in *Fifteenth-Century England*, ed. S. B. Chrimes, C. D. Ross, and R. A. Griffiths, Manchester, 1972, 146–7; P.R.O. Min. Acc. 1216/2 m. 5; 1216/3 m. 3; A. B. Emden, *A Biographical Register of the University of Cambridge to 1500*, Cambridge, 1963, 615; R. A. Griffiths, 'The Glyndŵr Rebellion in North Wales through the eyes of an Englishman', *Bulletin Board of Celtic Studies* xxii, part iii, 1967, 151–68.

[20] P.R.O. Exchequer, E. R., Warrants for Issues, 29/112; Min. Acc. 1153/1 m. 1d; E. Foss, *A Biographical*

As prince, Henry had staffed the most important southern castles with constables from Herefordshire who knew one another and the chamberlain, John Merbury: Sir John Scudamore at Carmarthen, Andrew Lynne and John Burghope at Cardigan, and Richard Oldcastle at Aberystwyth. Of all the English shires, this county had easiest access to west Wales; moreover, part of it lay with Carmarthenshire and Cardiganshire in the diocese of St. David's, and a substantial Welsh-speaking population lived in its attractive vales. Appropriate to a military establishment in the aftermath of fierce rebellion, at least four of these constables were soldiers (Scudamore, Lynne, Burghope, and Sir John Griffith), and two others had military inclinations that took them to France soon after appointment. But above all, they were devoted to the house of Lancaster and especially (since five were already his retainers or servants) to Henry himself. They formed a coterie of tried and trusted soldiers who knew something of Wales and had much else in common.

Such ties were weaker among the northern constables, for the dubious loyalty of Cheshire in the recent past probably restrained Henry from choosing his constables exclusively in this, the nearest recruiting ground. However, four of them hailed from Lancashire, Staffordshire, Cheshire, and Salop,[21] and the same dependence on Henry as his esquires or bachelors is as evident here as in the south: Sir William Newport at Beaumaris and Sir John Bolde at Conway had fought with him in Wales, while he employed John Norreys simultaneously as a transport expert and as constable of Conway castle. The only Welshman appointed was Sir John Griffith, to Aberystwyth in 1422, but his estates in midland and northern England were more important to him than those in Cardiganshire, and his English forebears allowed him to slip past parliament's legislation.[22]

The qualities Henry sought in his sheriffs of north Wales were no different, though their social origins less exalted. Three of Anglesey's sheriffs, Ralph de Barton, Richard atte Wode, and John Walsh, came from Cheshire, the latter brought to the principality by Lord Talbot, whom he had served before; another, Roger Strangeways, lived in Lancashire.[23] Others had seen military service in north Wales, and, like Barton, were vitally concerned in Henry's French enterprises. The trained administrator acquainted with Wales was therefore at a premium, but the personal connection

Dictionary of the Judges of England, 1066–1870, London, 1870, 358. Huls was also from Cheshire: G. Ormerod, *The History of the County Palatine and City of Chester*, 3 vols., London, 1875–82, iii. 464.

21 J. H. Wylie and W. T. Waugh, *The Reign of Henry the Fifth*, 3 vols., C.U.P., 1914–29, i. 336, 456 n. 4; ii. 308; *C.P.R., 1422–9*, 15, 56; P.R.O. Exchequer, T.R., Council and Privy Seal, 31/91; *C.P.R., 1416–22*, 46; B.M., Add. Ch. 26597 m. 3, 4; *Reports of the Deputy Keeper of the Public Records*, xxxvii, part 2 (1876), 636–7; R. Somerville, *History of the Duchy of Lancaster*, London, 1953, 462.

22 Griffiths, 'The Glyndŵr Rebellion in North Wales', loc. cit. 157; J. H. Wylie, *History of England under Henry the Fourth*, 4 vols., London, 1884–98, i. 147, 243, 247, 431; ii. 19; iv. 243, 245; *C.P.R., 1399–1401*, 338; ibid. *1413–16*, 160, 413.

23 P.R.O. Min. Acc. 1305/5 m. 1; 1152/7 m. 8, 9, 10d; *C.C.R., 1405–9*, 253; Ormerod, op. cit. ii. 749; *D.K.R.* xxxvii, part 2 (1876), 808, 809, 759–60; A. J. Pollard, 'The Family of Talbot, Lords Talbot and Earls of Shrewsbury in the fifteenth century' (unpublished University of Bristol Ph.D. thesis, 1968), 25 n. 1.

with Henry was equally strong: two sheriffs were his esquires, and Hugh Huls, sheriff of Caernarvonshire in 1411–13, was a royal justice.[24] Needless to say, no Welshman could safely be entrusted with a northern shrievalty, but in the south Rhys ap Thomas ap Dafydd, the loyal Cardiganshire esquire, was made denizen and sheriff of Carmarthenshire in 1413—and steward of Cantrefmawr and Cardiganshire soon afterwards. Rhys's experience in government and as a soldier, and his devotion to Henry IV and Henry V place him alongside other royal servants in Wales. The same can be said of Thomas Walter, royal attorney in south Wales in 1411–36, and a deputy-chamberlain and deputy-justiciar; he was an Anglo-Welsh lawyer from the borough of Carmarthen who was proud of his English loyalty.

Henry did not deny the native Welshmen access to his patronage, but common security dictated that only minor offices be offered them. When William Stalworth and John Vernon, yeomen of the Chamber, became woodward of Penllyn and Tal-y-bont (Merioneth) in 1418, they joined a fraternity of commote officers who were almost exclusively Welsh (some of them, indeed, former rebels); if Henry had not been at Bayeux when he issued the appointment, he might not have made this exception.[25]

The king, however, dug deep into his Welsh coffers for annuities for his personal servants. This was less likely to outrage Welsh opinion than if they had monopolized the influential, archaic, and profitable offices. South Wales supported more annuities than the north, perhaps because its involvement in the revolt was less deep-rooted and its recovery quicker. Even before 1413 Henry had granted £245 worth of annuities there to nine persons, one of whom, Henry's companion-in-arms, Richard Beauchamp, earl of Warwick, received 200 marks. Although he added another six, in 1422 only seven (worth £217 per annum) were still payable. Most annuitants were Henry's personal servants and three (including Warwick) were retained by him for life. It is significant that three were also Herefordshire esquires, who could seek assistance from friends in the administration to collect their cash; Nicholas Merbury, a £20-annuitant since 1408, was the chamberlain's brother. The only Welshman on the list was the ubiquitous Rhys ap Thomas ap Dafydd, whose favours were unrivalled among Welshmen of his day.[26]

The pattern was similar in north Wales. In 1413 three annuities (worth £23. 6s. 8d.) had already been granted, and King Henry issued a further nine, totalling £152, especially to Household servants and esquires; the largest (£100 from Twrcelyn commote) was received by Sir William Harington, knight of the Garter, Henry's

[24] P.R.O. Exchequer, K.R. Sheriffs' Accounts, 57/28 m. 1; Min. Acc. 1175/10 m. 5; 1203/6 m. 2; E. Breese, *Kalendars of Gwynedd*, London, 1873, 69; *D.K.R.* xxxvii, part 2 (1876), 647; Wylie and Waugh, op. cit. i. 109, n. 4, 456, n. 4; P.R.O. Exchequer, E.R. Warrants for Issues, 39/57; 40/172; *C.P.R., 1422–9*, 53; Ormerod, op. cit. ii. 749.

[25] *D.K.R.* xli (1880), 700; P.R.O. Min. Acc. 1305/5 m. 1.

[26] R. A. Griffiths, 'Royal Government in the Southern Counties of the Principality of Wales, 1422–1485' (unpublished University of Bristol Ph.D. thesis, 1962), 385; P.R.O. Min. Acc. 1222/14 m. 5, 6; 1223/5 m. 9; *C.P.R., 1413–16*, 42, 99, 164; *C.C.R., 1405–9*, 45; Griffiths, *Principality of Wales*, 132, 249.

standard-bearer and a commander in France. Several others were in recognition of war service in Wales or France, but not one annuitant was a Welshman.[27] Under Henry V there is less evidence of the northern Welsh being willing to collaborate with the government—and therefore attracting royal favour—than those from the south.

At first, the Minority Council did not alter radically the distribution of royal patronage at its temporary disposal. But as the years passed a shift of emphasis occurred which throws light on the relationship between Englishman and Welshman, on the Council and, as the king grew older, on the Household. Henry V's sudden death at an unusually early age after a brief reign left a mere baby to succeed him barely six years after Glyndŵr had disappeared. These facts made the Council cautious, and in the principality it looked to two prominent aristocrats to head the government. Thomas Beaufort, duke of Exeter and justiciar of north Wales from February 1423, was the late king's uncle; he was one of the two dukes on the Council and had taken charge of the baby king. Thomas had had a distinguished military career in Wales and France, and was justiciar of Chester from 1420. The Council chose a younger man for the south, Lord Audley: although his experience was limited, as a marcher lord he had a personal interest in south Wales. These two men represent a return to the type of justiciar appointed by Prince Henry. Exeter's death in December 1426, when the rift between his brother, Bishop Beaufort, and Duke Humphrey of Gloucester was widening, produced a stop-gap appointment in the person of James Strangeways, Henry V's serjeant-at-law and a royal justice who had been deputy-justiciar in 1413–14. When the bishop left England in March 1427, Humphrey took steps which in May secured for himself the justiciarship of north Wales and Chester. Conciliar politics had invaded provincial government by means of royal patronage.

James Audley was encouraged to be a conscientious justiciar by his possession of estates in south Wales. He used a deputy infrequently, and then usually Staffordshire men whom he, as a Staffordshire magnate, would know and trust. William Legh acted for him on several occasions, and when Audley went to France in 1430–1 a panel of lieutenants was formally constituted: Sir Richard Vernon, Thomas Mollesley, and Legh were from Staffordshire; Sir Edward Stradling was chamberlain of south Wales, and Sir John Scudamore was so experienced that he could hardly be excluded. As a group, these deputies were connected with one another, while Vernon and Stradling were associated with the Beauforts; furthermore, Legh, Vernon, Scudamore, and Mollesley served the Stafford family, of whom the earl was married to Bishop Beaufort's niece. One of Gloucester's lieutenants in the north was William

[27] *C.P.R., 1422–9*, 49, 57, 61, 88; ibid., *1413–16*, 106, 108, 143, 169, 184; ibid., *1416–22*, 60; ibid., *1436–41*, 163, 482–3; *Rot. Parl.* iv. 184; P.R.O. Min. Acc. 1152/7 m. 3d, 7d; Exchequer, E.R. Warrants for Issues, 22/256; 31/326.

Burley, a Shropshire lawyer who was sufficiently trusted by Humphrey to be nominated by him as deputy-justiciar in north Wales and Chester. For all this suspicion of conciliar connection, these deputy-justiciars were skilled administrators.[28] The remaining lieutenant in south Wales was Dafydd ap Thomas, whose Lancastrian loyalties earned him letters of denizenship in 1427, but who so allowed personal ambition to triumph over loyalty that he was dismissed for partiality in 1436.

Rank and connection appealed just as forcibly to the Council in its choice of chamberlains. The Anglo-Welsh landowner Sir Edward Stradling became chamberlain of south Wales in 1423; if he could justifiably claim that there was 'noo chamberlein there this hundred wyntres that maad bettre levee of moneye due', his marriage to Bishop Beaufort's niece is equally significant. In the north, Richard Walkestede, the Oxfordshire knight appointed chamberlain that same year, had appropriate experience as constable of Beaumaris castle, clerk of the market in Henry V's Household, and as a military administrator in France. If Stradling had the Beauforts' endorsement, Walkestede was likely to receive that of the martial Gloucester and Bedford. Walkestede's successor in 1434, Sir John Radclyff, was from the same mould. A soldier-administrator in Gascony from 1419, Radclyff was of Cheshire origin and served in France under Bedford, who was in England when he was appointed chamberlain.[29] Political sponsorship now ranked with merit as a prerequisite for the chamberlainship.

The choice of deputy-chamberlains, however, continued to respond to the chamberlain's own wishes. Thomas Dawkinson (Walkestede's deputy, and escheator of Caernarvonshire and Merioneth in 1417–8, and sheriff of Merioneth in 1430–2) and John Foxwyst (Radclyff's lieutenant) were Cheshiremen, while Sir Geoffrey de Radclyff was one of Sir John's kinsmen.[30] In breaching the legislation of 1401–2, Sir Edward Stradling stood alone. Although he relied on William Burghill, a Herefordshire gentleman with whom he had served elsewhere and who had been deputy-constable of Cardigan castle, and on the Kidwelly burgess, Thomas Castell, he also employed two Welshmen. One, Gruffydd ap Dafydd ap Thomas, was the son of the denizen whom Henry V had found reliable. The other, Gruffydd ap Nicholas, owed less to his family than to his extraordinary ability and powerful instinct for self-preservation and self-advancement. Thus, although political motives unconnected with Wales were increasingly directing patronage in the principality, the door was

[28] J. S. Roskell, 'William Burley of Broncroft, speaker for the Commons in 1437 and 1445–6', *Trans. Shropshire Archaeological and Natural History Soc.* lvi, 1960, 263–72; B.M., Add. Ch. 26597 m. 4.

[29] R. A. Griffiths, 'The Rise of the Stradlings of St. Donat's', *Morgannwg, Trans. Glamorgan Local History Soc.* vii, 1963, 22–6; *C.P.R., 1416–22*, 65; M. D. Lobel, 'The History of Dean and Chalford', *Oxfordshire Record Soc. Publications*, xvii, 1935, 58–9, 114 and n.; *D.K.R.* xli, 1880, 716, 718, 753; xlii, 1881, 358, 390, 397, 406–7, 425–8, 433, 438, 447, 450; M. G. A. Vale, *English Gascony, 1399–1453*, Oxford, 1970, 86, 96, 97–8, 102, 103, 105, 245–7; Wylie and Waugh, op. cit. iii. 73, 313; *D.K.R.* xxxvii, part 2 (1876), 603–6; P.R.O. Exchequer, E.R., Warrants for Issues, 45/140, 156.

[30] B.M., Add. Ch. 26597 m. 2; P.R.O. Min. Acc. 1216/3 m. 1; 1216/4 m. 6, 9; *D.K.R.* xxxvi (1875), 140; xxxvii, part 2 (1876), pp. 120, 183, 496; Vale, op. cit. 98; P.R.O. Exchequer, K. R. Sheriffs' Accounts, 57/28 m. 1; Breese, op. cit. 69; Ormerod, op. cit. iii. 668.

opening for Welshmen of a new generation to achieve power as lieutenants of the greater officers.

The constraints felt by Henry V in the choice of constables for the royal fortresses still operated after 1422, and none of the experienced soldiers appointed by him was replaced. At Caernarvon Thomas Barneby died in harness in 1427, and so did Sir John Bolde at Conway in 1436; others lasted even longer. However, the Council's two appointments in north Wales are significant. At Caernarvon John Stanley, Henry V's Cheshire esquire, had been sheriff of Anglesey since 1425, and his advancement enhanced the Stanley tradition of service in north Wales and Cheshire. The appointment of the war captain Sir Ralph Botiller to Conway in June 1436 was a striking political nomination without the guarantee of merit which residence or experience in Wales could give; he spent most of his time in the king's company and the need for deputy-constables was acknowledged in his patent—provided they were English.[31] Continuity was equally apparent in the south. Christopher Standish at Dinefwr was the first to be replaced in 1425 by his soldier-son, Sir Roland, one of Bedford's retinue. The lieutenant-constables, too, are predictable. At Cardigan, John Burghope relied on two Herefordshire men with whom he was doubtless acquainted, William Burghill (1426–43) and Hugh Eyton (1428–9); whereas Scudamore at Carmarthen looked to his son-in-law, Gruffydd Dwnn, for assistance. On the other hand, at Dinefwr, where the Standishs were unlikely to attend to their duties in person, two Welshmen nosed their way into positions of authority: in 1428–9 Rhys ap Gwilym ap Philip, a Carmarthenshire gentleman from Kidwelly, and in 1429 the forceful Gruffydd ap Nicholas. The vindictiveness of Henry IV's Parliaments was evaporating even with regard to the royal castles.

More disturbing were the political purposes to which patronage was put towards the end of the minority. Despite Scudamore's record, in August 1433 Edmund Beaufort destroyed his career by recalling that provision of 1402 which made ineligible for office in Wales any Englishman married to a relative of Glyndŵr. He used the statute for partisan motives, for Beaufort was anxious to counter Scudamore's claim to those of Glyndŵr's estates granted to John Beaufort in 1400. Two years later, Edmund succeeded Sir John Griffith as constable of Aberystwyth castle, and south Wales's most important fortresses were thereby placed at the disposal of the Beaufort faction. The northern shrievalties were open to political pressure too. When it needed to replace Henry V's appointees, the Council continued to enlist experienced men of modest fortune preferably near at hand in Cheshire. But John Stanley (sheriff of Anglesey from 1425 and of Merioneth in 1433) and John Hampton of Staffordshire (sheriff in Merioneth from 1433) were also Household men of long standing.[32]

---

[31] Griffiths, 'The Glyndŵr Rebellion in North Wales', loc. cit. 157, n. 4; P.R.O. Min. Acc. 1216/4 m. 8; 1216/7 m. 5; B. Coward, 'The Stanley Family, *c.* 1385–*c.* 1651: A Study of the Origins, Power and Wealth of a Landowning Family' (unpublished University of Sheffield Ph.D. thesis, 1968); Breese, op. cit. 35; *Complete Peerage*, xii, part i, 419–21.

[32] *D.K.R.* xxxvii, part 2 (1876), 343, 571; Breese, op. cit. 35; J. C. Wedgwood, *History of Parliament, Biographies of Members of the Commons Houre, 1439–1509*, London, 1936, 415–17, 797–9.

This feature is graphically illustrated lower down the official scale. Whereas Henry V was reluctant to assign the near-sinecure offices to carpet-baggers, the Council began to insinuate Household servants into them. The courtly influence of William, earl of Suffolk, may have been partly responsible, for he was steward of the Household by 1433 and this pattern of patronage persisted until he retired in 1447. Of the eight non-Welshmen to become *rhingyll, amobr* collector, or woodward in north Wales during 1422–36, six were yeomen or grooms of the Household, Thomas Bateman was cofferer of Queen Katherine's household, and another was clerk of the privy seal; almost all had served either Henry IV or Henry V. Furthermore, these grants were concentrated between February 1432 and February 1435, at the beginning of Suffolk's regime as steward. In south Wales Household intrusion into the commote constableships occurred earlier, during Prince Henry's time, but it was never as extensive as in the north.

The Council was at least inhibited from granting life annuities during the minority, and in Wales it did not add to those issued by Henry V. However, it was determined to exploit Wales's income by using bills of assignment to satisfy Exchequer annuitants. Those who, accordingly, collected their annuities from the chamberlains were quite different from those to whom Henry V had granted annuities in Wales. Foremost among members of the royal family who were promised (and were largely paid) large quantities of cash in this way were Margaret, widow of Henry V's brother, Duke Thomas of Lancaster (£1,739), the Queen Dowager Katherine (£1,627), and even Henry IV's widow, Joan of Navarre (£417), who had lived under a cloud for some years after 1419; Gloucester was assigned £910, Bedford £767, and John, earl of Somerset £500. The Council was especially generous after Gloucester's victory over Beaufort in 1426, and again after the duke renewed his attack on the cardinal in 1431. Thus, from the beginning the aristocratic Council looked after its own. In the early 1430s, it also granted profitable offices to Household servants, probably at the prompting of Suffolk in the king's Household, although such men received no life annuities in Wales. After 1433 larger sums even than those assigned to the greater aristocracy were diverted from Wales to the royal Household, where the earl stood ready to supervise their expenditure. 'Where money was so acutely short, political power was used to secure preference for its disbursement . . .'; the same could be said of profitable Welsh offices—and even before Henry VI came of age.[33] Single-faction government was in the making.

Henry VI played an active part in government from the autumn of 1436, though Earl William of Suffolk continued to direct his patronage just as the duke of Bucking-

[33] G. L. Harriss, 'The Finance of the Royal Household, 1437–1460' (unpublished University of Oxford D.Phil. thesis, 1952), 2; Griffiths, 'Royal Government in the Southern Counties', op. cit. 391–6; P.R.O. Exchequer, E.R. Receipt Rolls, 703–48 *passim*. See also B. P. Wolffe, *The Royal Demesne in English History*, London, 1971, 87–8.

ham, as Lord Steward, did that of Charles I. The king's personal intervention did mean that grants hitherto made during pleasure were increasingly conferred for life; even some that pre-dated 1436 became life tenancies and a few were extended to the recipient's heir. This made the king's patronage less flexible and, as farms could not be increased or entry fines imposed, and as entrenched officers were tempted to abuse their position, the Crown was steadily impoverished.[34] Such ill-judged developments had disastrous consequences for government in Wales.

By June 1438 Suffolk had replaced Audley as justiciar of south Wales, and soon afterwards he transferred to the north, where patronage was greater and many of his Household subordinates were already installed. Duke Humphrey moved to Carmarthen as justiciar in February 1440 ostensibly to 'ease the great debates' there. This change was probably the earl's idea; it was unlikely to be Gloucester's, for at that moment he was lambasting Cardinal Beaufort and confessing by the way that he no longer had the king's confidence. The chamberlainships had already been recast. Within the space of a month, Sir Ralph Botiller was appointed to south Wales and Sir William Beauchamp, the king's carver, to the north. When the latter was replaced in 1439 by the controller of the Household, Sir Thomas Stanley, Suffolk's influence increased, and in 1443 he went so far as to associate Stanley with him as joint-justiciar of north Wales and Chester in survivorship—a unique step in fifteenth-century Wales.[35]

This change of gear after 1436 was more marked and more rapid in north Wales than in the south, and signalled a veritable Household invasion. The occasional life grant began to be issued in April 1437; with the formal reappointment of Henry's Council in November this turned into a flood. Minor offices, perquisites, and estates, as well as influential positions, were disposed of: twenty-three of the thirty-seven northern grants recorded on the patent roll between 1436 and 1461 were made during 1437–40; in the south, seventeen out of thirty-two were so recorded. Half of these forty patents were for life. Henry VI in his Household was indubitably affixing the seal—in many cases his signet—and within months of grasping his prerogative, he had given away (often for life) a third of the Welsh offices, in north Wales more than half. Most of these appointments were of Household servants: twenty-seven of the thirty-seven made in north Wales during Henry's mature years, sixteen of them during 1437–9; the comparable figure for the south is at least ten out of thirty-two appointments, eight in 1437–40. All minor officers appointed in the north were Household men, except John Fray, a baron of the Exchequer.[36]

[34] Ibid. 88, 108; P.R.O. Exchequer, T.R., Council and Privy Seal, 58; *C.P.R., 1429–36*, 188, 513; ibid., *1436–41*, 20, 50, 78, 171; *Rot. Parl.* v. 366–7.

[35] *English Historical Documents*, vol. v: *1327–1485*, ed. A. R. Myers, London, 1969, 254–6. Stanley also secured in 1443, the marcher lordships of Mold and Hawarden in fee tail: J. S. Roskell, *The Knights of the Shire for the County Palatine of Lancaster, 1377–1460* (Chetham Soc., new series, xcvi, 1937), 162–72.

[36] P.R.O. Privy Seal Office, Warrants, 1/7/372. For the increased size of the Household itself by 1445, see A. R. Myers, *The Household of Edward IV*, Manchester, 1959, 8–9; and for the disposal of the Crown lands generally, Wolffe, op. cit. 106, 108–10.

Suffolk's acquisition of the northern justiciarship is, therefore, readily explicable: it enabled him after 1440 to extend protection to his Household subordinates there, and in this he was assisted by the Lancashire knight, Sir Thomas Stanley. There was less patronage available in south Wales, where Suffolk encountered Herefordshire men, some of whom were retainers of Duke Richard of York. Moreover, since 1433 Edmund Beaufort had held the two most important castles there, and there was no need to challenge his influence. But when Gloucester died in 1447, the coping-stone was placed on this Household edifice by the nomination as his successor of Sir John Beauchamp of Powick, treasurer of England three years later and steward of the Household after that. A battery of similar appointments to the castle-constableships and shrievalties ensured that by 1450 the northern principality especially was a Household preserve—and with a distinctly Cheshire flavour. Notable were Sir Ralph Botiller, constable of Conway castle until 1461 and Suffolk's successor as steward of the Household, and John Stanley, usher of the Chamber and Sir Thomas's kinsman. John's earlier appointments as constable of Caernarvon castle and sheriff of Anglesey were extended for life in 1437, and he had other positions there besides. The escheatorships were also fair game, and one new escheator, Ralph Legh, a king's esquire from Cheshire and serjeant of the catery, was later on to exploit another office for profit.[37] Equally blatant was the intrusion of Household men into offices rarely occupied by absentee non-specialists in the past. The most unlikely individuals took charge of the king's works and artillery after 1437: grooms of the cellar and pages of the kitchen incongruously became armourers, master carpenters, and masons. Scarcely an influential or profitable office was not reserved for a Household servant at some time during Suffolk's regime as steward, and a few that had long been forgotten were revived to furnish financial reward for a favoured servant. The distinction between effective and archaic offices was gradually blurred—with fatal consequences for Anglo-Welsh relations and royal authority: '. . . yf hit were yt the kyng hade .ij. gode shirreffs a bidyng upon thair offys in Caern'schir' and Anglesey . . .', lamented one clerk![38]

Suffolk's patronage in Wales was unrivalled and the protection he could offer to fellow Household officers was powerful indeed. Yet, when Duke Humphrey castigated Cardinal Beaufort and Archbishop Kemp in 1440 for their monopoly of government, he did not link Suffolk's name with theirs. Indeed, the earl's dominance in the Council seems to have become irresistible only from 1441, when Gloucester's duchess was publicly disgraced. One can readily believe in King Henry's 'ready accessibility and uncontrolled largesse', but the installation of so many personal servants in the principality may reflect more forethought than 'inanity' on the king's

[37] Wedgwood, op. cit. 797–9; P.R.O. Exchequer, T.R. Council and Privy Seal, 72/7; 763/3; *C.F.R., 1430–7*, 314; Breese, op. cit. 35; Min. Acc. 1216/7 m. 9; *The Paston Letters*, ed. J. Gairdner (6 vols. 1904), iii. 142; *D.K.R.* xxxvii, part 2 (1876), 451; Ormerod, op. cit. i. 69; iii. 765.

[38] P.R.O. Exchequer, T.R., Council and Privy Seal, 76/19, 69/68; *D.K.R.* xxxvii, part 2 (1876), 602–3; P.R.O. Exchequer, E.R., Warrants for Issues, 58/104, 110–11; Min. Acc. 1216/7 m. 7.

part. Resumption was the only means of challenging this Household ascendancy, but most Household servants with patronage in Wales successfully petitioned for exemption in 1449–51, and the parliament of 1453 confirmed this.[39] The one instrument capable of restoring the balance between patronage and the needs of government, between those inside and those outside the Household, was seriously blunted. However salutary the effect of resumption on the Crown's finances, it did not fundamentally alter Crown patronage in Wales. Rather was the whole structure jeopardized by Suffolk's fall, for far fewer appointments of this sort were made thereafter. But when Richard of York landed in 1450 the Household servants among the officers of north Wales were still there to bar his path.

During the next ten years patronage in north and south Wales followed divergent courses, partly because Edmund Beaufort, the king's new favourite, retained his strategic power in the south, and partly because the Herefordshire remnant there was linked with the duke of York. The rivalry between these two dukes, each with a foothold in south Wales, enmeshed the patronage of the southern principality in national politics before 1455. When Beaufort was killed, York seized his offices, whereas the latter's men, Sir Walter and Hugh Scull, already occupied Cardigan castle and the stewardships of Cardigan and Carmarthen. James Ormond, once York's annuitant but by 1455 a devoted royalist, was sheriff of Cardigan and Carmarthen. This projection of national rivalries on to a provincial screen opened the way for Welshmen like Gruffydd ap Nicholas and his sons to win a prominent place in local government and society.

This solvent was absent from the north. After Suffolk's assassination, Sir Thomas Stanley lost the justiciarship and the chamberlainship, and several household men associated with north Wales were named in the Commons' attack on the Court in the winter of 1450. By July 1452, however, Stanley was back in the saddle and stayed there until 1461; having survived the acts of Resumption, Household influence in north Wales re-emerged as strong as ever. So did the Stanley family and its Cheshire connection. Several Household servants were appointed to major and minor office during Somerset's ascendancy, though instructively not one was patronized by Protector York, to whom unwise patronage and resumption were important concerns.

The Stanleys were a serious obstacle to outstanding Welshmen in north Wales acquiring political power in the way that Gruffydd ap Nicholas did in the south. Despite Sir Thomas's place at Court (and he was Henry's chamberlain during 1455–9), his estates in the north-west sustained his interest in Lancashire, Cheshire, the marches, and the principality. His Cheshire kinsman, John Stanley, buttressed his authority in the region. Few Welshmen of the calibre of William ap Gruffydd ap Gwilym (Stanley's deputy-chamberlain by 1453) were able consistently to fill the

---

[39] Wolffe, op. cit. 120, 124, 127–8, 132, n. 30; *Rot. Parl.* v. 186–99, 267–8; P.R.O. Min. Acc. 1216/8; 1217/1; *C.P.R., 1446–52*, 470; Griffiths, *Principality of Wales*, 218, 252, 539; Griffiths, 'Royal Government in the Southern Counties', op. cit. 412–17.

higher posts in the northern principality, whereas Gruffydd ap Nicholas was regularly deputy-justiciar and deputy-chamberlain of southWales in the 1440s and 1450s.[40]

Lancastrian patronage had a fundamental effect on Welsh society and government, and on relations between Wales and the Crown. In the south its subjection to national considerations made the Welsh indulgent towards a government that allowed them to benefit from the absence of Beaufort, York, and Jasper Tudor, although the mutual political hostilities of these aristocrats undermined public order. In the north (and to some extent in the south) Henry VI and Suffolk employed patronage after the fashion of Richard II to create an exclusive citadel of Household power which would incorporate Cheshire, Lancashire, and, eventually, the queen's midland estates. Sir Thomas Stanley was its focus, with benefit to himself but restricted opportunities for Welshmen. In the process, effective government was paralysed and political stability eroded, especially in Merioneth, as English and Welsh officials were inadequately supervised. Henry VI had none of the perseverance and shrewdness required to provide a remedy. The prince's Council, under Queen Margaret's guidance, exhibited signs of reasserting superior control, but it could hardly have been aware of the fundamental problem when it retained Stanley and Beauchamp of Powick as justiciars and appointed a Household magnate, Lord Dudley, as chamberlain of north Wales in 1459.[41]

In these circumstances, it is remarkable that there was no recurrence of the bloody resentment which similarly insensitive rule had helped to generate in 1400; now Welshmen had sufficient autonomy for them to tolerate a Lancastrian regime which practised little of the judicial and financial oppression of which Richard II was capable. The principality did not itself rebel during the 'Wars of the Roses', and at times Gruffydd ap Nicholas threw his weight behind Henry VI; but Edward IV had great difficulty in subduing the principality after a generation of carelessness and neglect.

[40] J. R. Jones, 'The Development of the Penrhyn Estate up to 1431' (unpublished University of Wales M.A. thesis, 1955), chs. iv, vi; P.R.O. Min. Acc. 1217/2 m. 1.
[41] Ibid. 1217/3 m. 1, 2, 4–7; Griffiths, 'Wales and the Marches', loc. cit. 154–5; *Rot. Parl.* v. 366–7.

The Chancellor, the Chancery, and the Council at the End of the Fifteenth Century

NICHOLAS PRONAY

THE first half of the fifteenth century saw the medieval Council reach the high point of its power and competence. Under the Lancastrian kings the Council was the seat of political power, administrative initiative, and also, to a very real extent, of judicial policy. It came to be composed of the greatest men of the realm according to the medieval definition of great men; its capture was the aim of the political factions amongst the higher nobility, and the dominant figures of the Lancastrian period such as the Beauforts and the De la Poles succeeded by dominating the Council. The Lancastrian Council was the ultimate development of the medieval ideal of kingly rule guided by the formalized advice of the king's natural born councillors directing his ministers. Under the Council there were the clerical officers, the 'celibate civil service', separated from the centre of decision-making by great disparities of prestige, wealth, and birth. By the end of the fifteenth century there emerged a different pattern. Under Henry VII the Council was dominated by the king's chief ministers, professional administrators who were at the head of the great departments of the state. Under them in their departments there appeared a new layer of top civil servants, highly educated, trained and much-travelled men who regarded themselves as not all that inferior to the men of birth and, as much as they, men of affairs. They saw themselves as being in line to the offices which gave the chief ministers their position, and it was indeed from their ranks that the Wolseys, Cromwells, and Burghleys of the Tudor period came. The power of the chief ministers manifested itself in the network of special courts which came into being composed of departmental heads *ex officio*, and in which they themselves could exercise the most important coercive powers of the Council. The new system was co-ordinated by the Chancellor and by the greatest of these departments, the Chancery. It was natural, therefore, that the Chancellor should have emerged at the end of the century as the king's chief minister, far more than one of the members of the Council which he had been before, and he was soon on the way to be the official *alter ego* of the king. The king himself was raised higher than before by this development: it was easier to dismiss a chief minister than to dismiss a great noble from the Council for the chief minister however powerful was the king's own creation; he could not claim to be there because of what he was, there could be no issue of law or principle.

The emergence of this successful but transitory system—for in the long run a thorough reform of the Council was required—depended on three factors. The development of an independent jurisdiction in Chancery, the rise of the legal authority of the Chancellor in conjunction with the other great officers of state over much of the Council's domain and the creation of a strong and clear basis for them in the law through Parliamentary legislation. A contributory factor which was perhaps of equal importance was the emergence of suitable personnel from the Universities. In the longer perspective, it was the fact that the growth of the new authorities came through the legislative channels of the past and grew within the old framework of the law, which was of the greatest significance. It preserved continuity with the medieval world and its ideas about a legal and moral approach to government. It also emphasized the usefulness of Parliament for making changes, even quite major changes, *within* the existing system and thus harnessing the long-term forces of custom instead of opposing them.

The feature which characterized the emergence of the Chancery in this period more than any other was that the many different judicial and administrative functions of the Chancellor remained undifferentiated in practice. It was as a result of the inter-play, even confusion, of these many different and sometimes mixed functions that Chancery grew as a court and as an administrative centre. It was not a result of special provision in equity: that came later. The growth in the number of cases which litigants wished to bring before the Chancellor was not itself the primary reason for the growth in the Chancellor's importance in Government either, for the cases multiplied in his Court as a result of the changes in the Chancellor's position *vis-à-vis* the Council. Yet the growth in his authority in the end was bound up with the evident success of his Court and the consequent building up of a highly qualified legal personnel, for it extended the scope of Chancery at a time when expansion in government was called for. Nevertheless, the growth in the number of petitions is a primary indicator of the changing position of Chancery.

There are some 789 surviving petitions between 1387, when petitions addressed to the Chancellor began to be calendared and also perhaps to be kept separately, and 1426. This represents an annual average of no more than twenty cases. Of course this is an uncertain figure which cannot be taken as more than a very rough and rudimentary indicator of the volume of cases in Chancery.[1] However, by 1432 we are on more certain ground partly because the jurisdiction of the Chancellor had settled into

---

[1] This figure does not take account of the undated petitions which were addressed simply to 'the Chancellor'. For an analysis of the cases from Kent and Essex see Margaret E. Avery, 'The History of the Equitable Jurisdiction of Chancery before 1460', *B.I.H.R.* xlii, 1969. I am puzzled by the figure given by Miss Avery for petitions before 1417 (p. 131, n. 1), which is 104 for all petitions. This appears to be the number of petitions in Bundle 3. But Bundles 4, 5, 6, and 7 *all* contain petitions addressed to Langley, Beaufort, and Arundel and some of them at least definitely belong to their tenure of the Chancellorship before 1417.

a pattern and partly because petitions were by then addressed more uniformly and were kept more carefully. For the eleven years of the Chancellorship of John Stafford as bishop of Bath and Wells, 1432–43, there are 1,502 petitions including the 259 which were addressed to his Master of the Rolls, John Frank, who kept the Great Seal during Stafford's absences. This gives us an annual average of 136 cases, which remained in fact substantially the same for the rest of the Lancastrian period. The number of petitions fell to 110 cases per annum for the very disturbed years of the Chancellorships of Richard Neville and Thomas Bourchier and rose to 126 per annum again for the tenure of William Waynflete between October 1456 and July 1460, when, with the accession of George Neville to the Woolsack, the Lancastrian epoch came to an effective end as far as Chancery was concerned.

The growth of the cases in Chancery appears to have been marked during the Lancastrian period.[2] Nevertheless, cases in the order of 130 per annum do not call for substantial changes in the organization of either Chancery or the time-table of the Chancellor himself. The chances of survival were probably worse in the case of Chancery petitions than in the case of the Rolls of the Common Law Courts,[3] but even so there can be little doubt that the volume of business in Chancery was small in comparison with the work of the Common Law Courts.

The Yorkist period, however, witnessed a remarkable further growth. During its first five years the number of cases doubled, to 243 per annum, while during the last ten years of the Yorkist epoch, 1475–85, it more than doubled again and reached 553 cases per annum. Thereafter, the numbers grew more slowly: 571 per annum during 1485–1500; 605 per annum during 1500–15. Under Wolsey the rate of growth slightly accelerated again to 770 per annum for his tenure as a whole.

It is clear that it was during the Yorkist period that Chancery changed from an administrative department with a certain amount of judicial business, to becoming one of the four central courts of the realm, though still much smaller than King's Bench or Common Pleas.[4] Neither the Lancastrian Chancellors, as Miss Avery had

[2] I accept in general the view that there has been an increase in the number of petitions all through the Lancastrian period, but I doubt whether the growth has been as marked as Miss Avery has claimed. Up to 1440 many petitions were oral. The changeover was gradual and was not completed before that date. We do not know how many oral petitions or even how many petitions contained on a brief note rather than a formal petition were dealt with during the earlier period. If there had been, however, only as few cases as Miss Avery believes then it would be difficult to account for the repeated attacks made by the Commons upon the court of Chancery during this early period. In 1415 for example they claimed that: 'Et les queux plees ne purront prendre fyn, sinoun per examination et serement des parties, solonc la fourme de ley cyvyle et leyde Seinte Esglise, en subvercion de vostre cummune ley' (*Rot. Parl.* iv. 84). I suspect we are in danger of confusing the number of written petitions with the actual volume of business conducted in Chancery. The fact is that when we reach the age of written petitions and when we can also date them reliably, there is not much growth for the remaining decades of Lancastrian rule.

[3] W. S. Holdsworth, *A History of English Law*, iv, London, 1923, 255, gives some approximate figures for the Common Law Courts for the first two terms of 1466. Common Pleas dealt with 13,452 cases; King's Bench with 1,601 cases; Exchequer with 77.

[4] Chancery outpaced Exchequer by the beginning of Henry VII's reign and was approaching the volume of King's Bench cases. Holdsworth, op. cit. iv. 256–7.

argued, nor Wolsey as Pollard believed, can be regarded as the fathers of the great 'Tudor' court of Chancery. During the Lancastrian period a Chancellor of average industry, supported by Common Law colleagues and assisted by his Master of the Rolls with the paperwork, could easily handle the numbers of cases involved while also discharging his other duties. By the time John Morton took over from the Yorkist Chancellors this would not have been possible even if he had not been Henry's most trusted and widely employed chief minister as he was in fact. Chancery had to change its personnel and routine to accommodate the needs of over 500 cases each year; each case was entirely paper-bound and could involve by this time ten documents or more, often lengthy and complex,[5] and also preliminary examinations. The Chancellor might well have remained ultimately responsible in person for judgements made in his courts but he simply had to have regular legal personnel to deal with them all.

Until the end of the Lancastrian period Chancery operated in matters of personnel like other medieval administrative departments, such as the Privy Seal. Clerks entered early in their life and rose slowly through the years in order of seniority which was sometimes accelerated by exceptional ability, patronage, or luck. On the whole the Chancery Clerks who reached the top of their profession, the Masters and the principal clerks of the Hanaper and the Rolls, were of the competent but undistinguished clerical officer pattern which this system had encouraged. In 1454, for example, eleven of the twelve Masters[6] were still men of this kind. Only one of them possessed more than a first degree, John Chamberlain who was a *Magister in Artibus*. Seven of them do not appear to have been at University at all, not even to the Oxford 'business-school' which Master Richard Fryston appears to have attended. Their average length of service by then exceeded 25 years from the first writ discovered under their name or the first time they were called Clerk of the Chancery on the Rolls, which in most cases must have been several years after they actually commenced their career in Chancery. Most Masters had had very long careers in fact, though few could equal Master Nicholas Wymbysh[7] who entered Chancery in the latter years of Richard II and was just about to retire to St. Leonard's hospital at York in 1454. None of the eleven Masters had legal training.

Their chief, the Master of the Rolls, was a man of the same stamp; Thomas Kirkby. He does not appear to have had a University education. He was already in Chancery as a clerk of the second grade by 3 November 1429, became a Master by 1 December 1437, Clerk of Parliament during the 1440s, Secondary to the Master of the Rolls, 29 March 1447, and Master of the Rolls from 26 January

---

[5] Many of the supporting documents are missing; even so there are still for example 295 documents for eighty-nine cases in Bundle 52. P.R.O., C1/52.

[6] They were: John Bate, John Cammel, John Chamberlain, M.A., John Fawkes, Richard Fryston, William Hill, William Morland, William Normanton, John Pemberton, Thomas Westhorpe, Richard Wetton, D.C.L., Nicholas Wymbysh. For Wetton, the first of the new personnel, see below.

[7] For a petition by Wymbysh himself referring to his fifty-four years of serving the king in Chancery, see *C.P.R., 1446–52*, 208.

1448.[8] He was, of course, a man of several rich benefices and some property, but he was, and remained, no more than a clerical officer. Both he and his Masters differed little if at all from their predecessors in the reign of Edward III.

Forty years after the appointment of 'Kirkby del Rolls', however, we find that a dramatic change had taken place. In 1487 the Master of the Rolls was David Williams, B.Cn.L., B.C.L., Doctor of Canon Law, former Keeper of the Prerogative Court of Canterbury and his secondary in the office of the Rolls was Master William Elyot, B.C.L. The list of the Masters tells its own story: Thomas Barowe, B.C.L., Lic. Cn.L.; Robert Blackwall (education unknown); William Bolton, '*Baccalareus legum*';[9] John Brown, B.Cn.L., Lic.C.L.; William Kelet (education unknown); James John described as 'Doctor' but not known of what; Edmund Martyn, B.C.L., Doctor of both Laws; John Morgan, Doctor of both Laws; William Morland[10] (education unknown); Richard Skypton, not a lawyer, Oxford business school; and William Smyth, Doctor of Civil Law. Thus at the beginning of the reign of Henry VII, Chancery was led by a very eminent civilian as the Master of the Rolls, at least seven and probably nine of the twelve Masters were trained lawyers, with no less than four being a Doctor or Licentiate of Law. Of course the department of the Protonotary, who was concerned with treaties with foreign powers, and which had been a preserve of civilians for some time, remained so; at this time it was in the hands of Dr. Henry Sharp.

The change from a clerical to a legal personnel had been gradual. It began in fact in the year when Kirkby took over the Rolls. In 1448, Richard Wetton, D.C.L., became the first Master in Chancery not to have risen through the ranks, probably through the exercise of the King's right of nominating one of the twelve Masters. Wetton remained the only lawyer in Chancery—apart from the Protonotary— until his death in 1465. It appears that the appointment to the Mastership of lawyers brought in directly from the Universities rather than from clerks of the second grade did not become a policy until the 1470s and it appears to coincide with the appointment of the first Doctor of Civil Law to the Mastership of Rolls itself, John Morton in 1472.

We do not know to whom this radical departure from the departmental custom of the previous century was due. It is, however, quite possible that the succession of notable civil lawyers to the Chancellorship at this time had something to do with it. In 1467 Robert Stillington, Doctor of Civil Law and reputedly one of the most famous civilians of his day, succeeded George Neville and then Lawrence Booth, Doctor of Civil Law and another well-known civilian, followed him. In any case,

---

[8] 3 Nov. 1429 is the date of the earliest writ found under his name, P.R.O., C. 93/4: see also *C.P.R.*, *1436–41*, 204, and *1446–51*, 32, 108.

[9] This is how he described himself in his will, *P.C.C.* 11, Moone.

[10] Morland is likely to have been a lawyer; he appears in a great number of cases involving churchmen and Canon Law as an arbitrator. He was also at this time the doyen of the Masters. He began his career in the 1440s and it is possible that, like Archbishop Rotherham, he taught himself while working in Chancery. For Rotherham, see below, p. 92.

after 1472, as each of the older generation of Masters departed one by one, they were replaced by young civil lawyers from the Universities, almost without exception, until, as we have seen, most of the Masters were civilian lawyers.

An illuminating sidelight on the transition is shed by the will of Thomas Rotherham, Chancellor from 1474 to 1483, He was a theologian by training, in fact a D.Th., who might well have been expected to look down on the technicalities of the Civil Law and administer 'equity' without recourse to more than the doctrines of Christian Church, as in fact the 'Ecclesiastical Chancellors' have been thought to do. At his death, however, he bequeathed a splendid set of Civil Law codices to his old college at Oxford, containing the standard works of the practising civilians of the period.[11] Rotherham was replaced as Chancellor in 1483 by Dr. Russell, a very learned lawyer himself, and with Henry VII came Dr. Morton, one of the first Principals of the Great Civil Law School at Oxford. Thus the people who shaped the work of the Court of Chancery during the crucial period when it settled into its stride were men who spent all the years of their University training in the study of Civil Law. Whatever they actually dispensed in the Court of Chancery was likely to have been a great deal more precise and juristic than 'common sense and common fairness'.

When we turn to the question of the types of cases which Chancery dealt with during this period we are faced with considerable problems. No final answer is possible until all the *c.* 15,000 cases from 1460 to 1500 have been analysed. Until such time we can, however, derive some fairly reliable data by analysing the contents of selected bundles. Sampling by localities leaves one of the most significant aspects of Chancery entirely obscured—that its jurisdiction had a special relevance to commercial towns. Bundle 59 appears to be typical of the business of Chancery during the Chancellorship of Rotherham, 1474–83, with the majority of the cases which it was possible to date coming from between 1480 and 1483. There are 210 cases listed in the Bundle: 202 separate cases in fact. Of these 202, 11 arose from detention of documents; 13 concern or derive directly from a Use; 13 allege riot, intimidation, or some other form of perverting the course of justice by main force; 14 allege perversion of justice through non-violent means, perjury, chicane, or vexatious litigation; 30 derive from one or other of the parties being an alien or the transaction itself having taken place abroad, including Calais; 22 concern wardship, marriage or testamentary dispositions, of which 11 cases might in fact involve an equitable trust; 10 request the enforcement of awards made by an arbitrator; 38 concern merchant-debts; 55 concern equitable debt/detinue, including allegations that the petitioner had failed on a technicality at Common Law. These specifically equitable cases are particularly difficult to identify, for there are only 17 petitions which either claimed failure at the Common Law on a technicality, or sought an essentially equitable remedy in the sense that their case was grounded on natural justice rather than the allegation of some point of law. An example of the former kind is the petition for a debt in the

[11] A. B. Emden, 'Thomas Rotherham alias Scot', *A Biographical Register of the University of Oxford to 1509*, Oxford, 1961.

case of a debtor who had become a monk (P.R.O., C1/59/64), and for the second type there is a petition from Richard Kelsey, sometime chaplain to George Neville, the disgraced and by this time dead archbishop of York, who was a surety for a debt incurred by his master from the bishop of Lincoln, and who sought to be released from the obligation. He had, of course, no ground at all but he hoped the court would understand the predicament of a young chaplain, etc. (P.R.O., C1/59/104).

There are naturally great difficulties in classifying sensibly the cases of a court which did not operate a formulary system like that of the Common Law. How does one classify the plea from Prioress Elizabeth Croft (P.R.O., C1/59/97)? She alleged that John Kirkby Esquire charged excessive rents to the Nunnery in breach of an agreement made between them—apparently without specialty—and had forcibly taken away all their deeds, and refused to return them because he asserted that he had actually founded the Nunnery, as far as I can ascertain, without a licence in the first place. Such cases might justifiably be classified under several headings or none at all. The reader might like to know that I classified this case under Detention of Deeds because the first thing the Court had to do was to make Squire Kirkby disgorge the deeds for examination. All cases in which detention of deeds was the prime obstacle were 'equitable' in the sense that they had to be dealt with outside the Common Law since it was not capable of effectively securing the production of documents. We might, however, be wise to distinguish such procedural equity cases based on the power of the Chancellor to make a defendant actually do something without which the court could not have a clear idea of the case before it, from those types of cases where the Chancellor might be applying different notions of law and justice.

One of the more interesting aspects of the work of Chancery at this period was the relatively small proportion of cases directly concerning feoffment to use. Here again there are problems of classification since some of the testamentary cases really concerned the creation of a use by will. Clear instances of that have in fact been classified under Uses and there are perhaps another eleven behind which lurks a Use. Nevertheless, they still form a relatively small proportion of the whole. This contrasts with the findings of Miss Avery and needs to be explained.

All through the fifteenth century a very substantial part of the cases in Chancery came from the towns. The ten 'staple-towns' in Bundle 59 account for two-thirds of all cases. Miss Avery on the other hand studied the Lancastrian Chancery through the cases which came from the counties of Kent and Essex and there is good reason to believe that the predominance of Uses in her analysis is primarily due to the method of selection. For example, Kent and Essex provided 25 of the cases in Bundle 6 (Henry Beaufort) which were analysed by Miss Avery. The *total* number of cases in Bundle 6 is 333 of which, however, the towns account for over half the cases. In our own Bundle 59, Kent produced 14 cases and Essex 6 cases, while London alone accounts for 52 cases, a quarter of the whole Bundle. But 5 out of the 6 Essex cases are about Uses and the majority of the cases from Kent concern either a Use or gavelkind. (The creation of a Use was an easy and common way of extending Kentish notions of partible inheritance to possessions acquired outside Kent (e.g. P.R.O., C1/59/16).) If we classify all these 'Kentish' cases as a Use—which is perhaps legitimate—then we find that Uses predominated amongst Kentish petitions too. In fact Uses and the often related testamentary, wardship and marriage matters vied with perversion of justice as the main *rural* reasons for applying to Chancery. The great bulk of Chancery petitions, however, came from towns and were mercantile in nature. Also from the towns came many of the large category of petitions concerning aliens and in the main involved also mercantile law. Moreover, 24 of the 55 of the equitable debt/detinue cases in Bundle 59 themselves came from trading towns and were often very close to mercantile debts. A substantial portion of cases of the perversion of justice by non-violent means alleged malpractices by town officials or courts, such as P.R.O. C1/59/39 in which the Piepowder Court of Southampton was subpoenaed to appear on a charge of corrupt verdict in a debt case. So was the winner of the verdict, also a merchant.

Thus while it is true that a substantial and growing proportion of cases from landowning classes asked the Chancellor's Court to protect the various arrangements of equitable use made by them, these cases were still a small proportion of the whole and cannot be regarded as the real foundations of the growth of the Chancellor's jurisdiction. The Year Books themselves are perhaps misleading in this respect. Uses very often involved the Common Law as well and hence there were frequent consultations concerning Uses between the Chancellor and the judges. These take up a disproportionate share of the Year Book reportage, for that reason.

It was the mercantile community, whether of aliens or natives, which provided at least one of the main pillars upon which the Chancellor's court was built during the Yorkist period. These cases provided in the first instance the financial incentive for Chancery to adapt its personnel and organization to dealing with a large volume of business. Whatever benefits the Chancellor and the king might have derived in this world or the next from providing a court for those who were either too poor to sue at Common Law or too weak to face an opponent in its arena, that was not revenue and in the last resort not all that much political capital. If there was not a great deal of money for the King in rendering judicial services to the weak and the poor there was not much financial incentive for Chancery officials either. The mercantile cases were, however, a different proposition. They could provide the money which paid for the time the Masters spent on examinations and for the services of the clerks of the second grade who travelled around taking depositions and who checked accounts. In general these cases paid for the evolution of that highly paper-bound system which enabled the Chancellor to get through, even if in name only, all the cases which came into Chancery, and eventually could make a post in Chancery attractive enough for the highly educated civil lawyers needed to run it. *Justitia est magnum emolumentum*— where there are no profits we seldom find much development. Chancery is only another illustration of this old medieval truth.

We can only touch upon the way in which it became worth the while of Chancery personnel themselves to foster the development of the Court of Chancery, which was, apart from legislation, the real key to its growth. What happened in brief was that Chancery clerks living in the midst of the increasingly international mercantile community of the City came to exploit their official position and privileges to offer a congenial and sympathetic tribunal for mercantile disputes. Access to the dorse of the Close Rolls has been a customary perquisite of Chancery clerks—it came to be used to provide a convenient register of mercantile agreements, which offered the further attraction of security, because agreements so entered could be enforced by the court of Chancery. It was a very much more businesslike form of registering agreements than the Common Law offered and did not suffer from the territorial limitations of the mayoral rolls of towns, such as London. By using the two in conjunction, however, a further profitable though ultimately illegal, refinement was possible—interest-bearing arrangements in the nature of mortgages could be made for the purpose of raising capital, which skated over the laws of usury.[12]

Developing from bonds such double recognizances in which a merchant pledged his goods and chattels without actual possessions on the one Roll and a sum of money on the other circumvented the law of the land and the Church alike since it also avoided death duties extracted by the Church courts. This system of double recognizances offered a more flexible yet stronger security for mercantile capital—provided the precautions were taken to 'bring in' a Chancery Master and if a sufficiently large sum was involved, someone at the Court too. The extent to which a Chancery clerk could become involved was truly remarkable, even before this business had really become a going concern. William Hill,[13] one of the Masters in 1454 who had a relatively short career of 27 years and in fact died at the end of 1454, appears in no less than 170 such deals recorded on the Close Roll. The list of his 'partners' by occupation tells its own tale: Armourers, Broderers, Butchers, Brewers, Cordwainers, Drapers, Fishmongers, Fruiterers, Glovers, Goldsmiths, a 'Hurer', Hostelers, Hackneymen, Haberdashers, Ironmongers, Jewellers, Mercers, Taylors, and one Vintner. Master John Bate who served in Chancery from 1429 to 1467 when he retired voluntarily to Tamworth and who was not quite as keen on business as Master Hill, was nevertheless in the happy position to be owed £475 by two of his partners in a single though complicated deal.[14] This was no mean sum considering that the Chancellor himself received only £500 per annum for the maintenance of himself *and* the whole chancery.

While the clerks of Chancery had thus every incentive to help alleviating the limitations placed upon mercantile finance by the laws of usury and the Common Law, Chancery itself received the fees from the enrolments and exemplifications which went with it. Although it was the privilege of Chancery clerks to have access

[12] For the London half of these double-recognizances, see P. E. Jones, *Calendar of Plea and Memoranda Rolls . . . at the Guildhall*, Cambridge, 1954, vol. 5, xxiii–xxvi.

[13] Hill had close connections with the Mercers' Company, but he is not to be confused with a Mercer of the same name. Our Wm. Hill, came 'from a noble race' and from Lincoln Diocese. *Cal. Papal Letters*, vol. 8, 656.

[14] *C.C.R., 1475–85*, nos. 430 and 433. His partners were merchants of the staples of London and Hull.

to the dorse of the Close Rolls and to bring cases in which they were parties themselves into the Court of Chancery, the appropriate fees were rigorously extracted by the Hanaper, the fee-collecting department of Chancery. One of the reasons in fact why the Hanaper remained in a relatively prosperous state even during the latter years of Lancastrian rule was the mounting income from such fees.[15] The Chancellors of the Yorkist epoch were themselves involved in the financial pickings as much as their officials and so were Edward's favourites, such as Lord Hastings. The king himself soon became aware of this lucrative development in Chancery and, troubling himself as always more with the financial benefits available than with ethical aspects, annexed the Hanaper to his Chamber,[16] the first king to do so, and thus condoned and encouraged this already flourishing business.

The Yorkist Chancery thus undoubtedly had the financial and the personal incentive for developing its jurisdiction in commercial law and for moving closer to the combined worlds of the mercantile and the civil laws to oblige its mercantile and alien clientele. Yet it would be a mistake to assume that these personal and financial interests would have been sufficient to ensure the development of a new court, especially one which dispensed different procedures and principles from the Common Law unless there was a strong basis in legislation to build upon. In fact the power of the Chancellor to offer remedy in cases of mercantile transactions derived from two sources, both strongly grounded in Statute law: his appellate and supervisory jurisdiction over Staple towns and from his position as protector of 'strangers of the king's amity'. Since most of the aliens were merchants and most of the business they conducted was in Staple towns, these two powers most effectively and usefully overlapped. The legislation which gradually transferred from the Council to the Chancellor the appellate jurisdiction over Staples and aliens is a subject on its own which we cannot, alas, enter here. The most important aspects of this legislation (which began with the Staple Acts of 1353 and 1362 and was effectively completed by the Act of 1453) from our point of view here were twofold. Firstly, the legislation concerning the Staple towns gave explicit statutory authority to the Chancellor to depart from the course of the Common Law and to use the Merchant process instead. Secondly, the legislation making him the guardian of aliens gave him authority by statute to exercise both criminal and civil jurisdiction, to punish as well as give damages and to select at his own discretion whether to use the conciliar process of Subpoena or the Common Law process of Capias to compel attendance—this was a power as we shall see, which was explicitly denied to the Council itself. It was also a feature of this legislation that it linked protection of aliens with riot and similar offences against the machinery of law enforcement and in its final form empowered the Chancellor to form a tribunal made up of himself and two judges of his choice for exercising both

[15] Nicholas Pronay, 'The Hanaper Under the Lancastrian Kings', *Proc. Leeds Phil. and Lit. Soc.*, 1967, 83.

[16] There were several stages in channelling the income into his own coffers, but the crucial step was the appointment of Thomas Vaughan the Treasurer of the Chamber to become the Controller and Surveyor of the Hanaper. *C.P.R.*, 1467–7, 125. For earlier experiments, see: ibid., 1461–7, 82, 85, 137.

conciliar and Common Law powers indiscriminately. It was the development of such tribunals around the Chancellor, and also other officers of state, which grew up in the fifteenth century in order to deal with the crippling tendency to pervert the machinery of justice, that illustrated best the changing positions of the Chancellor and the Council for it carried the growing recognition that the Council was not capable of dealing with this problem or at any rate was not the best suited to deal with all its manifestations.

The first Act specifically connecting the Chancellor to one of these manifestations (13 Henry IV, c. 7) was in the case of riot, in 1411.[17] Riot was to be punished according to the discretion of the king and the Council, but if there was traverse of the indictment before the Sheriff or the Justices then the traverse was to be determined in King's Bench. If the accused failed to appear for that hearing, then he had three weeks to present himself before either the Council, or King's Bench or in Chancery in time of vacation. This Act restated the *status quo* at the end of the fourteenth century, which was that Chancery had no other function in such matters determinable by the Council except as a sort of *poste restante* in times of vacation. In other words, here the Chancellor acted merely as a temporary delegate of both the Council and the Courts, for limited procedural purpose.

Three years later there is, however, a marked change. It was then enacted that if the Sheriffs, Under Sheriffs, and Justices of the Peace had failed to take vigorous action against riots, maintenance, and cognate offences against the machinery of the law, a special commission shall go out made up by 'sufficient and indifferent persons at the nomination of the Chancellor for the time being and that the said Commissioners shall return presently to the Chancery' their inquests. Moreover, if the Chancellor should receive information of such a riot, etc., he should cause writs to be sent out to ensure that the J.P.s do in fact take action.[18]

It is clear that the rationale of this Act is that he is made responsible for seeing that the Justices of Peace do their duty. This is in fact a logical extension of his administrative responsibility for the appointment of the Justices of the Peace. He had long been involved in the selection of Sheriffs[19] and Escheators, and similar responsibilities devolved upon him concerning the Justices of the Peace, who were gradually replacing the Sheriffs as the chief local law-enforcing agency. When the Commons petitioned in 1399 that J.P.s were not of sufficient standing and therefore encouraged maintenance of quarrels, brocage, etc., they were told by the king that he would charge the Chancellor to see that J.P.s were of sufficient standing.[20] In 1414 it was enacted that J.P.s shall be made by advice of the Chancellor *and* the Council.[21]

[17] *Statutes of the Realm*, vol. 2, 109. References in the text to the Statutes are given in the standard form of king's regnal year and name, followed by the number of the clause.

[18] 2 Henry V, c. 8, ibid. 184.

[19] For the authority of the Chancellor concerning Sheriffs and Escheators, as well as some other officers and the relationship with other departmental heads such as the Treasurer during the reign of Edward III, see B. Wilkinson, *The Chancery Under Edward III*, Manchester, 1929, 31–40.

[20] *Rot. Parl.* iii. 444, echoing somewhat 35 Edward III.

[21] 2 Henry V, Stat. 2, c. 1, *Statutes of the Realm*, vol. 2, 187.

The position of the Chancellor in respect of the Justices of the Peace was finally clarified in 1439 (18 Henry VI, c. 6) when it was enacted that they should have at least £20 per annum, be of good fame, and be learned in the law, but the Chancellor shall have power to 'put other discreet persons learned in the law on such commissions' if there are not sufficient persons possessing such incomes available.

It was out of his responsibility to ensure the effective operation of the law by the J.P.s and Sheriffs that his authority grew in respect of riot and other violent perversions of the machinery of order. In 1429 (8 Henry VI, c. 14) it was enacted, following upon the experiments begun by Henry V, that if persons suspected of riots, unlawful assembly, insurrection, and the like offences could not be indicted because they fled from their counties 'in order to avoid the Execution of the Common Law' the J.P.s were to lay information to the Chancellor who at his discretion could then proceed against them by Capias and Proclamation. In 1452 in the case of intimidation of women by abduction or violence (31 Henry VI, c. 2) it was enacted that the Chancellor upon information may issue Proclamation to bring the suspects before him, or before a special commission appointed by him to try them locally. This Act conferred on him the power to delegate his authority which was a further step in his progress towards his eventual wide and independent authority. In both of these kinds of cases he was authorized to do what the Common Law could not do and what only Council could do in the past: to proceed at once with both civil and criminal powers, and also to order restitution as well as costs and damages.

The stage which had been reached in the development towards the independent position of the Chancellor by the end of the Lancastrian period is strikingly illustrated by the Act of 1452 (31 Henry VI, c. 2). The Act rehearsed, rather desperately, that many persons who had been summoned by the Council by writ or Privy Seal letter to appear before it have disobeyed these commands. The purpose of the Act was to remedy this abuse and it enacted that from henceforth the Chancellor shall have power to deal with those flouting the Council: he had the power which the Council did not have, to issue Capias and Proclamation and he was empowered by this Act to pursue those who disobeyed the Council with these powerful writs. The point was, of course, that Capias and Proclamation might lead to the loss of freehold or even life and the Council had lost the power to touch freehold or life by its own processes in the reign of Edward III.

By the end of the Lancastrian period thus there had been a substantial legislative development which provided the basis for Henry VII. With his characteristic ability to discern the emerging principles within this piecemeal legislation he proceeded to systematize and complete the new structure.

In the case of the Chancellor's supervisory powers over J.P.s there was, despite the many several powers and extensive legislation no over-all legislative authority for appeal to the Chancellor, or any clearly defined hierarchy of appeal. The Justices of the Peace Act of 1487 established that all complaints on account of any failure by any J.P. to do justice would lie in the first instance to another J.P. then to a Judge of

Assize and then if there was still no satisfaction 'to the King's Highnesse or his Chancellor for the time being'.[22]

In the case of perversion of the course of justice the Chancellor's cognizance had in fact been extended over most of the judicial and administrative aspects of that many faceted evil by the Lancastrian legislators, as we have seen, through several differently constituted courts, including Chancery itself. Yet there was still an unresolved overlap with Common Law and in many instances such as conspiracy, maintenance, and riot there was also a confusion between the specialized Common Law meaning of these terms and the wider sense in which these terms were used in the legislation which authorized various special courts around the Chancellor to deal with them. It was vital to bring together these essentially cognate and in practice often linked offences on the basis of their common rationale and equally to rationalize the various jurisdictions over them. This was precisely, and no more, what the celebrated Act of 3 Henry VII, c. 1 (erroneously but popularly known as the Star Chamber Act) had accomplished. It pulled together the legislation of the previous century, identifying as cognate offences maintenance, livery, indentures, retaining, embracery, the impanelling of corrupt juries, the false returning of verdicts, and riot and unlawful assembly for overawing courts. It also brought together the various special courts already established and clarified as well as centralized their processes. Information was to be laid to the Chancellor who, by this and previous acts had become the official recipient of all such information. The Court was now constituted of the Chancellor, Privy Seal, and Treasurer, or two of them, together with one judge each from the two Benches and one lay and clerical councillor. This well-thought-out Act omitted one particular form of perverting the course of both justice and administration: perjury by the parties themselves or by the panels of the inquests.

In 1495 (11 Henry VII, c. 25) it was enacted that complaints of perjury were to be presented to the justices who tried the case; they were bound to receive them and to transmit them at once to the Chancellor. He was authorized to summon the suspects before himself, the Treasurer, the Chief Justices, and the Master of the Rolls. The reason for this composition was that the Act extended also to perjury before the Council and in the Court of Chancery, creating for the first time a recognized machinery of appeal for these courts, in the case where it was really needed and should have been provided before. For what the makers of the Act faced here intelligently was the unpalatable fact that the inquisitorial procedure employed to combat corruption in the Common Law process was particularly susceptible to perjury. Hence the presence of the Master of the Rolls who was responsible for the conducting of the examinations and was, probably, the most experienced inquisitor in the service of the king.

These Acts and others of the reign of Henry VII rationalized and consolidated the century-long process whereby the Chancellor and the great officers of state acquired a new position in the constitution. Yet there is one initially mysterious aspect to this legislation: with the exception of the power to issue Capias, none of the

---

[22] 4 Henry VII, c. 12, *Statutes of the Realm*, vol. 2, 537.

quasi-judicial, quasi-executive powers conferred upon the Chancellor either singly or in association with the Treasurer, Privy Seal, or the judges were powers not already exercised by the Council, of which they had been and remained the leading members. Since there were no reasons why the Council should not have informally delegated the trial of any matter to any of its members or a group of them, what was the point of all this legislation? It is also well known that quite often petitions addressed to the Chancellor were in fact dealt with by the Council and that the Council continued to deal with matters which might have been dealt with by the special courts around the Chancellor.[23]

An early clue may be given by a Commons petition of 1402 in which it was prayed that relief may be given to Commissioners who had not in fact received the Commissions sent to them and who were being distrained by the Exchequer for their failure to discharge their Commissions. The Commons requested that the said Commissioners should be allowed to appeal to the Chancellor against the distraint. The king agreed to the substance of the petition and added: 'et ait mesme: le Chancellor en autres cases poair *per auctoritate du Parliament*, appellez a luy tieux justices come luy plerra s'il embosoignera de purroir de remede de temps en temps solonc leur discretion' (my italics).[24]

The same point is brought out by another common petition 20 years later, in 1421. The Commons asked that the 'Exception that remedy is available at Common Law' should dismiss all cases tried in Chancery 'except those which are there by authority of Parliament'.[25]

We need not read political implications into the phrase 'by authority of Parliament' for it is simply the standard form meaning by authority of Statute, of legislation. The point which it illustrates is that the purpose of the legislation was to give authority to the Chancellor by the only means whereby his acts might have the force of law to act independently alongside and instead of the Council, without of course pre-empting the Council's right to act also. The Council was and remained undifferentiated, and it did not acquire 'committees' by legislation; instead, however, there were established courts, properly within the law as it was understood at the time, which by authority of Statute exercised a more flexible and effective procedure than either the old Common Law Courts or the Council were able to operate.

The legislation also defined the vague but for a long time perceptibly twofold position of the great officers of the state. As trusted servants of the king they were naturally 'of his council' whose influence depended on their ability to persuade the king. But they were also, which other councillors were not, at the head of the great departments of state to which belonged much judicial and administrative authority progressively built up by legislation and prescription. Their position had in fact

---

[23] See I. S. Leadam and J. F. Baldwin, *Select Cases Before the King's Council, 1243–1482*, Selden Society, xxxv, 1918, pp. xxxii–xxxv.

[24] *Rot. Parl.* iii. 498, and 4. Henry IV, c. 9 which enacted a compromise between the Commons and the king, containing this provision but not allowing the J.P.s to handle some of the depositions.

[25] *Rot. Parl.* iv. 156.

changed and there was need to redefine their identity *vis-à-vis* the council and it was this which Henry's legislation provided.

This stage had been reached, in fact, by the reign of Edward IV. Perceptive observers such as Fortescue—who was of course involved in much of the legislation which had brought it along—already recognized the new position of the Chancellor. In the make-belief world of 'government in exile' where one could more or less pick the post one wished to have, Fortescue chose to be the Chancellor. It was also as Chancellor that he spoke in the *De Laudibus Legum Angliae*. But it remained for the orderly mind of Henry VII—aided perhaps by the advice of John Morton who spent many years in exile as the only intellectual companion of Fortescue—to perceive the logic of this development: the men in charge of the great departments had to be identified primarily with their departments. Edward IV had continued with the earlier medieval practice of moving his councillors around. Lawrence Booth, Alcock, Russell, Rotherham, and Morton moved in and out of the Keeperships of the Rolls, the Privy Seal, and the Great Seal; their real position in government remained as one of his Councillors whether in or out of such offices. Henry VII, in contrast, identified his officers with their office. Courtney held the Privy Seal until his premature death in 1487, thereafter, Richard Fox held it for the whole reign of Henry VII and for many years after it. John Morton was Chancellor from his return in February 1486 until his death in 1500. When he died Fox was not moved into the Chancellorship, although he held the king's favour as much as ever. The Privy Seal was treated as an office in its own right and not as a stepping-stone to the Chancery. Morton was succeeded by two men who died within two years (and not even then was Fox appointed) and then Warham, Master of the Rolls, received the office and held it until 1515 when Wolsey came. While there had been nine treasurers during the twenty-two years of the reign of Edward IV (though he began to improve his system himself after 1471) there were two between 1485 and 1522.[26] Continuity in the great offices also helped to impart a sense of permanence and continuity—for the majority of the king's lesser subjects and also for many of the more important subjects such as J.P.s, the government appeared in the persons and in the names of the great office-holders. Even in Parliament, it was the Chancellor whom M.P.s heard explaining the policies of the government. Continuity was a stabilizing and normalizing influence, badly needed at the time, and it helped to foster, perhaps even re-create the illusion that it was not merely the frail and changeable victor of Bosworth, but the impersonal, undying forces of the law and the state with which men had to deal.

The Chancellor had appeared already as 'the kyng's chief judge of his ream' to a petitioner of the Parliament of 1472.[27] He was called 'prime minister' by foreign

[26] Bourchier, Tiptoft, Grey, Mountjoy, Rivers, John Langstrother, Bp. Grey, Tiptoft, Bourchier (the last three for a second term of office): John Dynham, 1485–1501, Thomas Howard, 1501–22.

[27] *Rot. Parl.* vi. 103. The petition gives a vivid account of Chancery proceedings and the kind of mixed case with which it dealt.

ambassadors in the reign of Henry VII who observed that he alone shared the king's table at ceremonial functions. It was not long before Wolsey practically substituted himself for the Council and demonstrated that the development had gone too far and new definitions were required for both the office of the Chancellor and the Council.

The changing pattern of administration wrought a quiet revolution in personnel. The Chancery was staffed by men trained in the civil law. Civil lawyers filled the prerogative courts, the privy seal, and the royal secretariat, they stood by the king at his arrival and were strong on the Council. Henry might well have found them congenial, reminiscent as they were of the government he witnessed in Brittany and France where the lawyers of the Capetian kings have long had great influence. To what extent they actually applied specific civilian doctrines in Chancery, Star Chamber, Admiralty, and Requests we do not know and perhaps it is a hopeless quest. It would be difficult to believe, however, that a University training as long as theirs could have left no lasting mark. Even if it went no further than 'the application of the current ideas of the canonists of the fifteenth century regarding the moral government of the Universe to the administration of the law of the state',[28] as Holdsworth believed, that could lead far. The current ideas of the civilians of the fifteenth century were moving quickly towards the notion of the reason of state, and increasing impatience with the law of nations. Perhaps more important in the short run was the fact that all these men around Henry shared with him the double-edged quality of not being insular. If they were not educated abroad, as his secretary Dr. Kyng, or as his Privy Seal Richard Fox were, they had all travelled a great deal. His Chancellor John Morton had spent nine years in the France of Louis XI, apart from embassies. They could, like Henry himself, look at the events of the past twenty-five years with a detached and comparative eye—and their training led them to think in terms of political laws of universal application. We have a glimpse of the mind of one of these men; a Doctor of Law, a Chancery man, an ambassador and councillor of Edward IV who wrote the Second Continuation of the Crowland Chronicle. The most astounding quality of this Canon lawyer is that he has a more secular approach to politics than his lay compatriots who appear still imbued with the medieval Christian-ethical outlook, shown in the Tree of Commonwealth. He is sarcastic about the ordinary folk who hope to see the hand of God in political turns of events; he applauds Edward IV as 'this prudent Prince who acted more upon the needs of the moment than upon irrational custom' when he ignored the Peace of God on the holiest day of the Christian calendar, Easter; he managed to write what was supposed to be a monastic chronicle without mentioning the death or consecration of a single bishop. But he could perceive of the Yorkist age as a historical period after which there were new political realities calling for new policies. His recipe was for a cold, calculating government which distrusts its people and rules by eternal suspicion and vigilance. If the thinking of this man was as typical of his fellow civilians who surrounded the

[28] Holdsworth, op. cit. v. 216.

new king and who filled the most important offices under him as what we know of his qualifications and career, then we may be nearer to penetrating Henry's reign. It may well be the key to understanding the transformation from the merry but unstable England ruled by Edward to the tame, sullen, and tense land inherited by Henry VIII.

Prophecy, Poetry, and Politics in Medieval and Tudor Wales

GLANMOR WILLIAMS

AT some point which cannot be more precisely dated than the second half of the fifteenth century the last of the great poets of Wales to commit himself almost exclusively to the composition of prophetic verse, Dafydd Llwyd o Fathafarn (*fl. c.* 1447–90), addressed himself to an imaginary conversation with a seagull. In this and many other poems he identified himself unhesitatingly with what he believed to be an unbroken continuity of close on one thousand years of prophetic poetry. He traced the origins of his own muse back through medieval poets all the way to the sixth-century fountainhead of Welsh prophetic verse, to 'Taliesin ddewin ddoeth' ('Taliesin, wise soothsayer') and 'Myrddin burddysg mawrddoeth' ('Myrddin of pure learning and great wisdom').[1] Looking at the whole corpus of Dafydd Llwyd's verse we can readily discern that he was the heir to a good many other prophetic materials besides the indigenous Welsh ones. He could draw on the whole miscellaneous mass of medieval prophetic motifs: those of the Christian religion, the Sibylline oracles, Joachim of Fiore, Geoffrey of Monmouth, miscellaneous divinations widely current in England and Scotland, and the murky and esoteric science of astrology.[2] Yet he was justified in his conviction that the hard core of it, to which all the rest could be expendable accretions, was the native tradition which he had inherited from the countless generations of his poet-predecessors. Admittedly, none of the Welsh prophetic poems which have come down to us can be traced back further than the ninth or tenth centuries, even though they may be spuriously fathered on the sixth-century poets, Taliesin or Myrddin. Yet there is no reason to suppose that those founding-fathers of Welsh literature were not prophets. It has been convincingly argued that Myrddin, none of whose poetry is known to have survived, as well as Taliesin was a sixth-century poet and that the chief claim of both to fame and remembrance among their bardic successors was precisely their preeminent reputation as prophetic poets.[3] Nor need we doubt that the role of the poet as prophet goes back even further to the Celtic druids. One of the striking features of

---

[1] W. L. Richards, *Gwaith Dafydd Llwyd o Fathafarn*, Caerdydd, 1964, 50–1.

[2] See M. E. Griffiths, *Early Vaticination in Welsh with English Parallels*, Cardiff, 1937, for a comprehensive survey of prophetic materials in early and medieval Welsh literature; A. O. H. Jarman, *The Legend of Merlin*, Cardiff, 1960.

[3] Rachel Bromwich, 'Y Cynfeirdd a'r traddodiad Cymraeg', *Bulletin Board of Celtic Studies*, xxii, 1966, 30–6.

Celtic pagan religion was its addiction to those animal deities of dragons, boars, ravens, and the rest, which were also among the most persistent and widely employed vaticinatory symbols in the poetry of early medieval Wales.[4]

However, it would be very unwise to embark on highly speculative excursions into the misty uncertainties of early Celtic religion in order to uncover the roots of Welsh prophetic tradition. Let us start at a clear and well-established *terminus a quo*, the Welsh prophetic poem *Armes Prydein* ('Prophecy of Britain'), which Sir Ifor Williams conclusively dated to the early part of the tenth century.[5] For a period of some six centuries after that, down to the age of Dafydd Llwyd o Fathafarn, it is quite evident that the prophetic tradition remained virile and evergreen among Welsh poets. It was not the product of a rigid and unimaginative conservatism on the part of poets too unintelligent or uninspired to find new themes; rather was it the fruit of a powerful and necessary myth which served a deep and enduring social need.

Having stressed the power and continuity of the prophetic tradition over these six centuries, let us at once concede that within that period there were marked differences of individual emphasis and approach. The *Armes Prydein* and other pre-Norman poetry obviously reflects the political and military problems of the Welsh in the Anglo-Saxon era. The poetry of the *Gogynfeirdd*, the court poets of the twelfth and thirteenth centuries, is equally clearly closely geared to the needs and policies of the native princes in the confused and tumultuous centuries after the advent of the Normans. Geoffrey of Monmouth injected a new and immensely potent stimulus into prophecy in Wales and elsewhere.[6] The disasters of 1282-3, when Welsh political independence and the princely house of Gwynedd were extinguished, were a traumatic experience for the poets, as the heartbroken desolation of the elegies to Llywelyn ap Gruffydd unmistakably reveals; and yet, the prophetic theme, improbable as it might have seemed, survived this débâcle. In the fourteenth century it continued to place its hopes on a resurgent Welsh prince—an Owain Lawgoch ('Owain of the Red Hand') or an Owain Glyndŵr.[7] After the failure of the Glyndŵr rebellion early in the fifteenth century, visions of Welsh political independence seem to have been abandoned by the Welsh poets in favour of capturing power within the English political machine by means of a William Herbert or a Jasper Tudor.[8] Their prophetic appeals could be and were ingeniously adapted to the exigencies of this kind of power politics. They were brought to what many Welshmen believed to be their consummation and fulfilment in the victory of Henry Tudor in 1485. Nor was

---

[4] Anne Ross, *Pagan Celtic Britain*, London, 1967.

[5] Ifor Williams, *Armes Prydein, o Lyfr Taliesin*, Caerdydd, 1955; cf. Thomas Parry, *A History of Welsh Literature* (transl. H. I. Bell), Oxford, 1955, 12–14.

[6] The Galfridian literature is endless, but see especially Griffiths, *Early Vaticination* and R. Taylor, *The Political Prophecy in England*, reprinted New York, 1967.

[7] For Owain Lawgoch, see *A Dictionary of Welsh Biography*, London, 1959, *s.n.* Owain ap Thomas ap Rhodri and references given there; for Owain Glyndŵr, see J. E. Lloyd, *Owen Glendower*, Oxford, 1931, and Glanmor Williams, *Owen Glendower*, Oxford, 1966.

[8] Eurys Rowlands, 'Dilid y broffwydoliaeth', *Trivium*, ii, 1967, 37–46; cf. H. T. Evans, *Wales and the Wars of the Roses*, Cambridge, 1915, 179–80.

their potential even now fully exhausted. When young Rhys ap Gruffydd, head of the house of Dynevor, became restive against his Tudor sovereign between 1529 and 1531, one of the accusations solemnly brought against him was his use of ancient prophecies to popularize his cause.

Numerous and diverse the emphases may have been, wide the variations in tactic and exploitation; and yet within and through them all there ran certain basic and unchanging motifs. The Welsh were held to be the heirs and descendants of an ancient and honourable race, the rightful owners and rulers of the island of Britain. They had been wrongfully and treacherously deprived of their patrimony by the Anglo-Saxons. However, the tables would be turned on the offspring of Hengist and Horsa by the return of a great British hero or heroes—Cynan and Cadwaladr, or Owain, or Arthur. His reappearance would presage great cataclysms, furious battles, and copious bloodshed. Finally, these tribulations would be surmounted and crowned with complete victory, in which the Welsh, reinforced perhaps by allies from Scotland, Ireland, and Brittany, would be wholly and lastingly triumphant.

The consideration about these grandiose expectations that will immediately strike a modern observer is that they must have been disappointed with leaden and monotonous regularity again and again over the centuries. It is no wonder that from time to time there should be expressions of chagrin and resentment on the part of the disappointed poets. A fourteenth-century poet, keyed up to await the coming of Owain Lawgoch, expressed his bitter mortification that his hero had been killed before he could claim his inheritance;

> Er edrych am ŵyr Rhodri,
> Llyma och ym lle ni chawdd.
> Lleddid a diawl ai lladdawdd.[9]

('Though I looked for the grandson of Rhodri, what grief it is to me not to have had him. He was killed and it was a devil who killed him.').

Nor is it surprising that for long periods the prophetic theme seems to have disappeared or at least to be dormant. There are other occasions when poets appeared only to be 'going through the motions' of voicing prophetic themes when their patrons were known to be holding office under the English Crown and fully co-operating with the English authorities. This led a historian as sensitive and percipient as the late Glyn Roberts to suggest that there might really have been no substance in the prophetic themes after 1282, that they were merely reflecting a kind of morbid or unthinking curiosity of the sort that leads people to read Old Moore's Almanack.[10] Was the prophecy indeed just some fossilized vestige which had now become meaningless sentiment? It is difficult to accept it as such. Poetry of this kind was

---

[9] Glanmor Williams, 'Proffwydoliaeth, prydyddiaeth a pholitics yn yr Oesoedd Canol', *Taliesin*, xvi, 1968, 32–9.

[10] Glyn Roberts, 'The Significance of 1284', *Wales through Ages*, i. 128–37, especially 136; *idem*, 'Wales and England; Antipathy and Sympathy, 1282–1485', *W.H.R.* i, 1960–3, 375–96.

commissioned by patrons who were often 'hard cases'; experienced leaders who knew what o'clock it was in the political and military world of their time—Owain Glyndŵr, William Herbert, Jasper Tudor, or Rhys ap Thomas. It is not easy to see them as men indulging in nothing better than sentimental commonplaces. Was it, then, cynical manipulation? Exploitation for selfish political ends by unscrupulous careerists of a genuine but uninformed loyalty on the part of the mass of the people? Henry Tudor has in recent times in Wales been cast in this role. It is impossible to deny that Henry was an astute political operator who knew how to capitalize his assets effectively. Professor Chrimes, his latest biographer, has also warned us against exaggerating the king's Welshness, and Dr. Anglo has reduced to its proper proportions the influence of the 'old British history' on the early Tudors.[11] Yet it is difficult to escape the conclusion that these prophecies penetrated to some deep strata in Henry's complex and multi-layered personality. This is not the place to examine the issue in detail, but to take one single and seemingly crucial instance: the choice of the name Arthur for the king's eldest son. This must have appeared to many of his contemporaries as a bold and startling innovation. In so strongly dynastic an age, when so much depended on the heir to so fiercely contested an inheritance, this almost unprecedented choice of a royal name may perhaps be best explained in terms of a fascination which the prophetic theme exercised over Henry, who, as a king, was anything but a political gambler.[12]

Whatever we may think of the influence of prophecy on Henry VII there seems little doubt that for many of his Welsh contemporaries the whole complex of prophetic hopes, longings, and predictions still retained its substance, that it was still capable of triggering off deep and powerful responses. Why had it been able to do this for many centuries and why could it still do so? The answer seems to be that it had been a great and necessary myth. It was the myth which for the Welsh made sense of their past history and their future destiny. Like many other peoples at an early stage of their development they found it necessary to render the past intelligible and the future meaningful by the selection of some focus or foci. That is precisely the function served by myth before much formal history exists. In Wales, as in other countries, myth received its literary expression mainly in poetry. It was the poets who were the conservators of the past and the heralds of the future. They had a vital role to fulfil for the society of which they were members. What M. I. Finley has written of the poets' function in ancient Greece can almost equally well be applied to Wales:

Group memory, after all, is no more than the transmittal to many people of the memory of one man or a few men repeated many times over. The act of communication, and therefore of preservation, of memory is not spontaneous and unconscious, but deliberate, intended

[11] S. B. Chrimes, *Henry VII*, London, 1972, 3; S. Anglo, 'The *British History* in Early Tudor Propaganda', *Bulletin of the John Rylands Library*, xliv, 1961–2, 17–48.

[12] For the fascination of things Welsh for Henry VII, see Christopher Morris, *The Tudors*, London, 1955, 60–1. The significance of the name Arthur was certainly not lost on the Welsh poets; Richards, *Dafydd Llwyd*, 27–9.

to serve a purpose. Unless such conscious, deliberate activity occurs in each generation the memory of any event will disappear for ever.[13]

This kind of myth did not call for a detailed, accurate, and continuous narrative of the past; it would indeed have been encumbered by it. Very few early peoples enjoyed such knowledge. They knew far less about the past than we do, but they felt a much keener sense of continuity with it.[14]

The essence of this Welsh myth was that it embodied a messianic hope. Recent studies by social psychologists and anthropologists, as well as historians, have brought out more strongly than ever how widespread and potent messianic hopes have been and still are. In all parts of the world in many different ages there has been an infinite variety of messianic expectations founded on traditional myths. Nearly all of them have a core of characteristics in common: belief in a Golden Age, the source to which a society must return in order to find fulfilment; expectation of a millennium which is to be preceded by dire cataclysms and catastrophes; confidence in the appearance or return of a charismatic deliverer—a very common motif in these beliefs is expectation of the return of the dead; and conviction that the hero's emergence will be quickly followed by final victory, the ejection or subjection of the erstwhile conquerors, and the re-establishment of the Golden Age. The powerful aesthetic as well as emotional attraction of such a myth, which appears so harmoniously and organically to join past, present, and future in common unity, can hardly be overestimated. The situation in which it most naturally arises is that in which acute anxiety is felt at the prospect of disaster or threatened disaster, in which the autonomous social and cultural values of the group concerned are threatened with extinction. Among the Welsh it was pressure first from Anglo-Saxon rulers and later from Norman kings and lords which naturally enough evoked such fears. They persisted throughout the Middle Ages. As late as the turn of the fourteenth century we have a note on a Welsh manuscript prepared for Hopcyn ap Thomas, renowned in his day as 'master of Brut', in which the copyist, having mentioned earlier disasters experienced by the most eminent Welsh princes, refers to the contemporary 'pain and want and alienage (or oppression)' ('poen ac achenoctit ac alltudedd') which made the Welsh feel like exiles in their own land.[15] The reference is all the more significant because of the extreme rarity with which a littérateur or manuscript-copier gives his own reaction to the contents of a manuscript he was copying. In the face of this age-long fear of destruction of identity, if not of physical extinction, it was the strength of the myth which provided social cohesiveness and emotional compensation. This was not the product of morbid psychology, or eccentricity, or collective derangement. It was a perfectly healthy and normal reaction which could be intensified into unwonted excitement in

[13] M. I. Finley, 'Myth, Memory, and History', *The Listener*, 23 and 30 Sept. 1965, 449–51, 490–2, especially 491.

[14] Hans Meyerhoff, quoted by Finley, *The Listener*, 30 Sept. 1965, 492.

[15] B. F. Roberts, 'Un o lawysgrifau Hopcyn ap Thomas o Ynys Dawy', *Bull. Bd. Celtic Studies*, xxii, part iii, Nov. 1967, 223–7.

times of stress or crisis. It was not peculiar to Wales in the Middle Ages but exercised a comparable fascination in other Celtic lands, and there were similar motifs at work in other European countries.

This kind of myth was widely associated with religion. Though in Wales, on the face of it, it was wholly secular in content, there were some subtle interrelationships with religion. Some of these are far from clear, and much more detailed examination needs to be undertaken before any confident assertions concerning them can be made. There is, for instance, the question of a possible connection between the old Celtic religion and the prophetic tradition. It is known quite certainly that there were well-marked prophetic elements in the old pagan religion and that the return of the hero and the revival of the dead were familiar to it. Christianity itself has a most powerful eschatological content, and one of the most striking repercussions in many pagan communities in the modern world into which Christianity has been introduced is that it has led to rediscovery of and re-emphasis upon traditional pagan prophetic myths earlier cherished. It is not out of the question that something of the same sort happened in early Britain. It may have been conflict between two rival sets of values, one of them having a 'tainted' pagan origin, which led Gildas to assail the bards so violently and later to the tension between priest and poet, which was always latent in medieval Wales and occasionally burst out into acrimonious controversy.[16]

However, no myth of this kind could have continued to flourish in Wales throughout these centuries if it had been pagan or antichristian; it had perforce to operate within the Christian framework. The intellectual and ideological content of that framework, nevertheless, was not as monolithic as is sometimes supposed. It may be true that early British history was interpreted by Gildas and Bede in a characteristically Christian fashion, i.e. that the defeat of the early British and the alienation from them of much of their territory was a divine punishment laid upon them for their sins. But such an interpretation was not subscribed to by all British clerics, especially those of Wales. As long as the Roman and Celtic churches remained separate it was natural that the Celtic church should defend its national as well as its ecclesiastical tradition; nor could the one be separated from the other. It is this which may account for the persistence of one remarkable trait throughout the whole of the poetry—the close and frequent association of St. David with it. He was clearly the symbol for the autonomy of the Welsh church and of the hope of its renewal in association with the victory of the national hero. He was invoked in the *Armes Prydein* and he was present in the prophecies at a number of critical points all the way down to Dafydd Llwyd o Fathafarn on the eve of the Tudor victory. There were even prophecies attributed to his authorship.[17] He finally came into his own at the time of the Reformation, when Welsh reformers tried to set the record straight after centuries of what they saw as spiritual calumny. They maintained that it was not the sins of the British

---

[16] Glanmor Williams, *The Welsh Church from Conquest to Reformation*, Cardiff, 1962, 183 ff., 237–9.

[17] For St. David and the prophetic tradition, Griffiths, *Early Vaticination*, 99, 109, 135, 165, 182, 186; Richards, *Dafydd Llwyd*, 46–8.

that had been punished by Anglo-Saxon victory. On the contrary, the British had fallen into Roman idolatry and wickedness only when forced to do so at the point of Anglo-Saxon swords. The true vindication of the ancient prophecies, so the Welsh Protestant humanists argued by inference, was the spiritual renewal associated with the introduction of reformed doctrine.[18]

Despite the existence of these religious associations and overtones, however, the myth remained an essentially secular one. When we ask ourselves what were its perennial sources of appeal and stimulation, we find that the first and deepest source of satisfaction that any myth could bring was that it helped to relieve the tension caused by the disparity between the actual and the ideal. Real life in medieval Wales brought pressures that were oftentimes well-nigh intolerable: the threat of defeat, enslavement, and even annihilation by external enemies. Perhaps the only way in which the disintegration of the people's morale could be prevented was by an appeal which transcended the anxieties of a disordered present by drawing sustenance from the supposed *mores* and achievements of a glorious past which were to be reinstated in the future.[19] Moreover, one of the particular tribulations of the Welsh was their own fatal proneness to internecine feuds. It can hardly be an accident that an essential feature of the myth was its concentration upon a united past and a united future under a common deliverer. Again, the emphasis upon the awesome disasters and upheavals, bloodshed and battles that must precede final victory was stressed in Wales, no doubt as in other countries, in order to brace men to make those greater-than-normal efforts and sacrifices that would be needed 'to take arms against a sea of troubles'.

That the poets should shoulder the prime responsibility for conveying this message from one generation to another was to be expected.[20] They were historians and genealogists, not just for the prince himself but for the whole community associated with him. Descent and lineage were his and his subjects' claim to land and authority. The poets, too, were the ideologists, propagandists, and morale-builders, who were as conscious of their obligation to posterity as of their debt to ancestry. As such their influence was not confined to princes, noblemen, and literary patrons; it ramified throughout the free population of Wales—an unusually large proportion of the populace—from whom the rulers and gentry hoped to recruit military and political support. The status and prestige of the poets were acknowledged by their own people in the honoured position they were accorded at court and in the laws. Their influence was recognized also by their adversaries, especially by some of the English kings, who identified the bards as the most dangerous organs of opinion and resistance in Wales.

At this point, two serious objections could well be raised: that the bards were, to

---

[18] For the Reformers' view of church history, Glanmor Williams, *Welsh Reformation Essays*, Cardiff, 1967, 207–17.

[19] Thomas Jones, 'Historical Writing in Medieval Welsh', *Scottish Studies*, xii, 1968, 15–27; R. W. Hanning, *The Vision of History from Gildas to Geoffrey of Monmouth*, New York, 1966, 140 ff.

[20] There was also, of course, a good deal of prose material relating to the prophecies—translations of Geoffrey of Monmouth's works and commentaries on them, and the like. These were thoroughly familiar to the poets and, sometimes, to their patrons.

a large extent, the creatures of their patrons; and that the latter could induce them to manipulate the aspirations enshrined in the prophecies to serve their patrons' immediate political ends. Both are valid. Very often the grandiloquent vaticinations of the poets wrap up the power politics of Welsh princes or gentry. Their fine phrases, stripped of bardic rhetoric, may mean nothing more than the assertion of one Welsh prince or gentleman of his own and/or his faction's right to land and authority in some part of Wales. Large-sounding prophecies were commonly used in the same way in other parts of Britain and Europe to advance relatively narrow ends,[21] and contemporary politicians are no strangers to the art of identifying sectional advantage with the common good. However, the really interesting consideration remains that these Welsh poets and their patrons should nevertheless think it indispensable that they should go to the trouble of casting their ambitions in this particular prophetic mould; they believed it eminently worth their while presenting themselves as the true heirs to the myth. It would be easy, but foolish, to be cynical about them. Of course their motives were a mixture of personal ambition and patriotic pride; and the proportions of the amalgam varied widely from individual to individual. Could we expect it to be otherwise? Has there ever been an age when this was not so? Self-seeking and opportunism are constant ingredients in the chemistry of political activity; but if the myth and the ideology it encapsulated had been no more than the tool of private ambition it could never have lasted so long or exerted so profound an influence. Only as a response to a more broadly based and deeply felt social need could it have renewed itself repeatedly over so many generations. That is not to say that many, if any, of the medieval Welshmen expected the prophecy of the re-establishment of Welsh rule over the whole island and the permanent subjection of the English to be literally fulfilled. It did, however, embody for them two indispensable assumptions about their forebears, themselves, and their progeny; assumptions which they would never willingly or lightly relinquish. The one was that they were descended from one of the most ancient and honourable stocks in Europe, which gave them a separate identity as a people that they wanted to see preserved.[22] The other was that their status as a people made them unwilling to submit to being treated as a race of conquered and untrustworthy barbarians; that whoever their theoretical overlords might be, the only men whose right they recognized to bear direct authority over them were men of their own race or those who had identified themselves with it. Again and again they could be induced to respond to the leadership of men who were able successfully to appeal to them on the basis of the vindication of these rights. In a glimpse we get from Archbishop Pecham of the attitude of the common people, as penetrating as it is rare, he warned Edward I that the 'people of Snowdon say that even if the prince would intend to hand them over to the

---

[21] Taylor, *Political Prophecy*, 48–9, 91–2, 104, 114; cf. also N. Cohn, *The Pursuit of the Millennium*, London, 1957, *passim*, and Marjorie Reeves, *Prophecy in the Later Middle Ages*, O.U.P., 1969, *passim*.

[22] Michael Richter, 'Giraldus Cambrensis', *N.L.W. Journ.* xvi, 1970, 193–252, 292–318, especially 293–6.

king, that they had no intention to do homage to a foreigner (*alicui extraneo*) whose language, laws, and customs are completely unknown to them'.[23]

★   ★   ★

Interest in prophecy did not disappear in the sixteenth century. On the contrary, there is abundant evidence that it continued to grip popular imagination, especially in times of crisis. This was as true of England as Wales. There was a whole crop of prophecies circulating at the time of Henry VIII's breach with Rome, during the last year or two of Henry's reign, and in the shadow of the Armada.[24] Dissident nobles like the dukes of Buckingham and Norfolk, or the earls of Northumberland and Essex, encouraged the preservation and promulgation of prophecies favourable to their interests, as did the rebels associated with John Ket.[25] In Wales, during the troubles in which the house of Dynevor became involved in the 1520s and 1530s, prophecy had its part to play. This family, with its highly evocative and emotionally charged arms of the three ravens, had long been associated with prophetic poetry. Among the charges brought against the young head of the house, Rhys ap Gruffydd, was one that he had encouraged seditious prophecies that the king of Scotland, together with the Red Hand ('Llawgoch') and the ravens would conquer all England. When Rhys himself was executed in 1531 his turbulent and ambitious kinsman, James ap Gruffydd ap Howell, went abroad unreconciled to the house of Tudor and bent on scheming against it.[26] Some twenty years later, in the course of furious altercations between Robert Ferrar, a Yorkshireman who became bishop of St. David's, and his leading clergy, one of the most serious accusations brought against him was that he had tried to curry favour with the Welsh in his diocese by stirring up old prophecies of Merlin that the Welsh were again to rule the whole island.[27] Welsh Catholic exiles of Elizabeth's reign were much concerned to uphold Geoffrey of Monmouth's history and the possibility that prophecies propitious to their cause might still be fulfilled.[28] As late as 1600, in a remarkable letter to Sir Robert Cecil, a disgruntled Welsh correspondent, Lod[ovic] Lloyd,[29] claimed that 'the old Romans were not as addicted to their Sybils, the Egyptians to the priests of Memphis, nor the Frenchmen to their superstitious Druids', as many in his country were 'given to the

---

[23] Quoted by Richter, *N.L.W. Journ.* xvi, 312.

[24] G. R. Elton, *Policy and Police*, Cambridge, 1972, 58–62; John Bowle, *Henry VIII*, London, 1964, 177; D. M. Loades, *Two Tudor Conspiracies*, Cambridge, 1965, 147–8; Garrett Mattingley, *The Defeat of the Spanish Armada*, London, 1959, 159–60.

[25] Taylor, *Political Prophecy*, 84–5, 106; Hist. MSS. Comm.: *Hatfield MSS.* xi. 135; J. A. Froude, *History of England: the Reign of Edward VI* (Everyman ed.), London, 1926, 128.

[26] W. Ll. Williams, *Cymmrodor*, xvi, 1903, 33–4, 40–1. Owain Lawgoch ('Red Hand'), the last representative of the house of Gwynedd, had been engaged in attempts in the 1370s to regain his inheritance. The ravens were the arms not only of the house of Dynevor but also of Owain ap Urien Rheged, one of the heroes of earliest Welsh history and legend.

[27] Williams, *Welsh Reformation Essays*, 133–4.

[28] Donald Attwater, *The Catholic Church in Modern Wales*, London, 1935, 20; cf. Geraint Bowen, 'Apêl at y Pab ynghylch dilysrwydd *Historia Regum* Sieffre o Fynwy', *N.L.W. Journ.* xv, 1967, 127–46.

[29] This may have been the writer and literary figure, Lodovic Lloyd, for whom see *DWB, s.n.*

prophecies of Merlin, or to the fond fables of Taliessin; . . . the Jewish Rabbins wrought not so much upon Moses' Pentateuch in their Talmuds, or the Turks upon their sacred Musaph in their Alcorans, as they which they call "Bardi Brytannorum" wrought of Merlin and Taliessin and others'. Were he sheriff that year in Cardigan he would bring 'such volumes of prophecies that after reading them Cecil should make better fire of them in London than Duke Ogis made in Athens of all the writing tables of usurers'.[30] In the following year another of Cecil's correspondents, John Garnons, wrote of his fears that the earl of Essex and his confederates might derive support and confidence from the rather cloudy prophecies of a Welsh 'priest and soothsayer', Lewis Devett.[31]

There was no doubt, either, of the continuing popularity of the 'British history' and Geoffrey of Monmouth. Welsh scholars put up an ardent and spirited defence of the Galfridian version of history in reply to the 'calumnies' of Polydore Vergil and other critics. This did not necessarily mean that they thought the prophecies associated with it had been or were still to be fulfilled, but without belief in the traditional Welsh view of the past there could be no substance or meaning in the prophecies. The sixteenth century was, moreover, the age of the first great antiquary-collectors and copyists. Among the materials zealously sought after and preserved by them were the poetry and prose-writings associated with the history and prophecies. Such an interest was not confined to a select handful of littérateurs and scholars. It was reported of Wales that

upon Sundays and holidays the multitude of all sorts of men, women and children of every parish do use to meet in sundry places . . . where their harpers and crowthers sing them songs of the doings of their ancestors, namely of their wars against the kings of this realm and the English nation, and then do they rip up their pedigrees at length, how each of them is descended from those their old princes.[32]

Despite this evidence of continuing interest in history and prophecy, a rapid and unmistakable decline came over Welsh prophetic poetry in the sixteenth century. Like other medieval forms of expression it found the soil and climate of Tudor Wales uncongenial. The living essence was drained out of it and no new growth took place. It found virtually no niche in contemporary verse, in either the customary fixed metres or in the new free verse now emerging. There was no longer any poet whose reputation was chiefly based on his knowledge of divination or his skill in expounding it. Prophetic themes had clearly ceased to have the same meaning and attraction for patrons that they had once enjoyed. Interest in them among the literary men of the age was largely confined to antiquarian curiosity, and prophetic poetry had no relevance as a weapon to be used in contemporary politics. Whatever difficulties there may be in trying to trace the dawn of Welsh prophetic poetry, there is no doubt that its sunset has to be placed in the sixteenth century.

[30] Hist. MSS. Comm.: *Hatfield MSS.* x. 369.   [31] Ibid. xi. 135.
[32] Quoted in Francis Jones, 'An Approach to Welsh Genealogy', *Trans. Cym. Soc.*, 1948, 390.

No single reason will suffice to explain this sudden eclipse. Partly it was brought about by the decay from within of the bardic order itself. Though the circumstances which brought this about are as yet far from having been fully explained, it is clear that the medieval system became fatally weakened in the sixteenth century and by the end of it was in full decline. The whole function and status in society of the poets were placed in grave jeopardy during the period. This crisis in the fortunes of the bardic order, the originators, guardians, and mentors of the poetic prophecies, must grievously have impaired the continuing composition of them. Yet it can hardly provide the complete explanation, because the prophetic poetry withered much sooner and faster than other kinds of conventional verse and long before the general decline in Welsh poetry had reached crisis proportions.

The decay of the traditional poetry was paralleled by the rise of other cultural values and interests. This was the age of the Renaissance and the Reformation when Welshmen's eyes were turned to new horizons, which sometimes led to an adjustment of perspective that was sceptical and critical of customary Welsh literary criteria. No doubt this helped to contribute to the enervation of some features of the old literary order. But too much stress should not be laid on this point. Everywhere in Europe Renaissance scholarship could be happily if incongruously married with some medieval conceptions. Wales was no exception; and Welsh Renaissance scholars were among the most ardent admirers of the earlier Welsh literary achievement and of the 'matter of Britain', whose cause they so warmly espoused. It is possible that particular Welsh views of the Reformation may have done more to deprive the older prophecies of their impact than the Renaissance did. Welsh Protestant humanists contended that the coming of the Reformation to Wales did not represent the imposition of anything new-fangled or foreign, but that it was the reinstatement of the pristine faith of the ancient British in their Golden Age, the restoration of the one cardinal virtue that, above all others, had made them great. Here indeed, it could be argued, was the true vindication, the supreme consummation, of the prophecies.[33] Yet this exposition came relatively late, long after the prophetic poetry could be seen to be far gone in its decay and can hardly have been a primary reason in accounting for it.

Much more weighty than any of the considerations so far adduced was the belief of many of the Welsh that Henry Tudor's victory at Bosworth had fulfilled the Cymric destiny. The last front-rank stalwart of the poetic tradition of prophecy, Dafydd Llwyd o Fathafarn, certainly thought so. He sang of Henry:

> Ag ef ni bu neb gyfuwch
> Dan y nef nid â dyn uwch.[34]

('No one reached as high as he; under heaven no man will go higher').

---

[33] Williams, *Welsh Reformation Essays*, ch. ix.
[34] Richards, *Dafydd Llwyd*, 56; for other poems to Henry, ibid. 25–6, 27–9, 54–6, 61–6.

Many of his compatriots saw Henry's triumph in the same light. The Tudor had a very plausible case, particularly for those who wanted to believe it. Through his grandfather, Owain Tudor, he could claim to be sprung from illustrious Welsh lineage, and poets were prepared to acclaim his descent from the stock of Cadwaladr himself.[35] In advance of his invasion his sympathizers had sedulously tried to whip up support for him in Wales as 'mab darogan' ('son of prophecy'). After his accession he had, on the whole, treated his Welsh subjects decidedly more favourably than earlier English rulers had done. To the general Tudor myth of the dynasty as the healers of the wounds of civil strife and the sole bulwark against another lapse into anarchy was added in Wales the image of Henry VII as the Moses who had led his people from bondage into freedom.[36] Yet even here we have only part of the answer to our problem. The Tudors after Henry VII did nothing to identify themselves with the 'matter of Britain' and made no effort to encourage this notion of the fulfilment of the kind of prophecy associated with it. Not only did they not foster that prophecy but they showed considerable sensitivity on the subject of prophecy in general, and Tudor parliaments enacted a number of statutes to try to suppress 'fond and fantastic prophecies'.[37] The hostile attitude of local Welsh clerics to Ferrar's references to Merlin's prophecies and the views expressed by Cecil's correspondents suggest that people in Wales were well aware of the regime's disapproval of prophecies.

While we should be unwise to dismiss as of no consequence the genuine pleasure undeniably derived by many of the Tudors' Welsh subjects at the sight of what they believed to be a Welsh dynasty ruling on the English throne, it is hard to accept that this alone accounted for the extinction of the prophetic poetry. The critical factor was whether or not Welsh emotional satisfaction at the victory of the 'Welsh' Tudors was underpinned and perpetuated by the latter's willingness to meet the political, social, and economic ambitions of the ruling class in Wales. This class wanted to preserve in the sixteenth century the two indestructible assumptions of their predecessors in early medieval Wales; that they were descended from one of the most distinguished peoples in Europe, and that the right to rule in their own localities ought to be reserved to Welshmen. It was to assert the former that they continued to cling so tenaciously to the old British history. But the prophecies had been invoked primarily to defend the latter, and were now no longer really necessary. What had decisively changed the situation was that the Welsh gentry's right to bear rule and authority in Wales had been made clear beyond all doubt and safeguarded by statute. The real key to the Tudors' success in Wales lay far less in their Welsh descent than in their willingness to align the interests of the Crown and those of the Welsh landowners. That is the secret revealed by the panegyrics of George Owen, the most authentic and articulate surviving voice of the Welsh Tudor gentry. He drew the sharpest

---

[35] Dafydd Llwyd hailed Jasper and Henry Tudor as being of 'hil Cadwaladr paladr per' ('of the stock of Cadwaladr, the bright ray'), Richards, *Dafydd Llwyd*, 82.

[36] George Owen, *The Description of Penbrokshire*, iii, London, 1906, 37.

[37] Taylor, *Political Prophecy*, 105–6.

contrast between the pre-Tudor kings, 'who by open hostility and wars as by providing of extreme intolerable laws sought continually the subversion, ruin and impoverishing of Wales', and Henry VII and his son 'who came to redress those enormities and to establish good and wholesome laws among them and to give them *magistrates of their own nation*' (my italics)[38] It had been the acceptance of this concept of the relationship between the Tudors and the Welsh which, more than anything else, had outmoded the prophetic poetry and rendered it superfluous.

[38] Owen, *Penbrokshire*, iii. 55.

The Crown and the Provincial Immigrant Communities in Elizabethan England

LIONEL WILLIAMS

ELIZABETHAN England welcomed and made use of two essentially different categories of foreign expertise. The first comprised those who usually came in response to a specific invitation intended to create or further develop industries other than textiles. Their relationships with the Crown were almost invariably those of monopolistic patentees. The second category comprised those who came in consequence of religious persecution, political upheaval, and economic dislocation in their homelands. Their reception and subsequent treatment were primarily influenced by the character and causes of their migration, their number, and the experience so many of them possessed in the manufacture of those textiles known as the 'new draperies'. Although the majority of them had not emigrated voluntarily, to describe them simply as Protestant refugees tends to obscure the evidence that many of them had been principally motivated by economic considerations. About 35 per cent of the 7,143 aliens recorded in London in 1573 said that they had come solely in search of employment. Seventeen of the sixty-four alien craftsmen living in Blackfriars in April 1583 were recorded as having come 'for . . . consciens saeke', compared with twenty-four who had come 'to get [a] living'. Imperfect as such data are (for nineteen of the Blackfriars group no reason was recorded),[1] they nevertheless indicate that the desire to escape from religious persecution was not the sole cause of the migration, though it was no doubt the most compelling. Those who came from France as a result of intensive but intermittent religious persecution tended not to settle; those who came from the southern Low Country did. Their influx into England, which was part of a three-directional movement which took others to the northern Low Country and to friendly German states, had begun by 1559. In the second half of the fifteen-sixties, the mid seventies, and mid eighties it was intensive. The numbers involved in migrations of a dramatic character are liable to contemporary exaggeration; moreover, the mainly transient nature of the French influx of the sixties could not be foreseen. When, during that decade, the Elizabethans were seeking solutions to their migrant problem, they were, therefore, almost certainly thinking in terms of a settlement number that was larger than proved to be the case. The denization grants issued between 1509 and 1603 in respect of just under seven thousand aliens are of little use in estimating the number of immigrant settlers

[1] Hist. MSS. Comm.: *Hatfield MSS.* xiii. 219–27.

in Elizabethan England, for they barely reflect even the trend of that immigration, still less its volume.[2] But the evidence obtained from returns of aliens made in London and the provincial settlement towns by order of the privy council in the fifteen-seventies produces a total of about twelve thousand.

The second influence on the Elizabethans' reception and treatment of their immigrants was a legacy from the past which, until the fifteen-forties, was mostly negative and discouraging in character. Whereas medieval governments, in varying degrees aware of the industrial benefits possibly to be derived from immigrants, had normally tolerated and occasionally welcomed them, English artisans had reacted against them since the fourteenth century with mounting suspicion and some violence. During the first half of the sixteenth century, this hostility was sharpened by the fear that immigrant labour would exacerbate the problems of unemployment and poverty. The unsuccessful attempts of a few foreign entrepreneurs to diversify textile manufacturing seemed an equally unpromising portent. Their late fifteenth-century schemes to introduce cloth-finishers and dyers to teach their skills to the inhabitants of Southampton came to nothing; so did a project to establish silkweaving there in 1536. Only in East Anglia was a very minor degree of diversification effected by foreign expertise: at Coggeshall in the fifteen-twenties and at Norwich, in combination with local capital and with the assistance of the city, in the forties and fifties. Nevertheless, the small-scale introduction of Low Country fustian-makers to Norwich in 1554 foreshadowed the major migrant-created diversification of an industry handicapped by its depressed worsted manufacture which was initiated in the sixties. Similar foreshadowings are visible elsewhere in the later forties and early fifties, when the official welcome extended to Protestant refugees and a tentative appreciation of their potential economic value denote the approaches to a turning-point in the sixteenth-century treatment of immigrants. The Crown's financing of sail-clothmaking Bretons at Abingdon (1547–50), of Low Country hop-planters (from 1550), and of German silver-miners in Ireland (1550–3), its contract with some Venetian drinking-glass makers (1549), and the broad-glass monopoly patent (1552) departed only in degree from past precedent. But the extension of religious freedom to Protestant refugees and the settlement of some of them in a weaving community at Glastonbury (1551–3) contain significant elements of subsequent Elizabethan practice. The idea of a provincial settlement was apparently put to Protector Somerset by Valérand Poullain, a pastor who had arrived in England from Strasbourg in 1548 bringing with him a considerable proportion of his Walloon congregation. Somerset was seeking to promote the economic development of his ex-monastic estate at Glastonbury. His initial idea, which was to use a group of Low Countrymen to establish hop-planting there, was replaced by the clothmaking project which, after his fall from power, was brought into existence by and financed on the authority of the privy council. Most (though not all) of its features anticipated those of the

[2] *Letters of Denization and Acts of Naturalization for Aliens in England, 1509–1603* (Huguenot Soc. of London, Pub. VIII), ed. W. Page, London, 1893, tabulated list of 6,901 denizations, lii–liii.

Elizabethan provincial settlements: the mixture of immigrant, governmental, and episcopal creation; the acceptance of a foreign church; the general supervision of the community by the privy council; some initial local hostility; the description of the settlers by those sympathetic to them in terms which were to become clichés—godly, honest, sober, and willing to teach their skills to Englishmen; the manufacture of 'saye', which must have been akin to (if not definitely) one of the new draperies; the large size of the community (about 230) relative to the town; the grant to the settlers of a cloth-sealing hall and its management by wardens chosen by their community.

When Protestant immigrants once more sought asylum in England, the Elizabethan government, the Church, certain towns, and the politically conscious element in society quickly extended a general welcome to their requests to be allowed to settle. This welcome was both religious and economic. The Church was prepared to welcome the newcomers as persecuted brethren. Jewel countered papal condemnation of them and Spanish protests about their reception with expressions of outrage at their victimization. Grindal embarked benevolently on his new duty as superintendent of the revived London foreign churches. Radical puritans, among them John Field, became intimately involved in the activities of these churches, whose godly example, they hoped, would help to promote a presbyterian restructuring of their own Church. The principal economic considerations motivating the general welcome were a desire to profit from the immigrants' industrial skills, particularly in clothmaking, and the hope that increased native employment would result. For there was already a degree of urban awareness of the existence of genuine unemployment and the theme of 'setting the poor on work' was rapidly becoming a commonplace of economic literature. The Elizabethan government's response to contemporary economic problems was not the drafting of an integrated plan designed for their solution. Its economic actions—often half-hearted, and compounded of a hotchpotch of inherited practices, paternalistic habits, and responses to the loudest and most persistent of various competing interests, pressure from the Commons, or immediate crises—display both consistency and its opposite. Economic considerations were subordinate to the priorities of political survival amid dangers from within and without. Thus the only 'economic policy' safely attributable to the Elizabethan government is the pursuit of those priorities.[3] Not surprisingly in view of the powerful interests involved, the industry which aroused most concern was clothmaking. Its major problems comprised an over-dependence on the manufacture of white broadcloth in the West Country which was geared to risky Low Country and north German markets, the continued expansion of rural clothmaking, and the chronic

---

[3] Peter Ramsey, *Tudor Economic Problems*, London, 1963, ch. v, contains the best brief critical résumé of opinions about Elizabethan economic policy. Vincent Ponko, jr., 'The Privy Council and the Spirit of Elizabethan Economic Management 1558–1603', *Trans. Amer. Phil. Soc.*, N.S., 58, 1968, surveys the council's economic behavioural patterns, concluding that its 'activity in the field of economic management may be termed multiple administrative brinkmanship on behalf of a balanced society', p. 59. Ponko, though seemingly impressed with the council's efforts to control and supervise immigrant settlers, devotes only a brief paragraph to them, p. 26.

depression of Norfolk worsteds for which the growing manufacture elsewhere of kerseys was no compensation. The first and comparatively recent problem entailed frequent governmental consultation with merchants and clothiers throughout the reign, productive of actions dictated by expediency and of dubious benefit. The second and very much older problem had been tackled in the fifteen-fifties with singularly ineffective legislation which was on the verge of abandonment as a solution a decade later. The third problem, which had developed earlier in the century, was about to be overcome by a major diversification of manufacture: the successful introduction of the new draperies. Half-worsted in composition though many of them were, they were nevertheless genuinely new cloths whose commercial manufacture had developed in the southern Low Country during the early sixteenth century, with off-shoots spreading into the northern provinces and into parts of France and Germany. Crucial to their successful introduction into England on a scale sufficient to put down quickly flourishing and healthy roots was the presence of numerous Low Country refugee immigrants.[4] Equally crucial was a desire by certain towns to receive settlements of these immigrants, and the actions taken to promote them by a swiftly responsive government. The intention was to assist some economically depressed towns by encouraging in them the manufacture of the new draperies and thereby to promote the diversification of the English textile industry. For diversification—not expansion as such—was what that industry needed, what Cecil appeared to favour,[5] and what principally motivated governmental action.

This action had to be undertaken with as much prudence as the pressures of time, apparent immigrant numbers, and the limitations of governmental power and administration would permit. For the conversion of a general welcome of refugees into a specific acceptance of them as settlers—with the minimum risk to a precariously established religious uniformity, to national security, and urban social harmony—demanded the rapid improvisation of safeguards and controls. Careful superintendence of the settlers' religious practices was required in order both to isolate the Church of England, its clergy, and the laity from too close a contact with them and to avoid reviving the informalities and idiosyncratic freedom of the Edwardian refugee churches. Vigilance was demanded lest anabaptists, hostile plotters, and intelligence agents should infiltrate in the guise of refugees. Neither the government nor the authorities in the settlement towns could with certainty predict that the immigrants

---

[4] D. C. Coleman, 'An Innovation and its Diffusion: the "New Draperies"', *Econ.H.R.*, 2nd s., xxii, 1969, 417–29 traces the complex origins of the cloths and stresses the refugee-impetus governing their successful implanting. The Publications and Proceedings of the Huguenot Society of London are an indispensable source of information about the settlements. Recent economic case-studies are J. E. Pilgrim, 'The Rise of the "New Draperies" in Essex', *U. of Birmingham Hist. J.* vii, 1959–60, 36–59, and K. J. Allison, 'The Norfolk Worsted Industry in the Sixteenth and Seventeenth Centuries' (part 2), *Yorks. Bull. of Econ. & Soc. Research*, 13, 1961, 61–77.

[5] Despite the dangers of reading too much significance into Cecil's economic memoranda, his strictures on white broadclothmaking and his acceptance of dyed and finished clothmaking in his memorandum of 1564? (*Tudor Econ. Docs.* ii. 45–7, ed. R. H. Tawney and Eileen Power, London, 1924) seem neatly to summarize official attitudes to clothmaking.

would promote urban economic revival, let alone create employment for the native 'poor'. Indeed, they had to face the likelihood of an increase in the latter's well-known xenophobic jealousy during the critical initial stages of urban settlement. Thus immigrant encroachment on existing crafts had to be prevented, immigrant teaching of new skills promoted, and the apparently numerous immigrant poor not allowed additionally to burden hard-pressed citizens and magistrates. The nurture of disaffected Low Countrymen, particularly in London, needed to be rendered less diplomatically offensive. The situation in London was an immediate problem for other and more pressing reasons. The Edwardian tendency for the capital to attract large numbers of refugees looked like being repeated in the early and mid sixties, with the predictable consequences of renewed artisan protest and an intensification of overcrowding, poverty, and disease, and of city companies' complaints about the difficulties of effective craft supervision. Despite orders from the privy council that returns be made of London's 'strangers' and that registers of newcomers be kept, despite an early dispersal of a small proportion of them, their supervision in the metropolitan area, shared between initially poorly co-ordinated agencies, was unsatisfactory to the government. Moreover, it was likely only marginally to improve unless immigrant numbers could be stabilized or, better, reduced.[6]

That provincial dispersal was one method of relief had been grasped very early in the sixties. Practised then and later, particularly in the mid seventies, it did seemingly reduce London's immigrant population. The element of compulsion in the dispersal gives a misleading impression, however, of a procedure which could only be effected by a tripartite collaboration between government, urban authorities, and the settlers themselves. The government's push was in fact met considerably more than half-way by an urban and settler pull. The outcome was the creation between 1561 and 1575 of six principal settlements at Sandwich, Norwich, Colchester, Southampton, Maidstone, and Canterbury. It was a three-stage process: preliminary discussion about a possible urban settlement; detailed negotiation, often assisted by some person of influence; and final governmental consent to a settlement of precise size. Immigrant groups expressed a willingness to settle at Sandwich, Southampton, Maidstone, and Canterbury before governmental permission had been sought, and probably also at Norwich and Colchester. The authorities of all six towns were ready to accept them because of their need for economic revitalization. Sandwich, with its silting harbour, was prepared to welcome immigrants in 1561. Colchester, whose small coloured-cloth manufacture was declining, approached the privy council about a settlement in 1563. Norwich, already a marginal beneficiary, made a similar approach in 1564. Southampton, suffering from the concentration of English external trade on London, expressed its willingness to receive a settlement in May 1567; Maidstone, not yet

---

[6] The totals of London aliens reported to the privy council were not unduly large, but they were rising (from 4,500 to 6,700 in 1563–8), and there was a risk-bearing concentration in certain districts. Bishopsgate Ward in 1568, for example, probably contained one alien for every eight natives, Irene Scouloudi, 'Alien Immigration and Alien Communities in London, 1558–1640' (London M.Sc. (Econ.) thesis, 1936), 60.

recovered from the consequences of its participation in Wyatt's Rebellion, did so in June; Canterbury, no longer a centre of lucrative pilgrimage, recorded its willingness in July. The negotiations between these urban authorities, the prospective settlers, and the government were then completed with varying degrees of smoothness and dispatch. Sandwich, using Roger Manwood, its M.P. and recorder, as intermediary, secured the letters patent which authorized its settlement easily and very quickly in July 1561. It cost the town £50, to which the settlers contributed £20. Norwich obtained its letters patent just as easily, not quite so quickly, but at the duke of Norfolk's expense and with his assistance, in November 1565. For reasons that are unclear, Colchester experienced a long delay. The transfer of some settlers from Sandwich was arranged in 1565; by August 1570 fifty had come; reporting them to be honest and godly, the town obtained an equally pleased privy council's permission in March 1571 to receive another two hundred, though when a formal licence was granted is uncertain. At Southampton, where there is a similar uncertainty, the pace of negotiations was rapid but contentious. The settlers' quite genuine poverty led them to seek unusually extensive privileges, and there was the possibility of an alternative settlement at either Salisbury or Winchester. Differences between the port's authorities and the prospective settlers were, however, resolved by Cecil, assisted by the bishop of Winchester. At Maidstone, in contrast, Cecil's role was routine; Nicholas Barham, a Maidstone M.P., assisted in drafting letters patent for his inspection, and they were issued in November 1567. Canterbury, after a long delay for reasons which are obscure, received a major settlement only in 1575. It was the result of determined efforts made by Cobham, Lord Warden of the Cinque Ports, to reduce the number of immigrants at Sandwich. He suggested to the privy council that some of the Walloons there be moved to Canterbury to join eighteen French refugees who had just arrived from Winchelsea and sought permission to make new drapery. The council, informed of Canterbury's willingness, instructed Cobham to select clothmakers (avoiding the indigent) and to send them to Canterbury, whose authorities concluded a formal agreement with them in March. An acceptance of this agreement by the privy council and the Crown's law officers, rather than the issue of letters patent, apparently sufficed as the settlement's authorization.

Most of the principles governing the establishment of all the provincial settlements are contained in the letters patent granted to Sandwich: the promotion of economic revival, the relief of immigrant pressure on London, the establishment of new-drapery making, the permission granted to the settlers to rent property and to dwell and work in the town, and a maximum permitted settlement number. This was fixed at 200–300 for Sandwich, 300 for Norwich and perhaps also for Colchester, 200 for Southampton, 360 for Maidstone,[7] and for Canterbury perhaps the hundred families which the city declared its willingness to accept. The letters patent for the

---

[7] Maidstone's letters patent authorized a settlement of thirty households each of twelve servants, and then put the settlement ceiling at 200 'householders, children or servants, men not women', *C.P.R., 1566–9*, no. 347, 39–40.

Norwich and Maidstone settlements also mentioned the promotion of new industries additional to textiles (those of Sandwich had additionally mentioned only fishing), and provision for replacements resulting from death or departure; Maidstone's included the prohibition of settler retail trading. Southampton's agreement with its settlers included their undertaking to preserve religious propriety, their seven-year privilege to export at natives' rates, and special apprenticeship arrangements. Canterbury's agreement recognized the settlers' freedom of worship, residence, property-renting, wool-buying, and new-drapery making; they were forbidden to retail; they undertook to practise certain crafts only for their own needs and to pay local dues at natives' rates; their large measure of autonomy would include their own system of poor relief.

A further half-dozen or so provincial towns contained immigrant textile workers. In 1576 some Colchester settlers, with the assistance of Sir William Waldegrave and the consent of Walsingham, secured permission for a settlement of thirty families at neighbouring Halstead. In Norfolk, however, the privy council in 1574 refused to permit a group of Norwich immigrant mockado-weavers to move to King's Lynn, where some of their fellow craftsmen were already at work; a few Low Country bay-makers from Norwich had also set up at Thetford. In Lincolnshire, Cecil permitted a group of Low Country dyers to settle on his property at Stamford. There were sixty-six immigrant textile workers at Dover in 1571, but the government discouraged settlement there and most of them probably soon departed inland. The foreign community at Ipswich in the sixties and seventies was mercantile, and the town's later attempt to use Low Country clothmakers to provide work for the unemployed inmates of Christ's Hospital seemingly failed. At Rye, a residue from the series of large influxes by often destitute French refugees was permitted to settle, but it contained no identifiable new-drapery craftsmen. Neither did the permitted settlement at Great Yarmouth, whose primary purpose was fishing. At Christchurch in Hampshire, John Hastings perhaps employed some Low Countrymen to effect his frizado monopoly patent of 1569. The presence of immigrant textile workers elsewhere in the provinces rests on unsubstantiated tradition. Their known distribution, therefore, was almost entirely confined to East Anglia and the south-east. For this, the immigrants themselves were very largely responsible. A tendency to remain together (which may have as much influenced immigrants then as it apparently does today), the welcome they received from the authorities of the major settlement towns, distance from ports of entry, and the end of major influxes after the mid eighties probably inhibited the creation of more than a few minor subsidiary settlements. The history of the Halstead settlement, as we shall see, illustrates the decisive character of settler decisions. It also suggests that whether or not a town wished to receive immigrants was not always crucial. In most cases, however, it was. At both Norwich and York, traditional textile manufactures were seriously depressed. But whereas the authorities of Norwich welcomed and profited from immigrant new-drapery makers, those of York—sponsors though they were from 1569 of sporadic clothmaking projects—did not, presumably because of their powerful anti-alien prejudices. Yet immigrants would have improved York's decayed linen industry, and would probably have been more effective creators of fustian and worsted manufactures than the city's unsuccessful schemes of 1597 and 1619. The government's responsibility for the settlement pattern was probably slender. Once the dispersal decision was made, its role was almost entirely confined to approving settlement proposals made to it. Strategic considerations probably explain its discouragement of settlement at Dover; why mockado-weavers were not permitted to move from Norwich to King's Lynn in 1574 is not apparent. There is no evidence that the government contemplated a settlement in a town which neither asked for nor was prepared to accept one: such was the magnitude of the risks involved in provincial dispersal. The government would doubtless have vetoed proposals for any very remote settlement of refugee immigrants: the numerous German miners and technicians working for the Mines Royal Company in the extreme north-west were neither refugees, nor were their skills likely to encroach upon those of natives; but it may be significant that Cecil refused their request for a German-speaking pastor in 1568 and told them to attend their parish churches.

Because of the risks undertaken in promoting the immigrants' provincial dispersal, the collaboration between government, urban authorities, and immigrants which had effected it remained hardly less essential thereafter. The government's role, however, gradually altered from one of detailed control to a more generalized supervision of the activities of the authorities in the settlement towns and of the settlers' own lay and spiritual leaders. This role was exercised by the privy council, the secretaries, the lord treasurer (after 1572), using as intermediaries the Lord Warden of the Cinque Ports, the archbishop of Canterbury, bishops whose dioceses contained settlements, and local notabilities. In the settlement towns, formalized relationships were created between the immigrant communities and the urban authorities which, despite differences in structural detail, exhibited common characteristics. In these relationships, and in those of an informal character between the settler communities and the government, the settlers' churches fulfilled from the outset an indispensable function. A total of ten Dutch and four Walloon French churches was permitted to come into existence in thirteen provincial towns (Norwich having Dutch and Walloon churches). The government was, however, careful not to grant them formal legal recognition; this was the significance of its rejection of a request from the revived Dutch church in London for the reissue of its Edwardian charter. In addition, the revived London churches were, unlike the Edwardian, placed under episcopal superintendence, as were the new provincial churches. They were presbyterian in structure, their consistories comprising pastors, elders who 'disciplined' the entire membership, and deacons who organized the relief of their community's poor through the careful distribution of collections, donations, bequests, and loans, in both money and kind. The churches were maintained at their communities' expense. But their creation reflected much more than refugee piety. For each was an essential component of the apparatus of supervision and control exercised over the immigrants by the government and the settlement towns, which endeavoured to enforce compulsory church membership. To a very considerable extent, each church was responsible for its members' behaviour to the urban authority and, indirectly, to the government. Each church intervened in every public and private aspect of its members' lives in its dual concern to maintain the secular as well as the spiritual reputation of its community. The standards of conduct expected were high and, for many, evidently difficult to maintain; in the bigger communities, some settlers managed to avoid membership altogether. Contacts between the London and provincial churches were close and became formalized in occasional colloquies, when as many as possible of the pastors and elders of either the Dutch or the Walloon French churches met to discuss matters of doctrine and discipline. Sixteen Walloon French colloquies met between 1581 and 1603, and eleven Dutch between 1575 and 1599. Contact between the immigrant churches and those of their homelands was close; this aroused some governmental suspicion; in 1581, for instance, the Dutch churches were forbidden to submit to rules drawn up by a synod which had met at Middelburg.

Formalized relationships between the immigrant communities and their host towns were embodied in written agreements, 'orders', and institutions. At Norwich in 1567, twelve immigrants were apparently chosen to share responsibility for the good behaviour of their community with the two church consistories. But disagreements in 1570 between the city and its settlers, particularly over the latter's economic rights, had to be resolved by the privy council which, having heard delegations from both parties, imposed a revised 'Book of Orders' on them in 1571. These provided for the settlement of native–immigrant disputes by the mayor and two aldermen, the keeping of a mayoral register of each immigrant's name and trade, the reporting of newcomers who might remain at mayoral discretion, the payment by the settlers of certain parish dues and watch money, and the detailed regulation of the settlers' economic activities. The Book of Orders also required the Dutch and Walloon communities to choose eight and four, respectively, of their number. Known as the 'Politijcke Mannen' or 'The Eight and Four', they were confirmed in office by the city and empowered to resolve all minor inter-settler disputes, present serious offenders to the city's magistrates, imprison any committed to them for that purpose by the ward constables, and to offer general counsel to their compatriots. At Canterbury, the consistory of the Walloon French church was initially responsible for its members' adherence to the formal settlement agreement of March 1575. Despite its eagerness to share this responsibility, twelve 'politic men' were not chosen until 1582. At Sandwich, the twelve settlers chosen by their community to superintend the inspection and sealing of their new draperies may well have come to act as 'politic men'. This could also have happened at Maidstone, whose settlers tended to model their behaviour on those of Sandwich. At Colchester, the two Governors and twenty-two Assistants of the Dutch Bay Hall, annually chosen by the immigrant bay- and say-makers and confirmed in office by the town's bailiffs and magistrates, added a general oversight of the settler community to their specific cloth-regulating duties. At South-ampton, the Walloon French consistory probably acted for their community, as had happened temporarily at Canterbury. As we have seen, the privy council played an important role as mediator in the creation of the apparatus of immigrant supervision at Norwich. There is every reason to suppose that its approval was sought for similar arrangements at the other settlement towns, though confirmation of this is in some instances wanting.

The Crown's closest fiscal involvement with the settlers occurred when parliament granted subsidies. The wealthier paid a double-rate on personal chattels worth over £3 and on land worth over £1 a year; the poorer—and they were the majority—paid a poll tax, initially of 4*d*., rising in 1571 to 6*d*. The threat of an additional fiscal burden appeared in 1576, when William Tipper was granted a patent to supervise the hosting of alien merchants. This threatened revival of obsolescent practice alarmed the settlers, particularly when Tipper won a test case concerning London. In the provinces, however, the threat proved more apparent than real; the authorities at Norwich compounded with him for 100 marks; perhaps those of the other settle-ment towns followed this example. More serious was the alnage patent of 1578. The new draperies were not adequately covered by the existing alnage arrangements whereby each cloth produced for sale paid an alnage fee and a subsidy. The remedial device selected was the creation of the office of the Alnagers of the New Draperies and Collectors of the Subsidy. Until 1605, it was held by Sir William FitzWilliam and Sir George Delves who (like the existing alnagers) functioned through their deputies. They were to examine and seal all new draperies offered for sale, taking a fee of ¼*d*. and collecting a subsidy of from ¼*d*. to 4¾*d*. on each cloth. Norwich sought exemption, protesting to Burghley that the grant was a breach of the city's privileges. In 1579 the privy council took legal opinion and from 1580 Norwich was permitted to collect and retain the new-drapery alnage fees and subsidies in the city and its environs on payment of £300, of which its settlers had to find £77. 15*s*. When the alnagers' first patent expired in 1585, Norwich failed to secure a twelve-year lease of new-drapery alnage rights for itself and it was still seeking exemption from the system as late as 1602. In 1592 the privy council appointed commissioners to investi-gate the new draperies with an eye to revenue, but the only result seems to have been a thorough (and understandable) confusion in the commissioners' minds about the variety and nomenclature of these cloths. Until 1604, export duties on the new draperies were fitted into the unrevised Book of Rates of 1558, being partly, at least, rated as 'short cloths'.

The administrative problems resulting from immigration and subsequent pro-vincial settlement necessitated a far greater volume of governmental action. Among the earliest problems of this sort was the control of immigrant numbers. From the early fifteen-sixties, a few enterprising individuals were devising schemes for this. The best known was that of William Herle who argued in 1571 that because immi-grants were provoking artisan discontent, encroaching on housing, curbing native employment opportunities, and pushing up prices, an office of surveyor should be created to register aliens' movements. This and other similar proposals were rejected. Essentially impracticable, their acceptance would have resulted in nothing more than lucrative private rackets. London's drastic proposals for controlling aliens, submitted to the privy council in October 1571, were also sensibly rejected. With a commendable grasp of realities, the privy council instead sought later that month—and quickly obtained—information from the maritime counties, the settlement towns and their bishops about immigrant numbers, origins, occupations, and church membership, and estimates of any potential danger to state security and to social harmony in the existing settlement towns. When it ordered similar returns a year later, it emphasized that its major concern was with potentially dangerous immigrants. That is why, for example, it ordered the Lord Warden in 1576 to investigate any surreptitious landings within his jurisdiction. This official also had to deal with Sandwich's laxity in exceeding its settlement limit, which had happened as early as 1562. The privy council censured Sandwich and ordered Cobham to remove the excess. But even after that was done, numbers at Sandwich so increased that at the beginning of the seventeenth century natives were outnumbered by those of immigrant origin. At Norwich, numbers rose to just under four thousand in November 1571: the native population was perhaps 13,200. The privy council kept an anxious eye on the settlement's growth during the seventies, but the city repeatedly assured it that its settlers were well behaved; despite severe plague losses in 1579–80, they numbered 4,679 in 1583. The privy council was apparently unconcerned about numbers at Canterbury where, between 1582 and 1592, Walloon French church membership rose from an estimated 1,679 to 3,312. Numbers at Colchester, which reached 1,148 in 1584, caused some concern (as we shall see), but no governmental pressure to reduce them seems to have resulted. It is unlikely that the settlements at either Maidstone or Southampton much—if, indeed, at all—exceeded their authorized limits.

The government was particularly sensitive about even minor manifestations of native jealousy towards settlers. When in the mid seventies, the immigrant community at Sandwich complained to the Lord Warden and Burghley about a quarterly urban due newly imposed on its fifteen denizens, the mayor and recorder were summoned to London to answer for their action, which reflected a native jealousy from which only Maidstone seems to have been free. Trouble at Canterbury in November 1575, possibly over the interpretation of the March agreement between the city and its settlers, was thought sufficiently serious by the privy council to require its intervention. A group of politically motivated plotters in Norfolk in 1570, who apparently intended to expel aliens from Norwich and elsewhere, was drastically dealt with, three of the ringleaders being executed. At Colchester in 1580, native resentment at immigrant numbers and threats of expulsion induced the bailiffs to order that no settler might remain unless he belonged to the Dutch church. Four of the town's Anglican clergy sought Walsingham's protection for the settlers, assuring him that their number was supportable, that they were godly, well behaved, providers of work for the local unemployed, and that prices (contrary to native allegation) were cheap. So far as is known, neither Walsingham nor his colleagues thought their intervention necessary. Their most revealing intervention came a decade later. As we saw, some settlers moved from Colchester to Halstead in 1576; their bay-making skills were soon imitated by natives who, in 1586, secured Walsingham's unwise consent to clothsealing arrangements which extended to their inferior-quality product the prestige of settler-made bays. Finding protests ineffective, the settlers returned to Colchester in 1589. In 1590 leading Halstead residents, local notables, and villagers formerly employed by the settlers petitioned Walsingham and the privy council to effect their return. The privy council assured the Dutch at Colchester that the sealing customs of those who returned to Halstead would be respected and that local justices—and, if necessary, the privy council itself—would arbitrate in any future dispute. But its repeated commands to the Dutch pastors and the bailiffs of Colchester to send settlers back to Halstead were totally ineffective. Halstead never regained a settlement whose brief history illustrates native folly, immigrant obstinacy, and the limits of both urban and governmental authority.

The settlements' religious affairs required little governmental action and, since their superintendence was an episcopal duty, only a very general supervision. Precautions against anabaptist infiltration were ordered, principally in 1560 and 1575, and from time to time orders were issued about enforcing immigrant church-membership. Their effectiveness, however, depended on the localities' response, which was unenthusiastic. They seem to have done only the unavoidable minimum. Immigrant non-membership of their churches remained a chronic problem in London and, to some extent, in the larger provincial settlements, indicating both the strength of economically motivated immigration and the authorities' inertia or weakness. Episcopal superintendence very occasionally required forceful intervention. Thus in 1562 Grindal was involved in the expulsion on doctrinal grounds of one of London's Dutch pastors. Three years of dissension within the Dutch church at Norwich involved the city, the archbishop of Canterbury, and the bishop of Norwich; the latter deprived all three pastors in 1571, much to their church's resentment.

In economic matters, the authorities in the settlement towns endeavoured to ensure that their immigrants' efforts were directed towards making the new draperies and other new products, and teaching their manufacture to the inhabitants. The government endeavoured to ensure that these ends were achieved with the maximum benefit to both natives and settlers, but with the minimum disturbance of existing interests and waste of its own time. It was the responsibility of the urban authorities to create the necessary economic machinery. For the new draperies, this meant regulating the buying and selling of wool and yarn, the manufacture, inspection, and sealing of the different cloths, the collection of various fees and of the settlers' farm for their economic privileges, and cloth sales (to maximum native profit). When the government did intervene, it was in response to settler complaints, which its actions were then intended to redress. At Norwich, for example, the settlers complained about the city's arrangements for both wool purchase and cloth sales. To redress the first grievance, the privy council said that settlers were not bound to buy their wool from the four aldermanic monopolists whom the city had licensed in 1571 to buy wool for subsequent sale to natives and settlers alike. It also hoped that the licensees would so exercise their monopoly as to reduce the settlers' sense of grievance. The settlers' complaints about cloth sales focused on article eleven of the city's 'Book of Orders' of 1570 which would have prevented them from retailing their own cloths. After very heavy privy council pressure, the revised Orders put into effect in 1571 allowed them to sell to natives and aliens both in Norwich and other towns. An apparently straightforward problem could have almost incredible ramifications, as at Southampton where immigrant serge-makers' protests about a proposed monopoly for pressing (a finishing process) sought by one of their community came to the privy council's attention in 1597. By 1599 it had entangled native serge-makers, Sir Robert Cecil, the pastor and elders of the Walloon French church, and the archbishop of Canterbury in a seemingly insoluble serio-comic dilemma.

Immigrants who were able to introduce into a settlement town some new non-textile craft (and they were very few in the settlement towns themselves) presented no problem either to the urban authorities or the government. But the former were very much concerned with immigrants who practised already existing crafts, for their proportion in relation to new-drapery workers could be quite high. At Sandwich in 1582 it was 32 per cent, and encroachment on existing crafts was sufficiently troublesome to require the intervention of the Lord Warden. As a result of the ever-conscientious Cobham's pressure, the town restricted the number of immigrant bakers, brewers, bricklayers, carpenters, coopers, cordwainers, cow-keepers, masons, shipwrights, smiths, and tailors. Sandwich also imposed special restrictions on certain of its immigrant craftsmen in addition to the usual urban requirement that they make and sell by retail only to meet the needs of their own community. Very strict control, for instance, was imposed on building workers who, 'more reasonable in their takings, and lesse wasters of time by a greate deale than our owne',[8] invariably aroused strong native jealousy. These were not, however, matters normally requiring governmental intervention, whether at Sandwich or the other settlement towns, where restrictions similar to those of Sandwich were imposed. The government's attitude was summed up in the privy council's order to Rye in 1568: it must permit refugees to practise their accustomed trades in order to relieve their poverty, provided native interests were not harmed. A bill displayed by the Speaker in the Commons in 1593 to debar aliens from practising such crafts as cordwaining was thought to be merely part of a political manœuvre on the part of alien merchants seeking to defeat another bill promoted by London commercial interests intended to prevent their alien competitors from retailing foreign commodities. The control of immigrant craftsmen was left in urban hands, and was in practice largely exercised only after

---

[8] William Harrison, *An Historical Description of the iland of Britaine*, ed. F. J. Furnival (New Shakespere Soc., ser. vi, part 1), London, 1877, 238.

pressure on a town from its native artisans and (where they existed) craft gilds. Only exceptionally was an appeal made to a higher authority, as when Rye in 1573 informed Cobham about an enterprising settler who had set his compatriots to candle-making, cornered the market, and used an export licence to create local scarcity; or when the settlers at Norwich in 1583 obtained a privy council order to the city that it assist them against vexatious native informers—a not unusual settler problem.

The collaboration between the government, the authorities in the settlement towns, and the immigrant communities successfully created new-drapery making, beginning thereby the necessary major diversification of the English textile industry. In this sense, the impact of the new draperies on the structure of that industry 'may properly be regarded as revolutionary'.[9] In the areas of immigrant settlement, most had been achieved by 1603 in East Anglia. At Norwich, native artisans quickly and successfully adopted the manufacture of some, though by no means all, of the very wide range of immigrant new drapery, and others were employed by the settlers. In consequence, the heavy burden of native poverty was eased from the mid seventies. Colchester's rapid economic recovery rested on a very narrow range of new drapery, whose manufacture spread among natives there and in five other Essex towns, their surrounding villages, and to Glemsford and Sudbury in Suffolk. In parts of Norfolk, Essex, and Suffolk, villagers were also employed in spinning for settler and native new-drapery makers. In Kent and Hampshire, however, the new draperies remained an essentially urban manufacture. At Sandwich, bay-making flourished and remained important throughout the seventeenth century. At Maidstone, whose settlers were never a particularly wealthy community, natives had taken over woollen new-drapery making by the beginning of the seventeenth century, as they later did the immigrants' linen thread speciality. At Canterbury, the settlers' mainly woollen initial emphasis began to give way to silkweaving during the fifteen-nineties, thereby laying the foundations of an important post-1675 industry (a similar trend was evident in London from the fifteen-seventies). Some of the inhabitants of South-ampton learnt from their settlers how to make serges and rashes, though their combined efforts probably engendered only a marginal economic improvement. In 1603 the immigrant communities whose skill had implanted the new draperies still retained their secular and spiritual identities. The former was beginning to fade. But the latter was not, and it was soon to reawaken a suspicion of its influence which culminated in Laud's efforts drastically to curtail it. During the Elizabethan period, however, governmental supervision of the settler communities and their churches, which was initially close and never became entirely routine, had been guided by a more shrewdly tolerant spirit. The Crown—through its privy councillors and agents, lay as well as ecclesiastical—had contrived successfully to blend considerations of

⁹ Charles Wilson, Introduction to reprint of William Cunningham, *Alien Immigrants to England*, London, 1969, xiv. The 'revolutionary' impact of the new draperies is touched on by Pilgrim, *ut supra*, 59, and is summarized in Lionel Williams, 'Alien Immigrants in Relation to Industry and Society in Tudor England', *Huguenot Soc. Proc.* xix. 4, 1956, 152–60, 169.

economic advantage, its own security, urban social harmony, and Christian compassion. Its motto could well have been

> Thou shalt not be the worse,
> o england, if thou nourse
> Theise exiles come of late.[10]

In nearly every case when its assistance was sought by the settlers, it endeavoured to act on their behalf, but to an extent which stopped short of an insupportable pressure on native interests and which, once the provincial dispersal had been effected, refrained from attempting a detailed control for which it had neither the resources, the time, nor the inclination. Its actions displayed consistency and a realistic awareness both of what they could and could not effect, and of wider urban and even national interests. The Crown and those who governed in its name, centrally and locally, extended a shrewd, civilized, though patronizing and sometimes smug, welcome to the immigrants. That this welcome became a lasting acceptance of their presence was the result of their refugee character and economic potential, a shared hostility towards Spain after 1585, the pervasive growth of puritanism and, above all, of the fact that no one prominent at Court or in the settlement localities—except momentarily in Norfolk—found it expedient seriously to utilize for his own ends the popular xenophobia that was never far below the surface of Elizabethan society.

[10] 'If England will take heed', *c.* 1570, in *Old English Ballads 1553–1625*, ed. H. E. Rollins, Cambridge, 1920, no. 26, 182.

Lawmaking in the Second Protectorate Parliament

IVAN ROOTS

THE history of Stuart parliaments has been written largely in terms of confrontation over large political and religious issues. The medicine of the constitution has been seen as its daily food—an impression encouraged by such collections as Gardiner's *Constitutional Documents of the Puritan Revolution 1625–1666*, which depict a sick patient enduring, or rather collapsing under, the ministrations of a horde of enterprising, even reckless, physicians. It is all ills and pills. Of a constitution in normal, moderate health almost nothing. This picture of crisis at once long-drawn-out and intense is deepened by recourse to some of the more substantial collections such as Rushworth's and Nalson's. But a different aspect is glimpsed in *The Statutes of the Realm* which prints in full the public legislation of these parliaments and (unfortunately only) the titles of private Acts.[1] It is clear at once that these parliaments cannot have spent all their time locked in conflict over major reformatory or destructive measures. Here is a mass of laws, some certainly on the urgent and weighty matters always referred to in the summons, but a good many on more routine matters, economic, social, and administrative. Many are evidently in some agreed interest of the commonwealth generally. Others are of a more particular concern, meeting the requirements of this or that locality, undertaking, institution, community. Some are for a group of named individuals, some even for a single person. Parliament even in 'the iron age of the constitution' has always had more to do than to chew over the grievances of the realm in a Grand Remonstrance or to rewrite an Instrument of Government. 'The great eye' of the nation could light upon clerks of the market as well as upon a traitorous Lord Deputy. The readiness of members of parliament to take note of the interests of individuals, groups, and communities within the framework of the nation can be established by working

---

[1] *The Statutes of the Realm 1235–1713*, 11 vols., 1810–28. 'There never has been a sharply drawn legal distinction between the two classes of bills. It must be sufficient to say that a private bill is one which is founded upon a petition from the person or persons in whose special interests Parliament is requested to lay down certain legal rules or to confer certain privileges, while a public bill is introduced into parliament as a measure affecting the whole community, as a transaction in the life of the state, and originates with one or more members of the House'; J. Redich, *Procedure of the House of Commons*, London, 1906, ii. 257. See also [G. Bramwell] *Manner of Proceeding on Bills in the House of Commons*, London, 1833, 10–18, and *Erskine May's Treatise on the Law, Privileges, Proceedings and Usage of Parliament*, ed. Sir Barnett Cocks, 17th edn., London, 1964, ch. xxxiv.

through the day-by-day entries of the *Commons Journals*,[2] not seeking references to some selected theme, but trying to experience the activity of the House as any assiduous M.P. must have done. Can these dry bones live? Yes, with some imagination, a knowledge of procedure—'the essence of parliament', said the speaker in 1656—and with recourse to the material on debates recorded patchily in parliamentary diaries, not all of which are indifferent to the routine and the seemingly trivial. In this way something of the true inwardness of these parliaments can be approached, even now and then perhaps grasped. The conflicts are there all right, but in their proper setting, one which may, in fact, enhance their impact.

A parliament which seems particularly apt for this sort of treatment is the second one of the Protectorate (17 September 1656 to 26 June 1657 and 20 January to 4 February 1657/8), called after great arguments in Council to finance the war with Spain.[3] Even for the most vocal advocates of that war money was not its *alpha* and *omega*. The Council was as much a mixed batch of individuals as a ragged representation of the various interests, civil and military, fostering survival of the regime. For them all, not least for Oliver Cromwell himself, here was another opportunity for healing and settling, though just what were their aspirations that way it is hard to say. In his welcoming speech, one long and rambling but, *pace* W. C. Abbott, never dull, devoted chiefly to justifying the break with Spain, Oliver mentioned necessary reforms, notably of the law and of manners.[4] His defence of the 'system' of the major-generals suggests that in September he looked for no fundamental governmental change, though it need not be supposed that he had set his face against it. In the event this parliament not only saw to supply, but following the putting down of the swordsmen and decimators, inaugurated a second Protectorate with a new constitution, one, unlike the Instrument of Government, backed by a vote of the Commons. It is possible that all this was planned. No doubt conservatives like Lord Broghill among the Protector's entourage, perhaps even Oliver himself, were anxious to shake off his damaging military associations. But the major-generals were not politically murdered, they almost but not quite committed suicide. Their discomfiture was the occasion, hoped for rather than meticulously plotted, for bringing in the Remonstrance out of which the first edition of the Humble Petition and Advice emerged. The excision of kingship from the second version showed that Broghill's triumph was less than complete. The major-generals, even Lambert, were as much in evidence in parliament during June 1657 as they were in September 1656. As for the second session of parliament, so different in structure that it might be best considered a separate one, it rapidly turned out to be a catastrophe for almost everybody.

---

[2] The Journals for the second protectorate parliament are printed in vol. vii. 423–592.

[3] Vols. v and vi of T. Birch, *Thurloe State Papers*, London, 7 vols., 1742, contain much material and comment on the decision to call parliament, on the elections and on proceedings in the Commons. See also I. Roots, *The Great Rebellion 1642–60*, London, 3rd edn., 1972, chs. xxi–xxiv and references there.

[4] W. C. Abbott, *Writings and Speeches of Oliver Cromwell*, Cambridge, Mass., 4 vols., 1937–47, iv. 260–79.

This outline of the history of the parliament puts rather more stress on the contingent than does Professor H. R. Trevor-Roper in his plausible study of 'Oliver Cromwell and his Parliaments'.[5] His six pages (out of forty-five) make 'the victory' of Broghill's 'kinglings' too much the intended effect of brilliant planning and the assertion that they 'quickly took control of the House' pays little attention to the narrative of what actually happened. There is no mention of 'the case of James Naylor'[6] which took up so much parliamentary time in December 1656 and by raising unexpected issues, large and small, helped to prepare the minds of men inside and outside of parliament for some of the constitutional changes later embodied in the Humble Petition and Advice, among them the revival of a second chamber. The 'case' was a happening, not a playreading.

There is in fact both rather more and rather less in the history of this parliament and to Cromwell's relations with it than is allowed for in Professor Trevor-Roper's thesis. This is even more true of the impatient account by Professor W. C. Abbott in his *Writings and Speeches of Oliver Cromwell*. Certainly much of the day-to-day activity of parliament was in itself unexciting, but in context is as vital a part of its story as the more spectacular aspects. This parliament was a constituent assembly, in Naylor's case it was a court of judicature, but most of all from start to finish—of the first session, anyway—it was a law-making institution which produced a stack of statutes after an expenditure of time, effort, and thought, which deserves the historian's attention and respect.

Bills were presented for the Lord Protector's assent on three occasions during the first session: 26 November 1656 and 9 and 26 June 1657. The first batch contained 11 of which 5 were public and 6 private; the second 38 (9 public and 29 private), and the last, marking the end of the session, 22 (13 public and 9 private).[7] The Protector rejected one public Bill on 9 June using the phrase, an echo of the old royal veto, 'I am desirous to advise of this bill'. The mere total of Acts brought to fruition in this parliament represents surely a formidable legislative achievement. Their content reinforces this conclusion. Some were long and detailed. The Protector remarked on 5 June 1657 of 'the multitude of bills' offered for his consent that 'he had read one . . . and if he should rise at 4 in the morning he could not read them in a whole day'. In the second session Sergeant John Maynard said that 'this parliament did pass more in one month than the best student can read in a year, and well if he can understand it then'.[8] We could guess that the time taken in the House and the committee rooms —the Speaker's Chamber, the Inner Court of Wards, the Duchy Chamber, and

[5] In H. R. Trevor-Roper, *Religion, the Reformation and Social Change*, London, 1967, 345–91, esp. 380–5.

[6] For Naylor see I. Roots, op. cit., ch. xxii, and T. H. Wilson and F. J. Merli, 'Naylor's Case and the Dilemma of the Protectorate', *U. of Birmingham Hist. J.* xi, 1967–8.

[7] The printed public acts can be found in H. Scobell, ed., *Collection of Acts and Ordinances*, London, 1658, and C. H. Firth and R. S. Rait, *Acts and Ordinances of the Interregnum*, 3 vols., London, 1911. The private acts have disappeared.

[8] J. T. Rutt, ed., *Diary of Thomas Burton*, London, 4 vols., ii, 1828 (reprint, ed. I. Roots, New York, 1974), 180, 461.

elsewhere—preparing these measures—to say nothing of the specialized work of the Clerks in engrossing them and so on—must have been considerable. Examination of the Journals, backed and extended by Burton's *Diary*, confirms this. It does more. It cries out that this completed work in no way reflects the true legislative burden shouldered in this parliament. We must take account of the whole mass of Bills which were contemplated (some never reaching the drafting stage), introduced, read over, committed, reported, amended, debated, but which for various reasons, all worth exploring, failed to go through all the processes necessary for ultimate protectoral acceptance. There were well over a hundred of them, some public, some private, some major, some minor, none without appeal to at least a few members, many of concern to almost all active members. Some brought in members who might otherwise have stayed away. Some were quite short—one was described by a sponsor as 'a little bill no bigger than my thumb'.[9] Others were elaborate. Short or long, a number occasioned what Burton calls—and sometimes confirms in his text to be— a 'great debate'. Even obviously trivial Bills could set off heated debates, shedding light on things other than great matters of state about which prominent members and backbenchers alike could be exercised. The pity is that Burton, who had an eye and ear for such things, was not present all the time to take down what men said and to make his occasional illuminating comments.

Among the topics about which someone thought there ought to be a law were the erecting of a court of law and one of equity at York; making malt at unseasonable times; draining lands in Hampshire; settlement of the Merchant Adventurers into a corporation; the maintenance of ministers in cities, corporations, and market towns; the sale of lands to settle Hamlet Latham's debts; indemnification of Col. Markham; gaming; holy days; wages; common lands; timber; 'undecent fashions' and marriage portions. The range of provenance was as wide as the range of subject. Some were obviously government inspired. A few respond to the Protector's call for a reformation of manners, and to his invitation (besides providing the wherewithal for the Spanish war) to inspect and improve the uneasy revenues of the state. A number would revise, revive, or continue existing legislation, such as the measure relating to probate, for which Sir William Strickland and Sir Thomas Wroth, growing old and thoughtful of their graves and posterity, tried vainly to get priority.[10] A few of these were in fact taken up in the Act showing how far 'acts and ordinances made since 20th April 1653 and before 3rd September 1654 . . . shall be of force', about which I have written in detail elsewhere.[11] Besides promoting measures which in its view contributed towards the settlement of the commonwealth, government support was forthcoming for private Acts which 'tended to the establishing of men's estates and families'—gestures which might strengthen precarious loyalties and win those who were showing signs of wanting to come to terms with the regime. Hard

---

[9] Ibid. 304.   [10] Ibid. 237.

[11] 'Cromwell's Ordinances' in G. E. Aylmer, ed., *The Interregnum: The Quest for Settlement 1646–1660*, London, 1972, 143–64, 212, 229–30.

cases make bad law it is true but in dealing temperately with them it is possible sometimes to check dissatisfaction with existing or contemplated general provisions. Even 'hard-liners' could see that. Major-General John Lambert attempted 'very feelingly' on the morning of 25 June, the last day but one of the session, to get priority for a Bill for the relief of Lady Worcester over 'the bill for Attainder of the Irish Rebels'. He failed then but the Bill was brought in again on the 26th, pushed through a third reading—time was found even for adding a proviso—and passed in time to be offered with the other completed Bills for the Lord Protector's assent. Earlier on the second reading (2 May) another member of the Council, Strickland, had also spoken 'very favourably on Lady Worcester's behalf'.[12]

Not all public Bills were government-inspired, hardly a matter of surprise considering the diversity of view among the councillors and leading officials. The minutes of the Council contain little reference to parliamentary proceedings, though they may have been informally discussed. The Catechism Bill, an intolerant measure long in gestation, certainly ran counter to the wishes of some of 'the merciful men' among the councillors and was as we have seen rejected by the Protector on 9 June. Its leading backer was the very active member for Exeter, Thomas Bampfield, a 'presbyterian' whose experience and expertise as chairman of the committee on religion helped to win him the Speakership in Richard's parliament. He took the veto very badly, saying that 'his Highness never did himself such an injury as he had done this day'. Another voluble M.P., Lambert Godfrey, queried the action of the Clerk in offering the Bill separately to the Protector and after consent had been given to the other Bills. It looked as if the Clerk had had some prior intimation of what was in Cromwell's mind.[13] A Bill for which the Council clearly did not have collective responsibility was the 'short' one introduced by Major-General Disbrowe on Christmas Day 1656, when the House was thin, for 'continuance of a tax upon some people for maintenance of the militia' (the decimation tax). This was a private enterprise, as Cromwell later tartly reminded them, of some of the major-generals. They got their first reading, but soon lost the Bill against the votes of civilian colleagues and other men close to the Protector. On Christmas Day, too, men of 'the court' were divided over the introduction of a Bill to prevent the superstitious keeping of Christmas and other festivals.[14]

There was never anything monolithic about the Cromwellian front in the parliament, nor, and this is important, were the divisions fused along permanent lines. Major-Generals might argue with one another over Naylor but come together on the Decimation Bill. The final form of the Humble Petition and Advice brought together some military men and civilians in support of it, others in at any rate a quizzical attitude towards it. Taking together the names of tellers in divisions recorded in the *Commons Journals* with the speeches and gestures reported in Burton's *Diary*, we can see that many Bills were tackled as much on their merits as individuals

---

[12] Burton, *Diary*, 102, 305.   [13] Ibid. 205–6.
[14] Ibid. 230–43; Speech of 27 Feb. 1657/8, Abbott, op. cit. iv. 418–19; Burton, *Diary*, 228–30.

(even councillors) saw them as from any previously agreed position. Men's views were sometimes as affected by what they heard in the debates as by their discussions and associations outside the Chamber. Professor Trevor-Roper has assumed the docility of this parliament, presumably because the Scottish and Irish members were not freely representative of their constituencies and because around a hundred members were excluded by the Council under Clause xxi of the Instrument, while perhaps another fifty voluntarily abstained from attendance. No doubt some very independent, outspoken, energetic, and intelligent men were kept out though no one has analysed the list sufficiently to establish just what was objectionable in them all, if anything was. What is certain is that many men remained in the House who were by no means government clients or timid time-servers but had views of their own on matters of the day, including intended legislation of great or little consequence, and who were not afraid to express them, though sensibly enough many of them took the line that their interests might best be served by tact, moderation, and the constructive employment of the procedures of parliament rather than by obstructionism that gloried in its frankness. They recognized that the regime would take some handling. In their turn so would they, even if the government had taken a Tudor line in management. That was never really on the cards. The Lord Protector recognized it, and the result of his recognition aided by circumstances (Cromwell always drew on Providence) and some initiatives by others on his behalf (another perennial factor in his career) was a limited but by no means tiny achievement in June 1657.

To return, as parliament itself was daily doing, to the lawmaking process we may consider something of how the members of all persuasions persuaded themselves to allocate their time. To start with they met in the mornings only from nine till noon. Afternoons were set aside for Committees of the Whole, Standing, or for particular Bills. Some of the committees were large, the number of them rapidly increased and an assiduous member could find his time heavily engaged even in the early days before big issues like Naylor's case or the proposed new constitution came along. The Speaker, Sir Thomas Widdrington, soon found it hard going. The Venetian ambassador considered him a competent man, entirely devoted to the Protector. His handling of the House proved him to be neither. The business of the House got sadly out of schedule. He dithered—on one occasion, casting his vote, said *yea* when he meant *no*, precipitating a debate which reflected on his capacity. His health deteriorated and he had for a period to be replaced by Bulstrode Whitelocke. He showed on at least one occasion that he could put his pocket above his concern for government business by allowing a private Bill in contrary to the orders of the House —almost certainly for the fees.[15] If Cromwell had contemplated an Elizabethan pilotage of the commonwealth here was no Elizabethan Speaker firm in control. But he had no great difficulty getting the members off the dangerous topic of the excluded members. Certainly there were strong feelings which would burst through a little at odd times all through the session. If the House had fought the issue, so great was the

[15] *Calendar of State Papers, Venetian, 1655–6,* 266; Burton, *Diary,* i. 337–41, 369–70; ii. 70–1, 192.

need for money, the Council might, just might, have compromised. More likely there would have been deadlock broken by further exclusion or dismissal. If the former 'the rag of parliament' would have had so little respect it would have served no purpose and the moves towards moderation of the regime would have been checked, even more likely following a dismissal. It was better that a bitter pill should be swallowed in order that parliament survive—to comment, to co-operate, not slavishly but sensibly. There were perhaps some political forces in the sixteen-fifties so inimical to stability that it was death to associate with them. The protectorate was not one of these. A parliament sitting could be a parliament working in what this or that interest among its members could consider the national interest. So they went on, in the shadow of an impending dissolution, with the great—and it may be added, the small affairs of the nation.[16]

Within a few days measures—public and private—were before the House and its committees. By November the burden of work was already acting as a slipping brake on any programme contemplated by any grouping. On 3 November committees were urged to dispatch their Bills. On 26 November the Lord Protector gave his consent to the first batch of Bills.[17] The procedure for this was an occasion for discussion bringing out a determination for everything to be done in a parliamentary way. Burton's *Diary* makes clear throughout that members of this parliament shared their predecessors' sense of the dignity and high status of the institution. The public Acts included one repudiating Charles Stuart's title, nothing novel in that, and one for the protection of his Highness's person, an encouraging gesture. Another confirmed the 1645/6 abolition of the Court of Wards, an attempt to resolve some doubts. Another on the exportation of native products showed a concern for the trading welfare of the nation. The last public Act stated baldly that the acceptance of the Bills offered that day did not determine the sitting of parliament, a confirmation of post-1641 practice and an assertion of a will to go on. Significantly, there was no lavish grant of money to make government feel independent of parliament, but there were measures for supply and other matters of public concernment 'on the anvil' as the Speaker put it. So co-operation was invited. The private Acts dealt with a wide range of individuals, localities, communities. A pattern was not imposed on a scratch lot but something like one emerges. It was a good augury for survival.

By the end of November parliament was plodding ahead with some corporate sense, not unanimity but practical harmony. Private business proliferated and resolutions were being made to hear no more for specified periods, resolutions easily broken. Soon specific days were put aside for private business but no one contemplated stopping it altogether. One might suspect a conspiracy by obstructions to use it to bring the machine to a halt, but its provenance from so many different directions suggests otherwise. The proliferation of private petitions and private Bills argues a

---

[16] Full references for this paragraph and some others are too numerous to give here. They are chiefly to *C.J.* vii and Burton, *Diary*, i and ii.

[17] The Acts are listed in *C.J.* vii. 459.

respect for parliament, an inkling of its role as trustee of the members of the commonwealth, a place for redress, a court of last—sometimes first—resort. If private business had been effectively excluded the whole atmosphere of the House would have changed, as some members pointed out. If too much private business discouraged some members from attending, others came precisely because there was private business. Not every private matter was of minor significance. Any might lead to a discussion on a point of principle or precedent that could have far-reaching consequences, and members were quick to see these things and express their fears. Moreover, a local or a private initiative could provide an example for a national provision. The Bills for improving ministers' maintenance on a local basis were an argument for keeping up discussions for a general Bill to resolve one way or other one of the most difficult of all public issues in the period, one which Cromwell had referred to, with no great guidance, in his opening address.

Working through the *Journals* and Burton's *Diary* we can see the role of private business extending. No wonder some impatient men complained that it jostled all else out. But one notices two other things. First, that in spite of everything some great matters got the attention they deserved—Naylor's case, the new constitution—mostly by lengthening the working day, the House sitting in the afternoons (sometimes until after dark, and on a couple of occasions going without its dinner), committees meeting now and then at seven in the morning. Secondly, no one wanted to exclude private business permanently. When priority was given to certain matters—'the first business', 'nothing to intervene'—it was sometimes given to private Bills. This meant that the time-schedule got out of hand. A reading set for a particular day was postponed to another, sometime *diem in diem*. A few Bills disappear altogether, a committee ceases to meet and has to be revived. Much depended on the determination and regularity of the backers of particular measures. With days for reading or reporting so uncertain chance might play an important part in the fate of a measure—illness or a pre-engagement on outside affairs prevent attendance. Burton was put off coming once by heavy rain. Some were bored by the debates and left before a vote. On a couple of occasions the whole House grew weary, debates ground to a halt while members looked at one another in puzzled silence or collapsed in laughter. No amount of management by subtle politicians could ensure certitude in an age in which what men called 'parties' were merely shifting groups of individuals whose 'interests' would only rarely rise into principles and whom there were no whips to bring into line. Professor Trevor-Roper believes that Cromwell's parliaments might have been easily managed, indeed at times were, though not by himself. The evidence for this session of parliament can be read through to a different conclusion.

No Bills, public or private, came up for protectoral assent between November 1656 and June 1657. But at no time did the legislative process grind to a halt, in spite of the distractions of Naylor's case and the long-drawn-out framing and acceptance of a new written constitution. It meant more or less regular afternoon as well as morning sittings. On 19 February it was resolved to meet at 8 a.m. every day (except

Sunday), to have a private Bill read and then to receive reports from committees till 10 a.m., when supply should be considered. Soon afterwards Saturday all day was put aside for money and later even more time was scheduled. No one quite forgot that it was for money that the House had been summoned and that too cavalier an attitude to the government's needs would put its survival at risk. From time to time resolutions were made deferring private business for periods of a week or more. By the time the Humble Petition and Advice was presented the excise, assessment, and other revenue Bills were well out of schedule in spite of resolutions to quicken the pace. The Protector's seemingly dilatory consideration of his reply dissipated the elation that some members had shown in 'the time of hammering' of the Petition. Attendance figures dropped and remained low for the remainder of the session. But the rejection of the Crown and the acceptance of the revised, many might have said 'emasculated', petition was followed by a stepping up of work on Bills public and private in the expectation of a new installation of the Protector. It was argued by some (including the Speaker and the Master of the Rolls) that all Bills not completed would be automatically on 'the changing of the government'. Others thought that no Bill could now become law without the concurrence of 'the other House'. The final decision was that all Bills presented to the Protector before the end of the session would be of force. Bills still in the pipeline could still go forward in a second session. It encouraged action.

On 25 May in accepting the Petition Cromwell had spoken of what the parliament was doing and could do for 'the liberty' and 'for the good of these nations'. Next day the House resolved to take on no new private business for a fortnight. The debate was a lively one. Major-General Whalley was for 'meddling with none for a month, but what you are already possessed of'. A former member of the Long Parliament, Denis Bond, preferred a week since 'if you have not private business, you will have no House'. Mr Speaker agreed, 'for when private business was excluded for two months, you did less public than when you took in private'. 'Haply you may not sit a month', he went on—the date for prorogation though not yet fixed was expected to be an early one. Mr. Disbrowe was 'sorry that private business should be the only reason of the House coming together', but it was so. 'I have known private business hinder men from coming, I mean by excluding private business such as have not a day fixed'. Sir Gilbert Pickering sagely suggested no exclusion at all, 'because of the difficulty to distinguish'. The House could decide on the nature of each measure as it came up. It was 'equal that poor people that cry to you should be relieved'—whether by a private measure or a public.[18]

The knowledge that adjournment would be towards the end of June was a spur— but to private as well as public business, though some argued that 'your time will not afford it'. For Major-General Disbrowe 'our life and being [was] to perfect the Petition and Advice'. Someone else told the Speaker 'if you will go on with private business'—as he was notoriously inclined to do—'and leave the public, you may sit

---

[18] Burton, *Diary*, ii, 133-4.

by yourself'.[19] In the event June was a hectic month, with morning and afternoon sittings. If the money Bills advanced, so did some private ones. A proviso to a Bill 'for settling Blarney Castle, etc., upon Roger Boyle, Lord Baron of Broghill . . . in satisfaction of all his arrears and demands unto 28 June 1650' aroused particular interest. Col. Castle could not 'but observe the great zeal of this House in private business and so careless of the public'. He wanted no private debts paid till the public were satisfied. Lambert was 'not against the thing but the manner of it' and appealed to procedure to delay it—a thing he was not always inclined to do. But Col. Jephson, an Irish member, close and known to be close to Broghill, and the man who had first raised the notion of kingship in this parliament, expostulated that 'when you are upon acts of private justice, you are always minded you neglect the public. I wish those gentlemen's memories would serve them to tell it you some other time.' In the end the proviso was accepted but only after a division. References in the debate to dangerous precedents underline how any private business could be related to the public welfare.[20]

When the House assembled at 8 a.m. on Monday 8 June there was no minister to take prayers. Some were for going on without them but Bampfield insisted that there could not be such haste in business that they could not wait 'to take a blessing along with them'. 'Some said the Speaker used to exercise in the absence of a minister. Others said, the Clerk; but nobody coming, the House proceeded without any prayer.' Immediately 'a long bill for naturalizing' was read the third time 'notwithstanding the late order to exclude all private business'. 'The House grumbled', says Burton, but accepted the fact that Mr. Speaker was determined to get his fees and went on to debate amendments, which relating to trade and revenue, could be shown as 'of public concernment'. Even so, when the Bill passed, Bampfield pointed out it was now past 11.30 'and all taken up with private business'. Somewhat embarrassed the Speaker apologized. He had not thought 'it would have held so long'. 'Till Tuesday se'nnight you shall not have a private bill read.' In the afternoon it was resolved (on the motion of Major-General Disbrowe) that 'nothing shall be admitted to intervene for six days, but that which concerns the raising of money and settling the nations; and that Mr. Speaker do put the House in mind of this order'.[21]

Next day (9 June) the Protector was to give his consent to some Bills. Suddenly Major-General Goffe, 'observing the House at a stand having nothing to do until his Highness give us notice of his being in the Painted Chamber', moved the third reading of 'the short bill' for the relief of Mrs. Bastwick, widow of an egregious victim of Charles I's 'personal government'. There was a half-hearted objection to 'a private business [that] makes a breach in your order'. But, says the diarist, 'the House having nothing to do' passed the Bill which went along with the rest to the Protector.[22] Thirty-eight Bills passed that day, eight or nine of them public (an assessment of Ireland, settling the postage, abolishing purveyance, repressing vagrancy, etc.). The Act for mitigating the rigour of forest administration in the Forest

[19] Ibid. 170–1.   [20] Ibid. 175–9.   [21] Ibid. 191–6.   [22] Ibid. 204.

of Dean is a doubtful one but Scobell later included it among the public Acts of this parliament. The private measures included several for naturalization, for the improved maintenance of ministers in various localities (pending a general Act any member could bring in a particular Bill and several had done so), the breaking of certain entails and changing the day of Carlisle market. Another rag-bag, some obviously significant, others 'of little consequence'. Some had been on the anvil for months, others were quite fresh.[23] Their passage left a great mass of Bills still to be processed, some of them obviously major measures, all potentially controversial, such as the Bill for 'the continuation of several Acts and Ordinances made since 20 April, 1653', a date whose significance was obvious. These things would have made the closing weeks of the session busy enough, without the Additional Petition and Advice pressed by Secretary Thurloe who was now very much in evidence in proceedings. There were some long and lively debates. Under the strain the Speaker fell ill. But the pace did not slacken. On 24 June they sat till 9 p.m. with candles brought in. On the 25th, last day but one of the session, they were still debating the detail on third reading of the Bill for Attainder of the Irish Rebels. 'Provisos came in so throngingly' till 1 p.m. 'that the House was forced to vote that all . . . not now brought to the table should not be heard'.[24] Half-way through the debate Burton's *Diary* for this session peters out as if exhausted by the effort all were making. Next morning a Bill 'for amending the river Ouse at and near the City of York' passed. A Bill for adjourning parliament until 20 January 1657–8 was read twice, committed, engrossed, reported, discussed, and passed. Time was almost up. In a faintly royal ceremony on 26 June the Protector consented to twenty-two Bills, including the Additional Petition. Later that afternoon the House resolved to have their public Acts printed at the public charge and a collection of Acts and ordinances made since 1640 to be made and published by their Clerk, Henry Scobell. The session was over. Members dispersed leaving hopefully on the books a mass of uncompleted Bills against the next session. But in fact the legislative work had been achieved.[25]

During the hurried second reading on the morning of 26 June of 'the bill for the adjournment of this present parliament', a clause was added after the words 'until the 20th day of January next ensuing': 'at which time all such persons as have been duly elected and returned to serve in this present parliament, being qualified according to the qualifications in the Humble Petition and Advice, and not disabled thereby, are required to give their attendance accordingly'.[26] It meant the excluded members and those who had voluntarily withdrawn could come back—a triumph for liberty and parliamentary privilege. It was also a disaster. Nominations to the other House of men apt for its functions as envisaged by the framers of the Petition meant that the Commons was deprived of some of its best members, experienced as well as loyal, able to do things in a parliamentary way. Their empty benches were to be filled with men of diverse viewpoints and capacities, but among them ex-Rumpers

---

[23] For the list of the Acts passed, see *C.J.* vii. 52–3.
[25] *C.J.* vii. 577–8.
[24] Burton, *Diary*, ii. 305.
[26] Ibid. 575.

like Hesilrige and Scott, embittered but self-confident, voluble, agile, and by now quite negative in their approach to the problems of settlement. Remedial legislation, public or private, had little appeal to them. Instead once settled in they began in the words of Ludlow, a sympathizer, 'to call in question all that had been done in the former session'. This would have undone not only the Humble Petition and Advice, whose ambiguities bred quibbles anyway, but have torn up a mass of legislation, public and private, some of it still in draft, most of which had seemed to help to settle men's estates and to provide for the nation's welfare. Worse, Hesilrige and his cohort grabbed the opportunity for discord offered by the uncertain status and function of 'the other House'. They made a great deal of noise, but a reading of the debates suggests that in truth they did not (*pace* Professor Trevor-Roper) have it all their own way. There is irony in the fact that as Black Rod came to the door of the Commons to summon them to hear the Protector's dissolution of the parliament Sergeant John Maynard was asserting his belief that 'a check is necessary upon us'— an echo of the Naylor debates—and putting a motion 'that you will call them by the title of Lords'. But by then it was too late. Alarmed at 'a spirit of contradiction' everywhere about him, set off he suspected (perhaps so advised by 'some fierce men and flatterers') by the proceedings of the Commons, the Protector had decided on abrupt dismissal. 'Let God be judge between me and you'. 'At which *many*'—not all —'of the Commons cried, "Amen" (4 February 1657/8.)'[27]

If parliaments were in the interests of the nation, as many men in the seventeenth century believed and some still do, then it was worth keeping them in being. Inept parliamentary tactics had forced Charles I into an 'Eleven Years' Tyranny', which but for such external accidents as the Scots rebellion might have led to a permanent royal ascendancy, if not absolutism on the continental model. Cromwell might consider he had suffered in the same way. Faults lay on both sides in both instances, it is true, but the second session of the 1656–7/8 parliament showed that something could be done given goodwill in reciprocity. What was achieved then was hastily thrown away in the second session—in the name, but perhaps not really in the cause, of liberty. True, Cromwell was frustrated and died, the protectorate of Richard soon collapsed, while in a few more parliamentary debates Hesilrige, growing almost as tedious as the senile Sir Walter Erle, was able to 'speak 'till four o'clock'.[28] But there was no ready and easy way to establish a free commonwealth. Very soon Charles II was back on his throne. Hesilrige was in the political wilderness, and Scott was dying bravely but to no great purpose on the block.[29]

[27] C. H. Firth, ed., *The Memoirs of Edmund Ludlow*, 2 vols., Oxford, 1894, ii. 33; Trevor-Roper, op. cit. 384–5; Burton, *Diary*, ii. 461–2; Abbott, op. cit. iv. 728–32.

[28] Burton, *Diary*, ii. 437.

[29] The most recent consideration of the fall of the republic is by A. Woolrych, 'Last Quests for a Settlement 1657–1660', in G. E. Aylmer, op. cit. 183–204, 213, 232–4.

The Financial Settlement in the Parliament of 1685

C. D. CHANDAMAN

THE parliament of 1685 has received a notably bad press from historians. This may be partly attributable to the fact that the composition of the lower House was so obviously partisan and one-sided. Assisted by the strong loyalist reaction which had followed the collapse of the exclusion campaign in 1681 and by the remodelling of many corporations through the Quo Warranto attacks on borough charters, the elections of 1685, skilfully and not too obtrusively supervised by Sunderland, had produced a loyalist Tory landslide. James II is reputed to have said, when the election returns were known, that there were not above forty members, but such as he himself wished for. It is not, however, the party bias or the committed loyalty of the parliament which comes under direct fire but the apparent timidity and servility of its behaviour, a weakness thrown into sharper relief by the formidable, independent-minded nature of the parliaments— the Exclusion Parliaments of 1679–81 and the Convention Parliament of 1689— which preceded and followed it. Burnet considered that 'in all England it would not have been easy to have found five hundred men, so weak, so poor, and so devoted to the court, as these were', so 'resolved to recommend themselves to the king by putting everything in his power'.[1] This is the opinion of a prejudiced Whig observer, but the most judicious of recent writers on the period epitomizes modern historical opinion on the parliament of 1685 when he describes it as 'servile' and 'ultra subservient'.[2] And in no respect, we are given to understand, was this servility so clearly and so dangerously shown as in the financial settlement at the beginning of the new reign, when a Catholic king with authoritarian leanings was so lavishly over-supplied that he was freed from any possibility of parliamentary restraint. 'Never before or since', says James's best biographer, 'has there been a Parliament so lavish of public money, and they had not the excuse that they were working in the dark: they were well aware that Charles had had to do his best with a supply calculated to yield a revenue of £1,200,000, and that if it had not fallen short of the estimate he would have had almost enough; they knew also that the present charge of government was not more than £1,300,000, and yet they gave the King . . . a revenue little less than

---

[1] G. Burnet, *History of My Own Time*, ed. M. J. Routh, Oxford, 1833, iii. 17, 94–5.
[2] J. R. Western, *Monarchy and Revolution: The English State in the 1680s*, London, 1972, 80, 356.

two millions.'[3] A more recent writer goes even further in condemnation of the
'unparalleled generosity' of the grants made to James II in 1685: 'Fuddled by loyalty,
bemused by his threatening injunction to "use me well", the House of Commons
voted him an unconditional revenue little short of £2 million per annum. It was a
piece of craven irresponsibility.'[4] It is the purpose of this article to try to demonstrate
that these strictures on the parliament of 1685 are to a large extent unjustified.

That the parliament should have acted with such reckless prodigality seems on the
face of it inherently improbable. The ethos of Toryism placed as much emphasis on
loyalty to the established Church of England as on loyalty to the Crown and to
suppose that the post-1681 reaction in favour of the monarchy blinded the members of
parliament in 1685 to the risks involved for the national church in the accession of a
Catholic king is to ascribe to them a degree of trusting naïveté which is simply not
supported by the evidence. Far from their showing any eagerness to over-endow the
new king, there appears to have been a move, among the members gathering in
London before the opening of the parliament, to limit the revenue grant to James
to a period of three years at a time, instead of granting it for life as with his predecessor, in order to ensure that 'Parlaments might be consulted the oftner'.[5] Burnet,
with his determinedly low opinion of this parliament as viewed from his refuge
abroad, considered that this move was 'a little talked of' and supported by only
'some few'; but Reresby, who was himself a member of the parliament, maintains
that revenue limitation was 'the question', and it apparently took a preliminary
meeting of M.P.s arranged by Ailesbury and a sharp warning on this point by the
king in his opening speech to the parliament, to lay this particular bogy.[6] As a typical
Tory squire of the middling sort, Reresby doubtless expressed the opinion of the
bulk of his fellow members, whom he describes as 'loyall gentlemen . . . however,
good patriots and Protestants', when he says: 'In all this concern I ressolved to doe my
duty to the Crown, but yet with a good conscience to my religion and country.'
And what this good Tory conscience might require was to be demonstrated very
soon after the opening of the parliament. In spite of James's assurance, both informally
at his accession and more publicly in his opening speech to the parliament on 22 May,
that he would maintain the existing position in church and state as it was then by
law established, the loyal Tory Commons nevertheless unanimously decided on 26
May, much to James's anger, to address the king to put the penal laws in execution
against all non-Anglicans.[7] It is true that an expression of James's intense displeasure
at this implied mistrust of his word secured the withdrawal of the intended address

[3] F. C. Turner, *James II*, London, 1948, 273–4. I omit Turner's assertion that the parliament also granted
James a capital sum of 'four millions at once', a wholly mythical grant which results from a misinterpretation of the evidence.

[4] H. Roseveare, *The Treasury: The Evolution of a British Institution*, London, 1969, 67.

[5] *Memoirs of Sir John Reresby*, ed. A. Browning, Glasgow, 1936, 362.

[6] Burnet, iii. 17, 39; Reresby, 362; *The Memoirs of Thomas Bruce, Earl of Ailesbury* (Roxburghe Club
1890), i. 100–1; *L.J.* xiv. 9.

[7] *Parliamentary History of England*, ed. W. Cobbett (1806–20), iv. 1357; Reresby, 368–9.

and induced the Commons to express their willingness to rest content with 'His Majesty's gracious word and repeated declaration to support and defend the religion of the Church of England as it is now by law established; which is dearer to us than our lives',[8] but the whole episode bears unmistakable witness to the existence of some anxiety on the score of religion. That in spite of this anxiety the Commons should not only have abandoned the idea of limiting the duration of the revenue grant but should deliberately have bestowed on James a financial settlement so lavish as to free him from all possibility of parliamentary restraint and indeed to equip him for a considerable extension of his activities in a variety of unknown, and possibly undesirable, directions, is one of the unexplained mysteries of James's reign.

There can be very little doubt that this mystery arises from a misinterpretation of the facts of the financial settlement. These can be simply stated. At his accession, James automatically entered into possession of the hereditary revenues of the Crown, that is to say, the whole of the ordinary revenue of Charles II apart from the customs and that half of the excise which had been granted to Charles for life in the Restoration settlement. The question of the ordinary revenue settlement in 1685 therefore related solely to these revenues and it was over the possible limitation of these grants that the initial difficulties arose. The fact that these revenues accounted for something approaching two-thirds of the total yield of the ordinary revenue underlines the importance of the issue and helps to explain why James marred the generally reassuring moderation of his early actions as king by continuing to collect these expired revenues without legal authorization during the interval between his accession on 6 February and the first meeting of parliament on 19 May. There can be little doubt that, as he told the French ambassador, he intended by this move (justified as it was by pretty flimsy pretexts) to force the parliament's hand in the matter of securing the regranting of these revenues to himself for life.[9] The fact that the parliament ultimately yielded to these pressures is hardly surprising. Given James's assurances on the score of religion, the fact that he had already in effect taken possession of the revenues in question, and that a refusal to regrant them to him for life (particularly in the face of his direct demand) would be a major, and in the case of the customs even a revolutionary, departure from past practice, it would have been much more surprising if the parliament had indeed embarked upon this startling innovation. On 30 May, apparently without further discussion and maintaining a tactful silence on the subject of the unauthorized collection of the revenues since February, the parliament granted to James for life the expired life revenues of his brother.[10] This was the revenue

---

[8] *C.J.* ix. 721.

[9] J. Dalrymple, *Memoirs of Great Britain and Ireland*, 1771–3, ii. 103–4. The continued collection of the customs was justified on the ground that an intermission would cause confusion in trade, but as Burnet points out (iii. 9–10) this could have been avoided by simply taking bonds for the later payment of the duties after their regrant by parliament. The pretext in the case of the excise was that Charles had entered into a farming contract a few days before his death, but this 'farm' was fictitious.

[10] *L.J.* xiv. 21; 1 Jac. II, c. 1.

settlement of 1685, the first and most important element in the general financial settlement.

In graciously accepting what he had been determined to obtain, James drew the attention of the Commons to the debts left outstanding by his brother, the depleted condition of the Navy and Ordnance, and the expense which would be involved in suppressing Argyll's rebellion in Scotland (a point reinforced by the landing of Monmouth in England on 11 June) and asked for additional supplies for these purposes. The Commons responded with three grants. Two—additional customs duties on wine and vinegar for eight years from midsummer 1685 and on tobacco and sugar for the same period—were for the payment of outstanding debts and for making good deficiencies in the Navy and Ordnance.[11] The third—a combination of additional customs and excise duties on linen, silk, and spirits for a period of five years from 1 July 1685—was to defray the cost of suppressing the rebellion.[12] This was the full extent of the grants made to James II. A further supply projected later in the year for the temporary maintenance of the additional forces raised to deal with the rebellion was caught up in the dispute over the appointment of Catholic officers and was lost in the prorogation of 20 November.

That these additional grants all took the form of indirect taxes imposed for a period of years—a type of taxation normally associated with the provision of ordinary revenue—has tended to obscure the essential fact that they were not in any sense additions to the royal revenue but extraordinary supplies to meet specific extraordinary expenses. On the face of it, it does seem surprising that indirect taxation over a period of years, rather than one of the recognized forms of direct taxation capable of yielding a fairly rapid lump sum, should have been so generally used in 1685 for the purpose of extraordinary supply, particularly in the case of the Monmouth rebellion which raised, in however modest a form, those considerations of national emergency, as in war, for which direct taxation had hitherto been regarded as particularly appropriate. The reasons for this unusual concentration on indirect taxation as a means of extraordinary supply in 1685 are tolerably clear. 'Such a landed Parliament', says Ailesbury, 'was never seen',[13] and it is hardly surprising that the members should have felt in a particularly keen form that disillusionment with direct taxation which had grown steadily during the reign of Charles II because of its tendency, despite all efforts to ensure an equitable distribution, to come unerringly to rest with its main weight upon land. The government itself appears to have strongly favoured the use of taxes on trade. James apparently told Ailesbury, who was much in his favour at this time, that the supply ought not to be raised by the taxation of land because this was the last resource in war. ' "Lay it", said he "on Luxury, as chocolate, tea, coffee, East Indian commodities as not necessary for the life of man and" (with warmth) "on wine", (for he was a most sober prince).'[14]

---

[11] Ibid. c. 3 and 4.
[13] Ailesbury, i. 98.
[12] Ibid. c. 5.
[14] Ibid. 105.

His financial advisers, Sir Dudley North and the Chancellor of the Exchequer, Sir John Ernley, who piloted the new duties through the Commons, may not have shared their master's moralizing sentiments but doubtless recalled, from the experience of Charles's reign, that indirect taxes were more difficult to tailor to a precisely delimited yield.[15] The experience of Charles's reign had also shown that it was perfectly practicable to use duties granted for a term of years as a fund of credit for an immediate supply, so that with government and parliament both agreed on the desirability of using indirect taxation there was nothing to prevent the adoption of this method in 1685 even for the urgent purpose of suppressing the Monmouth rebellion.[16] But if the method adopted for the additional grants of 1685 calls for some explanatory comment, the nature of the grants themselves does not. They were, quite simply, extraordinary supplies granted for extraordinary purposes and, although the additional duties were collected by the existing customs and excise organizations, they were accounted for quite separately from the yield of the ordinary revenue.

To judge the parliament of 1685 by what the financial settlement produced rather than by what it was expected to produce is to fall into the simplest kind of historical error. Viewed from the standpoint of contemporary intention and expectation, the settlement appears in a very different light from that in which it is seen, with the advantage of hindsight, by later observers. In regranting the expired life-revenues to James II for life, the Commons bestowed upon him, in conjunction with the hereditary portion, precisely the same ordinary revenue as had been granted to Charles II in the Restoration settlement, a revenue which had then been estimated to be worth £1,200,000 per annum and which had for twenty years conspicuously failed to produce this sum. It is true that with improving economic conditions the yield of the ordinary revenue had been in process of expansion during the closing years of Charles's reign, bringing it for the first time up to, and indeed beyond, its estimate, but even if we assume that the ordinary member of parliament in 1685 possessed reliable knowledge of recent financial developments, or means by which such knowledge could have been acquired, an investigation into the accounts of the last full financial year, 1683–4, would have shown a net revenue yield of little more than £1,300,000[17]—an increase of approximately £100,000 over the revenue projected

[15] The government may well have been influenced also by mercantilist considerations. In again supporting indirect taxation to provide the abortive supply for the forces later in the year, Ernley expressed the opinion that 'a Tax on Commodities . . . for balancing of Trade, may better be charged than not' (A. Grey, *Debates of the House of Commons, 1667–94*, 1763, viii. 356–7).

[16] This grant contained explicit credit provisions designed to make the bulk of the supply available immediately (1 Jac. II, c. 5, s. 7). The Commons had originally considered a tax on new buildings about London for this purpose, but this was soon dropped (Grey, viii. 351).

[17] Here and later in this article figures for the total yield of the revenue in any given year are based upon the dovetailing of numerous separately calculated components, for which it is impossible to give full explanation and references here except at inordinate length. Full documentation of the total revenue figures will be provided in my forthcoming book on *The English Public Revenue, 1660–88*; meanwhile, anyone wishing to check the figures given should consult my doctoral dissertation of this title in the

at the Restoration which could hardly have been regarded as excessive for the purpose of the new settlement in view of the increase of normal governmental expenditure since that time.[18]

Similar considerations apply with equal force to the additional supplies. The grant for the suppression of the Monmouth rebellion presents no problem. The cost involved was estimated, with an unavoidably high degree of conjecture, at £400,000 and the new silk, linen, and spirit duties were calculated to produce this sum.[19] Unfortunately, owing to the meagreness of the evidence of parliamentary debates at this time, we possess no reliable parliamentary estimate of the value of the other grants, made for the liquidation of debts and the refurnishing of the fleet and stores.[20] But we are not without fairly strong indirect evidence of the value placed upon these grants. The wine and vinegar duties imposed in 1685 were a precise repeat of duties which had been granted to Charles II in 1670 and which had then been in force for more than a decade.[21] During the years of their uninterrupted operation, 1670–7, years of quite buoyant trade before the constriction imposed by the three-year parliamentary prohibition of trade with France in 1678, these duties had produced an average of £137,250 per annum[22] and it is difficult to see how the dutiful Commons, expertly guided by North and Ernley, to whom this knowledge was available, could have placed a value on the same duties in 1685 much in excess of this figure. No previous estimate of the tobacco and sugar duties was available, but they were to prove, on the whole, slightly less productive during James's reign than the duties on wine and vinegar, and it seems unlikely, in view of the experienced guidance of North in particular, with his extensive personal knowledge of foreign trade, that they were rated at a much higher value.[23] If we assume that the two grants were regarded as of roughly equal value, it therefore appears probable that the additional duties granted in 1685 to free the new king from debt and to make good the earlier neglect of the fleet and stores were designed to produce around £275,000 per annum, or about £2,200,000 during the eight years of their operation.

The generosity of this grant can only be judged by reference to the needs it was designed to supply and, in particular, to the size of the debt which was bequeathed by Charles II to his successor. The latest detailed estimate, during the reign of Charles,

Institute of Historical Research (University of London). In all cases, except where otherwise stated, years cited later in this article refer to the financial year from Michaelmas to Michaelmas.

[18] An estimate made at the opening of James's reign shows a level of normal expenditure, even allowing for an inflation of pensions, not far short of £1,300,000 per annum (B.M., Add. MS. 15896, ff. 56–56d).

[19] *C.J.* ix. 740; Grey, viii. 351.

[20] Clarges's estimates in November (ibid. 363) are plainly exaggerated in order to reinforce his argument against making any further supply for the newly raised forces. This is shown, in the one case which we can check, by his over-stating the estimated value of the grant for the suppression of the Monmouth rebellion by about 50 per cent and by other wild calculations.

[21] Compare the rates in 22 Car. II, c. 3 (extended for three years to 1681 in 30 Car. II, c. 2) with those in 1 Jac. II, c. 3. [22] B.M., Sloane MS. 3329, f. 116.

[23] For the work of North as a financial adviser to the government at this time, see *Lives of the Norths*, ed. A. Jessopp, London, 1890, ii. 209–12.

of the floating debt of the government (i.e. excluding the 'funded' debt to the bankers resulting from the Stop of the Exchequer) relates to the position in March 1683 and shows the following:[24]

Anticipations on the three great revenue branches	£682,069
Departmental debts and arrears	£841,816
Arrears of salaries and pensions	£504,140
Other particulars	£12,000
	£2,040,025

The closing years of Charles's reign, in contrast to what had gone before, were years of revenue increase, careful management, and debt reduction, and there can be little doubt that the debt shown in March 1683, itself a reduction from the level in 1681, was further reduced by February 1685 when James succeeded to the throne. Only in the case of the anticipations on the three great branches of the revenue do we possess positive evidence of the extent of the reduction—to £549,747 at the time of Charles's death.[25] Since the anticipations were the most public and pressing of the interest-bearing debts, with a direct claim on the revenues upon which they were secured, there can be no reasonable doubt that their repayment carried a higher priority than the other elements of the floating debt, but even if we assume (most improbably in the case of the arrears of salaries and pensions which showed a tendency to progressive accumulation rather than decrease) a proportional reduction in the floating debt as a whole of the same magnitude as that in the anticipations, it is difficult to see how the debt bequeathed by Charles to his successor could have been less, on the most optimistic valuation, than about £1·6 million–£1·7 million, if it was not substantially more.[26] In relation to a debt of this size, the need to make some provision for interest (since the liquidation of the debt was to extend over a period of years), and the expense involved in building up the Navy and Ordnance, which had been allowed to run seriously down, a parliamentary supply designed to produce around £2,200,000 cannot be regarded as excessively generous, let alone as wildly extravagant.

In view of what has been said, it is difficult to sustain the charge of irresponsibility in the financial settlement of 1685. It seems tolerably clear that what the Commons intended to do, in the various grants they made, was to furnish the king, in the manner of the Restoration settlement, with a permanent ordinary revenue roughly commensurate with the current level of ordinary governmental expenditure, to free him from the encumbrance of debts and deficiencies inherited from his predecessor, and to defray the cost of suppressing a rebellion against him. If any charge at all

---

[24] B.M., Add. MS. 15896, f. 60. The figures are rounded to the nearest whole pound.
[25] Bodleian, Carte MS. 268, ff. 65–65d; *Accounts and Papers* (1868–9), xxxv (366), pp. 444–5.
[26] Dr. W. A. Shaw, who is on the side of the critics of the parliament of 1685, estimates the floating debt outstanding at Charles's death at £2 million (*C.T.B.* VII. xxxiii).

lies against the parliament of 1685, it is not that the members consciously or recklessly over-supplied the Crown, but that they made no real attempt to assess the current value of the ordinary revenue[27] and that, in a period of trade expansion, they chose or were persuaded to grant the additional supplies by the method of indirect taxation. These were sufficiently serious errors, as events were to prove. Two developments, which were destined to falsify all the Commons' calculations, were in unsuspected operation when their apparently reasonable financial settlement was made. One was the rapid growth of the movement of trade expansion since 1681 into a positive boom, which imparted a strong stimulus to the yield of a royal revenue composed overwhelmingly of taxes on trade and consumption.[28] Scarcely less important was the effect of a major reorganization in revenue administration. Of the three great branches of the ordinary revenue, the customs had been brought under direct governmental collection as early as 1671, but the wasteful and restrictive system of farming was abandoned in the Excise and the Hearth Tax only in 1683 and 1684 respectively. Although it took a little time for the full effects to appear, the removal of two of the major revenues from the straitjacket of farming at a time of mounting economic prosperity was also to make a powerful contribution to the expansion of revenue yield. These were developments which it was impossible in the early summer of 1685 for the ordinary members of parliament, mainly Tory squires, to assess. While doubtless aware in a general way of the buoyancy of the economic situation, they could have had no reliable means of gauging its fiscal significance, and the reorganization of the Excise and Hearth Tax was too recent for any accurate prediction of its effects to be made.[29]

The effects can be traced in the revenue figures. The expansion of the net yield of the customs by an average of about £75,000 per annum during the three years 1685–8, compared with the yield in the year 1684–5 during which James's financial settlement was made, had been foreshadowed by trade developments since 1681.[30] Much more startling was the expansion in the yield of the Excise and the Hearth Tax. Under the double stimulus of favourable economic conditions and administrative reorganization, the joint yield of these revenues leapt from approximately £635,000 in 1683–4 to £845,000 in 1687–8.[31] As a result of these developments, the total net yield of the ordinary revenue, which had been little more than £1,300,000 in 1683–4 and only about £1,370,000 even in 1684–5, rose to an average of approximately

[27] In fairness to the parliament, however, it must be recognized that the urgency of the need to settle the revenue, the peremptory nature of the king's demand, and the fact that what he demanded was simply a renewal of a very long-standing grant, containing nothing that was new, made it exceedingly difficult to justify investigation and delay.

[28] The trade boom of the 1680s is shown in the accounts of the Receiver-General of the Customs (P.R.O., Declared Accounts, E. 351/1069–80; A.O. 1/763/833; A.O. 1/764/842).

[29] In the financial year 1683–4, the net yield of the Excise actually fell; it was only during the course of 1684–5 that the real effects of the reorganization began to be felt. A sharp, though temporary, set-back in the rising yield of the customs in the year 1684–5 was also likely to create a misleading impression.

[30] See the accounts referred to in footnote 28.

[31] P.R.O., Declared Accounts, E. 351/1323–8, 1409–13; A.O. 1/1442/2; Tax Accounts, E. 360/204.

£1,600,000 per annum during the three years 1685–8. The additional grants tell the same story. Estimated, if our calculations are correct, to produce about £275,000 per annum the additional duties on wine, vinegar, tobacco, and sugar in fact together produced an average net yield of around £330,000 per annum during the years 1685–8.[32] And the supply for the suppression of the Monmouth rebellion, estimated to yield £400,000 over a period of five years, in fact produced approximately this sum in the period of little more than three years before the Revolution.[33] All in all, James's total receipts from all sources would indeed appear to have amounted to around £2 million per annum during the greater part of his reign.

To say, however, that an income at this level was at the free or 'unconditional' disposal of James is once again to misinterpret the nature of the additional grants. As extraordinary supplies, they were designed, if not committed, to meet the cost of a number of extraordinary charges. The need to suppress the Monmouth rebellion, to take the most obvious example, involved the commitment of funds to an unavoidable extraordinary expenditure; and so too, though in a less compulsive form, did the obligation to pay the debts of Charles II and to remedy the depleted condition of the Navy and Ordnance. Whatever his other failings, James was a man of probity in financial matters and clearly made a genuine effort to pay off the debts of his brother. The extent to which he succeeded in doing so, before the Revolution supervened, is not entirely clear, but according to an estimate submitted to the Convention Parliament early in 1689 he appears to have reduced the anticipations to approximately £278,000 and the departmental debts to about £300,000 by the time the Revolution occurred.[34] If we add to these reductions, the payment of more than £265,000 on arrears of salaries and pensions,[35] about £60,000 in interest on the Stop debt,[36] and some unidentifiable, but not negligible, sum for interest on the diminishing debt by anticipations, then it appears that the total amount expended by James in honouring his brother's obligations cannot have been very far short of £1 million. The additional expense involved in restoring the Navy and Ordnance to full efficiency cannot be easily separated from ordinary expenditure on these departments but what evidence we have suggests that it was fairly substantial. There is no evidence of additional expenditure under these heads up to the spring of 1686 and the Exchequer account of issues for the half-year Easter–Michaelmas 1686 is unfortunately missing, but if we compare the Exchequer issues to the Navy and Ordnance for the two years 1686–8 with the average for the three years 1681–4 we find an increase of nearly £150,000 per annum.[37] Some part of this increase almost certainly reflects the repayment of departmental arrears outstanding on the Navy and Ordnance at Charles's death, which has already been allowed for in the calculation of debt

[32] P.R.O., Declared Accounts, E. 351/958–61, 988–91, 1146, 1148–9, 1212–14.

[33] P.R.O., Declared Accounts, E. 351/1019–22, 1178–80; B.M., Harl. MS. 1898, ff. 66–7, 6013, ff. 8–9; Add. MS. 11597, ff. 44–5.

[34] *C.J.* x. 55.   [35] Bodl., Carte MS. 268, ff. 65–65d; *C.T.B.* viii. 929–30.

[36] P.R.O., Declared Accounts, E. 351/1317–28; A.O. 1/897/35.

[37] P.R.O., Declaration Books, E. 405/322–5, 327, 410–15; *S.P.* 46/154 i and ii.

reduction, but it seems most unlikely that this factor alone can account for an increased expenditure of this magnitude.

The additional grants of 1685, which are often so casually included in calculations of James's 'revenue', would therefore appear, in spite of the fact that their yield greatly exceeded their estimates, to have made surprisingly little addition to the resources freely available to the king. On the admission of the government's own representatives, the Monmouth rebellion, owing to the comparative ease of its suppression, did not involve the government in an expense of more than about £200,000, so that approximately half of the supply for this purpose was in the nature of a windfall for the king;[38] but if the above assessment of debt reduction and other necessary expenditure on the Navy and Ordnance is correct, the payment of obligations outstanding from the reign of Charles II would appear to have absorbed at least the whole of the sum of a little more than £1 million produced up to the Revolution by the other additional supplies.[39] The resources freely available to James therefore appear to have consisted, as they were intended to consist, basically of the ordinary revenue and it was the unexpected expansion of the yield of this revenue to a level of approximately £1,600,000 per annum during the three years 1685–8, supplemented by some £60,000–£70,000 per annum saved from the Monmouth supply, which was responsible for over-supplying the king. The possession of an income at this level enabled James not only to meet the normal demands of governmental expenditure but to maintain additional military forces costing about £300,000 per annum above the normal establishment, without the need for recourse to parliament.[40] This was a sufficiently disturbing state of affairs, but not quite as potentially disastrous as we are often led to believe. To ascribe to James 'an unconditional revenue little short of £2 million per annum', endowing him with almost unlimited resources with which to finance his attempt to establish an authoritarian regime, is a gross distortion of the true situation during the three years of his reign. With ordinary expenditure running at about £1,300,000 per annum, the maintenance of his standing army would in fact appear to have put him almost at the limit of his resources.[41]

It would therefore appear that there are two fallacies in the accepted view of the financial settlement of 1685. One is the belief that the parliament, however loyal, ever intended to grant to James resources in excess of his legitimate needs; the second, that, even allowing for the unexpected inflation of the yield of the supplies, James ever received an 'unconditional' or freely disposable revenue of £2 million per

---

[38] Grey, viii. 356, 363.

[39] See the accounts referred to in footnote 32.

[40] During the course of James's reign, the military forces appear to have involved an expenditure of approximately £610,000 per annum, compared with £283,000 per annum at his accession (*C.J.* x. 54–5; B.M., Add. MS. 15896, ff. 56–56d; *C.T.B.* vii. 1087).

[41] This is true of the actual period of his reign but might not have remained true if he had reigned longer. Given the rate of his outlay on the obligations inherited from his brother, it seems clear that these would have been completely discharged well before the expiry of the eight years' duration of the additional supplies, so that if James had reigned as long as this he would have gained quite heavily from the whole transaction during the later years.

annum. When the parliament of 1685 becomes the subject of serious historical investigation, a task long overdue, we may predict with some confidence that it will be found to have been far less weak and foolish generally than the opinion of Burnet and other whig writers has led historians to believe. For the time being, however, we have been concerned only with the most damaging criticism levelled against it and from this charge of a reckless prodigality in matters of finance the members of the parliament of 1685 should surely at long last be exonerated.

The Role of the Justice of the Peace in Social Administration

DOROTHY MARSHALL

THE activities of the justices of the peace are in general considered to be of interest mainly to students of legal, constitutional, and administrative history. This is to denigrate these activities. In the study of history, as in much else, the obvious receives little attention. The object of this article is not to throw fresh light on the office of justice of the peace, but rather to direct that light from a different angle, the angle of the social historian. From at least the sixteenth century until 1834, and in rural districts until 1888, to the mass of the population the justice of the peace was the local and visible embodiment of the authority of the State. It is easy to forget the tremendous impact that he could, and often did, exert on the lives of the labouring poor, quite apart from keeping order and punishing crime. In the sixteenth century the magistrates exercised in embryonic form the functions of both a court of industrial relations and a department of social security. To illustrate this point two Elizabethan statutes can be adduced, the Statute of Artificers (1563) and the codification of the poor laws in 1601. By the former the justices in each county, meeting in Quarter Sessions after Easter, were ordered, having regard to 'the plentie or scarcity of the tyme and other circumstances, necessarily to be considered', to draw up official lists of wages for both workers in husbandry and for the major categories of craftsmen and artisans. Such rates, which went into considerable detail, were to be reassessed or confirmed each year. The penalty for giving higher wages than those so ordained was ten days' imprisonment or a fine of £5, at that time a considerable sum; the penalty for receiving higher wages was twenty-one days' imprisonment. This clause by itself placed enormous economic power in the hands of the Bench, but in addition it was the responsibility of the justices to see that the entire provisions of the statute were enforced, being ordered to 'make a special and dyligent inquirie' into the 'good execution of the same' twice a year. Among the clauses to be enforced was that which authorized two justices to order any woman between the ages of 12 and 40, who was unmarried, to be bound as a servant for a year 'for such wages and in such reasonable sort and manner as they shall think mete' on pain of being committed to ward until she agreed. Even a single justice had considerable power over the labouring poor. For instance in hay or harvest time he could order any craftsmen and 'persons as be mete to labour' to work in the fields on pain of spending two days and a night in the stocks if they refused.

If an apprentice suffered ill treatment or neglect at the hands of his master or if the latter found his apprentice idle or insolent, then again a single justice acting alone was empowered either to sort out the difficulty by his 'wysdome and dyscreation' or, if he failed, to refer the matter to Quarter Sessions. No apprenticeship could be voided without the authority of a justice.

Even if the powers of the justices had been limited to the regulation of industry and the fixing of the rewards of labour these must have made them economically influential, but by the end of the sixteenth century both these were already being overshadowed by the part which was assigned to them in the administration of the emerging Poor Law. Though the day-to-day administration was the business of the parish officers, the overseers, and churchwardens, the oversight belonged to the justices. It was they who in theory, though not in practice, appointed the overseers; it was they who passed the parish accounts and who authorized the rates. It was to them that appeals against injustice, whether suffered by paupers or ratepayers, were to be made. Until the end of the personal government of Charles I the justices themselves had been supervised by the Council, acting through the Judges of Assize, but after the Restoration they were left very much to their own devices and to their own initiative; they could be zealous or slack so long as they kept within the framework of the law. Moreover, new legislation in the Act of 1662 had made explicit what had previously been implicit, namely their right to control the mobility of the great mass of the population. After that date any parish officer, on the authority of two justices, could move any persons attempting to gain a settlement in their parish whom the parish might consider 'likely to become chargeable' unless they fell into certain exempt categories, or rented a house of the annual value of £10 when the average labourer paid £2 or £3. It is true that the initiative lay with the parish which, for reasons I have examined elsewhere, made only a limited use of it, but the final decision as to whether poor men and women should be confined to the parish in which they had a settlement or should be allowed to seek better employment elsewhere, lay with a couple of justices with appeal to the Bench at Quarter Sessions if their decision was disputed. The result was to place great economic power in their hands at a time when the population was growing and when industry was not only expanding but was also continually on the move.

Nor did the power of the justices stop there. Originally, the parish had been left to judge to whom and to what extent it should give relief but by 1693 the pressure of the paupers and the kindness, or weakness, of the overseers had made it seem desirable to transfer the responsibility to the justices. Accordingly, a new Act provided that no person should be relieved, except in a state of emergency, until such relief had been authorized by a justice. The Act worked badly. Enterprising claimants, by-passing the parish, had gone to the nearest magistrate who had a reputation for being sympathetic to a poor person's hard-luck story. As Chadwick was later to observe, a shilling a week meant so little to a gentleman that he was apt to award it without any genuine investigation as to the character of the applicant or the circumstances that made it necessary. To stop up this legal loophole a new Act in 1722 said that no pauper was to approach a justice unless he had first been refused by the overseers. In which case the justice was to call both parties before him, a circumstance infinitely more troublesome to a busy man serving the office of overseer than to an idle pauper. But, whether approached first or last, after 1693 the final amount of relief that a poor person could receive was determined by the justice, a responsibility which, viewed from the national angle, placed in their hands power that today would belong to the Department of Social Security and Parliament itself. Any body of men who were legally authorized to control wages (though as industry became more flexible, this power was less and less used), and determine the levels of poor relief, as well as the circumstances in which it was to be granted cannot but be of concern to the student of social history.

From the closing decades of the eighteenth century a growing population and increasing industrialization combined to face the justices with even more formidable versions of these problems. Though the more enterprising of the rural population circumvented the restrictions of the laws of settlement the majority remained on the land rather than seek employment in the growing towns. This meant that in the countryside too many people were chasing too few jobs. Moreover, from a combination of circumstances more and more of them were becoming dependent on the wages they could earn when these were being depressed through competition and when England was facing a period of growing inflation. It was no longer a question of a few unfortunate individuals or families in each parish being forced for a time to rely on the parish but of large sections of the community being unable to earn a living wage. The House of Commons, when urged by Whitebread to pass a minimum wage Bill, refused to do so, probably wisely in face of its own lack of experience in this field of social legislation and of the absence of the administrative machinery which would have made its implementation possible. This meant that the only persons with the authority to do anything were the justices. Their solution has come to be known as 'the Speenhamland system' based on a resolution of the Berkshire justices in 1795 by which, though refusing to fix the wages of day labourers, as by law they were still empowered, they decided to fix a scale of relief to be paid to 'all poor and industrious men and the families who to the satisfaction of the Justices of their Parish shall endeavour (as far as they can) for their own support and maintenance'. In other words they were prepared to supplement the wages of the industrious poor when these fell below a certain level. Too much emphasis is apt to be put on their resolution. They were not the only or even the first set of magistrates to fumble their way to this rate in aid of wages. It was merely an adaptation of an earlier practice of making a small allowance to a man 'over burdened with children'. Though the rate moved up and down with the price of bread there was no uniformity, no 'system'. Each Bench made its own recommendations which varied both as to the amount given and the size of the family needed to qualify. Nevertheless, the policy so haphazardly worked out by the justices of southern England proved to be one of the most important factors influencing the lives of the labouring poor until, some fifty years later, the power of the magistrates to dominate the granting of relief was swept away by the Poor Law Amendment Act of 1834. That a policy the wisdom and propriety of which has been so bitterly debated, both by contemporaries and historians, and which had the most profound influence on the society of their day, should have been left to undirected justices to formulate, is in itself a massive testimony to their social importance. Whether, if some other way of dealing with the crisis had been adopted, or whether, if wages had been allowed to find their own level, the situation of the agricultural labouring poor would have been better or worse is open to argument. What is not open to argument is the decisive part played by the Bench in both framing and implementing a policy so vital to the nation, a policy as a result of which large numbers of their countrymen were forced to accept as charity what in justice should have been part of their wages.

At the same time in the North and the Midlands some justices were becoming increasingly involved in the problems posed by the emergence of a new type of industrial society. To some extent these new activities can be regarded as merely an extension of their traditional ones. The care of poor apprentices and the regulation of the relations between master and man had always been part of their quasi-judicial, quasi-administrative duties. It was natural therefore that when in 1802 Parliament passed an Act to regulate the conditions in which these pauper apprentices could be employed in the new cotton mills that its enforcement should be left to the justices. It is indeed difficult to see to whom else this duty could have been entrusted. Accordingly, it was provided that in every county where such mills were to be found the Bench should appoint two persons, one a clergyman, the other a justice, to visit factories employing pauper apprentices, in order to see that the provisions of the Act were being observed. To ensure the impartiality of such visitors they were to be 'persons not interested in, or in any way connected with any such mills or factories'. It is generally assumed that this supervision was totally ineffective. Such generalization may be too sweeping, at least in so far as it suggests a complete lack of interest on the part of the justices, among whom there were some men of benevolence and driving energy. Even so, an inspection carried out by a country gentleman or cleric quite unfamiliar with the economy of the new mills and dealing with ignorant and bullied children was not likely to be very searching. When Robert Owen, campaigning for legislation to improve the working condition and hours of the so-called 'free children', i.e. those who remained under their parents' protection, he was anxious that paid inspectors should be appointed. This, however, seemed too great a break with tradition and in the 1819 Act enforcement was once again left to the justices. When finally in 1833 three official inspectors replaced them they found themselves both overwhelmed by the number of mills for which they were responsible and constantly thwarted by acts so badly drafted that unscrupulous mill-owners could drive the proverbial coach and horses through them. When it is remembered how many of these small water-driven mills were built in isolated valleys and how difficult even the first paid inspectors, men like Horner, found their task, it is clear that the State had been asking from the justices services which they were no longer fitted to perform.

The same charge can be made with regard to other responsibilities which they were forced to assume in connection with the growing cotton industry. Here again tradition played its part. As early as 1563 the justices had been empowered to arbitrate in a summary way between master and man, a task not beyond the competence of a magistrate of common sense at a time when manufacturing processes were both simple and traditional, but a matter of more difficulty as processes became more elaborate. This practice had a continuing tradition behind it. An act of 1773 for instance gave to the Middlesex Bench and to the Quarter Sessions for the City and Liberty of Westminster the power to fix the rates of pay for the journeymen weavers in the silk manufacture at Spitalfields and later that same year Sir John Fielding reported that this had been done 'by a numerous and unanimous bench to the entire satisfaction of those masters and journeymen weavers who appeared there in behalf of their respective bodies'. The enforcement of the award was left to the magistrates, two of whom could sentence any master who paid either more or less than the official rate to a fine of £50. Journeymen weavers who asked or took more or less wages, or who entered into a combination to do so, or who tried to 'decoy, solicit or intimidate' others to quit his master's service, or any workmen who assembled 'in numbers exceeding the number of ten' to present petitions concerning wages, on the oath of one or more credible witnesses, could be fined forty shillings. If this were not paid immediately the offending workman was to be sent to the House of Correction and put to hard labour of any period up to three months. The only exception to this prohibition against organizing petitions for an increase in wages was when the petition in question was presented to Quarter Sessions itself.

This power of the justices first to settle wages, albeit in consultation with the trade, and then for merely two to enforce the award by fine, backed by imprisonment, gave the magistrates as a body a great deal of power over what would now be called industrial relations. By an act of 1800 they were similarly drawn into disputes in the cotton industry. Here they were to act as final arbitrators if masters and workmen failed to agree on rates of pay, particularly those to be given for new types of work, an important cause of dispute at a time when industry was undergoing continual change and expansion. In the first stages of a dispute each side was permitted to choose its own arbitrators but if these failed to agree then a single justice, after having heard the points at issue, was entitled to settle the matter out of hand. No magistrate who was a cotton manufacturer could act in such cases, a provision which, if it secured impartiality, at the same time denied to both parties the services of an expert who could be expected to understand the finer technical points of the dispute. As in every other sphere of their authority there is the bland assumption that an honest gentleman is competent to give judgement on any matter brought before him.

Such legislation foreshadowed the power placed in their hands by the Combination Acts of 1799 and 1800. These in themselves were mainly a restatement of the views of the ruling classes as to the necessity of disciplining and controlling the labour force: their purpose was not to enact new principles but to provide for their more rapid and sure enforcement. In future two justices were to constitute a court of summary jurisdiction, though an appeal against their sentence could be made to Quarter Sessions. The maximum sentence they could impose was three months' imprisonment. In giving these powers to the magistrates Parliament was following the traditional policy of enforcing the authority of the masters in the interest of a smooth running economy, but by 1799 the motives of ministers and members were at least as much political as economic. Rising prices and the difficulty of keeping markets open under the pressure of the Napoleonic wars led to fluctuations in employment that, as industry expanded, affected more and more people. The world of labour was in ferment, a ferment increased by the post-war depression, and the government was afraid. The heads that had rolled under the guillotine were still a recent memory and the propertied classes were prone to see revolutionary fervour when they should have seen economic desperation. Society itself was changing and an emerging working class, conscious of its own aspirations and identity, was beginning to replace the old labouring poor. The involvement of the justices in the enforcement of the Combination Acts was therefore significantly more socially important than the role they had played in earlier Acts, which had aimed merely at securing the maximum production by the prevention of strikes over wages and hours, because it reveals their attitude towards the industrial strife and political undercurrents of protest that was to characterize so much of the industrial North and Midlands in the early decades of the nineteenth century.

In spite of wide differences in personality and outlook between the individual magistrates it was inevitable that the Bench as a whole should be influenced by the general outlook of the hierarchical society of which they were a part. Though some gentlemen, individuals such as Cartwright and Sir Francis Burdett, held radical views, the propertied classes, from whom the justices were appointed, were 'Establishment men'. They were appointed to 'keep and cause to be kept all ordinances and statutes for the good of our peace'. By the terms of their commission therefore they could not fail to be concerned with industrial unrest when this led to disorder. Of this there was plenty in the first two troubled decades of the nineteenth century. Sometimes this was no more than an orderly parade of weavers; sometimes it took the form of intimidation by their more discontented workmates of men who, left to themselves, would have been willing to work: at moments it even took the form of destruction. In the Midlands the framework knitters broke the frames of masters who employed women and apprentices on the broad frame, which made cheap cut-up goods. In the West, and later in the North, the destructive element was supplied by the croppers, or shearers, who broke the hated gig machines, used for mechanical shearing. Collectively, this army of violent men gave their allegiance to that shadowy figure, King Lud. Even if the local Bench had been inclined to turn a blind eye to the violence engendered by economic suffering the government would have made this impossible. In previous centuries, when the fabric of society seemed unthreatened, ministers at Westminster appear to have interfered very little with the local magistrates but one effect of the long war with France had been to make them anxious to get reports from the justices wherever disorder broke out. Behind their anxiety, which was shared by many of the magistrates themselves, lurked the fear that industrial anarchy was merely the cloak for revolutionary doctrines and that even if the workers themselves had no long-term revolutionary objectives men who had were using industrial unrest to wreck traditional society. As early as 1799 John King, an Under Secretary of State, was suggesting the advisability of infiltrating trusted agents into suspect working-class organizations. Later in 1801, and again in 1818/19, when industrial Lancashire was in a ferment of strikes by both weavers, who for the most part were still handloom weavers, and cotton spinners employed in the new power-driven mills, the ministry kept in close touch with the leading magistrates, sometimes receiving almost daily reports. Even if they had wished to stand aloof they could hardly have resisted this ministerial pressure.

It is clear from the Home Office papers edited by Professor Aspinall that in many cases the justices themselves were only too anxious to seek advice and help from the Home Office. Not all the reports that they sent in were the result of ministerial pressure; some were active and willing instruments in this business. Magistrates such as Colonel Fletcher, John Norris, R. A. Farrington, and the Revd. Robert Hay were in constant touch with Lord Sidmouth and the Under Secretary Hobhouse. From their letters it is possible to reconstruct a detailed, almost blow by blow, account of the workers' grievances and the reactions of the masters, extremely important material which illustrates one facet of early trade unionism. From this correspondence some interesting points emerge. Neither magistrates nor ministers were primarily concerned with the disputes between masters and men over wages. In contrast to earlier beliefs such matters were no longer considered to fall within the province of government. Indeed in 1814 that part of the Statute of Artificers which had provided the machinery for wages to be fixed by Quarter Sessions had been repealed to remove the embarrassment of a law to which most inconveniently, according to *laissez-faire* thinking, the workers could still appeal. What the government feared was that social revolutionaries might use the current economic distress to create political dissatisfaction. The same John King who had urged the desirability of infiltrating trusted agents into suspected associations had also urged that the magistrates should arrange for a meeting of the Bench as soon as possible in order to demonstrate to the weavers that the justices as a whole were sympathetic to their distress and that they were more likely to be more effective in devising means of alleviating it than the ill-disposed and seditious persons who, for their own purposes, were endeavouring to persuade the weavers to take the law into their own hands. Combined with this carrot, by way of a stick, King pressed the magistrates to emphasize their determination to use the full force of the law against any illegal proceedings or any breaches of the peace.

This advice coincided with the attitude of the more active magistrates. Their letters make it clear that they were not necessarily on the side of the masters in the bitter disputes that raged over wages; their sympathies were often with the men. In 1818 the Revd. W. R. Hay expressed the opinion that the employers could well have afforded to raise the wages of their spinners, while three years earlier another clerical magistrate, the Revd. R. Grey, writing to Lord Sidmouth from Wearmouth, told him that the Tyneside seamen had a good case had they not spoilt it by supporting it by illegal methods. Nor did they all see the spectre of political revolution lurking behind every industrial turn-out. For instance in the August of 1818 another magistrate, James Norris, informed Lord Sidmouth that the Lancashire weavers had been very temperate in asking for an increase in wages and that there were no political undertones to their demands. This was an allusion to the clamour for parliamentary reform which a year later was to explode at Peterloo. One reason for holding aloof from wage disputes was, as Norris explained to Sidmouth in another letter, that when the magistrates had to hear cases involving the Combination Acts the workers would be more inclined to accept their judgements as impartial. This attitude did not commend them to the mill owners, who considered that the civil power should have done much more to back them up in their struggles with their recalcitrant work-people. Some of the justices, men like Colonel Fletcher, would possibly have preferred to have done so. He thought a dangerous precedent was established whenever the lower orders succeeded in dictating their own wages and that the result must be a mob oligarchy leading to universal anarchy. Norris was more inclined to blame the spineless behaviour of the manufacturers, who were ready enough to run to the magistrates and ask that the troops be called in whenever the situation threatened to get out of hand but who, faced with the knowledge of an illegal combination, were apt to turn a blind eye and not prosecute for fear of reprisals from the mob. Nobody wanted to be the one to 'bell the cat' but unless the masters were prepared to bring charges there was nothing that the Bench could do to eradicate these illegal combinations which organized and fermented industrial strikes and demonstrations.

The position of the magistrates was therefore a difficult one. However scrupulously they might try to remain on the side-lines the fact that the weapons of the workers were demonstrations backed by crowd violence and the magistrates were responsible for law and order inevitably involved them. This put the more active members of any Bench into situations which were often threatening and could be dangerous. Before the establishment of a local police force, or indeed before the days of any police force, the only method by which the mob could be restrained was to call in the military. But before the soldiers were prepared to go into action a justice had to read an order calling upon the crowd to disperse, a proceeding inaccurately described as 'reading the Riot Act'. When for example a Stockport magistrate, a Mr. Harrison, began to read the proclamation both he, the constables, and the cavalry, who were being held in reserve, had brickbats and stones hurled at them and suffered some injury before the mob, after breaking some windows, dispersed. This respite proved to be only temporary; the crowd next launched an attack on the mill of an unpopular manufacturer, in itself an illustration of the risks a mill owner faced when he took the lead in any struggle against the workpeople. On this occasion windows were broken and several people hurt and some twenty persons arrested before order was restored. Such incidents were not uncommon. Sometimes a tactful and popular magistrate managed to persuade an ugly gathering to disperse, sometimes alarmist messages were sent to the nearest barracks for a troop of cavalry and sometimes violence broke out. Much therefore depended on the calibre of the local magistrates.

Nowhere was this to be so tragically demonstrated as at Peterloo. Here the conflict was not one of wages but a deep fissure between the political 'haves' and the unfranchised masses. It was an event that was to have widespread repercussions on the society of the day; an event that no student of the nineteenth century can ignore. The situation that faced the representatives of the Lancashire and Cheshire Benches was a difficult one. There is evidence that the more 'respectable' Manchester householders were alarmed and in anticipation of trouble the Borough Reeves and Constables of Manchester and Salford had posted up notices advising the 'well-disposed inhabitants' to keep within doors. Undoubtedly, feelings in Manchester were running high and the intention of Orator Hunt to address a huge rally in St. Peter's Fields had alarmed the local magistrates, who had twenty years' experience of the threat to law and order posed by a riotous mob. This makes it easy to understand their feelings when faced by a vast concourse of people who had come into Manchester from the outlying towns, each with its own history of strikes and turbulence. Nevertheless, these crowds, marching under their own flags and banners, were in the beginning a good-tempered crowd, out almost in a holiday mood to enjoy the satisfaction of politically and emotionally charged speechifying. It must be remembered that the magistrates, watching from a near-by house that commanded a view of St. Peter's Fields, had first-hand knowledge of how a crowd, originally peaceful, could be whipped up into violence by fiery oratory. Its grievances were very near the surface. It is easy to condemn the magistrates for waiting until Orator Hunt, the idol of the crowd, had mounted the rostrum and begun speaking before sending in the constables to make an arrest. It is easy to understand why the deputy constable, entrusted with this dangerous task, should ask for the backing of the yeomanry. What followed then has been a matter of continued controversy, some averring that the yeomanry attacked the defenceless crowd, others that an aggressive mob was itself turning to the attack. It is easy to understand the confusion, the bloodshed, and the horror that followed. Whether by a more adroit handling of the situation by the magistrates the great mass rally could have passed off peaceably must always be open to question. There can be no question that to the working classes their handling of the situation was the final demonstration that the magistrates were the representatives of everything that they condemned in contemporary society. In the industrial North such ancient respect as there had been for them vanished with the charge of the cavalry on 16 August 1819.

The rural poor had their own reasons for disliking the magistrates, though this dislike was certainly tempered by the fact that the justice of the peace was, until 1834, often the poor man's best ally against a harsh overseer. The relationship between the justices and the rural poor was governed by non-legal as well as by legal considerations. In the country the magistrate was also the squire, the occupant of the 'Big House', the centre of employment and charity, in short the pivot around which local life revolved. He could therefore exert pressure as a landlord, as an employer (most of his servants came from the village), and in the neighbouring market town as an important customer, as well as being the embodiment of law and order and the authority of the Crown. The average countryman would have been hard pressed to say where the one ended and the other began. So too, for practical purposes, would the justices themselves. This is well illustrated by the dual identity of justice and squire in the enforcing of the hated Game Laws. Here few magistrates could be regarded as impartial; they were judges in their own case and nothing made them more disliked in rural England. The attitude of the various sections of the community to poaching almost more than anything else reveals the hidden tensions in rural society. The average country labourer refused to recognize the snaring or shooting of game and rabbits as a criminal act and suffered from a deep sense of injustice at not being able to supplement an often too meagre diet in this way. The country gentleman, who in the eighteenth and nineteenth centuries was becoming more and more addicted to sport, and who often laid out considerable sums in the stocking of his coverts, regarded the game as his property and his alone, and because country gentlemen predominated in Parliament the Game Laws gave legal sanction to this conviction. Even tenant farmers were usually forbidden to shoot over the land they farmed. The result in many parts of England was almost unofficial war between the gamekeepers and the poachers. Not all the latter were hungry villagers. Organized gangs from the towns were as violent as the smuggling gangs that brought in tea or French brandy. Such men were too often difficult to apprehend; the poacher seized by a gamekeeper and dragged before the justice was more likely to be a local man known to both. Admissible evidence in a countryside where the majority of the inhabitants were in sympathy with the offender was not easy to come by and in consequence the charge often levelled against the justices is that they used their authority in a high-handed manner, accepting the evidence of their own gamekeepers and convicting on flimsy evidence any villager about whom they harboured suspicion. Even if trials of poaching offences had been scrupulously conducted they would still have caused bitter resentment. Two justices could sentence anyone convicted of poaching at night to three months in gaol if he were a first offender and on his release demand that he give security not to so offend again. For a second conviction the penalty was six months in prison with hard labour together with a further year's detention if no surety could be found. A third conviction could lead to seven years' transportation. This was a very great power to place in the hands of prejudiced country gentlemen; the fact that they were able to exercise it in the name of the Crown bred a contempt for the law that exploded in the agrarian riots of the nineteenth century. Here therefore the attitude of the justices must be considered as providing one important ingredient in the unrest that time and again characterize rural society.

Some of the tasks imposed on the justices are interesting not so much because they influenced society, or created tensions within it, as because of the way in which they illustrate contemporary social thinking. Possibly this had its roots in a combination of the tradition of a paternal monarchy and the religious pattern of a medieval past as a result of which the Crown, somewhat spasmodically, continued to regard itself as the guardian of public morality. Overlaid on this substratum of religious and monarchical tradition was the eighteenth- and nineteenth-century conviction that, both from the angle of a stable social structure and from that of a flourishing economy, the mass of the people must be industrious, frugal, and deferential. The result over the centuries had been a series of laws which aimed at achieving these ends by both forbidding undesirable activities and by punishing the outward signs of depravity. There were laws against profane swearing, against tippling in alehouses, against riotous games that might attract and inflame a crowd, against bull baiting or against coursing with dogs on Sundays, all of which it fell to the magistrates to enforce. In the interests of a sober work force they were also entrusted with the licensing of alehouses and the punishment of the persons who tippled within them. After 1729 regular sessions, known as the Brewsters' Sessions, were held each September at some principal inn in a convenient market town. Here licences were granted or revoked, complaints against disorderly alehouses heard, and the character of new applicants for licences investigated. At least this was the theory; how seriously the average magistrate took his duty to keep England moral and sober may be doubted. Their own contemporaries charged the majority of the Bench with laxity, corruption, and favouritism. Whether slackly enforced or not such legislation tended to press more hardly on the poor than on the rich; it was easy if any one cared to do it to drag the village drunkard before the justice, less easy when the offender was a gentleman. This too was in line with eighteenth-century social thinking. The morality of the rich was very much their own concern; that of the poor the concern of society which depended on their sobriety and industry on which its prosperity rested. The attitude of the poor law towards bastardy illustrates this point. Any pregnant unmarried woman could come before a magistrate and swear to the father of her unborn child. The man was then summoned and unless he could give security that the child when born would not be chargeable to the parish he was liable to be clapped into gaol. This was not a punishment for immorality but merely a precaution to prevent him absconding before the birth of his reputed child. In the same way the mother of a chargeable bastard could be imprisoned, though in practice this seldom happened; but to give birth to an illegitimate child was not a punishable offence. In such matters there was very definitely one law for the rich and another for the poor. It was not so much immorality as the economic consequences of immorality that between the Puritan regime and the rise of the Evangelical movement was the concern of Parliament. The conviction that the enforcement of morality in order to save souls was a national concern received official recognition when in 1787 George III issued a Proclamation calling for a stricter enforcement of the laws against vice and immorality. How much the main body of the justices would have responded had it not been for first the formation of a society for the enforcement of the proclamation and later because of the excesses of the French Revolution, which seemed to threaten the stability of society as a whole, must remain open to doubt. It was the combination of these two factors, together with a widespread superstitious fear that England's lack of success against the French stemmed from the Almighty's displeasure with the prevailing laxity in every stratum of society, that made national moral spring-cleaning more acceptable and there is some evidence that the magistrates were more active in this way. In this, as in so much else they mirrored contemporary thinking.

Both the powers conferred on the justices and the social position of the men on whom they were conferred can be used as a barometer to measure changes in the structure of society over the centuries. The early generations of justices were substantial country gentlemen endowed with authority by the Crown as a make-weight to the over-mighty subject. So useful did they prove that by Tudor times, in Lambard's well-known words, their backs were in danger of being broken by stacks of statutes. Until the collapse of the royal authority in the seventeenth century they remained very much an instrument in the monarch's hand but by the eighteenth century they had become almost independent rulers of the county, though technically they still held by pleasure not good behaviour, and as such were liable to the kind of purge to which Walpole in building his Whig supremacy subjected them. But, though for political reasons individuals might be omitted from the commission, the power of the landed gentry in a hierarchical society, where a man's possession was measured by the possession of land, was great. It was to ensure that the wide powers with which they were entrusted remained their preserve that a House of Commons, itself mainly composed of country gentlemen, passed an Act in 1722 which fixed the minimum qualification for the office of justice of the peace as the possession of land to the annual value of £100 because 'the constituting of persons of mean estate to be justices of the peace may be highly prejudicial to the public welfare'. In their person therefore was united all the power and authority that society conferred on the substantial landowner, together with all the authority conveyed by the 'stacks of statutes'. There can hardly be a better example of the close connection between the structure of society and the exercise of power within it than the eighteenth-century justice of the peace.

By the end of the century, however, changes in the structure of society were beginning to be reflected in the changing social standing of the men placed on the commission. This was no longer the almost exclusive preserve of the squirearchy. The system had fitted into the needs of a rural society where people accepted the philosophy of 'the rich man in his castle, the poor man at the gate', and where, in spite of the material gulf between the rich and the poor, both had belonged to a homogeneous society. The squire and the local justice might be benevolent or a bully but both he and the people over whom he exercised authority accepted its habits and practices. They were not alien to one another as later the factory hand was to be alien to the country squire. It was the growing urbanization and industrialization of the late eighteenth and early nineteenth centuries which, by creating a new kind of society, made the old type of justice and the belief that an honest country gentleman was capable of carrying out the duties of the office, inadequate. The problem was twofold. In the first place it was difficult to find the right kind of man to be a justice in such areas. The squirearchy had an instinctive dislike of towns, except for the small market town, which presented no problem, as it was merely an extension of rural society, a gathering place for countrymen. More important county families probably spent some part of each year in London while Parliament was sitting. Less important ones, under female pressure, might spend a couple of the winter months in one of the provincial capitals, such as Norwich, or take the waters at a spa. But fundamentally towns were alien territory; country gentlemen neither understood their problems nor wished to do so. Each year as industrial sprawls encroached upon the countryside their vicinity became less and less attractive to them. Birmingham is reputed to have had no resident magistrate nearer than fifteen miles. In those areas where the need was greatest there was often a chronic shortage of magistrates.

This was particularly true of London, apart from the City, which had its own magistrates and which had always been the preserve of merchants and bankers. Middlesex gentlemen were prepared to deal with county business and to sit on the Bench at Quarter Sessions; they were not prepared to deal with the drunks and drabs that abounded within the city of Westminster and within the urban sprawl that was only technically a part of the county. Because gentlemen were in short supply, though occasionally financial necessity or a sense of duty drove such men as Henry and his half-brother John Fielding to accept office, the gap had to be filled from non-traditional sources. In this way the justice of mean degree and the trading justice came to be well-known figures in the London scene. They were not all necessarily corrupt, though in general they had a bad reputation, but they all of them depended on the fees which they and their clerks were entitled to charge. The greater the business the greater the fees; Fielding described the money that came to them as some of the dirtiest money on earth. Only gradually did it come to be realized that both in London and in the growing towns the solution lay in the appointment of a well-paid and well-qualified stipendary magistrate.

The office of justice of the peace, though honourable, could be troublesome and not all the gentlemen who were placed on the commission were prepared to serve even in the rural areas. In the semi-industrial parts of the North and Midlands there was an actual shortage of landed gentry. In both cases one solution was to include the local beneficed clergy in the commission. Such men were reasonably well educated and perhaps more capable than some country gentlemen of dealing with the increasingly complex cases that came before them. But, though they were exceptions, the appointment of clerical justices tended to widen the gap between the labouring poor and the Established Church. Enforcing the Game Laws in the country and the Combination Acts in Lancashire and Cheshire did little to endear them to the vast majority of their nominal flock. In these counties the second source of supply was provided by the more prosperous mill owners or merchants, though their usefulness was limited by the provisions of several statutes that a justice who was a mill owner might not hear any case in which they or their relatives were involved. That mill owners and manufacturers should have been on the commission at all was in itself a testimony to the changes that were taking place. Formerly, few northern industrialists were substantial landowners; men like Josiah Wedgwood and Sir Robert Peel were the exception not the rule. But in the first decades of the nineteenth century they were buying land, sometimes as investments, sometimes for prestige. Even so, many of the justices who were most active in the industrial troubles of the northern counties were clergymen; John Norris, an active correspondent with the Home Office, was a stipendiary magistrate. In the North and Midlands the traditional pattern was breaking down rapidly in response to social and economic change. In rural England, though their powers were nibbled away by successive legislation, they were still rulers of the counties until 1888.

Though much of what the magistrates did over the centuries was directed to disciplining the mass of the population in order to secure social stability and economic prosperity, a discipline which entailed a constant and considerable interference in their lives, many of the justices' more purely administrative functions were important for society as a whole. Lack of space makes it impossible to examine them, but one at least must be mentioned. Before the coming of the railways England was neither a social nor an economic whole because of the inadequacy of her internal communications. It would be unfair to blame the justices of the peace for the shocking state of many of the country's roads but it is worth remembering that a matter of such economic importance, like so much else, was left to the parishes and the supervision of the Bench, unless they had been relieved of their responsibility by the creation of a Turn Pike Trust. From whatever angle therefore the student of social history looks at the activities of the justices of the peace they are found to be deeply involved in the day-to-day life of the mass of the people. They are part of social, as well as of legal and administrative history.

Jeremy Bentham and the Machinery of Social Reform

URSULA HENRIQUES

I

IF a study is made of the reforms in the poor law, factory regulation, prison administration, sanitation and public health, lunatic asylums, and elementary education carried out in the first half of the nineteenth century, it will be seen that certain elements are apt to recur among them. These elements can be listed as:

1. A series of parliamentary select committees inquiring into a contemporary social problem.
2. In some but not all cases, one or more royal or government commissions also inquiring and proposing solutions.
3. Legislation authorizing a centrally operated inspectorate to enforce the remedy established by law and to impose a degree of uniformity upon local agents.
4. A central body controlling the inspectors and laying down regulations. This could be a brand-new administrative commission (as in the poor law) or a section of an existing government department (e.g. branches of the Home Office for factory regulation and prisons), or the inspectors themselves in corporate form (as in the Lunacy Commission).
5. Where appropriate, an independent unit of local government partly controlled by the central body and its inspectorate.
6. More or less organized voluntary bodies acting as pressure groups for reform, often supplying ideas to the committees and commissions of inquiry, as well as personnel to the subsequent administration, central and local.
7. A voluminous and vigorous debate by pamphlet, periodical, and newspaper.

The last four elements were as interesting and important as the first three. However, it is proposed in this essay to concentrate on examining the use of select committees, royal commissions, and inspectorates. In the second part consideration will be given to an aspect of the controversial question of who was responsible for the development of this machinery of reform.

The opening years of the nineteenth century saw a large number of parliamentary select committees of inquiry. According to Clokie and Robinson there were 543 select committees between 1801 and 1834, many producing a series of reports.[1] Although a traditional and respected method of gathering information, they had limitations. As they were composed of members of parliament, they were tied to the metropolis. They were also tied to the parliamentary session which lasted about five months, and were interrupted, sometimes suddenly, by the end of it. Although frequently reconstituted from session to session, they broke up when parliament dissolved. As Bentham put it, they ran out of time every seven years or earlier.[2] They could compel the production of documents and the attendance of witnesses, and examine the witnesses on oath, often by powers defined in the motion which authorized the committee. However, the House of Commons committees in practice did not do these things while the Lords committees did. Some members sat on several committees, and there were complaints that these were apt to meet simultaneously.

As an instrument for deciding policy and recommending action the parliamentary select committee also had limitations. House of Commons committees normally contained about twenty-one members (although they could have many more) until 1836, when they were reduced to fifteen with a quorum of five. Provided a day's notice had been given, the M.P. who had successfully moved for the committee then proceeded to nominate the list of members.[3] Unless challenged, these were appointed, and the mover became chairman. Lords committees were constituted in much the same way, though they had no special rules regulating their appointment and constitution.

The 1854 report of the Select Committee on the Business of the House of Commons described the ideal at which the appointments aimed. 'In addition to Members moving for, or taking a special interest in the inquiry, Committees should comprise some Members of standing and experience, as well as a fair representation of different parties. in the House.'[4] That this was not always easy to realize is suggested by the Speaker's unsuccessful proposal (backed by Erskine May himself) to the Select Committee of 1854 that members of public committees should be appointed by the Committee of Selection, because it would get rid of a great number of inconvenient debates 'which are very invidious, because they relate to the names of Members proposed to be placed upon Committees'.[5] None the less, House of Commons Committees of Inquiry did generally include representatives of different sides of controversial questions. This, while it enabled constitutional theorists to praise them as truly representative of Commons and people, disqualified them for the task of taking decisive action in difficult problems. For instance, the Select Committee of

[1] H. M. Clokie and J. W. Robinson, *Royal Commissions of Inquiry*, Stanford U.P., 1937, 62.

[2] Jeremy Bentham, 'Constitutional Code', *The Works of Jeremy Bentham*, ed. John Bowring, 1843, ix. 187–8.

[3] *Erskine May's Treatise on the Law, Privileges, Proceedings and Usage of Parliament*, ed. Sir Barnett Cocks, 17th edn., 1964, 637.

[4] S.C. on the Business of the House, *Parl. Pap. Reports from Committees*, 1854, VII. vi.

[5] Ibid. xix. It is difficult to get details of these debates as they were not reported in Hansard, nor in the House of Commons Journals.

1840 on the Factory Act of 1833, despite serious complaints of misuse of the law, against the masters and some of the inspectors, could do nothing but tinker with the Act.[6]

While select committees were praised for their fairness and impartiality, they could be influenced, or even packed. A small knot of determined members, prepared to attend regularly, could ask most of the questions, and ask leading questions which affected the information obtained. Francis Place discovered at the Select Committees on Trade Unions in 1824 and 1825 that it was possible to select and coach witnesses to give the right answers. With the help of the chairman it was possible to obtain a one-sided body of evidence, as the cotton masters complained was done by Sadler's Factory Committee in 1832. The proposed members of the committee could not be changed without a public parliamentary wrangle, but there were ways of obtaining power over the selection. In 1837 John Walter, M.P. for Berkshire and proprietor of *The Times* moved for a select committee into the operation of the poor laws, intending to attack the Poor Law Amendment Act of 1834. The Home Secretary, Sir John Russell, a convinced supporter of the Act, moved an amendment narrowing the scope of the inquiry to the administration of poor relief under the regulations issued by the poor law commissioners. Then, in a conciliatory speech in which he indicated that he would support an inquiry into everything but the main principles of the Act he persuaded the House to induce Walter to withdraw his motion. The amendment being accepted, and despite Walter's hope that, 'the House would watch with jealousy the names of the committee, and that it would not give to them its unreserved confidence',[7] Russell nominated a committee with a large majority of supporters of the new poor law. Despite determined opposition from Fielden and one or two others, the committee brushed aside nearly all the complaints brought against the commissioners, and confirmed the Victorian workhouse system.

More remarkable than the large number of select committees was the rise in the first half of the nineteenth century of the royal commission as a means of inquiry. Unlike the select committee, which had been in regular use since the seventeenth century, royal commissions had nearly (although not entirely) lapsed until they were revived by the appointment of the Commission to take into Consideration the Public Accounts, during the crisis of 1780. Between 1800 and 1831 some sixty or more commissions of inquiry were appointed, some with statutory authority, most without. Between 1830 and 1900 388 such commissions were created (356, excluding special commissions to investigate bribery), the peak period being 1850–60, when seventy-four new commissions were appointed.[8]

As a means of obtaining information the royal commission had certain advantages over the select committee. It did not have to be composed of M.P.s, and could include expert full-time investigators. It usually contained a small central body or

---

6 U. Henriques, 'An Early Factory Inspector: James Stuart of Dunearn', *Scottish H.R.*, 1971, 39–40.

7 Hansard, 3rd series, xxxvi (31 Jan.–6 Mar. 1837), 1102.

8 Clokie and Robinson, op. cit. 57–60, 75–9.

board of commissioners with a number of assistant commissioners who were sent round various parts of the provinces, armed with questionnaires, to collect information. These assistant commissioners were usually paid salaries averaging £600 a year, or proportionately less for a shorter time, with travel expenses. The royal commission was not interrupted by the seasons and terms of parliament. Its membership, appointed by the government, could not be challenged in the House of Commons, and was therefore not affected by party wrangles. Unlike the select committee it could not legally call for documents, compel the attendance of witnesses, or examine witnesses on oath; but it did these things. The historian Redlich somewhat naïvely claimed that a royal commission could appoint scientific experts as members, 'so as to secure a completely impartial treatment of the subject'.[9]

In spite of Redlich, the great advantage of the royal commission, as contemporaries well knew, was that it could be very easily packed. Members were nominated by the government, sometimes in a 'riot of jobbery'.[10] But this also meant that the choice of personnel might be influenced by anyone who could secure the ear of the minister concerned. In the 1860s royal commissions were beginning to develop majority and minority reports; but the great reports on social problems of the 1830s and 1840s, composed by one or two central figures, were both unanimous and decisive. Of course governments could use both select committees and royal commissions to delay difficult decisions; but in the hands of a Chadwick no better machinery than a royal commission could have been devised to cut the Gordian knot of controversy and political hesitation.

Royal commissions and select committees did not operate in isolation. The reports, minutes of evidence, and even witnesses could be handed down from one select committee to another, and from committee to commission. The 1828 Select Committee on the Relief of Able-bodied Persons referred to 'the luminous and benevolent views', and the mass of evidence collected by the Select Committees on the Poor Laws of 1817–19, and the Select Committee on Labourers' Wages of 1824.[11] The Revd. J. T. Becher, a witness before the Lords Committee of 1831, was re-examined by the poor law commissioners of 1834.

Royal commissions not infrequently completed the work of select committees. There were select committees on the poor laws or some closely related subject almost every year from 1817, reflecting the general concern with rising rates and growing pauperism. Then, after the labourers' revolt of 1830 the Royal Commission Report of 1834 cut short the indecisive debate, not with new suggestions for the cure of pauperism, but with a bold administrative plan for enforcing in detail suggestions already made. Later, the opposition aroused by the Poor Law Amendment Act

---

[9] J. Redlich, *Procedure of the House of Commons*, London, 1908, ii. 193.

[10] e.g. the appointment of the Factories Inquiry Commission of 1833. S. E. Finer, *The Life and Times of Sir Edwin Chadwick*, London, 1952, 52. According to Finer, the Poor Law Commissioners unlike the Factory Commissioners, were allowed to choose their own assistants.

[11] *Parl. Pap. Reports from Committees*, 1828, iv. 3.

evoked select committees of both Houses to investigate the complaints. This pattern of a royal commission of inquiry producing a plan for decisive action following a series of inconclusive select committees or inadequate Acts of parliament, became the hallmark of Edwin Chadwick and his friends.[12]

Where inquiries were of manageable scale or there was no 'Benthamite' prompting, the appointment of an expensive royal commission with its paid investigators was sometimes avoided. Each step in lunacy reform followed the report of a select committee, often called into being by some appalling revelation of ill treatment. Wynn's Act of 1808, enabling magistrates to establish county asylums, followed a select committee inspired by Sir George Onesiphorus Paul, the High Sheriff of Gloucester, who was concerned about the plight of criminal and pauper lunatics languishing in prison or chained up in cellars and ruins. The Select Committee of 1814–15 investigated cases of gross ill treatment in York asylum and Bethlem Hospital, but Lord Chancellor Eldon refused to take any action. The Madhouse Act of 1828 which substituted for the ineffective College of Physicians a commission of doctors and laymen followed a select committee of 1827. The reports of the commissioners persuaded the government to turn them into a national body in 1845. The reforming steps were strung out over a long period, without any decisive royal commission.[13] Similarly, a long series of select committees governed the slow course of prison reform. Here the change of policy from 'classified' towards 'cellular' prisons was influenced by two of the inspectors appointed under the Prisons Act of 1835, which followed the recommendations of a select committee of the House of Lords the same year.

Exceptionally a matter was too controversial for resolution even by a royal commission. In 1818 Lord Sidmouth set up a Crown-appointed commission to inquire into the misapplication of educational and charitable funds. This commission, of very limited powers, was really intended to forestall Henry Brougham, chairman of the House of Commons Select Committee on the Education of the Lower Orders in the Metropolis. Brougham was demanding a 'parliamentary commission' as a means of collecting evidence which would justify the confiscation of many fat and comfortably abused endowments to finance a national system of education for the working classes. Sidmouth's commission was to prevent, not promote, reform. By the 1830s popular education had become so involved in sectarian strife that no royal commission could have reached a politically acceptable conclusion. Lord John Russell had to attempt reform by Order in Council in 1839, and was only partly successful.[14]

[12] Not only Chadwick. Cf. Lord Grey's Royal Commission to Enquire into Church Revenues, 1832, followed by Peel's in 1835; both dominated by Bishop Blomfield.

[13] This process of step-by-step reform resembles that recorded by Oliver MacDonagh in the control of emigrant ships, from which he took his model. O. MacDonagh, *A Pattern of Government Growth, 1800–60. The Passenger Acts and their Enforcement*, London, 1961. There was a Commission on Emigration in 1831; but it lacked the decisive direction of Chadwick.

[14] Russell established the Committee of the Privy Council on Education by order in council, and insisted on inspectors, but he had to abandon the government teachers' training college. Mary Sturt, *The Education of the People*, London, 1967, 79–85, 94–9.

If royal commissions could supplement select committees they could also conflict with them. There was open party strife between Brougham's select committee and Sidmouth's commission in 1818. Since after 1830 Whigs and Peelites were generally in agreement over social reforms (which was the fundamental reason why they had such an easy passage), the conflict between Sadler's committee of 1832 and the Factories Commission of 1833 was outside normal party lines. However, after Sadler's committee had published all its evidence reflecting discredit on the mill-owners, the Factory Commissioners of 1833 instructed their investigators to re-examine the committee's witnesses on oath. It was hardly surprising that the workmen who had supplied many of these witnesses were convinced that the royal commission was a government device to overturn the evidence of Sadler's committee and to whitewash the employers. However, Chadwick had made up his mind that children up to the age of puberty ought to be protected by the state while adults ought not,[15] and this principle (modified, to Chadwick's disgust, by a clause limiting the hours of young workers up to eighteen) was embodied in the Factory Act of 1833. Thus the royal commission in zealous hands could facilitate decisive and unpopular action precisely because its experts were not 'scientific' and were not appointed on a party balance, but were already committed to a policy which they could use the information collected by a commission to justify. This was true of almost any commission in which Chadwick played a part, whether on factories in 1833, on poor laws in 1834, on police in 1839, on sanitation and public health in 1844 and 1845. In 1833 he had decided on a policy of sets or relays of children in cotton factories, to limit their hours without touching those of adults, well before the peripatetic commissioners had finished gathering the information on which he claimed to base his conclusions. Assistant Commissioner John Cowell, who was very much opposed to relays, while struggling to get information from the hostile operatives in Manchester, read in the evening papers that the government had announced in parliament its intention to introduce them.[16]

The committed, or propaganda nature of such reports could be detected in the way evidence was used. Conclusions were not based on statistics (although these would certainly have been presented in an equally selective way), but justified by stringing together quotations from evidence believed to support the commissioners' findings, and omitting or brushing aside the rest. Naturally this was perceived and resented by opponents. 'By the Commission of Inquiry', grumbled Toulmin Smith, 'all the real bearings of the case, all the actual facts and conditions and requisites, are distorted or effectually smothered, and a vast blue book is produced, which it may be safely relied on that no one will read, but with the pretended results proclaimed in the first few pages of which the indolent may find it most convenient to content themselves'.[17]

[15] See Chadwick's undated memorandum in which he argued out this principle, in the Chadwick Papers, 18. D.M.S. Watson Library, U.C. London.

[16] John Cowell to the Central Board, 20 June 1833. Chadwick Papers, 41. Cf. S. E. Finer, op. cit. 56.

[17] J. Toulmin Smith, *Government by Commissions Illegal and Pernicious*, London, 1849, 18.

Opponents dwelt on the different origins and practice of royal commissions and select committees rather than on their common function as means of investigating problems, and as instruments of reform. Toulmin Smith saw in the royal commissions the lineal descendants of the unconstitutional commissions of the Stuart kings and the instrument of centralizing tyranny. They were the tools by which 'three paid commissioners, being three Whig gentlemen of agreeable politics and easy disposition, and also very thick with the Whig aristocracy' sought to overturn the fundamental institutions by which English liberty was preserved. Smith was referring here to administrative not inquiry commissions. But he knew one followed the other. '. . . the grand end soon follows, and a General Board of paid commissioners is formed to carry out the work of experimental mischief.'[18]

Toulmin Smith and other critics of royal commissions were loud in their complaints of the increase of government patronage. But their arguments were contradictory. Government by patronage was government by inefficiency and corruption. Most of the commissioners, paid or unpaid, were uncorrupt and efficient. Service on commissions of inquiry trained a nucleus of officials who secured jobs in the administrative commissions or inspectorates to enforce the schemes at whose initiation they had assisted. Chadwick as poor law commissioner, and part author of the commission's report, as well as assistant commissioner for London and Berkshire, helped to draft the ensuing Bill, and became secretary to the administrative commission set up by it. Alfred Power and E. C. Tufnell were assistant commissioners in the inquiry commission and subsequently in the administrative commission. They also served on the Factories Inquiry Commission. Leonard Horner and the unsatisfactory James Stuart both served on the Factories Inquiry Commission before being engaged as factory inspectors. Cowell moved over from factories to poor law. Evidently the commissions of inquiry were acting as training-ground for a budding profession. But their scope was wider than this, reaching down into the witnesses. William Day, although not on the inquiry commission, had been a Sussex magistrate. He was chairman of the Uckfield Union, and author of a pamphlet on the poor laws, before being recruited to the administrative commission as assistant commissioner for Shropshire and North Wales. With other reforming magistrates he had also been consulted on the drafting of the Bill.[19] Thus royal commissions attracted a number of interested men who, despite the inevitable frustration of some of their ambitions and their plans in passage through ministries and parliament, saw more of their ideas realized than any other group before them without the trappings of political power.

Recent historians have recognized that the vital element in the administration of nineteenth-century social reforms was the paid professional inspectorate.

The principle of inspection was not new, but until 1833 its practice had been largely

[18] Ibid. 13 (quoting from *The Times* of 20 Nov. 1848) and 18.

[19] *An Inquiry into the Poor Laws and Surplus Labour and their Mutual Reaction*, 1833. Cf. R. A. Lewis, 'William Day and the Poor Law Commissioners', *U. of Birmingham Hist. J.*, 1963–4, ix. 163–95. Chadwick Papers, 18.

in the hands of unpaid magistrates. Since the Vagrancy Act of 1774 county gaols and houses of correction had been supervised by committees of visiting justices. From the same year private madhouses had been inspected by a commission elected from their members by the College of Physicians, and from 1808 county asylums had been managed and inspected by committees of visiting justices appointed in Quarter Sessions. A number of late eighteenth-century statutes had increased the control of the magistrates over the administration of the poor law. These in their judicial function dealt with bastardy and settlement cases, in their administrative role acted as a kind of appeal tribunal from the decisions of overseers on rating and on applications for poor relief. The justices were responsible under some of the earlier factory Acts for inspecting the mills and enforcing the statutory regulations about child labour.

Although the inspecting magistracy had produced many of the early reformers, such as the famous prison reformer John Howard, Sir George Onesiphorus Paul, pioneer of county asylums and separate discipline prisons, the Revd. J. T. Becher, and Revd. Thomas Whately, managers of 'well-regulated' workhouses, it was generally felt to have failed. Too many gaols were filthy and corrupt, and even the classified ones made no dent in the climbing crime rate. The northern justices were believed to be in the pockets of the millowners who were their relatives or associates; Hobhouse's Act of 1831, which incapacitated millowners or their near relatives from acting as inspectors, probably made little difference in a closely knit society. As late as 1844 the report of the Metropolitan Commissioners in Lunacy to the Lord Chancellor was an indictment of the callous inefficiency of visiting justices, and of their failure to secure the proper treatment of pauper patients in private asylums. Above all, the blame for the rise and extension of the allowance in aid of labourers' wages was laid at the door of the justices.[20]

By 1830 some centrally controlled bodies of inspectors were already in existence. The two voluntary religious school societies employed their own inspectors to supervise the expenditure of the subscribers' money in their schools and ensure that their own religious tenets were taught. From 1828 inspection of lunatic asylums was in its transitional phase, with a body of sixteen government-appointed commissioners (eleven unpaid laymen, six physicians at £1 an hour) responsible for inspecting and licensing private madhouses in the metropolitan area, while two local justices and a medical visitor inspected all houses in the provinces.[21] In Ireland where experiments in centralized administration were easier than in England, government inspection of prisons and schools was already in being. There was a groping towards the practice and principle of central inspection before the Whigs took office.

Once the poor law and factory inspectorates were established they were copied for prisons, asylums, charities (the poor law assistant commissioners were also charity

[20] Report of the Select Committee of the House of Commons on Labourers' Wages, *Parl. Pap. Reports from Committees*, 1824, vi. 7.
[21] W. Ll. Parry-Jones, *The Trade in Lunacy*, London, 1972, 16.

commissioners), public health (with additional officials under local government), and in other fields.[22] There has therefore been a tendency to lump all the inspectorates together, although in fact each of them differed in purpose, in powers, and in achievements. The poor law assistant commissioners were there firstly to promote the new unions of parishes, and then to see that they did not indulge in improvident spending. Their most effective means of control was their power to disallow spending and surcharge it on the boards of guardians. This was successful in the initial stages of establishing a deterrent workhouse regime, almost useless when the guardians, more skinflint than the commissioners, rejected efforts to improve poor law medical and educational services. The factory inspectors enforcing unpopular restrictions upon millowners and operatives had powers of summary fining. These were abandoned when they had appeared merely to increase working-class resentment, and the inspectors then had to rely on prosecutions before the magistrates whom they had replaced as inspectors.[23] Prison inspectors were intended to secure a more uniform administration of the local gaols according to the classification system approved in Peel's Prison Act of 1823. As the magistrates continued to manage the prisons, the inspectors' powers were mainly those of persuasion. Crawford and Whitworth Russell, inspectors for the Home District, were influential because they had the ear of the Home Secretary, and could extract grants for prison building when it took the form they favoured, of separate cells. But to have made separate confinement universal would have entailed rebuilding all the prisons. The lunacy commissioners in 1845, struggling to enforce reasonable standards of care for pauper lunatics, were at last armed with comprehensive inspecting and licensing powers over private madhouses. But they could not withdraw licences because of the desperate shortage of asylum places, and had to rely mainly on publicity; and public opinion, especially in the treatment of crime and madness, was often an unstable and illiberal tribunal. The school inspectors were there primarily to ensure the proper use of parliamentary grants to school committees and training colleges. Kay-Shuttleworth cleverly used the inspectors' powers to certify the fitness of schools and teachers for these grants to build up a complicated system of departmental control designed to transform the standards of accommodation and teaching. Under the Public Health Act of 1848, the General Board of Health, fighting powerful property interests to combat the diseases emanating from brand new slums, used inspectors central and local to set up boards of health and force the provision of drainage and water. Here the coercive powers went beyond mere regulation or restraint. For instance, the local board's surveyor could prescribe drains and privies for new houses, require a house-owner to instal a connecting drain, and in default have the work done and recover the cost.

[22] Chadwick gave a list in his unpublished Memorandum on Local and Central Administration and Proposals for Administrative Reform, written *c.* 1841, including factory, poor law, and prison, school, emigration, asylum, and slaughter-house inspectors. He foresaw railway, ship, police, sanitary, and highway inspectors. His contention was that all the inspectorates were appointed as the result of irresistible public demand! Chadwick Papers, 51.

[23] U. Henriques, *The Early Factory Acts and their Enforcement*, Historical Association, London, 1971, 15.

These were what Mr. R. A. Lewis has called 'aggressive functions' and they aroused proportionate opposition.[24]

The commissions and inspectorates had their growing pains. The quarrels between Chadwick and the poor law commissioners to whom he was officially secretary are well known.[25] The relationships between central commissioners or departments and assistant commissioners or local inspectors, and inspectors and their assistants, were all undefined. E. C. Tufnell had walked out on his colleague John Cowell while they were making inquiries for the factories commission in Lancashire, leaving his hotel bills unpaid.[26] James Stuart, factory inspector for Scotland, quarrelled with his superintendents and then with the other three inspectors so that the inspectorate failed to co-ordinate its policies as required under the Factory Act. The early school inspectors (who were remarkably harmonious seeing that they represented different sects in a period of sectarian strife) held differing views on the use of monitors, which Joseph Fletcher the inspector of nonconformist schools tended to condone but which the Anglican Henry Mosely as well as Kay-Shuttleworth heartily condemned.[27] And all of them tended to rush into print, publicizing their quarrels with each other and their grievances against their political masters.

None of this is intended to denigrate the importance of the new inspectorates. They offered the first serious prospect of actual enforcement of the laws. They played an almost equally important part in amending and extending these laws. The inspectors' published reports, their evidence before committees, their personal influence with political patrons, even their communications to the press, influenced the further development of reform. Once the initial step of their establishment had been taken, they were its dynamic.

Few of the social reform initiatives achieved full realization, especially as reforming vigour waned in mid century. Chadwick did not in the end secure his classified workhouses (which as he had been warned would have aroused even more opposition).[28] Many workhouses, especially in London, remained obstinately ill regulated. The workhouse test broke down in the North, and was never universally enforced in the South. Kay-Shuttleworth was succeeded at the Committee of Council for Education by the bureaucratic and insensitive Ralph Lingen who helped to shackle the development of elementary education in the system of payment by results. The General Board of Health was dissolved in 1854 although much of its work continued and developed in other hands. The attempt to reform criminals by separate confinement with religious instruction ended in disillusionment in the 1850s. Yet social

[24] R. A. Lewis, *Edwin Chadwick and the Public Health Movement*, London, 1952, 174, 279–300.
[25] S. E. Finer, op. cit. 113–207.
[26] John Cowell to the Central Board, 24 June 1833. Chadwick Papers, 41.
[27] See Fletcher's defence of monitors properly used. Minutes of Committee of Council on Education, Aug. and Dec. 1846. *Parl. Pap.*, 1847, xlv. 283–7.
[28] 'If the men are to be sent to one parish and their wives to another, and their children perhaps to a third, I fear this would create a considerable opposition.' Comments of Mr. Day of Uckfield on Measures Proposed. Chadwick Papers. Poor Law, 18.

administration never reverted to the fragmented chaos of the eighteenth century; its machinery had been too soundly established. This was at least partly owing to the nature of the machinery itself. Committees, commissions, and inspectorates had served to attract and focus upon social problems and their solution all the specialized interest and administrative talent available in the country, from magistrates, voluntary bodies, and interested individuals. This does not mean that the reforms were directed by public opinion, or that the masses were consulted in legislation. Mass movements of public opinion had other means of exerting influence (which could also be manipulated by interested parties), notably mass petitioning. The anti-slavery movement, the leaders of the fight against the property tax in 1816, the unsuccessful opponents of Catholic Emancipation in 1829, the northern anti-poor-law movement, the Sabbath Day Observance movement, the anti-Corn Law League and many others agitated the public and intimidated the ministers with giant petitioning campaigns. Most of the social reforms failed to arouse consistent public support, and some aroused bitter hostility. The poor law was detested by the working classes, the Factory Act was equally unpopular with operatives and masters, the sanitary regulations were resented by landlords, builders, and water companies, journalists periodically attacked what they thought was 'soft' treatment of criminals, the public oscillated between pity for lunatics and fear of madmen. The machinery of reform was successful because it circumvented public opinion (which it sometimes succeeded in educating later), while it provided effective means of action for zealous individuals and groups of committed reformers.

II

The question of who was responsible for the social reforms of the first half of the nineteenth century has produced one of those many-branched controversies which decorate the overcrowded historical scene. Starting as a critique of A. V. Dicey's classic *Law and Public Opinion in the Nineteenth Century*, first published in 1905, with its claim that Benthamite collectivism had gradually replaced the older ideal of individualistic liberty, it has piecemeal narrowed into a discussion of how far the various reforms were actually inspired and initiated by the followers of Bentham.

Prompted perhaps by Oliver MacDonagh's famous article, 'The Nineteenth Century Revolution in Government: a Reappraisal', and David Roberts's article, 'Jeremy Bentham and the Victorian Administrative State', the recent tendency has been to move away from the too narrow ascription of social reforms to any one group of men.[29] The foregoing pages may have suggested that many individuals of

---

[29] *Historical Journal*, 1–2, 1958–9, 52–67; *Victorian Studies*, ii, 1958–9, 193–210. In general agreement with MacDonagh and Roberts is Dr. G. Kitson Clark, *An Expanding Society*, Melbourne U.P., 1967, 133–50, and 'Statesmen in Disguise', *Historical Journal*, 2, 1959, 19–39. In somewhat vehement opposition to this school of opinion is Mrs. Jennifer Hart, 'Nineteenth Century Social Reform: a Tory Interpretation of History', *Past and Present*, 1965, 39–61. The most recent reaffirmation of Benthamite influence is S. E. Finer, 'The Transmission of Benthamite Ideas, 1820–50', *Studies in the Growth of Nineteenth Century*

differing political, religious, and social outlook used various parts of the machinery, in co-operation or conflict, sometimes for very different kinds of reform. Nevertheless a commanding figure emerges in the crucial poor law and factory legislation of 1833–4, and especially in the use of royal commissions and the establishment of pioneer inspectorates—Edwin Chadwick. Now among that amorphous group somewhat indiscriminately referred to as Benthamites, Chadwick was the arch-Benthamite.[30] But what is meant by Benthamite? It is proposed in the second part of this essay to attempt an assessment of how far the utilization and development of the machinery of reform can be credited to Bentham.

To begin with, how far did Bentham suggest or indeed appreciate the special use which could be made of select committees or of commissions of inquiry?

Bentham was probably a pioneer in his insistence on a proper basis of information for legislation. His passion for accumulating and analysing facts led him to make analytical tables which he passed on. A manuscript copy of his Table of Cases calling for Relief is among Chadwick's poor law papers in University College, London.[31] In the Constitutional Code he described a 'Universal Registration System', by which all public officials were to keep time books, stock books, accounts, diaries, and records in intolerable number and detail. He suggested local registrars, to be occupied in death-recording, marriage-recording, birth-recording, maturity-recording, post-obit-administration-granting, property-transfer-recording, contract-recording, extra-judicial evidence-recording, and a subjudiciary topographical function. All the information gathered would be available to what he called 'Evidence Elicitation Committees', by which he evidently meant select committees of inquiry of the House of Commons. In taking and reporting evidence such committees would aim at appositeness, clearness, correctness, impartiality, all-comprehensiveness, and non-deceptiveness;[32] that is, at those virtues recommended to the House of Commons by radicals in the eighteenth century and traditionalists in the nineteenth century on the supposition that they were the qualities contributed by the popular element to the constitution. Bentham wished to use as many Evidence Elicitation Committees as possible, and to strengthen them by giving them the same power of punishment for perjury or contempt, i.e. transportation for seven years, as was already possessed by the courts of law. He had little use for select committees of the House of Lords, which represented a corrupt aristocracy. Meantime he wrote about royal

Government, ed. Gillian Sutherland, Cambridge, 1971, 11–32. I agree with the wider view of the inspiration of social reforms, but not with the views of the 'Tory' historians as to the nature of such legislation as the Poor Law Amendment Act and the Factory Act of 1833. But these questions will be discussed elsewhere.

[30] It seems doubtful whether this term could ever be applied to a coherent group. Does it, for instance, include Nassau W. Senior who in 1833 was simultaneously co-operating with Chadwick over the new poor law, and attacking his intention to restrict the working hours of children in the Factory Act? It is hoped to discuss this question also, elsewhere.

[31] Chadwick Papers, 18. The question of Bentham's responsiblity for the statistical movement which started suddenly in 1833 needs separate investigation. Chadwick prompted the Registration Act of 1836.

[32] *Constitutional Code*. Bentham's *Works* ed. Bowring, 1843, ix. 182 and 186.

commissions in terms which must have been appreciated by Toulmin Smith, if the latter ever read them. Royal commissions, he considered, were instruments of the monarch, used to exclude rather than to promote reform. They lacked power to secure either comprehensiveness or impartiality, if such were really their desire. They could command the attendance only of government servants or others subject to them by corruptive influence: '*quality of the information*, such as may be expected from packed witnesses speaking to packed judges'.[33] Since even in the circumstances of the time it was impossible to exclude from House of Commons committees all who would not concur in the suppression of evidence to conceal the misdoings of ministers, the latter, prevented by shame from refusing inquiry, and by fear from trusting to the House of Commons resorted to packed commissions. The commissions, besides being a fertile source of 'jobs', produced reports which suppressed the questions and the names of the questioners, concealing them from public scrutiny to which the witnesses were exposed. 'The practice may be set down among the natural fruits of aristocratical oppression: presumptive evidence of intentional abuse of power on the part of as many as give in to it.'

Bentham saw the select committee as a democratic means of securing informed legislation, and the royal commission as an instrument of monarchical tyranny. Writing in the 1820s he had no inkling of the extra power needed to realize controversial reforms such as a new poor law which he himself desired. He did not foresee, let alone suggest, the utilization of commissions as Chadwick and his associates used them, to secure their reforms. Perhaps this is not surprising. He may have had Lord Sidmouth's Commission on Charitable funds in mind. Moreover Chadwick himself issued instructions to the factory inquiry commissioners that the inquiry was expected to be into 'the whole truth about the employment of children in factories'.[34] He expressed the ideal of comprehensiveness and impartiality, plainly unconscious of the way he was really utilizing the machinery of inquiry.

As a practical reformer Bentham had submitted evidence to two select committees of the House of Commons upon his plans for the Panopticon penitentiary. In the Holford Committee of 1811 his evidence was overborne by that of Sir George Onesiphorus Paul in the interests of separate confinement, and the Revd. John Becher who maintained that the plan sacrificed amenity to false economy, and would produce 'a watch tower . . . surrounded at a small distance with six rows of cages, nearly similar to those used for the restraining of wild beasts'.[35] The committee reported against Panopticon. Whatever Bentham's appreciation of informed legislation, it is clear that he did not know how to use select committees for the furtherance of his schemes of social reform.

What did Bentham contribute to the development of those vital enforcement organs, the inspectorates? This is a more complicated question.

---

[33] Ibid. 188. [34] *Parl. Pap. Reports from Committees*, 1833, xx. 2
[35] Report from the Committee on the Laws relating to Penitentiary Houses, ibid., 1810–11, iii. 42.

Bentham had always stressed 'inspectability' which, as its name denotes, was the leading feature of Panopticon. Whether used as workhouse, prison, madhouse, boarding school for young ladies, or 'school of industry', the shape of Panopticon would ensure that every inmate would be visible to the keeper in the central watch-tower. Thus 'inspectability' would guarantee security. It would also guarantee the efficient administration of the institution and the proper treatment of the inmates; for Bentham proposed to allow the public to visit to inspect the occupants, and talk to them through speaking tubes which ran from the cells to the central reservation.[36] The public would watch the keeper who watched the inmates. Now whatever might be thought of the efficiency of this device for good administration (and to the lunacy commissioners who deplored the exhibition of lunatics to casual sightseers at Bethlem and knew it had not prevented scandals in the treatment of patients there, it must have been a retrograde proposal), it had nothing to do with an inspectorate. Indeed, all Bentham's safeguards for prisons and workhouses assumed they were self-sufficient units independent of government supervision and interference. The keeper of his penitentiary would contract to pay fines for prisoners who escaped, or who died, if in excess of the average number of deaths for the areas concerned. These were devices for harmonizing the self-interest of the prison keeper with the general interest in the good government of the prison, necessitated by the fact that the penitentiary was intended to produce a profit from the labour of the prisoners for the keeper, who would also be the supplier and the overseer. Contracts of this kind which combined management of a prison or workhouse with management of its labour for profit had been an inducement to corruption and cruelty in many eighteenth-century houses of correction, and it was not surprising that the committee of 1811 expressed anxiety as to what might happen if Panopticon penitentiary fell into hands less respectable than those of Mr. Bentham.[37] Bentham had also provided his penitentiary with a management committee of High Court judges as a substitute for the local visiting justices whose zeal and efficiency he mistrusted. It is problematical whether these would have given more time or devotion than the justices; and there was no provision for government inspection.

Even Bentham's pauper kingdom of regional workhouses was to be run by an independent Joint Stock National Charity Company on the model of the East India Co.; taking it out of the realm of ministerial supervision.

Panopticon was still being promoted by James Mill in his article on Prisons in the *Encyclopaedia Britannica* in 1823. Up to that time there was no indication that Bentham had anything but mistrust and suspicion of central or government inspection.

With the writing of the Constitutional Code in the last decade of his life, Bentham at last lost his fear of government 'interference'. His constitutional Utopia, which

---

[36] *Panopticon; or the Inspection House*, 1791, *Works*, iv. 46, 84. There are further descriptions of Panopticon in *Principles of the Civil Code*, *Works*, i, and elsewhere.

[37] Report from the Committee on Laws relating to Penitentiary Houses. *Parl. Pap. Reports from Committees*, 1810–11, iii. 13.

combined an American presidential system of government with elements from French law and British parliamentary practice, provided such a separation of powers and such a checking and counter-checking of each part that corruption by private and 'sinister' interests must be eliminated. In addition to the constitutive (electoral), legislative, and judicial authorities, the Code provided an administrative authority, headed by a Prime Minister elected by the legislature every four years, with thirteen departments under him. The Prime Minister appointed the minister and the officials of each department, all holding for life unless removed by the legislature. Each minister inspected his own department and all the officials and subordinate institutions connected with it. There was no recognition that political parties played more than a peripheral role in the government of the country, and no distinction between political ministers and permanent officials. It was a bureaucracy; and to prevent bureaucracy getting out of hand, further checks besides 'dislocability' by the legislature were needed. So there was a draconian special court for the punishment of corrupt and oppressive officials. All officials were tested for 'intellectual and moral aptitude' by a long period of specialized training followed by a public examination. The Universal Registration System would keep the legislature and the public informed of all their activities; and last but not least, there was inspection by the minister or his deputy. Bentham described the purpose of the minister's inspection. He was to see that the registration system was fully carried out, and any deficiencies supplied; to get to know by personal experience what he had only read in reports; to ascertain the efficiency of functionaries with a view to their instruction, transfer, promotion, or dismissal; to listen to complaints about them or praise of them; to explain their duties in cases of doubt, and to settle disagreements among them.[38]

Bentham's inspection was internal, and was primarily a means of supervising government officials. He increased its efficiency by providing that institutions should be inspected by a variety of officials with different interests in them. Thus, 'establishments for education in conjunction with indigence relief' (pauper schools) were to be inspected by the Minister for Indigence Relief and also by the Ministers for Education and Health for their teaching and health aspects. This would also happen in other institutions, and the ministers would check each other. The Finance Minister (Treasury) would inspect everything.

Bentham's inspection system, however, did not remain merely a negative system of checks because he now visualized state activity as extending beyond the limits tolerated by other constitutional thinkers. There was to be a Ministry of Indigence Relief to run the workhouse scheme, Ministries of Education and Health. Inspection followed, and extended beyond government establishments to corporately and privately owned ones. The Minister of Indigence Relief would inspect 'eleemosynary establishments' maintained by the government, by local corporations and private individuals. Since there were too many, circuits could be constructed, and those establishments to be inspected chosen by lot. The Minister of Education would

---

[38] *Constitutional Code. Works*, ix. 204–14 and 257–8.

inspect government, local, and private schools. The Minister of Health would inspect dispensaries in London and county towns, chemist shops on appeal, and all hospitals. Bentham explained that establishments under private management were those in which inspection was most useful, since they were not subject to the security afforded by the Registration and Publication System; 'the light of publicity not being otherwise capable of being thrown, with adequate intensity, upon those minor objects'. Moreover, inspection included a 'melioration suggestive function'; in other words, the inspecting minister could suggest improvements, by report to the Prime Minister.

In so far as they went beyond the mere inspection of officials by other officials, Bentham's proposals for inspection were sketchy. Nothing was said about the inspectors' powers, what standards or improvements were to be enforced, nor, publicity apart, how they were to be enforced. They form a very small part of the voluminous Constitutional Code. So the question arises, can we attribute to them any part in the establishment of the inspectorates after 1833? Here we are in the realm of the imponderables. Short of a written acknowledgement to Bentham by one of the leading actors, we can only guess what went on in their minds. They probably read the Code, or, in view of its verbosity and labyrinthine style, parts of it. And the scheme for inspection was much more impressive when taken on its own, divorced from the constitution depicted as a whole.

The first proposal for the new poor law inspectors (not the first to be authorized, who were the factory inspectors and the emigration agent at Liverpool in 1833) came from Nassau William Senior. Senior in his first letter to the Lord Chancellor, of September 1832 proposed the appointment of 'paid and responsible Poor Law Magistrates'. In his second letter of January 1833 he set out a plan for a central commission of three, a corps of 200 full-time paid district inspectors, and some 4,700 paid overseers, each running a group of three parishes and answerable to select vestries in each parish. His reasons were clear. He intended to abolish outdoor relief to the able-bodied, and was convinced that unpaid overseers 'who have to give or to refuse public money to their Relations, friends, dependants [*sic*], customers, debtors and neighbours' would never possess the necessary firmness. The inspectors would replace the magistrates, whom, in the course of rejecting the idea of an appeal from the vestry to Quarter Sessions, Senior called 'unpaid, irresponsible Judges, from whom no previous legal or political Education has been required, who have long been in the habit of administering the present system, and many of whom have been the principal authors of its abuses'. He went on:

Every one admits that the present administration of the Poor Laws cannot continue. Everyone admits that the interference of the unpaid and irresponsible magistracy is one of the Principal Causes of the existing evils, and the abuse most urgently crying for amendment. Everyone admits that the alteration must consist either in leaving the parochial authorities uncontrouled or in controuling them by paid officers.[39]

[39] Nassau W. Senior. Second Letter to the Lord Chancellor. Jan. 1833. Chadwick Papers, 18.

Senior's inspectors were to be the middle rank in a hierarchy of paid officials. However, when Chadwick drew up a bill to be introduced, as he said, on the principles set forth in the Report of the Commissioners, he proposed a board of control of three commissioners with power to appoint nine assistant commissioners. The unions of parishes were to be far larger, like the Gilbert Act incorporations, but with more powers. Their boards of guardians would be elected by the ratepayers. Chadwick somewhat guardedly proposed that their paid officers should be appointed as well as dismissed by the Central Board, although in the end appointment remained with the guardians.[40] This, in essence, was the scheme realized under the Poor Law Amendment Act. Its nine assistant commissioners, each peripatetic in a large district, were now inspectors in the proper meaning of the word, supervising independently elected bodies which they had persuaded to constitute themselves under the terms of the Act.

Just why Chadwick made these changes is not clear. But a clue lies in Senior's admission that his scheme would be very expensive. He estimated it at about £574,000 a year. Chadwick, who was more awake to the need for economy, estimated his plan at £25,000–30,000. In none of the proposals was any acknowledgement made to Bentham. Chadwick, as precedent for the Commission of Three, referred to the barrister in charge of savings banks and friendly societies. He did, indeed, propose the board be kept small on the Benthamite ground that it would concentrate responsibility (Bentham detested boards, believing shared responsibility was diminished responsibility).[41] But neither Chadwick nor Senior proposed fewer than three commissioners, tacitly but clearly on the grounds that the pressures of unpopularity would be too much for one man to bear. Bentham had proposed inspection by heads of departments. Senior argued that poor relief should not be in the hands of central government since party politics and vote-catching would in the end be fatal to the continuation of firm treatment of the paupers. Chadwick was determined that the commission should be kept away from contact with the Government because, 'at the Outset, the Duties to be performed by the Board would be excessively troublesome and unpopular'. Moreover, the assistant commissioners were to be non-resident, to preserve them from the temptations caused by local social and political entanglements.[42] Even the well-regulated workhouses were attributed not to Bentham's Panopticon, but to the example of the parish reformers, several of whom (including William Day of Uckfield, Thomas Whately of Cookham, Henry Russell of Swallowfield, and Tidd Pratt, the barrister superintending friendly societies) were invited to

---

[40] *Measures Proposed with Relation to the Administration of the Poor Laws*, p. 3. Chadwick Papers, 18. There are five printed copies of the Measures, representing different drafts, two entitled *Measures Submitted by the Poor Law Commissioners to His Majesty's Ministers*, but the variations are of minor importance. Most references here are to a copy endorsed in Chadwick's handwriting 'Uncertain whether this paper is not the first proof and whether there were not subsequent revisions', 3, 17.

[41] Chadwick, *Measures Proposed*, 17, 2, 4 (*Measures Proposed* endorsed '1st proof—uncorrected'. 'Any evil practice, by being brought to one Neck, may be struck off at one blow.' This was subsequently omitted).   [42] Ibid. 16.

comment on the heads of the Bill. Chadwick enlarged Senior's small unions of parishes partly in the hope of weakening the narrow parish settlement laws, and partly because he appreciated the economies and administrative advantages of larger units. Then he allowed ratepayer franchise for the Boards of Guardians (following the select vestry), convinced that, once relief was regulated by the commission, they would have no significant power.[43] Perhaps some echoes of Bentham were to be heard in Chadwick's arrangements for detailed accounts open to multiple inspection, for reports and suggestions for amendments to the legislature to secure 'Progressiveness of Improvement', and in his hope that the board would be a depot of trustworthy information as to the actual state of the labouring classes. But in essentials, while Bentham had planned an ideal constitution, Senior and Chadwick were devising the practical machinery to enforce what they well knew would be, except among ratepayers, an exceedingly unpopular law.

While it is impossible either to affirm or to deny that the principle of central inspection was taken from the Constitutional Code, the details plainly owed more to the exigencies of the situation than to Bentham's blueprint. Except possibly in the sphere of law reform Bentham's detailed suggestions frequently betrayed his lack of administrative experience, if not of common sense. Thus he insisted that his qualifying examination for public officials should be followed by an auction or bidding in which the post went to the candidate who would accept the lowest salary.[44] Putting poor law medical posts up to auction was tried, evoked a chorus of complaints, and was dropped after 1837. The reformers already knew that to get honest and efficient service, officials (unless aristocratic and honorary) had to be properly paid.[45] They also knew that different levels of salary would recruit different levels of social class and education. Kay-Shuttleworth, for instance, used this knowledge to keep elementary school teaching in the hands of the lower middle and artisan classes, and school inspection in those of the clergy and gentry.

A thorough consideration of the extent of Bentham's contribution to nineteenth-century social reforms, through his writings as well as his disciples, has yet to be undertaken. What begins to emerge, however, is the outworn nature of some of his suggestions in relation to the situation of the 1830s. On the wider theme, the development of constitutional machinery, like the technical achievements of the Industrial Revolution, was the work of many hands. Attempts to ascribe responsibility may never produce an unchallengeable verdict, bringing as they do the historian face to face with the complexities of settling historical truth.

[43] 'The functions left to a Board of Guardians would be chiefly those of inspection', *Measures Proposed*, 17.

[44] *Constitutional Code*, 266. It appears from Bentham's notes on the *Code* that he was even prepared to put these posts up for what was, in effect, sale.

[45] Chadwick in a manuscript letter of 1853 protesting against a proposal to reduce the salary of secretaries to the Poor Law Board from £1,500 to £1,000 argued that official work ought not to be performed on an honorary basis. To this letter is pinned a copy in his own handwriting of an extract, not from Bentham but from Burke's 'Speech on Economical Reform'. Chadwick Papers, 51.

Some Limitations of the Age of Reform

NORMAN McCORD

THE period 1815–70 which Woodward chose as his 'Age of Reform', has probably attracted more attention from twentieth-century historians than any other. This is scarcely surprising, for in a whole variety of historical aspects those decades were of cardinal importance. They saw the development of one of the world's greatest empires, the evolution of the world's first great industrial society, and they still offer to the historian the engrossing spectacle of a decentralized rural society facing enormous and unprecedented pressures of economic and social change coupled with accelerating population growth—and facing those difficulties with a notably small record of internal conflict and bloodshed. In the development of government and administration too those decades were of crucial significance in the transformation of Britain from a little-governed nation to a modern state equipped with large and expanding agencies of official activity.

This 'Age of Reform' remains too a major focus of argument and disagreement among historians, largely because of its imagined close relevance to our own society. The assumption of close connection has led to the constant use of nineteenth-century history as a convenient source of ammunition with which to fight our own ideological and political controversies. This continuing involvement has been a major source of historical distortion, for in reality the differences between mid-nineteenth-century and mid-twentieth-century British society are more striking than any similarities.

This distortion has shown itself in a number of ways. The interpretations advanced by Marx and his followers have in the past been a useful stimulus to understanding, but it is increasingly clear that, whatever their relevance to wider problems, from the narrower historical problem of understanding nineteenth-century Britain they do not provide a satisfactory explanation. It is sad to see how much skill and ingenuity is still being expended in the futile endeavour to make our conceptions of nineteenth-century Britain fit into an ideological frame which is not the right shape. It is true that we still lack any very complete alternative synthesis, but it is much better to accept this deficiency for the time being, and recognize the limitations of our conceptual equipment, rather than continue to pursue a historical chimera. This is the more desirable, when the alternative leads so often to the deliberate or feckless distortion of the past for the purpose of exciting hatreds and sectional conflicts within the society in which we all live.

Another element of distortion is to be found in the persistent determination to judge the actions of past generations—and none more so than those of the 'Age of

Reform'—by higher standards of altruism and virtue than any human society has yet contrived to manifest in practice. Generous indignation is, no doubt, an admirable emotion, but when applied anachronistically by historians it is frequently a serious bar to understanding. The absence of trade unions from neolithic society, and the failure of Elizabethan England to create a national health service, are I daresay to be regretted, but this kind of approach is of singularly limited utility in history; an astonishing amount of twentieth-century interpretation of nineteenth-century Britain has differed from these patent absurdities only in degree. The primary task of the historian is to try to understand and explain the past, and not to distribute praise or blame from a position of assumed superiority. The need to avoid, in E. P. Thompson's splendid phrase, 'the enormous condescension of posterity', should be the historian's constant care, and the principle has a much wider ambience than Mr. Thompson's first application of it to the treatment of early radical groups.

The purpose of this essay is to consider some of the work of the governments which held office in Britain during the 'Age of Reform', and especially to discuss the ways in which the administrations of the 1830s and 1840s sought to use legislation and the expansion of the civil service as agencies of improvement. If these matters are to be appreciated they must be considered firmly in the light of the realities of that society and the resources which were available for these purposes.

It would be absurd to suggest that twentieth-century British society has solved all of its domestic problems; the truth is far from that, and it may well be that some of the deeper problems now emerging will prove more intractable than questions of material needs. Yet it is true to say that a greater amount of wealth, skill, and effort is now devoted to the care of the weak, the sick, and the aged than at any earlier period in our history. This development depends to a large extent on two features of the preceding century. One is the expansion of the national economy, and the much greater resources which this has made available. The other is the increased use of the state's powers of intervention, regulation, and taxation for social purposes. It is with some of the early stages of this second process that we are primarily concerned here.

It is easy for us to see that the expansion of government was to become a major method of tackling a variety of social evils. It is equally clear that this was a lesson learned only painfully and reluctantly by nineteenth-century society. The historian's function is to seek to understand why this was so, rather than to indulge from the comfort of hindsight in a variety of arbitrary criticisms. Before the use of legislation and government expansion for social purposes could become more widespread two ingredients had to be present; one was the actual resources in men and organization, the other was the will to create these resources, to use them and to expand them. If the problem is looked at from this point of view it may be possible to obtain a truer conception of the realities of government during the 'Age of Reform' and especially in the crucial decades of the 1830s and 1840s.

The 1831 census credited Great Britain with a population of only $16\frac{1}{2}$ millions.

Britain was still primarily a rural society, and largely dependent on agriculture. For the most part its people lived in much smaller communities than we do now, and for most people life was bounded by local considerations much more than it is today. These local considerations, however, existed in very varied forms, and this in itself posed difficulties in devising reforms which were to be applied on a national scale. For example, the impact of the 1834 Poor Law Amendment Act proved very different in its application to the Hendon and Pwllheli Unions.[1] In the former, close to the centre, wealthy and relatively sophisticated, the 1834 Act produced quite quickly an active local authority, willing to take action in matters of public health, education, and specialist provision of facilities for such groups as the mentally ill among the poor; the Pwllheli Union, in remote North Wales, extensive and poor, presented a very different picture in a situation in which it was said that 'even those who paid poor rates seldom ate meat and some of the Guardians are little removed from pauperism'. It is not easy for us, living in an age of speedy national, and indeed international, communication, with a variety of readily accessible mass media, to appreciate this kind of difference in society's nature. It does, however, seem probable that these smaller, and for the most part localized, communities still possessed a degree of internal cohesion which later developments have somewhat eroded.

Britain throughout the 'Age of Reform' was not at all an equal or democratic society; great inequalities of status, of possessions, of influence, of opportunity, were the norm. It is crucially important, however, to remember that there was nothing in the least new about this; no Merrie England of equality lies anywhere beyond in the past. Even the extent of democracy and equality which we have attained lay far in the future and was scarcely even a widespread dream in the early years of the nineteenth century.

In terms of the formal agencies of government early nineteenth-century Britain possessed very limited resources of administrative experience and expertise. When Sir Robert Peel became Home Secretary in 1822 the Home Office, the most important domestic department of state, possessed a staff of only about twenty.[2] The staff of the Board of Trade in 1840 numbered about 30.[3] Nor were the arrangements for the enlistment and retirement of these small groups of civil servants calculated to promote the highest standards of administrative efficiency. Patronage remained the normal basis for appointment, and arrangements for retirement and pensions were not systematically organized. An example can be drawn from the Admiralty, not only a mainstay of national defences but also one of the country's biggest spending departments; the key position of secretary there was held (with one brief interval) by Sir John Barrow from 1804 until his retirement at the age of eighty in 1845.[4]

[1] R. Grace, 'The Hendon and Pwllheli Unions, 1835–1871', paper summarized in *Bulletin of the North-East Group for the Study of Labour History*, no. 4, Nov. 1970, 15–16.

[2] N. Gash, *Mr. Secretary Peel*, London, 1961, 297.

[3] H. Parris, 'A Civil Servant's Diary', in *Public Administration*, Winter 1960, 370. This paper has a wider interest for administrative behaviour in this period.

[4] Ibid. 377. Sir John Barrow is also in *D.N.B.*

In considering, therefore, the history of government and administration in the 1830s and 1840s we must not think in terms of the existence of sophisticated governmental machinery, equipped with a wide variety of resources and information. When the Whigs took office in 1830, for example, there had been only three national censuses, each of them limited and imperfect in the information which they obtained. There were at that time not even reliable maps covering the country's terrain in any very systematic form. Arrangements for such a fundamental business as the drafting of legislation were still haphazard. In a whole variety of ways British government was singularly ill equipped, as far as the formal machinery of administration was concerned, to cope with the emerging problems increasingly posed by population explosion and economic and social change.

This weakness certainly limited the efficiency of government and administration, but was in some respects less damaging than might appear at first sight, because Britain in the early nineteenth century did not depend on the formal agencies of government as much as has been the case in later periods. British society throughout the 'Age of Reform', and especially in its earlier years, was still much more held together and effectively controlled by a great mass of essentially unofficial disciplines and controls emanating from factors outside the structure of government. In that inherently unequal society the power which derived from birth, possessions, or education was more important in controlling society than the power emanating from formal office in central or local government. The two aspects of power were not of course separate; the ruling minorities which essentially controlled the economic and social aspects of that society also dominated the politics of local and central government, and this concentration of official and unofficial power was a formidable one. The nature of the connection is well exemplified in one key office, the county magistracy which played a crucial role in local government. It was not in practice the case that a man became important and influential because he became a county magistrate; a man normally became a country magistrate because he was already important and influential in terms of birth, property, or status, and his unofficial dignity qualified him for the additional status and influence of the magistracy.

If, then, government in the early decades of the 'Age of Reform' did not possess extensive resources for the expansion of government activity, what of the will to use and expand the resources which did exist? For readily explicable reasons the ruling minorities—and not only those groups—were deeply suspicious of attempts to extend the range of government activities and the numbers of government agents. For example, it was well known that from time immemorial governments had used their powers of appointment for partisan political purposes; although by the end of the eighteenth century there was a distinct tendency towards higher standards of selection, and away from the unscrupulous use of government patronage for partisan purposes, the process was very far from complete, and it is not surprising that it was to be a long time before the wide suspicion of government patronage markedly declined. It is still not dead. If we consider some of the appointments made by the reforming Whigs in the 1830s to the important new civil service posts they established, it is very obvious that partisan considerations still retained an important place. James Stuart of the early factory inspectorate, Sir John Walsham of the poor law assistant commissioners, are examples of important appointments of men with close personal links to the party in power; it is worth noting, however, that if H. S. Tremenheere owed his first government appointment in part to his being 'the only Whig in the family', yet once established as a member of the civil service, he was subsequently entrusted with important new responsibilities by both Whig and Tory governments.[5] Nor was the continuing presence of patronage in the government service simply a wicked device of corrupt politicians; it was at least as much due to the enormous pressure for government jobs which descended on the head of any man in a position or believed to be in a position to influence appointments. The papers of prominent politicians of the 'Age of Reform' abound with pleas of this kind; apart from ministers themselves, members of parliament were expected by their constituents to ensure that a proper share of the sweets of office should be obtained for the benefit of the constituency, and a considerable amount of an M.P.'s time had to be devoted to the scramble for patronage. While this situation continued, it was not easy to maintain or present the civil service as an agency of disinterested public service.

The second important factor militating against the expansion of government agencies to cope with social problems was the cry for cheap government. This cry was frequently louder than any expressions of enthusiasm for bigger and better administration. Nor was this a demand confined only to a propertied minority of electors and taxpayers, for it existed in all reaches of British society. The concept of a greedy and selfish minority strongly ensconced in power refusing to listen to the cry of the nation outside for higher government expenditure for social purposes may be an attractive one, but it is essentially unreal. Even in contemporary radical propaganda, for example, accusations of waste, extravagance, corruption, and inefficiency appeared much more frequently than any constructive proposals for arming the government, by higher taxation, with new resources to tackle the major social problems of that society. When in the early 1850s the Small Tenements Act greatly extended the municipal franchise, the effect in practice was normally that town councils were faced with strident demands not for expensive municipal improvements, but that the rates be kept down. It is difficult to see in the Britain of the 1830s and the 1840s any widespread and continuous pressure for the increased government expenditure and proliferation of government agencies which hindsight tells us were one of the necessary means of substantial improvement. Where expansion took place, and expenditure increased, it was more often the product of small groups of devoted reformers, usually within the ranks of the ruling minorities and not infrequently within government itself, working with the inexorable facts themselves, than the

[5] For Tremenheere generally there is a very able paper by R. K. Webb, 'A Whig Inspector', in *Journal of Modern History*, 1955, 352–64.

result of any continuous or widespread demand for more government at any level of British society.

The demand for cheap government was one of the major limitations on the freedom of action of a government in the 1830s and 1840s and for long afterwards. The reforming governments themselves were by no means immune to this pervasive demand; the Whigs entered office in 1830 under the banner of 'Peace, Retrenchment and Reform', and for many of their supporters 'Retrenchment' was by no means the least significant item on the triad. Yet it is undoubtedly true that it was a society still effectively dominated by minority propertied groups which did, however reluctantly, lay the foundations for expanded government activity in the course of the 'Age of Reform'.

An examination of certain aspects of the reforms of the 1830s and 1840s in more detail may help to amplify some of these arguments. We may take first the Great Reform Act of 1832. It is sufficiently clear that this measure was not based on any very accurate knowledge or assessment of the nature of contemporary society. A cardinal point in the reformers' case was a broad but inherently vague concept of the virtues of a middle class which is difficult to recognize in reality in the shape accepted by the reformers. It is likely that in concrete terms the nearest approach to a coherent, articulate, and identifiable middle class actually existing in the early 1830s was formed by the tenant farmers, but it is clear that this was not the middle class envisaged by the reformer. The 'middle class' with which they comforted themselves was more of a political myth than anything else.

It was not only the reformers themselves who did not see their society objectively or accurately. A notable feature of the subsequent writing of the 1831–2 reform crisis has been the exaggerated importance which some historians and many students have attributed to the radical and working-class contribution to the triumph of reform in 1832. There was another factor at work which was more important in the terms of that society, and that was the very wide support evoked by the Whigs' reform proposals from within the dominant propertied interests. The 'country' interest had long regarded the pocket and rotten boroughs as the basis for widespread government corruption and extravagance, and the Whig Bill was eminently well suited to meet these long-standing beliefs within the landed interest—after all, that was the essential source of the proposals, and the substantial reduction of seats allotted to decayed boroughs, together with the substantial extension of county representation, admirably suited 'country' political ideas. The Tories knew by 1832 that in opposing the Reform Bill they had been deserted by large parts of their usual support within the landed interest; the Whigs knew that in pressing their reform they were supported, not simply by the noisy and distinctly embarrassing popular demonstrations, but by the bulk of 'respectable' opinion throughout the country. The 1831 general election, a key event which provided the Whigs with their decisive majority for reform, makes this point very clear. It was of course fought on the old unreformed franchise and distribution of seats. Certainly in some seats the popular agitation out of doors played an important part in the triumph of reform, but the overwhelming swing of the county seats to reform is not to be explained in these terms. In Northumberland, for example, a county very much dominated by the landed interest and normally with a strong Tory bias, a sitting Tory member, Matthew Bell, in normal times an influential and popular local figure, withdrew from the contest in 1831 after a very short canvass convinced him that even Northumberland could not be held against reform. The alignment was to be a temporary one, and a major reason for the decline of the Whigs in the later 1830s was their inability to hold on other issues the wide range of establishment opinion they had temporarily recruited for parliamentary reform in 1831–2. The point can be further illustrated by employing the counter-factual approach, apparently fashionable in some areas of history today. Had the landed interest been united, or anything like united, in opposing reform in 1831–2 the story would have been a very different one, in spite of all the popular demonstrations, and indeed it is difficult to see how in those circumstances any practicable Reform Bill could have been before parliament at all.

Some of the major practical difficulties faced by the Whigs in drafting their Reform Bill are of considerable interest in illustrating some of the problems of government and administration in the earlier decades of the 'Age of Reform'. Of course they approached their task in no spirit of democracy, and there seems no very good reason why they should be expected to have acted in so patently anachronistic a way. Instead, they were concerned to recruit to the political nation groups who could be seen as potentially useful repositories of stability and political sagacity. This attitude, however much decried by later conceptions of society, must be seen as a tolerably enlightened one for an aristocratic political party in the early nineteenth century. Their intention was to admit the safe few, and firmly exclude the dangerous many. But just how, in the Britain of the 1830s, were you to separate the sheep from the goats? If for example they had believed in the concept that wisdom comes with age, they would have faced the immediate difficulty that in a society without any formal machinery for the registration of births, legal proof of age could only have been obtained by some kind of expensive official machinery at a cost unlikely to appeal to a party of retrenchment. The key problem was to devise some kind of practical test or tests for the electorate which could be applied at very modest cost, and it is this real difficulty which lies behind the apparently anomalous property qualifications embodied in the 1832 Act. All of them were qualifications which could readily be tested by means of evidence which was already in existence in one form or another. In the counties the freehold, leasehold, and tenancy qualifications could be readily proved by tax or rent receipts. In the boroughs the celebrated £10 household qualification was in no way new; that kind of qualification, easily demonstrable from local rate books, had been employed for generations in connection with the house tax, and the £10 limit itself had been employed for that purpose as a limit of exemption as recently as 1825.[6] The Whig reformers knew very well that these devices for

[6] R. Blake, *Disraeli*, London, 1966, 333.

enfranchising the 'property and intelligence' of the nation were very rough and ready rather than precise, but they were seeking the best practicable solution to a genuinely difficult problem.

The same kind of limitation can be seen at work in the provisions for the registration of the new electorate. The aim was effective registration without any great additional government expenditure. For this the government needed a body of officials throughout England and Wales which could carry out the task of making and maintaining lists of those qualified to vote. The choice of this agency posed no practical difficulty, for only one body of men existed to meet this need—the poor law overseers—and the task accordingly devolved on them.[7] It was equally obvious that here again the solution was a necessary rather than a perfect one, and a modest system of supervision which did not cost very much was inaugurated. The part-time revising barristers and their annual revision courts had a long career ahead of them, and their courts proved to be an arena of party conflict in a way which the Whigs who inaugurated the system had clearly failed to foresee. Here again partisan considerations certainly played a part in the selection of these electoral judges, and it is not surprising that it was to one of these posts that H. S. Tremenheere was appointed ('the only Whig in the family') in 1839.

One final point may be made about the 1832 Reform Act. The bestowing of independent representation on many industrial towns has always appeared as a cardinal feature of the reform. It is just worth noting, however, what some of the more obviously industrial constituencies did with their new seats, for in a number of startling instances the new industrial Britain showed an unmistakable preference for representatives from the older ruling groups. The case of Milner Gibson, squire and ex-Tory, sitting for Manchester from 1841 to 1857, is remarkable enough, but even more striking is the behaviour of Wolverhampton, a borough which holds the record for a member's uninterrupted tenure; it was represented in the House of Commons from 1835 until 1898 by the Hon. Charles Pelham Villiers, son and brother of earls of Clarendon. The extent to which industrial Britain was truly radical can easily be exaggerated.

Another Act in which change was very obviously limited by considerations of expense and local autonomy was the Poor Law Amendment Act of 1834. The concept of cheap government seriously limited the level of new staff and new expenditure; the instinct for local action preserved important functions from central encroachment. The 'new' poor law was to a large extent made up of pieces of the old; the new Unions consisted of groupings of old parishes and townships, which continued to play important roles in poor relief. Another limitation was also effective here; there was only one reservoir of experienced officials to operate the new poor

---

[7] Different arrangements had to be made for Scotland and Ireland where the poor law machinery employed in England was lacking. This need to improvise the use of existing resources is not just a nineteenth-century phenomenon—consider the use of the available Board of Customs and Excise in the early administration of state old age pensions.

law, and that was the officers of the old. Inevitably, as in subsequent remodellings in the 1930s and 1940s, the reformed system had to rely on the services of those experienced and to some extent moulded by the practice of the older system.

This point may usefully introduce a further general limitation on the effectiveness of the reforms of the 1830s and 1840s, the great difficulty of finding the right people to carry out extended government functions in a society so little accustomed to bureaucratic procedures. The problem of satisfactory recruitment caused immense difficulty in the creation of the Metropolitan Police after 1829, and was to prove a besetting problem for other police forces in subsequent years. The poor law system after 1834 and the factory inspectorate after 1833 met recurring problems in trying to find suitable staff. There was no large reservoir of individuals trained to government service and its responsibilities, and the teething troubles of the new government agencies in this respect were not surprising.

In staffing the new elements within the civil service, however, government could draw on two advantages which are not perhaps apparent at first sight. There was one aspect of government activity which had recently experienced major needs to expand administrative expertise, and which disposed of reserves both of administrative experience and technical skills. These were the officers of the armed services, who provided in the earlier years of the 'Age of Reform' a useful reservoir of administrative talent on which governments drew to a considerable extent, this in addition to a notable contribution to the maintenance of internal security, where the officers of army and navy demonstrated a striking capacity for common sense, conciliation, and moderation in carrying out police duties which they did not enjoy.[8] The Royal Engineers provided (and provide) the railway inspectorate, and through their part in creating the Ordnance Survey they also provided one basic requirement for government activity, a precise mapping of the country. The army was at once one of the biggest administrative units and a major spending department; it was not, therefore, surprising that the creator of the reformed postal system should have a distinctively military background. H. S. Tremenheere, successively revising barrister, schools inspector, poor law assistant commissioner, and inspector of mines and collieries, came from a military family. Officers from the Royal Engineers frequently took part in sanitary inquiries, and naval officers were frequently called on to study the ways in which the nation's ports could be improved.

This was in a sense a specialized facet of the second advantage which government possessed, the presence of a sufficient number of men well ensconced within the existing ruling groups, who were willing to take on new administrative roles and forward the expansion of government activity. In the realities of British society in the 1830s and 1840s it was of crucial importance for the relatively smooth inauguration of administrative innovation that the government could command the services

[8] For one instance of the ability of the armed services to develop administrative systems in the early nineteenth century see N. McCord, 'The Impress Service in North East England during the Napoleonic War', in *Mariners' Mirror*, liv, 1968, 163–80.

of an important group of men of independent status and influence to act as inspectors of factories, railways, schools, or mines, or as assistant poor law commissioners. In that kind of society a man who was a civil servant and not much else might find it very difficult to implement new methods in the face of local vested interests, but if he himself enjoyed—to use a handy classical concept—a considerable personal *auctoritas* independent of his official position then his task could be considerably eased. Good examples of this kind of man were Leonard Horner of the early factory inspectorate—a public figure and scholar of some distinction; Sir John Walsham, Bart., of the assistant poor-law commissioners—a landed aristocrat with close personal and family ties to the political élite; and H. S. Tremenheere, already mentioned, who came from 'an ancient Cornish family', was the son of a distinguished soldier, and inherited a substantial family estate.[9] In all of these cases it is clear that the official's administrative work was markedly facilitated by his own personal status. It is equally clear that where local interests succeeded in impeding or thwarting their efforts this was usually due to the inclusion among their opponents of men of equivalent or superior social metal. Walsham, for example, was repeatedly defeated in his efforts to persuade the Castle Ward Guardians in Northumberland to build a new workhouse, by the efforts of a coalition organized and led by Sir Charles Monck, Bart., while in the Rothbury Union he faced much more serious difficulties, against an opposition including not only Tory landowning families like the Liddells but also the wealthy Rector of Rothbury, who was a Vernon Harcourt, son of an archbishop of York, and a considerable source of paternalistic charity within the district. Nevertheless the resistance of local vested interests to administrative innovation would have been much more serious if government had not been able to call upon Establishment figures to staff the key posts within the new administrative agencies. Men like Horner, Walsham, and Tremenheere played an important role in establishing the 'respectability' of the posts which they held, and in a sense paved the way for successors entering government service from other social levels and by other channels.

These recruits, together with the existing resources embodied in the older departments of state, made the task of staffing senior positions relatively easy. It was not so easy in the case of more junior appointments in a society where there was relatively little knowledge of the standards and responsibilities entailed by public service. The records of the early work of such agencies as the factory inspection system or the post-1834 poor law abound with instances of difficulty with staff below the level of inspector or assistant commissioner. H.M. inspectors of factories were assisted by superintendents (later sub-inspectors), and there was repeated trouble at this level,

---

9 Horner is in *D.N.B.*; for the factory reform movement generally see J. T. Ward, *The Factory Movement*, London, 1962. Another useful discussion of an early inspector of factories, which is relevant to some of the arguments advanced here is U. R. Q. Henriques, 'An Early Factory Inspector; James Stuart of Dunearn', in *Scottish H.R.*, 1971, 18–46. For Walsham, see N. McCord, 'The Implementation of the 1834 Poor Law Amendment Act on Tyneside', in *International Review of Social History*, xiv, 1968. For Tremenheere, see R. K. Webb, op. cit. and also O. A. O. MacDonagh, 'Coal Mines Regulation: the First Decade', in *Ideas and Institutions of Victorian Britain*, ed. by Robert Robson, London, 1967, 58–86.

ranging from simple inefficiency or prolonged physical incapacity to the more sinister figure of Mr. James Webster, who combined a disinclination to move away from Bath to perform his duties with more than a suspicion of serious corruption and embezzlement.[10] Within the poor law system too, there was a flow of drunken or inefficient relieving officers, absconding collectors, or embezzling workhouse masters; the post-1834 system seems, however, to have been somewhat more effective in weeding out the unsatisfactory officials than the old system had been. It is important too to remember the considerable inherent bias of our evidence, which naturally represents most clearly and strongly to us the occasions where something had gone wrong, however untypical they may have been; the continuance of relatively satisfactory normality is not usually the subject of parliamentary inquiry or newspaper coverage. It nevertheless remains true that the task of finding growing numbers of suitable men to staff junior government posts was perennially difficult, especially in the early decades of the 'Age of Reform', and that defaults or derelictions at this kind of level were responsible for much of the hardship which took place during the implementation of administrative innovations, especially in the case of the new poor law.

Already by the 1840s and early 1850s government was finding a need for the services of men with more specialized qualifications. This appears clearly in the case of the inspectorate of mines and collieries, where from 1850 onwards the inspectors included men chosen not so much for their general status and talents, but for more specialized knowledge of the particular field involved. It was not always easy to find men who combined technical expertise with suitable social qualities. In the 1860s, after a little experience of subjecting intended mining inspectors to the modest tests of general education then in use for many home civil service posts, the Home Office judiciously decided that in the case of H.M. inspectors of mines and collieries a test of their technical capacity was all that should be demanded of them. A typical example of this newer group of government agents was Matthias Dunn,[11] one of the country's leading experts on mining, appointed an inspector of mines and collieries in 1850. Dunn was not ideal bureaucratic material, as was instanced when the Treasury indignantly refused his first accounts which included a charge justified only as 'sundry expenses about home'.

It is easy for us to see the history of nineteenth-century Britain in wide perspective; it was not so for the men in key positions at the time, who had to respond to a society changing with unexampled rapidity and to work through a distinctly feeble array of administrative resources. Much of what was done, both in legislation and in administration, was pragmatic and experimental. Some statutes were timorous and damaged by the parliamentary opposition of vested interest. Some on the other hand were distinctly bold and adventurous; a notable example of this quality was

[10] For Webster see P.R.O., H.O. 87/1, Maule/Webster 24 Apr. 1837 and 27 July 1839. The H.O. 87 series contains much information on these staffing problems of the early years of the factory inspectorate.
[11] H.O. 87/2 Waddington/Dunn, 21 Nov. 1850. Dunn also appears in *D.N.B.*

Labouchere's Mercantile Marine Act of 1850—the antithesis of *laissez-faire*, embodying detailed codes of supervision for merchant shipping crews which aroused considerable opposition from the seamen in whose interests the proposed supervision had been drafted.[12] Statutes drafted by somewhat haphazard methods and often based on inadequate evidence, frequently mutilated in parliament, failed in many cases to be effective means of achieving the desired objective of the legislation, yet it is not easy to see how, in the circumstances of the time, these weaknesses could have been remedied to any very great extent.

In administrative conceptions and techniques too the 1830s and 1840s present an odd mixture of sophistication and improvisation. For example, if Chadwick as Secretary of the Poor Law Commission busily devised ever more elaborate office procedures and official forms and returns, Sir John Walsham in practice transacted much of his business with the poor law headquarters in long, gossipy, and frequently discursive letters, often directed to the poor law commissioner with whom he was on closest personal terms. Central government itself could often have had only woolly ideas of what it expected from its new agents. Here for example is part of Dunn's letter of appointment as mines inspector in November 1850

> You will keep a record of your visits to all the Collieries you inspect, and of the results of your inspection.
> You will bear in mind the confidential nature of some of the information which you may acquire in the performance of your duty, and you will carefully guard against any violation of the secresy, which, in such cases, ought to be observed.
> You will not fail to act with courtesy and forbearance in your official intercourse with all parties, and you will encourage a good feeling and understanding between the miners and their employers.
> Although it will not fall within your province to take any direct measures for promoting education among the miners, you may usefully avail yourself of any opportunity of pointing out to them its importance and advantages, and lend your influence to the encouragement of any well devised plans for advancing their moral and intellectual improvement. The District assigned to you will, for the present, comprise the Counties of Durham, Northumberland, Cumberland, and the Mining Districts of Scotland.

A substantial District indeed, especially in an age of limited communications!

An analogous set of instructions from a quasi-official context is comprised in the duties which the Great Western Railway allotted to its railway police in 1841.

> The duties of the Police may be stated to consist in the preservation of order in all the stations and on the line of railway. They are to give and to receive signals: to keep the line free from casual or wilful obstructions; to assist in case of accidents; to caution strangers of danger in the railway; to remove intruders of all descriptions; to superintend and manage the crosses or switches; to give notice of arrivals or departures; to direct persons into the entrance to the station or the sheds; to watch movements of embankments or cuttings; to inspect the rails and solidity of the timber; to guard and watch the company's premises; and

[12] I am indebted to Mr. Stephen Jones for information on this subject.

to convey the earliest information on any subject to their appointed station or superior officer.[13]

Two further examples may be cited to illustrate the difficulties which the realities of that society posed for reformers. The Municipal Corporations Act of 1835 looks at first sight like an admirable example of statutory reform after preliminary inquiry and the useful cleaning up of a sizeable slice of local government. The reality was somewhat different. Certainly a Royal Commission sat, produced evidence, and made recommendations, but it was far from an objective process. The key post of secretary to the commission went to Joseph Parkes, a keen radical closely connected with the Whig party. Political allegiance also played an important part in the selection of the assistant commissioners who gathered the detailed evidence and made regional reports. Parkes himself conducted an extensive private correspondence with local radical leaders opposed to the old corporations. It is not necessary to suppose that these local leaders possessed any very enlightened conception of the social utility of reformed municipalities. For example, at a time when population growth was presenting Gateshead with serious social problems of housing and public health, the radicals there saw municipal reform as a method of cutting expenditure rather than of expanding it to improve amenities in the town. Their leader, W. H. Brockett, by no means an unrepresentative figure in the Britain of the 1830s, was of opinion that 'a mayor, aldermen and other expensive machinery of that sort are of course out of the question', and he advocated a much more simple and limited form of local government which would 'answer every purpose and provide for a real economy in funds, as well as a watchful guard over the interest of the borough'.[14]

It is scarcely surprising with these views in the ascendant that the practical effects of the 1835 Act were distinctly limited; indeed it is obvious enough that in some cases —Newcastle upon Tyne was one—the reformed municipality was for many years a less effective agency of municipal improvement than the unreformed corporation it replaced. This is not, however, to say that no attempt was made to meet the increasingly grave problems of the towns, but only to say that very slight attempts were made to meet them by the use of the official agencies of local government, which were in the end to appear as one of the major agencies of reform. It remains true that British society throughout the 'Age of Reform' made ever-greater exertions to tackle problems of poverty and distress by the use of unofficial voluntary agencies, whether in the form of organized charities or by private individual exertions. It was only slowly that it was appreciated that these methods were not enough, and that the intervention of the state would enable faster progress to be made in reducing the fundamental causes of poverty and suffering.

If in practice the actual effect of the 1835 Act was to replace one urban oligarchy with another often even more reluctant to spend the ratepayers' money for social

[13] L. T. C. Rolt, *Red for Danger*, London, 1955, 30–1.

[14] Notes for speech to public meeting, Feb. 1833, in Brockett Papers, Gateshead Central Library. See also N. McCord, 'Gateshead Politics in the Age of Reform', in *Northern History*, 1970, 167–83.

purposes, nevertheless the Municipal Corporations Act did eventually provide a basic foundation on which later generations could build the local government systems which have played a major role in modern administration.

The early years of the factory inspectorate inaugurated by the Act of 1833 provide a classical example of the difficulties entailed in implementing social reforms in a little governed society. At first sight the stipulation in the Act prohibiting the employment in certain factories of children under nine seems simple and clear enough, but in a society without formal registration of births what was a child of nine? The law officers of the Crown could only advise that the surgeon who was responsible for issuing a certificate of age could be guided by the following criteria—'that the child had the ordinary strength and appearance of a child *at least nine* years of age, or *exceeding* nine years of age, as the case may be'.[15] This rough-and-ready solution may seem reasonably adequate, but a further question is also involved—who in the Britain of the 1830s, was a surgeon? The professional groups had not yet acquired a clear identity or organization, and the rough-and-ready further definition that had to be employed for the factory inspection system would not satisfy modern requirements—'any person acting as a Surgeon although not a Member of any College of Surgeons is a Surgeon entitled under the Factory Act to grant certificates'.[16]

If all the limitations which contemporary conditions imposed on government are appreciated, then the achievements of the architects of the 'Age of Reform' will seem more considerable than if they are seen merely as inadequate responses to increasingly urgent problems. Moreover, in two different ways the innovations of the 1830s and 1840s are significant more for their later than for their immediate effects. Once new administrative agencies had been brought into existence for one purpose, it was relatively easy to use their services over a wider range of functions. In this way the post-1834 poor law machinery was employed for the registration of births, deaths, and marriages, and the factory inspectorate could be used to carry out emergency public health measures in the industrial districts during an epidemic. Secondly, a major factor in the continuing expansion of government to meet social needs was the growth in the supply of accurate information on just what those needs were. The poor law commission, and H.M. inspectors of factories, among others, were obliged by statute to lay regular official reports on their proceedings before parliament, and these documents, as well as many other reports and proposals which emanated from within the growing structure of government, provided vital evidence on which to base the case for further intervention and regulation by the state. The new poor law machinery was frequently employed by successive governments as an agency for the collection of statistical and descriptive information on a national scale, sometimes in fields only very sketchily connected to the organization's main duties. Successive Home Secretaries fought with only moderate success against the persistent attempts of factory inspectors to publicize their own experience and concepts of how the factory inspection system should develop. In these ways even the moderate

---

[15] H.O. 87/1, Home Office/Horner, 31 Aug. 1836.   [16] Ibid., 11 Aug. 1836.

expansion of the state's administrative resources which was effected in the first half of the 'Age of Reform' marked a very significant stage in the development of Britain's modern shape.

It is indeed by no means clear that the term 'moderate' is accurate, say for the period 1815–50. These years saw the first major reform of the legislature, an eventually fruitful overhaul of local government, significant changes in the structure of the public agencies for the relief of poverty, the beginnings of serious state intervention in matters of education and public health, and the establishment of state agencies of regulation in the fields of education, factories, railways, mines. It was certainly to take a considerable time for these innovations to achieve substantial coverage and effectiveness, but the first steps counted for much. It is not enough to compare these changes with the more sweeping actions of later periods; they must also be compared with what had been done in earlier periods to improve the efficiency of the state's administrative machinery and to employ it for socially ameliorative purposes.

This is not of course to deny the extensive poverty and suffering which continued to exist. Nor is it to claim that governments did everything they could conceivably have done to remedy this suffering, nor that they contrived to do very well everything which they did attempt. It would seem unjust, however, to regard the record of those who governed Britain in these years as a failure. By any reasonably practicable standard of human competence and merit—though not of course by standards of Utopian perfection—the period showed an oligarchy, on the whole well-meaning, reacting with inadequate resources to complex and unprecedented problems. If the context in which they had to operate, and the materials at their disposal, are fully taken into account, it should be possible to spare those who had to take the responsibility for decision-making in that difficult period from some at least of what has certainly been—*pace* Mr. E. P. Thompson—the excessive condemnation of posterity.

The Prime Minister and Foreign Policy: the Balfour Government, 1902–1905

E. W. EDWARDS

BALFOUR'S period as Prime Minister was brief, from July 1902 to December 1905, and final. Though he was to hold high office in the future and to remain active in politics until his retirement in 1929 in his eighty-first year, he was never again head of government. In the general election of January 1906 which followed the resignation of his ministry in December 1905 his party went down in disastrous defeat, the consequence in large degree of internecine conflict publicly waged. Nothing of this concerned foreign policy. In a ministry remarkable for the number of resignations of senior ministers which it suffered in its short life there was unbroken continuity in the administration of foreign affairs. Lansdowne, whom Balfour had retained at the Foreign Office when he succeeded Salisbury as Prime Minister, was still there when the government came to its end. If, inevitably, the achievement of the ministry was limited in domestic policy—though the Education Act of 1902 was a major reform—its record in foreign policy and in the allied sphere of defence, with the Anglo-French agreement of 1904, the renewal of the Anglo-Japanese alliance, the first stages of the Moroccan crisis, and the establishment of the Committee of Imperial Defence, was of particular significance.

All Prime Ministers are necessarily involved in foreign policy questions. It has long been accepted that in so important an area of policy the Prime Minister has an unquestioned right of concern and intervention. Ideally his role has been defined as that of 'sympathetic critic and helpful adviser'.[1] There were of course wide variations in practice during Balfour's political lifetime. Some Prime Ministers were little interested and relatively uninvolved, some at the other extreme—Salisbury, and Ramsay MacDonald in his first ministry—combined both functions in their own person; Lloyd George, a masterful Prime Minister, conducted what was virtually a private Foreign Office, reducing his Foreign Secretary almost to the position of an Under Secretary;[2] Rosebery, a masterful Foreign Secretary 1892–4, virtually excluded Gladstone as Prime Minister from the field of foreign policy.

For Balfour himself the area, together with defence, was one of special appeal. In the judgement of Austen Chamberlain, writing with long experience behind him, 'No Prime Minister ever took a closer interest in or, except when also Foreign Secretary . . . a more active part in the conduct of foreign policy.' As Chamberlain

---

[1] Sir Ivor Jennings, *Cabinet Government*, 3rd edn., Cambridge, 1965, 195.   [2] Ibid. 187.

remarks, Balfour, when he succeeded Salisbury in 1902 had had considerable experience in the conduct of foreign affairs. On several occasions during Salisbury's last ministry he had acted as deputy Foreign Secretary and had charge of the Foreign Office at times when critical decisions had to be taken.[3] In these circumstances relations between the Prime Minister and his Foreign Secretary might have led to friction for Lansdowne, even if his period in the War Office, that grave of political reputations, during the South African war had inevitably diminished his stature, had himself a wealth of successful experience in responsible office as Governor-General of Canada and Viceroy of India. Moreover, he had succeeded Salisbury at the Foreign Office in November 1900, had conducted affairs coolly and ably and had been largely responsible for one major development, the Anglo-Japanese alliance, which he had carried through in face of a notable lack of enthusiasm on the part of his colleagues. That there should be some conflict between Prime Minister and Foreign Secretary was almost a convention. As Balfour himself was to put it in 1923,

It is the rarest thing when the Prime Minister and the Foreign Minister don't clash . . . you can't expect the P.M. not to interfere with Foreign Office business. It's only when you get a combination of two men who see absolutely eye to eye and work in perfect harmony that you can avoid it. Lansdowne and myself were one of the rare cases—but I could give you any number of instances of the other. The fact is that the Foreign Office cannot be in a watertight compartment.[4]

No doubt the consistent serenity of relations between Balfour and Lansdowne was to be explained in part by long acquaintance and friendship—Balfour had been Lansdowne's fag at Eton—in part by temperament, for both men were cool and restrained, but essentially it was the result of community of outlook upon the ends and means of policy. Balfour's intellectual superiority was not in doubt but then he was in this respect superior to all his colleagues; indeed, it was to be said of him that his was the finest mind applied to politics in his time. Behind the impression of languor and even indolence that he conveyed lay a capacity for application and absorption of essentials which gave him a remarkable command of business. A Foreign Office official who acted as secretary of the Committee of Imperial Defence in its early stages was struck by 'the complete supremacy which Balfour exercised over his colleagues . . . He himself took endless trouble to study the questions which were coming up for discussion and afterwards to see that my minutes accurately reproduced the decisions reached.'[5] Balfour's appreciation of the necessity for the

---

[3] Sir Austen Chamberlain, *Down the Years*, London, 1935, 209.

[4] B. E. C. Dugdale, *Arthur James Balfour*, 2 vols., London, 1936, ii. 292–3.

[5] Sir John Tilley, *London to Tokyo*, London, 1942, 40. G. W. Monger, *The End of Isolation*, London, 1963, 93–4, notes that the decision that the Prime Minister should be the only permanent member of the C.I.D. increased his power in determining foreign policy. Monger errs in describing Sir George Clarke as the first secretary of the C.I.D. Clarke was the first permanent secretary but preceding him were various temporary secretaries including Tilley from November 1903 to June 1904. Balfour attended all of the sixty meetings of the C.I.D. held during his last two years as prime minister. Lord Hankey, *Diplomacy by Conference*, London 1946, 86.

organizing of business and the accurate recording of decisions taken must have been sharpened by experience of the informality of Salisbury's Cabinets where ministers were often of differing mind at the end of a Cabinet as to what course of action had been agreed upon, a circumstance which raised doubts even in Salisbury's mind as to the wisdom of not recording Cabinet decisions.

I am beginning to think, he wrote to Balfour, 19 April 1900, that the rule, of which we are rather proud, that there shall be no record of a Cabinet's proceedings is a mistake. I had imagined that the Cabinet had unanimously, and rather energetically resolved that the dispatch of Roberts about Spion Kop was not to be published yet there it was in the papers yesterday morning. I have not yet heard any explanation but I have no doubt it will be that Lansdowne did not understand the resolution of the Cabinet as we did.

Balfour replied.

I agree with you that a brief record of Cabinet discussion would be a convenience. My own memory in such matters is very untrustworthy and I sometimes find it difficult, after our confused discussions, to recollect even the instructions which I have received on matters which I have myself brought before it.[6]

Balfour as Prime Minister did not, it seems, institute the 'brief record of Cabinet discussions' which he had once contemplated. Apart from his own letters of report to the king, no record appears to have been made but he did ensure that members were 'abundantly clear' as to the decisions taken.[7]

Lansdowne was more matter of fact, more reserved and formal than Balfour. 'He was said to take so much trouble with small questions that he quite lost sight of the big issues and often to be so busy correcting the English phraseology of dispatches that he forgot what the dispatch was about.'[8] This was an unjust verdict. Lansdowne certainly watched over details and did pay close attention to the drafting of dispatches, meticulously correcting and amending slovenly and inexact language, but he showed a firm grasp of issues as well as of details. He worked carefully and consistently, keeping in touch with developments in all areas of interest, drawing upon the expertise of his officials but forming his own views and maintaining a firm authority over his department. Balfour's own judgement of his Foreign Secretary, made in later years, was somewhat patronizing 'I shouldn't call him very clever. He was— I don't quite know how to put it—better than competent.'[9] Like Balfour his mind was not rigid. In a rapidly changing scene both men were flexible and pragmatic, ready to adjust policy to circumstances, their constant aim the defence, not the expansion, of British imperial interests, their constant care the limited resources, military and financial, which they could command.

[6] Balfour Papers, B.M., Add. MSS. 49691.

[7] Jennings, op. cit. 243.

[8] Sir Frederick Ponsonby, *Recollections of Three Reigns*, London, 1957, 128. In Ponsonby's personal opinion Lansdowne 'will certainly rank amongst the best Foreign Ministers'.

[9] Dugdale, op. cit. i.

Balfour's conception of the proper relationship between Prime Minister and Foreign Secretary was indicated at the time of Salisbury's retirement from the Foreign Office in his support for 'an arrangement which left Lord Salisbury P.M. and put the conduct of F.O. details into the hands of Lord Lansdowne'.[10] Certainly he involved himself deeply in major questions of foreign policy throughout his period of office. His private papers show how closely he was kept informed and consulted by Lansdowne on details as well as on issues of principle. But foreign policy was not the preserve of the Prime Minister and Foreign Secretary. Both, moulded in the Salisbury tradition, were careful to conform to the doctrine of Cabinet responsibility. There was, as is common to all ministries, an inner group which was more closely informed and more active, notably Joseph Chamberlain, Selborne at the Admiralty and from 1903, Austen Chamberlain at the Exchequer, but all important questions of principle were brought before the Cabinet where issues of foreign policy seem rarely to have caused disagreement. There is a striking contrast here with Salisbury's ministry where division and dualism had been marked with Joseph Chamberlain as the leader of a 'ginger' group urging a policy divergent from that advocated by Salisbury. Balfour and Lansdowne never experienced the loss of authority in matters of foreign policy that had been Salisbury's experience.[11] Possibly it was Joseph Chamberlain's absorption with tariff reform, which brought his resignation in September 1903, that ensured harmony for Balfour in foreign policy at the expense of fragmentation over the fiscal question for Chamberlain's transformation by 1902 into a vehement Germanophobe could have created serious division in the Cabinet. As it was his support of the opposition to the Cabinet's wish to participate in the Baghdad Railway venture contributed significantly to the failure of the proposal in 1903. Austen Chamberlain reflected similar views but lacked the authority and assurance of his father.

The influence of officials upon policy was limited, Lansdowne drew upon his experts but formed his own views. He maintained detachment and was not carried away by the strong anti-German current that developed in the Foreign Office. Balfour's private papers show attempts to influence him by at least one of this group, Louis Mallet, précis writer to Lansdowne, who addressed a number of letters to Balfour's private secretaries clearly designed to alert the Prime Minister to German enmity. In June 1904 he wrote,

> I don't know whether the King's visit to Kiel is likely to be raised in the Cabinet tomorrow, but it appears to me that the King should be given a good talking to by Ld. L. before he goes.
> It is unfortunate at the present moment in any case, in view of the Emperor's recent utterances at Karlsruhe and Saarbrücken but we should make every effort to limit it to a mere family meeting. The Emperor is, however, to be accompanied by *his Ministers* and

[10] K. Young, *Arthur James Balfour*, London, 1963, 191.

[11] J. A. S. Grenville, *Lord Salisbury and Foreign Policy*, London, 1964, 127–9; Zara S. Steiner, *The Foreign Office and Foreign Policy*, Cambridge, 1969, 27–8, 50.

Metternich is going over for it and I see the King is to take 10 men of war with him. Is this necessary? The Germans will do all in their power to give the visit an international and political character. The Emperor will not improbably try to lead the King into making some indiscreet reference to Japan . . . and offer his honest brokerage with Russia—but this would be fatal and anything which might arouse suspicion in Tokio should be carefully guarded against.

It is not likely that the Emperor will propose an understanding with England at present but if he did—the King should answer that we should be agreeable if he will add no more to his fleet. Until that day, we must remain on our guard.

When during the Moroccan crisis it was reported that Marschall von Bieberstein, one of the ablest of German diplomats, was to replace Metternich as Ambassador in London Mallet wrote that if Marschall did come it was to make a final assault on the Anglo-French entente.

The peace of Europe and our security depend entirely on the attitude we observe and on our loyalty to the understanding with France. For it must be remembered that unfortunately we have no treaty and no written engagement. If we had there would be no need for anxiety and I believe that we should never be troubled with German ambition again.

It is this uncertainty attaching to the course we should take if war breaks out which is at the bottom of the ceaseless intrigues of Germany which makes the international situation dangerous.

If Marschall comes here the more attention that Mr. Balfour can give to foreign affairs the better.

A fortnight earlier he had urged resistance to a probable demand by Germany to France for a port in Morocco.

. . . The interest for us is extreme. One of the objects of this Morocco demonstration is to prove to the French the valuelessness of an understanding with England in which they will succeed if we do not back them up.

How far are we prepared to go? I would not hesitate but let the French know—when they come to us—that we would fight if necessary.

It would not come to that for Germany would not fight both France and England. But the French have much more to lose for Mr. Arnold Forster's army cannot defend Paris and we may have to back them up. Here again is a great danger for we must avoid all appearance of egging them on.

In the meantime, how would our naval authorities like to see the Germans established in a Moroccan port e.g. Mogador? We ought to make up our minds what policy to pursue.[12]

---

[12] Balfour Papers, Add. MSS. 49747, Mallet to Sandars, 1 June 1904; to Short, 6 May 1905; to Sandars 20 Apr. 1905. The Balfour Papers contain several other letters from Mallet to Sandars on questions of foreign policy. Mallet also sought to influence Lansdowne against Germany. It was he who suggested to Lansdowne in Apr. 1905 that Germany might ask for a port in Morocco, Monger, op. cit. 188–91. Up to the end of 1902 when he became ambassador in Rome, Francis Bertie as assistant under-secretary in the Foreign Office did influence Lansdowne, Steiner, op. cit. 65.

Though action was taken on the question of the Moroccan port the initiator was Lansdowne not Balfour. It would seem in general, however, that such attempts to shape Balfour's views had little success.

As for the role of the king in the making of policy, this was very limited and was accurately summed up by Balfour. 'So far as I remember, during the years which you and I were his Ministers, he never made an important suggestion of any sort on large questions of policy.' Relations between the king and the two ministers were not close. The king seems to have actively disliked Lansdowne and this personal factor may have contributed to sharpen several conflicts over minor questions of policy. Lansdowne maintained courteous resistance in face of royal opposition to the award of the Garter to the Shah of Persia and confined his impatience at the king's interference in the matter of the choice of a king of Norway to his letters to Balfour.

The King has in spite of our entreaties been sending more telegrams about Prince Charles's candidature. It is a pity H.M. cannot keep quiet . . . He has got the German Emperor on the brain, and I am afraid that his constant abuse of H.I.M. is doing a great deal of harm.

In these issues Balfour gave firm support to Lansdowne, going so far over the Garter question as to threaten the resignation of the ministry. If, however, the king's role in the making of policy was negligible he was able to influence appointments in the Foreign Office and Diplomatic Service and his interest and help were responsible for bringing into posts of importance men who were to be significant in the future.[13]

The Balfour government in the field of foreign affairs had to deal with a rapidly changing scene of which certain aspects only can be considered here. When Balfour succeeded Salisbury in July 1902 the focal point seemed to be moving away from the Far East the problems of which had dominated Salisbury's period. The Anglo-Japanese treaty of 30 January 1902 had been followed by an apparently more moderate turn in Russia's attitude on the question of Manchuria and there appeared to be some grounds for believing that the conclusion of the alliance had achieved Great Britain's aim of establishing a balance of power in the Far East. In little more than a year such hopes were dissipated for by the summer of 1903 it became clear that Russia did not intend to withdraw the troops which she had sent into Manchuria during the Boxer rising and that, consequently, there was prospect of conflict between Russia and Japan. British interests in Asia and Britain's position as the ally of Japan made the situation one of acute concern. Policy under Balfour as under Salisbury had to be formulated above all in the shadow of crisis and conflict in the Far East. It was in this one area that the views of Balfour and Lansdowne showed, at times, significant divergence. While few of the Salisbury Cabinet had been ready to do more than reluctantly accept the Japanese alliance advocated by Lansdowne, Balfour alone had put a case in principle against it. Unlike his colleagues who seem to have viewed the

[13] Lord Newton, *Lord Lansdowne*, London, 1929, 236–8, 293; Ponsonby, op. cit. 128, 146–7; Balfour Papers, Add. MSS. 49729, Lansdowne to Balfour, 23 Aug. 1905; Steiner, op. cit. 70–1.

treaty in narrow perspective as a local Far Eastern arrangement Balfour saw it in the broad perspective of the whole area of great power relations. Even more than Lansdowne he held that Russia posed the great threat to British interests but he did not agree that alliance with Japan was the best way to meet it. His arguments were set out in a memorandum to Lansdowne in December 1901, the first paragraphs of which, incidentally, are a further indication of the somewhat informal way in which Cabinet business was conducted under Salisbury.

> In reference to our conversation of yesterday the difficulties I see in the present position of the question of Foreign Alliances chiefly arise out of the perhaps rather hasty decision come to at the first of our Autumn Cabinets with regard to Japan. No papers were circulated to me on this subject before the Cabinet: nor was there any warning that it was likely to be discussed.
>
> I was a few minutes late, and found the brief debate already in full swing, and the Cabinet not very anxious to hear any views on the general aspects of a problem which they were treating in the main as one confined to the Far East. I ought perhaps to have insisted on pressing my views, but was taken so much by surprise that I should probably have done them very little justice.

In this remarkable analysis Balfour pointed out that alliance with Japan carried for Britain the possibility of war over a wide area with France and Russia. He judged Japan to be of doubtful capacity as an ally and, seeing Russia as the major threat to India, the centre piece of the British Empire, argued that participation in the Triple Alliance was far preferable as a safeguard for British interests because the maintenance of Germany, Austria-Hungary, and Italy as a buttress against what he clearly judged to be the superior power of the Franco-Russian alliance was of major importance to Britain.[14]

In the end he accepted the Japanese alliance but retained his doubts about Japan's ability to withstand Russia. When Russo-Japanese relations came to crisis late in 1903 his influence seems to have been decisive in ensuring British detachment from a conflict which he judged with cold realism. Since April 1903 Anglo-French relations had become increasingly cordial, a development contributed to by the rising tension between Japan and Russia.[15] Negotiations were now in progress for a comprehensive settlement of questions which had for long caused antagonism and on which agreement would offer both powers insurance against involvement in the difficulties of their respective allies. Lansdowne vacillated over the Far Eastern situation. In October 1903 he was ready for financial assistance to Japan. By December, apprehensive as to the outcome of a Russo-Japanese conflict in which he expected Japan to be defeated, he was writing to Balfour, 'We must do what we can to prevent war . . .' and contemplating mediation. Selborne, First Lord of the Admiralty, argued that Britain

---

[14] Balfour Papers, Add. MSS. 49727, Balfour to Lansdowne, 12 Dec. 1901.

[15] E. W. Edwards, 'The Japanese Alliance and the Anglo-French Agreement of 1904', *History*, 1957, 19–27.

must be prepared to support Japan to the point of war if Russia seemed likely to inflict a crushing defeat on her. The king, too, called for mediation.

I confess to feeling very anxious at the tension between Russia and Japan, and I earnestly hope that our good offices may be brought to bear strongly on the latter country to induce them not to proceed to hostilities as it would indeed be a most serious matter if this country were drawn into the quarrel. That we should be engaged in another war so soon after the South African war has been brought to a close would be most disastrous and I cannot disguise from you that our great financiers are in abject horror at the mere thought of it, as it would inevitably cripple our resources most seriously.[16]

Balfour resisted these pleas for action and argued for a policy of strict non-intervention. He saw in a Russo-Japanese conflict a solution to the British dilemma—how to weaken Russia—all the more attractive because it would be undertaken by Japan, serving not only her own but British aims, too, at little or no expense to the British Treasury. His reply to the king stated his position clearly.

We are under no *treaty* obligation to fight unless France joins Russia against Japan. It may be confidently said that France will *not* join Russia unless we *first* join Japan.

We are not likely to be forced to join Japan either by public opinion here or by a cool consideration of our own interests, *unless* and *until* there seems a reasonable probability of Russia being about to crush Japan. Mr. Balfour submits that this contingency is exceedingly improbable.

Mr. Balfour entirely agrees with Your Majesty in thinking that we ought to offer Japan every kind of diplomatic countenance and assistance which she may reasonably desire. It would, however, probably be a mistake to urge upon her Government unpalatable advice, however excellent. If, for example, we put pressure upon them to examine any of their cherished schemes in Korea, they might yield, but the Japanese people would not easily forgive us, we should be regarded as false friends who were really backing up Russia, and the value to us of the Japanese alliance would be greatly diminished. We should lose Japan in trying to save it.

The interest of this country is now and always *Peace*. But a war between Japan and Russia, in which we were not actively concerned, and in which Japan did not suffer serious defeat, would not be an unmixed curse. Russia . . . would have created for herself an implacable and unsleeping enemy . . . Mr. Balfour concludes from all this that she would be much easier to deal with, both in Asia and in Europe, than she is at present. For these reasons Mr. Balfour would do everything to maintain peace *short* of wounding the susceptibilities of the Japanese people.[17]

Similar arguments advanced to his colleagues convinced the Cabinet and Lansdowne, despite his marked uneasiness, fell in. No mediation was offered to Japan and,

---

[16] Balfour Papers, Add. MSS. 49728, Lansdowne to Balfour 23 Oct. 1903, in which he puts a case for a guarantee by the British government of a Japanese loan which would enable the loan to be raised on the London market; Lansdowne to Balfour, 22 Dec. 1903; Selborne to Lansdowne, 21 Dec. 1903; Add. MSS. 46893, King Edward to Balfour, 25 Dec. 1903.

[17] Balfour Papers, Add. MSS. 46893, Balfour to the King, 28 Dec. 1903.

during the war no assistance beyond the limits of British obligations under the alliance. The outcome of the war, of course, more than justified Balfour's attitude. Japan had emerged as a much more formidable power than he had envisaged and there could be no question of her value as an ally. When in January 1905 the subject of the renewal of the alliance was raised there was no opposition from Balfour. Indeed it may be not without significance that Earl Percy, the Parliamentary Under-Secretary for Foreign Affairs, who seems to have initiated consideration of renewal, having properly brought the matter to the notice of Lansdowne, wrote directly to Balfour to put forward his views 'in case other questions may put them out of Lord Lansdowne's mind'. Balfour's doubts as to renewal twelve months before the decision need to be taken arose not from distaste for continuation of the alliance but from issues of constitutional propriety.

If we renew before the natural period for renewal arises, can there be any other inference drawn from it than that we do not trust our successors. The fact that we do not trust our successors is undoubted; but they will, for the time being, represent the people of this country, and it seems hard to justify a course which is, and which is intended to be a straining if not a violation of that part of the Agreement which gives liberty to each country to revise its engagements at quinquennial intervals.[18]

Lansdowne, in fact, was ready for an offer to the Japanese of renewal for a term of five years. The matter was considered by the Cabinet at the end of March and negotiations with the Japanese were concluded with the signature of the new treaty of alliance on 12 August 1905. Balfour's constitutional qualms had been stilled, possibly in part by his influential private secretary, J. S. Sandars, who wrote to him in January on

your point in which I admit there is a great deal of force, namely that we do not trust our successors, and that we therefore prejudice their title to consider the matter in all its bearings should the quinquennial period elapse during their term of office. It is a rather high minded view to take, and if we are satisfied that the real interests of the country demand it I am not sure that we ought to be so tender towards our political heirs. But in such a case I feel that your judgement is much better than mine.[19]

Sandars, who had discussed the whole question of the alliance and its prolongation with Lansdowne, expected that Lansdowne 'would bring the subject before Cabinet as it is obviously one for Cabinet to deal with either way'. Evidently the Cabinet set at rest any doubts which remained with Balfour for not only were negotiations proceeded with but Balfour determined to remain in office until the new treaty with

---

[18] Balfour Papers, Add. MSS. 49747, Percy to Balfour 13 Jan. 1905; Balfour to Percy 15 Jan. 1905. In raising the matter Percy was influenced by uncertainty about the life of the government, by a press agitation on the Continent suggesting that a Liberal government might 'back out of the Japanese connection', and by uneasiness about the attitude of popular sentiment in Japan towards the alliance.

[19] Balfour Papers, Add. MSS. 49729, Sandars to Balfour 17 Jan. 1905. On Sandars see Sir C. Petrie, *The Powers behind the Prime Ministers*, London, 1958, ch. 3.

Japan was safely concluded. Though defeated in the House by a small majority on an Irish issue in July he refused despite vigorous criticism from the Opposition either to resign or dissolve.[20]

By this time a marked deterioration had come in relations with Germany. When Balfour had succeeded Salisbury the change had been welcomed in Berlin.

'Lord Salisbury's retirement is looked upon as favourable to the gradual improvement of Anglo-German relations,' reported Paul von Schwabach, Rothschilds' well placed correspondent in Berlin, '. . . the prevailing opinion here is that the relations of both countries are likely to improve considerably within a few years. It is expected that under Mr. Balfour's Administration the occasional salting of sore places will cease. This would suffice to secure the gradual healing process . . . You will see from the above remarks that my friends look forward to the future with a certain amount of confidence.'[21]

This judgement was well founded. As his criticism in December 1901 of the Japanese alliance proposals had shown, Balfour saw Germany and her partners in the Triple Alliance as the natural support of Britain in counteracting the Franco-Russian alliance. As for Lansdowne, if he was more optimistic as to the prospects of reaching a satisfactory *modus vivendi* with Russia, he, too, regarded Germany as a stabilizing factor and, as his policy in the Salisbury ministry had shown, the one European power with which close co-operation was possible. That continued association with Germany was desired by Prime Minister and Foreign Secretary was made evident in the Venezuelan debts question in 1902–3 and still more by the decision to seek British participation in the Baghdad Railway scheme, a decision which met sharp and successful opposition from public opinion and within the Cabinet from Joseph Chamberlain. Relations with Germany were becoming cool by 1903; Germany's naval ambitions were causing disquiet and the resolve to establish a naval base at Rosyth, though no haste was shown in implementing it, was an obvious precautionary measure. The decision to open negotiations with France for a settlement of conflicting interests in colonial questions—in retrospect the most significant foreign policy decision of the ministry—was certainly influenced by considerations of general policy as well as by the intrinsic advantages. Lansdowne instanced the state of relations with Germany as well as with Russia as a reason for removing causes of difficulty with France and awareness that Germany would exploit British involvement in the Far Eastern conflict was a factor in Balfour's determination to maintain detachment there.[22] The essential issue arising from the Anglo-French *rapprochement* is the extent to which its likely effect upon Anglo-German relations was grasped by Balfour and Lansdowne. It was by Cromer who pointed it out to

---

[20] Ian H. Nish, *The Anglo-Japanese Alliance*, London, 1966, 331.

[21] Balfour Papers, Add. MSS. 49747, von Schwabach to Alfred de Rothschild, 16 July 1902 (copy).

[22] Monger, op. cit. 132–3; Balfour Papers, Add. MSS. 49747, Balfour to Spencer Wilkinson, 3 Jan. 1904, 'I trust that, whatever be the course of events in the Far East, this country will not be dragged into hostilities, as, for obvious reasons, this could hardly occur without involving half or more than half the world in a war which would benefit nobody but the neutrals—and chiefly, Germany'.

both and it was by Rosebery. It was appreciated within the Foreign Office by the Germanophobes. What is curious is their assumption that Balfour, despite his un-questioned capacity for large views and penetrating insights, should not have been alert to these wider implications.[23] The evidence, in fact, would not seem to support this assumption. Balfour and Lansdowne expected German reaction to the agreement and expected it to be focused on Egypt and Morocco and precautions—the obligation to diplomatic support—were included in the agreement. This provision of defensive support was insisted upon in face of French objections by Balfour in respect of Egypt and he made no objection when Delcassé then extended it to include Morocco.[24] Furthermore, when, in the negotiations over the Khedival Decree to reform Egyptian finances, Germany proved difficult the British reaction was firm. Germany's demand for a general treaty similar to that which Britain had concluded with France was termed 'a great piece of effrontery' by Lansdowne and the Cabinet agreed that anything in the nature of a treaty with Germany which could be compared with the recent Anglo-French agreement should be avoided.[25] What seems to be more convincing is that Balfour and Lansdowne, though well aware of large possibilities in the settlement with France, had limited objectives—an easing of relations with France which would leave Britain in a position of balance by neutralizing France and therefore to some degree Russia, too, as elements dangerous to Britain—but certainly not to form a counter group or to isolate Germany. It was not a new policy. Salisbury in 1895–6 had made an abortive attempt in the same direction.[26] What transformed the situation was the unforeseen completeness of Russia's defeat by Japan which destroyed the European balance of power, and Germany's attempt to exploit this situation by its Moroccan policy. It was this which necessitated a new direction in British policy and the strong British reaction—in striking contrast with the attitude of France—indicated that this was being given. In making the unsolicited offer to France in April 1905 of strong support in opposing any demand from Germany for a port in Morocco Balfour and Lansdowne seem to have been influenced more by desire to buttress Delcassé and the *entente* than by apprehension as to the effect on British interests if Germany secured a port. The British message went further than

[23] Marquess of Zetland, *Lord Cromer*, London, 1932, 274; Newton, op. cit. 285–6. Monger, op. cit., ch. vi, provides a close analysis of Anglo-French relations, 1903–4. His view is '. . . there is nothing to show that he [Balfour] understood the growing rivalry with Germany, or the effect that the French entente would have upon it', ibid. 233. An assessment by Balfour of the attitude of the British public towards Germany is contained in Balfour to Lascelles (British Ambassador in Berlin), Jan. 1905, Balfour Papers, Add. MSS. 49747, in which he writes that the public thinks 'that while Great Britain cherishes no designs against Germany, Germany is seeking, or, at the best, is waiting for a fitting opportunity for aggrandising herself at the cost of Great Britain. Those who entertain such views cannot but regard with suspicion every movement of German diplomacy. For they conceive that its main end is to raise up strife between us and other powers in the hope that Germany may profit by the exhaustion consequent on a conflict which she has occasioned but not shared. . . . The result of all this mutual suspicion is, in my opinion, deplorable.'

[24] *Documents Diplomatiques Français*, 1871–1914, 2e série, iv, nos. 364, 367, 370.

[25] Newton, op. cit. 329–30; RA, R.25, Balfour to the King, 14 June 1904.

[26] J. D. Hargreaves, 'Entente Manquée: Anglo-French Relations, 1895–1896', *Cambridge Historical Journal*, xi, 1953, 65–92.

the suggestion initially put forward by Lansdowne to Balfour, that the French government, in the event of a German demand, be advised 'not to accede without giving us full opportunity conferring with them as to manner in which demand might be met'. Its firm tone may well have resulted from Balfour's personal intervention. After receiving the telegram containing Lansdowne's suggestion he called on the Foreign Secretary and the two drafted together the terms of the British offer. Both ministers recognized that a German port in itself was no threat. It was the wider implications which mattered. As Lansdowne put it, 'I doubt whether Mogador or Mazaghan are worth much but the establishment of a German station no matter how insignificant at either of these places could have a very bad effect.'[27] The subsequent proposal by Lansdowne in May 1905 for close contact and general exchange of views, if more limited than the French Ambassador assumed, pointed in the same direction. The destruction of Russian naval power at Tsushima for a while gave the British a new assurance, a feeling that unquestioned naval supremacy, the essential element in British 'isolation', had been restored while the resignation of Delcassé destroyed confidence in the French. But within a short time the reality of the situation, the enormous superiority in military power now enjoyed by Germany, was becoming clear. No approaches were made by France to Britain for a pledge of military support in the time of the Balfour government[28] but the indications seem clear that Grey in 1906 in essence followed in relation to the new situation a policy already discernible in embryo in Balfour's response to the Moroccan crisis.

Balfour and Lansdowne, like Salisbury before them, whose heirs they were, were essentially pragmatists; their aim was to defend not to expand and they responded to circumstances in the measures they took. Had it not been for the changed circumstances, the weakening of Russia and the German challenge to France, the Anglo-French agreement could well have remained a colonial settlement, another *entente manquée*.[29] But even if the agreement had not existed it is difficult to believe that, in the situation of 1905, Britain would have remained detached in face of German pressure on France any more than she had in 1875 in the 'War in Sight' crisis. If, alternatively, and this seemed the more likely outcome in April 1904 when the Anglo-French agreement was concluded, Russia had defeated Japan, the power of the Franco-Russian bloc would have been enhanced and Germany and Britain, where all the traditional Russophobia could well have revived, might have drawn together.

---

[27] Balfour Papers, Add. MSS. 49729, Lansdowne to Balfour, 23 Apr. 1905; F.O. 800/127 (P.R.O.), Lansdowne to Bertie, 26 Apr. 1905; A. J. Marder, *Fear God and Dread Nought*, 3 vols., London, 1952–9, ii. 57, Balfour to Fisher, 26 Apr. 1905; Monger, op. cit. 188–92. Balfour's attitude to the question of support to France may have been influenced by Mallet's letter to Sandars, 20 Apr. 1905, cited above.

[28] J. D. Hargreaves, 'The Origin of the Anglo-French Military Conversations in 1905', *History*, 1951, 244–8.

[29] The British attitude in the negotiations with France over Chinese railways 1903–5 supports this view. Initial official reluctance to admit French interests to partnership gave way to acceptance influenced by a clear desire to maintain the *entente*, E. W. Edwards, 'The Origins of British Financial Co-operation with France in China, 1903–6', *E.H.R.* 1971, 315–17.

The resignation of the government ended a co-operation between Prime Minister and Foreign Secretary rare if not unique in its harmony. If the conduct of foreign policy between 1902 and 1905 is to be judged as capable and resourceful, as well it may be, Balfour must receive much of the credit. Balfour regarded the relationship between himself and Lansdowne, a Foreign Secretary ready to defer to and be guided by the Prime Minister, as a model which he himself followed when years later he took over the Foreign Office in Lloyd George's ministry. His relations with Lloyd George—in sharp contrast to those of Lloyd George with Curzon—seem to have been as equable as his own with Lansdowne because he recognized and accepted, as Lansdowne had done, the undoubted right of the Prime Minister to involve himself in foreign policy questions.[30]

[30] Dugdale, op. cit. ii, ch. xii.

The 'Coercion of Wales' Act, 1904

G. O. PIERCE

Attitudes to the Boer War had heightened internal dissensions within the Liberal party, but before it had come to an end A. J. Balfour, then Leader of the House of Commons in Salisbury's Unionist government, generously presented to that party an opportunity which they could scarcely have hoped would have come their way so fortuitously to close their ranks and to achieve credibility once more as aspirants to power. On 24 March 1902 he introduced his notable Education Bill in the House, and on the same day David Lloyd George greeted the occasion with a remark that in retrospect appears, to say the least, unexpected, 'a very great improvement it is . . . I rather like the Bill'.[1] Lloyd George's initial impulsive approbation was to be metamorphosed into vehement opposition in a remarkably short space of time when he began to appreciate, together with the remainder of his party, some of the implications of its provisions. The ensuing protest against the Act, Joseph Chamberlain's cabinet-wrecking campaign for Tariff Reform in the following year, and criticisms of the government's fiscal policy soon induced the feeling among government supporters and critics alike that the end of the administration was imminent. Like Charles the Second, however, it was an unconscionable time dying, and it survived under Balfour's leadership until the end of 1905. Indeed, it would appear that some of Balfour's own friends likened the process to a last-wicket stand during which no runs were being scored, while Balfour resolutely batted on.[2]

Whether runs were being scored or not is, admittedly, debatable. The Education Act is a case in point. Few would now argue that it was not the basis of virtually all subsequent developments in the British educational system, for better or worse. To contemporary nonconformists its greatest evil appeared to be that they were now required to contribute by way of local authority rates to the upkeep and maintenance of voluntary elementary schools, both Anglican and Roman Catholic; arguably, on educational grounds, neither a sound nor a logical criticism. To a section of high-ranking Anglicans, a point not always sufficiently emphasized, the prospect of their voluntary schools being controlled by what may be described as lay or secular authorities, the local education committees, was not particularly acceptable either.

The Act was passed in the face of mounting opposition. Eventually, as in the case of more than one unpopular measure for which Balfour's government was responsible,

[1] *Lloyd George Family Letters 1885–1936*, ed. K. O. Morgan, Cardiff and London, 1973, 132.
[2] Stephen McKenna, *Reginald McKenna 1863–1943*, London, 1948, 11–12.

H

the somewhat unsatisfactory procedural device of applying the closure to debate in the House was resorted to in order to secure the acceptance. As his most recent biographer has pointed out the improvement of the country's educational system was one of the objectives considered to be essential by Balfour and to which he had committed himself 'with powerful tenacity' since the time of the abortive Education Bill of 1896. In any case, the eighteen-eighties and nineties had seen a spate of Commissions which had clearly indicated the need for improvement in the co-ordination of the administration of education, both centrally and locally, culminating in the Board of Education Act 1899. In accordance with the pledge given by the Unionists at the time of the election of 1895, the Bill of 1896 had sought to remedy the financial position of voluntary schools which were at a disadvantage, since the Forster Act of 1870, in comparison with the rate-aided Board Schools. It had proposed the establishment of education committees by county councils to control and support out of the rates both Board, or 'provided' schools, and voluntary, or 'non-provided' schools. It had to be abandoned because of what the same biographer calls 'sheer mania, of the religious variety, (that) lay dragon-wise across the path of the educational reformer'. Balfour had felt this deeply. He had taken over from Sir John Gorst, the task of piloting the Bill during the second reading debate and had had to cope with such exasperating and tedious opposition tactics in Committee as the expenditure of 'five nights to pass two lines with 1,200 amendments yet to be moved'. His own subsequent Bill in March 1897 to secure an aid grant of 5s. per child in voluntary schools, again passed against stern sectarian opposition, he probably regarded as a poor substitute as it was merely designed to give temporary financial relief to those schools. But Balfour had resorted to more dubious procedural tactics in order to see his Bill through, refusing to accept amendments in Committee to avoid the Report stage.[3]

He had given warning, therefore, of his intentions and his determination to employ ruthless methods in parliament before returning to the educational fray in 1902, now actively supported by a formidable ally behind the scenes, R. L. Morant, the *eminence grise* at the Board of Education, and having succeeded his uncle as Prime Minister before the Education Act had received the Royal Assent.

As is widely known, sectarian opposition to the Act in Wales was so strong that it became known as a Welsh 'revolt'.[4] The most prominent feature of that revolt, but by no means its only or its most imaginative feature, was the refusal of the Welsh local authorities, twenty-nine in number,[5] to operate the Act to the satisfaction of the Board of Education. Local councils were strongly nonconformist and Liberal in

[3] K. Young, *Arthur James Balfour*, London, 1963, 207.

[4] The best account of the revolt appears in K. O. Morgan, *Wales in British Politics, 1868–1922*, Cardiff, 1963, 2nd edn. 1970, 181–98.

[5] Thirteen county councils, three county borough councils, and thirteen municipal borough councils and urban district councils. One other municipal borough, Bangor, Caernarvonshire, qualified by definition as a Part 3 authority (s. 1 of the Education Act 1902) but it relinquished its powers to the county council. Caerns. C. Cl. Minutes, Box EA 2, 1 (a).

composition. After the local elections of March 1904 the thirteen county councils in Wales had overwhelming nonconformist, or so-called 'progressive', majorities ranging from 30 per cent in Breconshire to 89 per cent in Merioneth. Few instances of individual passive resistance to the payment of rates are recorded, and those were mainly in the Wrexham borough area, but a recent commentator on the Edwardian scene tends to give the wrong impression when he states that the National Passive Resistance Committee in England not only received wide support east of Offa's Dyke but also 'most of all from rural Wales'.[6]

It cannot be denied that there was close contact between the leaders of the English resistance movement and those of the Welsh revolt, and there is a sense in which it could be said that what Wales saw was a form of collective passive resistance on the part of the local education authorities. But Welsh resistance also had far more distinct political overtones.

In Wales, it was to be the decision of the local authorities whether rates were to be levied for the maintenance of voluntary schools or not. They were the bodies which Lloyd George immediately recognized as being the key to the whole situation, and it was their conformity with his well-directed campaign against the formal implementation of the Education Act that was his constant concern. He assumed command of the situation and revived memories of ailing causes which had been sources of nonconformist radical strength in the past—the struggle for the disestablishment of the 'alien' Church, the nationalist aspirations of the *Cymru Fydd* movement, and sectarian fears made more acute by the renewed vigour of the Church from the middle of the nineteenth century onwards. Since January 1903 he had also been involving local authorities in a demand for educational autonomy in Wales, a Welsh National Council for Education under s. 17 (5) and (6) of the Education Act which allowed for a possible 'combining authorities' scheme for 'the general co-ordination of all forms of education'. Indeed, the abortive negotiations for the establishment of such a body forms the back-drop to the educational situation in Wales up to the fall of Balfour's government and for a time afterwards, and it certainly contributed towards sorely trying the patience of an unsympathetic Board of Education, and of Morant in particular.[7] It also contributed not a little to the fact that provisional local education committees in Wales were reluctant to come to a swift agreement regarding the appointed day from which the Education Act was to come into operation in the areas under their control, three having it postponed until as late as September 1904. Most of them had already passed 'no-rate' resolutions regarding the maintenance of non-provided schools.

In general, voluntary school managers had been informed that councils were not going to accept their full responsibilities towards their schools. The provisional education committee of Carmarthen County Council had passed a resolution as early as 1 October 1902 that the provisions of the Act would not be implemented in its

[6] Donald Read, *Edwardian England*, London, 1972, 159.
[7] L. W. Evans, 'The Welsh National Council for Education, 1903–6' in *W.H.R.*, vi, 1972, 49–88.

area without adequate public control over voluntary schools. Further, on 19 June 1903 the committee adopted an extremely hostile attitude and even rejected a motion that parliamentary grants only should be spent on voluntary schools. When the county council, in turn, refused to accept this recommendation, being in favour of using parliamentary grants if not additional rate aid, there was uproar at its meeting with members of the public crowding the Shire Hall at Carmarthen and even sitting among members of the council and demanding 'no right of entry for the Priest into the People's schools'. Thus intimidated, in August and September the county council adopted its education committee's recommendations to raise a further loan to be applied to its seventy-two provided schools but not to its sixty-two voluntary schools, and to refuse to appoint managers to the latter. However, two days before the appointed day, 30 September, it recovered partially its self-esteem and re-affirmed its earlier unpopular decision that 'so much grant only shall be paid to each Voluntary School as is received in respect of such school'. No notice was taken of requests by managers for information on matters such as the appointment of teachers, salaries, demands for fuel or school materials beyond a curt letter from the County Clerk quoting the council's resolution to forward grants only to managers; 'beyond this the Council declines to interfere with the management of the Voluntary Schools within its area'. The situation was soon brought to the attention of the Board of Education in numerous letters of complaint from the managers and the Board countered by asking the county council what steps they were taking to maintain and keep efficient certain named voluntary schools in the county under s. 7 (1) of the Education Act. The council informed the Board of its resolution and by February 1904 it was told that its treatment of voluntary schools was illegal. An inquiry was held on 24 and 25 March by Judge A. T. Lawrence who reported on 18 April, his report being 'in every way adverse to the County Council' and confirming its illegal actions, but no proceedings followed against the authority other than the enforcement of the obligation to pay the costs of the inquiry. It would appear that it was not the intention of the Board to exact the full penalty by writ of *mandamus* under s. 16 of the Education Act but mainly to publicize the authority's default, and consequently to prove the need for further powers to ensure the effective operation of the Act. That this line of action was quite deliberate was freely admitted, indeed, the ultimate aim was 'to gain time and protract the matter till Parliament were in a position to interfere and provide increased or improved powers'.[8]

The Carmarthenshire 'policy' had been anything but to the liking of Lloyd George. It appeared that this was being broadly followed by the councils of Merioneth, Rhondda, Mountain Ash, and Pontypridd where, incidentally, there was a heavier incidence of provided schools over the non-provided. In Merioneth it was 52:27, Rhondda 35:1, Mountain Ash 14:1; and Pontypridd 10:2. By January 1903 Lloyd

---

[8] Much of the information contained in these paragraphs, except where otherwise stated, is based on P.R.O. Ed. 24/577, *Confidential Memorandum on The Defaulting Authorities Bill*, 25 June 1904, and Ed. 24/578, *The Educational System in Wales (Revised)*, 27 June 1904.

George's outspoken criticisms of the Education Act had been muted somewhat. Always a realist, he may well have begun to appreciate that extreme nonconformist elements in some local councils could well, in their enthusiasm, antagonize their less fully committed colleagues. His political instincts alerted, and 'putting on the wisdom of the serpent, but doffing the harmlessness of the dove',[9] he published a manifesto in the Welsh press on 17 January which was followed by a National Liberal Conference at Cardiff on 20 January where he advised local authorities to follow moderate lines of policy, to operate the Act partially and, if at all possible, without appearing to break the law. This was the technique demonstrated by the Caernarvonshire County Council on which he himself sat as alderman. The Caernarvonshire 'policy' had in common with that of Carmarthenshire only the withholding of rate-aid from voluntary schools and the use of parliamentary grants alone for their maintenance, but in contrast Caernarvonshire assumed complete control over the non-provided schools, making the existence of their managers as unnecessary as was possible. It did not refuse to pay salaries of teachers, neither did it refuse to pay for and supply fuel and teaching apparatus. But instead of handing over the parliamentary grants directly to the schools they were retained in total as a fund from which payments were met without reference to the school managers. The council dealt directly with the teachers and they were given to understand that they were the servants of the council. The schools were also informed that they might not be maintained even in this manner unless they conformed with the requirements of surveys made by an architect in the matter of upkeep and maintenance of the fabric of school premises— an unlikely possibility unless they had further financial resources to fall back on such as the Diocesan Fund which the bishop of St. David's was organizing in his own diocese, and later, the organization of emergency committees in all Welsh counties to watch over the interests of Church schools.[10] By June 1904 the Board of Education judged that five other authorities followed the Caernarvonshire 'policy' in most respects. They were Breconshire where, perhaps significantly, there were more voluntary schools than provided schools, 45:38, also Radnorshire, 40:11, and Denbighshire, 72:47. The exceptions to this trend were Glamorgan, where the proportion of provided schools was greater, 131:81, and Merthyr Tydfil, 18:4.

The smaller authorities, borough councils that qualified as Part 3 authorities under the Education Act in particular, the Board of Education found difficult to categorize. In general they were regarded as maintaining voluntary schools

on a hand to mouth principle, supplying the needs of voluntary schools out of their common education fund, without any declarations of hostility, representing to local Nonconformists that the money used for voluntary schools was all 'grant' money . . . In these boroughs and other small authorities there is probably no strong Nonconformist majority, and a general desire to abide events without forcing the question to an issue.

[9] *The Welsh Leader*, 31 Mar. 1904.
[10] Eluned E. Owen, *The Later Life of Bishop Owen*, Llandysul, 1961, 51, 63.

Their lukewarmness, on the other hand, was another source of concern for Lloyd George and after the Carmarthen inquiry, on 6 April, he exerted considerable pressure on representatives of all local authorities (with the exception of the Llanelli district and the boroughs of Carmarthen and Pembroke)[11] convened to a conference at Llandrindod that inaugurated a Welsh National Executive Committee with himself as chairman, to bring them into a more united frame of mind and to enjoin them to follow the Caernarvonshire 'policy'. By May, Carmarthenshire had cautiously signified its intention to do so but had not yet committed itself in practical terms. Montgomeryshire still handed grants over to each voluntary school separately. Merioneth was in straitened circumstances, twenty-three of its twenty-seven voluntary schools showing an aggregate deficit of £932 already. It was also suspected that some of the smaller autonomous areas probably used the rates without admitting it and, in general, being still loath to assert hostility to the Act. Lloyd George, therefore, had his difficulties in seeking to ensure concerted action on the part of local authorities, but by June the Board of Education were assuming that most authorities would eventually follow Caernarvonshire, maintaining their non-provided schools on government grants and claiming that they were thus 'efficient' according to the requirement of s. 7 (1) of the Education Act, without the necessity of having to expend public money out of the rates upon them.

It was this claim to legality which the Board of Education was not prepared to accept. It maintained that but for the support given to voluntary schools by Church and Roman Catholic organizations many of them would have had to close down. Its case was closely argued. Supported by evidence gleaned from an examination of the portfolios of all voluntary schools in Wales, it sought to show that although the parliamentary grants now included a further *per capita* aid grant based on the number of scholars in attendance at all schools, and an additional subsidy proportional to the amount which would be produced from the rates,[12] Lloyd George's claim that the new grants were at least equivalent to the combined total of the old grants and contributions from the rates was not true of Wales as a whole. It was possibly true in general, but not in detail, of ten of the twenty-nine local authority areas. In Caernarvonshire, for instance, because grants were pooled in a common fund 'the gains of one school were used to mitigate the losses of another', and in other areas a larger population and a higher rateable value could influence the amount of the new grant. But in the other nineteen, with their total of 690 voluntary schools, where there was 'an aggregate difference on the wrong side of £12,000 a year, which comes to an average of £17 a school, or 3s. 2d. a scholar in average attendance', it was not true, so that the expenditure necessary to maintain voluntary schools and keep them efficient in those areas was not being met by parliamentary grants alone. Further large deficits were incurred where maintenance of the fabric of school buildings was concerned, especially in less urbanized counties like Merioneth and Montgomeryshire. The Board argued further that merely to contrast the old income from grants with the new,

---

[11] *The Welsh Leader*, 7 Apr. 1904.   [12] S. 10 of the Education Act 1902, 2 Edw. 7, c. 42.

and to do so mainly on the basis of averages, had no relevance in respect of the future when the increased costs of education, including teachers' salaries, were likely to make grant aid inadequate without the addition of rate aid. It added, 'the "no-rate" body contemplates only the standard of efficiency reached before the Act. Clearly the Act was intended to increase efficiency'. It concluded that 'in every school where the Managers have intentionally been left without funds, there has been a distinct illegality'. Similarly, where managers had been ousted from voluntary schools an illegal action was deemed to have been committed.

Such were the main considerations which led the Board of Education to seek further powers for the operation of the Education Act in Wales. In the meantime there had been feverish activity on the part of Church leaders to cope with the situation although opinion was divided on the best means of achieving a satisfactory solution from their point of view. This is best illustrated by contrasting the actions of two of the Welsh bishops. The Bishop of St. Asaph, A. G. Edwards, later to become archbishop of Wales, sought a compromise or 'concordat' that would permit the transfer of voluntary schools to public control provided facilities for denominational instruction could be safeguarded. He met with scant support, even from his own diocesan Board of Education, but he persisted in his efforts to the extent of introducing an Education (Transferred Schools) Bill in the House of Lords on 9 May 1904. It progressed no further than a second reading on 4 July.[13] The bishop of St. David's, John Owen, on the other hand, sought no compromise and was active in seeking to relieve the pressures on Anglican voluntary schools in the hope that the government would move on their behalf. He visited London frequently and was in constant touch with Morant, Sir William Anson, Parliamentary Secretary to the Board of Education, and other leading members of the government. Morant had assured him in a letter in February 1904 that what he called 'a Pistol Bill' would be introduced in Parliament after the Easter recess 'and we are to settle the drafting finally in the next five days'. Even Balfour himself wrote on 8 March to the worried bishop, 'I quite recognise that the problem of Welsh schools is a pressing one and the cure will cause much Parliamentary trouble but it can be met. I shall be careful to meet it by a general measure'.[14]

In the event, Balfour's anticipation that there would be 'much trouble' proved correct. On 26 April, Sir William Anson introduced the expected Bill which, when it became law, was to be cited as the Education (Local Authority Default) Act, 1904. Lloyd George observed during the second reading debate that it was designed to amend the law as promulgated in the Education Act, 1902.[15] This was, for once, an understatement. It supplemented the law, and was to be construed as one with the Education Act. S. 16 of that Act, which empowered the Board of Education, after holding a public inquiry, to enforce any order made for the purpose of compelling a local authority to fulfil its duty by resorting to the legal remedy of *mandamus*, was

[13] K. O. Morgan, op. cit. 188–9; Eluned E. Owen, op. cit. 37–44; *The Welsh Leader*, 7 July 1904.
[14] Eluned E. Owen, op. cit. 56, 57.   [15] *Parl. Deb.*, 4 Ser., cxxxviii, cols. 165–227.

not rescinded. The Default Bill consisted, in substance, of one all-embracing clause subdivided into three sections, the first being itself further subdivided into two. Briefly summarized, it empowered the Board of Education 'if they are satisfied that it is expedient to do so'[16] to take further action, to confirm as managers of a school any persons who were acting as such and make valid any act or payment which might otherwise have been invalidated by reason of an authority's default, to repay to managers any expenses incurred by them for which an authority ought to have made provision, to recognize any sums expended by the Board under the Act as debts due to the Crown which would be deducted from parliamentary grants paid to the authority, and to allow retrospective operation of these provisions. The Board, in effect, could step in and administer the 1902 Act themselves where an authority was considered to be in default, without resorting to the formality of a public inquiry or involving itself in what was considered to be the cumbersome and comparatively slow *mandamus* procedure. Although, as Balfour had intimated to the bishop of St. David's, it was 'a general measure', there can be little doubt that it was primarily directed against defaulting authorities in Wales.

Procedurally, the Bill was noteworthy for the nature of its passage through the various stages in the House. A comparatively long interval had elapsed since its introduction during which there was increasing tension in Wales. It was even rumoured that the government might not, after all, proceed with the Bill, and one of John Owen's confidants, Lord Cawdor of Castlemartin (formerly Viscount Emlyn and M.P. for Carmarthenshire 1874–85), soon to become First Lord of the Admiralty, wrote to Balfour seeking reassurance. He hoped the rumours were not true because he was of the opinion that the Bill would kill opposition to the Education Act in Wales, 'but if you drop the bill, it will be taken as a sign of weakness, and the County Councils will run riot . . . The great danger to my mind is not so much the administration of the Education Act, but the growth of the idea that Local Authorities can defy Acts of Parliament . . . if the feeling grows we shall not be far off anarchy', and in true British Raj tradition he added, 'with an impressionable people like the Welsh *firmness* is all important'.[17] The second reading eventually took place on 15 July, a Friday, and the Speaker applied the kangaroo closure to the debate in the late afternoon. Neither the hour, the day, nor the method of gaining the acceptance had been particularly amenable to the Welsh members. The debate, after some initial uncertainty, had been on a modified form of an amendment proposed by J. Lloyd Morgan (Carmarthenshire West).[18] A division on the wording of the Bill ensured that it passed

---

[16] It would appear that it was not possible to investigate by any court of law the grounds of the 'satisfaction' required. 'Only in the case of absolute *mala fides* on the part of the Board could a court of law interfere'. W. H. Aggs, *Chitty's Statutes of Practical Utility*, 6th edn., 1911, iv, 333, note f.

[17] Balfour Papers, BM., Add MS. 49709, Cawdor to Balfour, 26 June 1904. I am indebted to my colleague Mr. E. W. Edwards for this reference.

[18] He was later to be regarded with disfavour by Lloyd George, together with Bryn Roberts (Caernarvonshire, Eifion), for his criticism of the policy of defying the Act in Wales. N.L.W. MS. 20448A (Lloyd George MS. 2098). *Notes for Speeches*, 1904.

the second reading without modification. Having thus failed to achieve any success in their opposition to the Bill up to this stage, only in the remaining Committee stage, as a last resort, could the Welsh members hope to secure amendments to its structure. It was considered in Committee on 5 August with the deputy-Speaker, J. W. Lowther (Cumberland, Penrith) not only undertaking his duties as Chairman in Committee but also, because the Speaker was indisposed, performing the duties and exercising the authority of Speaker when the House reassembled to receive the Committee's report. It was again a Friday sitting in the late afternoon of a sultry day. A strange situation arose which was to become something of a *cause célèbre* at the time.

Winston Churchill who had earlier, in May, crossed the floor of the House, complained during the proceedings that the Prime Minister was grossly interfering with the liberties of the House. His protest was mainly directed against the subtle way in which the Bill had been drafted, but it also had wider implications. Loud were the protests of the Welsh Liberal press also against 'the coercion of the House' let alone the coercion of Wales. A closer examination of the circumstances, however, does seem to confirm that Balfour cannot be accused of having acted unconstitutionally, but rather that he was adroit and unperturbable as ever in his exploitation to the allowed limit of the rules and orders of procedure without ever actually contravening them. He also depended a great deal on the discretionary powers of the Chairman, a point not lost on one Welsh lobby correspondent who called the latter 'obsequious'.[19]

Before the House resolved itself into Committee, the deputy-Speaker ruled that a mandatory Instruction standing in the name of Ernest J. Soares (Devonshire, Barnstaple) to divide s. 1 into three clauses was out of order. In Committee,[20] the first amendment standing in the name of Ellis Jones Griffith (Anglesey) was immediately ruled inadmissible by the Chairman as it proposed the postponement of a sub-section of s. 1. The ruling was that only a complete clause could be postponed.[21] Jones Griffith then amended his amendment to propose the postponement of s. 1, which again, in effect, meant the postponement of the whole Bill and was an obvious comment on the skilful way in which the clause had been drafted. The government was accused, not unfairly, of collusion with the Board of Education, and of dealing with at least three substantially different matters which ought to have stood, if stand they had to, as separate clauses. Lloyd George averred 'that the object in thus drafting the bill was so as to be able to closure it in one motion'. He was right, as it transpired, although both Balfour and Sir Robert Finlay, the Attorney-General, referred to precedents. They strongly denied accusations that it was a government expedient to achieve the acceptance by applying the closure 'at a certain time in the afternoon when in their opinion the discussion ought to be closed'. Lloyd George, Churchill,

[19] *South Wales Daily News*, 6 Aug. 1904.   [20] *Parl. Deb.* 4 Ser., cxxxix, cols. 1220–69.

[21] This, and other matters concerning procedure and rules of order mentioned in this context are dealt with in *Erskine May's Treatise on the Law, Privileges, Proceedings and Usage of Parliament*, ed. Sir Barnett Cocks, 17th edn. 1964, 475, 548, 550, 630, 634.

Reginald McKenna (Monmouthshire North), D. Brynmor Jones (Swansea District), and Samuel Moss (Denbighshire East) protested further that unless the clause was dissected no opportunity would be given, according to the rules of procedure, to discuss or amend the various separate points which the clause comprised. It was at this point that Churchill accused the government of interfering with the liberties of the House 'by an entirely new invention—through the method of drafting a Bill, and lumping together conflicting ideas in a particular clause in order to get a simultaneous closure on the whole clause'. He failed to obtain personal assurances from the Prime Minister or the Attorney-General that they had not drafted the clause with this object in mind.

The Chairman ruled that Ellis Jones Griffith's proposal to postpone s. 1 could not be admitted as it was equivalent to a negative of the Bill, or as the Chairman put it, 'there is nothing to postpone the clause to'. He would only allow Jones Griffith to move the omission of a sub-section of the clause, and that if such a motion was accepted the sub-section could be brought up as a new clause. But the slim chances of success of such a proposal was not unappreciated by the Welsh members, and it was not pressed. Furthermore, the Chairman made it quite clear in reply to McKenna's persistent effort to get him to rule that 'sub-sections 2 and 3 should be brought up in separate clauses' that he had no power to interfere with the drafting of a Bill agreed upon in the second reading. McKenna then desperately resorted to the only proposal he could make in Committee in order to obtain further consideration of the structure of the Bill by seeking to close the sitting of Committee for the time being. He asked leave to move that 'the Chairman do report progress and ask leave to sit again'. The Chairman refused to accept this motion and again referred to his suggestion that Ellis Jones Griffith move to omit a section of the clause. This Griffith eventually did 'in order to give the Prime Minister an opportunity of justifying so gross a scandal as this'. This took the form of the question being proposed and put that the first words of sub-section 1 stand part of the clause, the opposition could therefore take the course of voting against it, which they did, but it was carried by 150 votes to 68, two Welsh Conservative members, the Hon. G. T. Kenyon (Denbigh District) and Col. E. Pryce-Jones (Montgomery District) voting with the government.

The second amendment to be moved was that which stood in the name of J. H. Whitley (Halifax).[22] He proposed the insertion of the words 'After holding a public inquiry at which all persons interested have been heard' at the beginning of s. 1, which was meant to challenge what he considered to be the placing of 'Russian power' in the hands of the Board of Education. It was strongly argued by the opposition that to allow the Board of Education arbitrary powers to intervene diminished the power of local authorities. Being the lesser of two evils, the enforcement of

[22] M.P. for Halifax 1900–35. Like the deputy-Speaker, Lowther, he became Speaker of the House in 1921, succeeding Lowther to office. An active opposer of the Education Act 1902, he declared his interest in the Default Bill as a general measure which could affect Yorkshire. There was an active Northern Counties Education League based on Leeds which later warmly commended the actions of the Welsh authorities declared to be in default. *The Welsh Leader*, 20 Apr. 29 June 1905.

an order by *mandamus*, as James Bryce put it, would at least require the Board 'to take the case before a court of law to show and prove to the satisfaction of the court that there had been default, or to make good its case by public inquiry'. Welsh nonconformist fears that local authorities were to be forced to oppress 'their fellow religionists' by having to allow the expenditure of public money on schools which taught doctrines to which they conscientiously objected, without public control, were expressed most forcefully as expected by Lloyd George. This was his first substantial intervention in the discussion, and he began to inject into it considerable heat. Mischievously he denied that he was saying that the Parliamentary Secretary, Anson, was doing anything that was deliberately unfair, but he was inclined to think that the instigation upon which the Board of Education would proceed to act under its proposed new powers would be letters that they had received 'not altogether from parsons, but from bishops . . . This Act was, in fact, the result of episcopal pressure'. As to the government's tactics in procedure, he poured scorn on its attempts to justify the drafting of the Bill; the government wanted to see the Bill through without amendment, he unerringly maintained, in order to avoid a Report stage, having its eyes 'on the clock and the thermometer', and was prepared to adopt arbitrary methods 'unknown in English law. It was borrowed from Siam—it was Oriental' and unfitted to a free community, the reference to Morant hardly needing emphasis. This prompted a keen reply from the Attorney-General who pointed out that it was not necessary to go to Siam for a parallel case, that it could be found in an act passed by a Liberal government, the Education Act of 1870 no less, which had empowered the then Department of Education to suspend School Boards in default without an inquiry, and in any case, had the member for Caernarvon forgotten that the ultimate resort in the case of a *mandamus* was the imprisonment of members of defaulting local councils? The Attorney-General went on to explain that it was not envisaged that imprisonment would enter into the new provisions at all, that the Bill merely proposed that expenses which ought to have been defrayed by a county council should be defrayed, with powers of recovery, and in case of default should be made good. Both he and Anson emphasized the delay in operating the 1902 Act as being the main reason for the Default Bill. To allow further means of delay by initiating public inquiries into every case of alleged default was obviously more than they were now prepared to allow. Balfour, accordingly, rose abruptly to move that the Question be put, and on being put, J. H. Whitley's amendment was defeated by 166 votes to 82.

That the feelings of members on the opposition benches had been acutely aroused was amply confirmed by what followed. If they had considered Balfour's action to be uncompromising, worse was to follow from their point of view. He moved in quite calmly and ruthlessly without a word of further discussion, and rose to apply the closure by claiming to move 'That the Question . . . be now put'. This was quite in order. The Question had to be put without amendment or debate. The only possible contingency that could have arisen was that the Chairman might have considered the motion to have been an infringement of the rights of the minority. He obviously did not in this case. The Question was put, tellers were named, and the division bells rung. Members sitting on ministerial benches entered the division lobby to record their votes. Some minutes of almost complete silence ensued during which the opposition members remained in their seats. They were then invited to enter the division lobby by the Chairman. Lloyd George, seated, and with his hat on, then addressed the Chairman and inquired, on a point of order, whether the closure could be applied as long as there remained on the notice paper substantial amendments to be discussed, quoting an amendment by Walter Runciman and declaiming, amidst opposition cheers, that 'it is a disgraceful thing that the closure should be applied in this way'. A wrangle followed on this theme mainly between Lloyd George and the Chairman, the latter, unfortunately for him, being strangely heavy-handed in his handling of the situation and giving Lloyd George ample opportunity to exercise further his considerable powers of scathing comment on the government's tactics. When the Chairman insisted on his right to judge the substantiality of amendments, to accept the closure, and to consider 'other circumstances', Lloyd George replied amid ministerial cries of 'Obstruction!' and 'Order, order!', 'What circumstances? The exigencies of the government? The exigencies of the Cecil family!' The Question was again put, and members on the ministerial benches again proceeded to the division lobby but the Welsh members and their opposition supporters still remained seated. Lloyd George insisted that this was a farce in which he had no intention of taking part, and declined a third invitation to enter the division lobby. McKenna tried to calm the turbulent atmosphere by seeking an assurance from the Chairman that he had accepted the closure not because of pressure from the Prime Minister but after exercising his own discretion in excluding the amendments that had not been discussed. This, McKenna was told, had been the case, and the Chairman for the fourth time asked the honourable members 'who have now made their protest in a dignified way' to proceed to take a division. Once again the request was refused, and so was a fifth, whereupon Churchill submitted that a deadlock had arisen. Having proved so perspicacious, he drew the attention of the Chairman to a Standing Order which provided that in the case of grave disorder in the House the Speaker could adjourn without the Question being put.[23] This suggestion was ignored. After ensuring yet again that the opposition absolutely declined to proceed to the division lobby, the Chairman proceeded to name the Hon. Ivor C. Guest, Reginald McKenna, George Harwood, Alfred Davies, and Lloyd George, who refused to leave, and he made known his intention to report the circumstances to the House.

On the resumption of the House, twenty-one members were named by the deputy-Speaker of which thirteen were Welsh members,[24] and they were asked to

[23] Cf. S.O. No. 26 (1963), *Erskine May*, 17th edn. 466 (5).
[24] William Abraham, Alfred Davies, Frank Edwards, Lloyd George, Ellis Jones Griffith, D. Brynmor Jones, William Jones, Herbert Lewis, McKenna, Samuel Moss, J. Wynford Philips, Herbert Roberts, and Sir Alfred Thomas.

leave 'for disregarding the authority of the Chair' despite Churchill's protest that it was tantamount to disfranchising Wales. The named members refused to leave, William Abraham (Mabon) declaring that he would have to be carried out. Whether (as reported) circumstances could have degenerated into 'a very violent scene' is questionable for in fact Lloyd George apologized to the Speaker for having to make his protest in the way it had been made, but at the same time he firmly declared that he and his supporters now refused to take further part in proceedings and were prepared 'to walk out and wash our hands of the whole business'. It was H. H. Asquith who finally ensured that no further 'unseemly scenes' occurred, and that, in fact, the Liberal protest culminated in an orderly and apparently dignified demonstration. He left his seat to confer with Lloyd George and then, after returning, rose to declare the opposition's full sympathy with him and the Welsh members, to express support for the protest that had been made, and to indicate their intention to take the course which Lloyd George had suggested. Asquith, Bryce, Herbert Gladstone, and other Liberal members then rose and walked out of the House followed by the whole body of opposition members, including the Welsh members.

Fortunately, in spite of Winston Churchill's earlier doubts, no motion had been made to suspend the named members from the service of the House, not that suspension would have been a new experience for Lloyd George. The Liberal members merely absented themselves for the duration of proceedings on the Default Bill which lasted about two or three minutes. The House resolved itself once more into Committee with the opposition benches completely deserted, the Question was again put and both clauses were agreed to. The Bill was then reported to the House without amendment and with the intention that it should be read the third time on the following Monday, 8 August: 'not a single cheer was raised.'

The third reading was taken eventually in the early hours of Wednesday morning, 10 August, the Welsh members having met the previous afternoon and having resolved that in view of the fact that the Prime Minister had prevented discussion in Committee on 'vital' amendments by a motion for wholesale closure, and in order that the effect of the protest already made might not be weakened by further profitless discussion, 'the Welsh Liberal members decline to take any further part in the Parliamentary proceedings on the Bill'. When the third reading was moved there was total silence on both sides of the House and the Bill was carried without a word of debate. Seven Welsh members only witnessed what must to them have been a sad formality. The Royal Assent was granted on 15 August. As was to be expected, Liberal press comment in Wales on the whole affair was bitter. The tyrannical method of 'government by closure' which ensured that the Act was 'being put on the statute book without debate' was much publicized, and some importance was attached to the fact that the Welsh members had not only secured the support of the whole body of Liberal members but also had made an effective protest 'no less in the interests of parliament and freedom of debate that in protection of the rights of the people'.[25] The Unionist press, on the other hand, was most uncomplimentary towards the un-parliamentary behaviour of Lloyd George and his supporters.[26]

However, another aspect of the criticism levelled against the government raised questions involving the principles of local government; that Balfour had introduced 'a scheme to interfere with the powers of duly-elected local authorities'. Lloyd George, at Caernarvon in January 1906, talked about 'the unquestionable, inalienable right of the authority which levies a rate to control the expenditure of that money'.[27] No doubt such criticisms took no cognizance of what is conveyed by the well-worn observation that local authorities are 'creatures of statute', but the Default Act was, nevertheless, the subject of more substantial legal comment which regarded it as having a historical importance in its relation to the increasing concentration of administrative powers and duties being bestowed upon locally elected authorities.[28] In many respects the operation of the 1902 Education Act was the first severe administrative test imposed on these comparatively recently created authorities. Some conflict between locally elected bodies and the central authority was to be expected, such as had been foreseen in the days of *ad hoc* bodies by the legislators of the Education and Public Health Acts of 1870 and 1875 respectively, in which provisions were inserted to ensure the operation of the Acts by the central authority in case of default, the cost to be defrayed out of rates that could be levied for the purpose. But the Local Government Act 1888 contained no such provision out of respect, so it was averred, to the status of the county councils to which duties were being transferred. Neither did the Education Act 1902; the *mandamus* clause was a common law remedy, a process of inquiry followed by the issue of a writ at the suit of the aggrieved party. The method of enforcing obedience to a writ of *mandamus* was by imprisonment, deemed to be a form of coercion to be avoided when dealing with collective units like local authorities especially where religious and even national scruples were involved. This was especially applicable to Wales where there was the additional political desire to avoid the creation of martyrs. In any case, should imprisoned defaulters have remained obdurate, the neglected duty would have remained neglected. That this line of thought was also partly responsible for the Default Act seems not to be much in doubt.

The powers that the Act conferred upon the Board of Education, however, were far less extensive than those which were included in the old Education Act of 1870 and the Public Health Act of 1875. There was no power provided to appoint new school managers, or to levy a rate. From any administrative point of view this still remained a weakness and it was exploited by some authorities in Wales during the post-Default Act period of the Welsh revolt. As soon as an authority was declared to be in default and the Board of Education stepped in to provide for the

[25] *South Wales Daily News*, 10 Aug. 1904. See also the issue of 6 Aug., which reports the events mentioned above.

[26] K. O. Morgan, op. cit. 193.   [27] *The Welsh Leader*, 4 Jan. 1906.

[28] *The Justice of the Peace*, Oct. 1904. The article is reproduced in *The Welsh Leader*, 20 Oct. 1904.

maintenance of non-provided schools, the nonconformist majority in the education committee could withdraw *en bloc* as well as the managers of provided schools in place of whom no acting managers could be confirmed in office. This could result in paralysing the educational system of such an authority for, in addition, the finance required to maintain both non-provided and provided schools would be far in excess of the parliamentary grants to which alone the Board could have recourse. Should all local authorities in Wales have followed this course of action not only would the consequences have been disastrous from an educational point of view but also the basic principle of obedience to the law which underlies the proper functioning of local government in relation to central government would have been repudiated.

This did not happen. But it remains a matter which still awaits thorough investigation why, in spite of all that was claimed for the Welsh revolt in terms of a national uprising, it ultimately proved ineffective.

Lloyd George's immediate reaction to the Default Act was to redouble his efforts to promote concerted action on the part of local authorities. This culminated in a massive convention held at Cardiff on 6 October 1904 at which the leading representatives of all the Welsh authorities were present, and in the evening meeting, Dr. John Clifford proclaimed the sympathy of the Free Churches of Scotland as well as England, and their intention to give support 'not only with words but with their pockets' against the tyranny of the Board of Education which was 'simply an executive of the Anglican and Roman Churches'. The convention carried five resolutions with acclamation, the main items being that in the event of the application of the Default Act, Welsh education authorities thus affected were to 'relieve themselves' of responsibility for maintaining all elementary schools, and were to call upon parents of children in attendance at voluntary schools to withdraw them from those schools and 'avail themselves of the educational facilities provided by Free Churchmen'.[29]

Between April and December 1905, whilst all the Welsh local authorities except that of the borough of Wrexham adhered to their 'no-rate' resolutions, five were found to be in default, those of Merioneth, Montgomeryshire, Glamorgan, and the urban districts of Barry and Mountain Ash. Several others, such as Merthyr Tydfil U.D., Caernarvonshire, and Carmarthen borough, were in dispute with the Board of Education over their minimal efforts to maintain non-provided schools without actually being declared in default.[30] Only in Montgomeryshire was there an outright withdrawal of members from the education committee. The case of Merioneth, which was also the first, was the most celebrated, in the popular sense, and in its way the most long-lasting. After the county had been declared in default and grants to the amount of £2,000 had been withheld by the Board of Education, a large

---

[29] *The Case for the Welsh Revolt. Full verbatim report of the proceedings of the Welsh National Convention, Cardiff, October 6th, 1904*, Conway, 1904, *passim*.

[30] Much of the ensuing information is gleaned from the pages of *The Welsh Leader* for the period indicated. This source is particularly valuable in this context. It was a weekly journal, published at Caernarvon, which bears the self-explanatory sub-title, *A Weekly Record of Education and Local Government in Wales*. The first number appeared on 24 Sept. 1903.

representative conference of 580 delegates was held at Bala on 2 May which inaugurated a Welsh National Campaign Committee with Lloyd George at the helm. A series of further county conventions to stoke up popular enthusiasm were planned under its auspices and held during the following months beginning with a meeting of the Committee at Shrewsbury on 18 May where the decision of the Bala conference, in accordance with the Cardiff policy, to withdraw every child of nonconformist parents as far as was possible from non-provided schools in Merioneth was confirmed. They were to be accommodated either in Council Schools or in emergency accommodation in chapel schoolrooms and similar places. A fund to meet costs of staffing and equipping the emergency schools was also begun. The withdrawal involved 896 out of 1,600 pupils in twenty-seven voluntary schools within the county, and the first 'revolt' school was opened on 3 July at the Wesleyan chapel of Llandecwyn, followed by another in the Calvinistic Methodist chapel at Maentwrog on 21 August. The first permanent revolt school was opened at Llawr-y-betws, near Corwen, on 14 August. The education committee continued to function. In a county whose council was composed of fifty-two 'progressive' members as against only three 'sectarian' members, and where Council Schools were used to accommodate children withdrawn from non-provided schools, the question of control hardly arose, although some localities within the county had Emergency Committees to promote the revolt schools. The County Council continued to refuse to maintain Church schools until the end of 1907 when Reginald McKenna, then President of the Board of Education in the Liberal government, had the distasteful task of considering the possibility of having to apply the Default Act himself, but the occasion did not arise and the situation gradually resolved itself.[31]

In the Barry district, the only non-provided school was the Roman Catholic St. Helen's, Barry Dock. The complaints of the managers, first directed against the authority's intention to reduce the staff and their salaries, by 10 June became general complaints that the authority had failed to keep the school efficient by withholding parliamentary grants. The authority was informed on 21 November that the Board of Education would proceed to pay the salaries of the school's teachers, who had been appointed by the managers without reference to the education committee, and that the sums involved would be withdrawn from grants under the Default Act. There were no critical repercussions, however. Despite a threat to do so, the progressive majority on the education committee did not withdraw. Indeed, by January 1906 it was the Board of Education which made a concession by recognizing the irregularity of the appointment of teachers to St. Helen's without the view of the education committee having been ascertained, and by 21 March the hatchet had been finally buried, the authority having agreed to keep the school efficient out of parliamentary grants.

Like Barry, the only non-provided school in the Mountain Ash district was also a Roman Catholic school, Our Lady's, and the bone of contention here was the

Board's demand that the authority should bear the cost of furnishing and equipping it. In July 1905, the Board expressed its intention to hand over to the managers what it considered to be the expenses incurred in maintaining and keeping the school efficient, and it carried out its threat. But by 12 September the education committee had capitulated, in spite of a declaration of intent by the authority's delegates at a meeting of the Welsh National Executive at Llandrindod to 'checkmate' the Board, and they agreed to appoint two managers to co-operate with the foundation managers.

Montgomeryshire was declared to be in default by the Board on 15 July, more particularly for withholding sums due to teachers in the Newtown National School, neglecting the fabric of the school buildings, and withholding salaries at three other National Schools in the county. The education committee rejected a motion by Col. Pryce-Jones, Unionist M.P. for Montgomery District, that they should meet these claims, and the Board of Education operated the Default Act in order to pay the teachers, as well as withholding further sums from the grants to meet the expenses of managers in other non-provided schools. As in Merioneth, a policy of withdrawing children from Church schools was put into operation, but on 19 September a more drastic course of action was taken by the education committee. The Chairman vacated the chair, declaring that he and the Liberal members of the committee could no longer be responsible for administering elementary education in the county. They withdrew, but did not resign, leaving but seven Conservative members who were not sufficient to form a quorum to continue that particular meeting. Although the Conservatives were subsequently able to muster a quorum to function as a committee, seventeen members being present on 9 October, they were in all executive respects subject to the sanction of the county council, and thus, in view of the large Liberal majority on that council they were virtually powerless. This raised problems for the Board of Education who had to act through the education committee, although Lord Londonderry assured Col. Pryce-Jones in a letter of 6 October[32] that the Board would continue to provide for the maintenance of voluntary schools under the Default Act. It was the Council Schools that now became the education committee's problem, for Council School managers also withdrew their services. Chaos was averted, however, for on the assumption to power of the new Liberal government, by the third week in January 1906 the full education committee had reassembled and had agreed to pay salaries to non-provided school teachers out of the grants. The 'no-rate' policy was still to be adhered to until such time as the new government should amend the 1902 Act as was expected of it following Birrell's announcement that the Default Act would not be applied in Wales.

Whether or not more Welsh local authorities would have followed the example of Montgomeryshire and Merioneth had there not been a change of government is one of those questions which are not traditionally considered to be profitable for the historian to ask, but that there was some vital ingredient missing from the Welsh revolt is, perhaps, a little more than suspect. Welsh resistance was not widely resumed

[32] Londonderry to Col. Pryce-Jones, *The Welsh Leader*, 12 Oct. 1905.

on the failure of Birrell's Education Bill in 1906 which had proposed the control of all public elementary schools by local authorities, with compromises on Cowper-Temple lines in respect of religious instruction, nor after further attempts at compromise by the bishop of St. Asaph, Reginald McKenna, and Walter Runciman in 1908. By 1913, the annual report of the Board of Education showed the number of Council Schools in Wales to have reached the figure of 1,218 (with 421,950 scholars) with voluntary schools numbering 649 (with 105,167 in attendance), whereas in 1903 there had been 926 provided schools and 800 non-provided schools, indicating that a gradual transference of voluntary schools to local authorities was already taking place, and the 1902 Act being administered legally.[33]

There is no reason to doubt the verdict that the unity claimed for the Welsh revolt in the years 1902–5 was superficial and illusory, that the extent of public interest was exaggerated despite the apparent catalytic effect of the religious revival of 1904–5, and that it was inspired essentially by the energetic leadership of Lloyd George. It represented not the high peak of expression of the nonconformist conscience but rather a stage in its decline as a 'relevant' force in changing social and political circumstances. There were, in reality, many cracks that were papered over by Lloyd George's enthusiastic campaigning in support of the revolt. Some of these existed among the nonconformist denominations themselves. It was only with difficulty at times that he was able to keep some authorities in line with his policy, and he had his Liberal critics among the Welsh Parliamentary Party. Concern was being felt at the neglect of education as such, and rightly so, in the pursuit of aims which were becoming increasingly outmoded. In this respect, the dogged perseverance of leading representatives of the National Union of Teachers in seeking compromises, in relieving the plight of unpaid teachers, and in stressing the damage done to the continuity of the education of children in poorly maintained schools deserves more attention than it has received.[34] It becomes apparent that further effective investigation into the circumstances and nature of the Welsh revolt will be in the hands of the social historian. This will be particularly the case concerning the more positive attempt to form a Welsh National Council for Education which ran parallel with the protest against the 1902 Act. Attempts to explain the eventual demise of the proposed Council merely as having been the result of local parochialism are not sufficiently convincing. The key is more likely to lie in attitudes to secondary education, that not unreliable barometer of social change, mobility, and aspirations.

Perhaps it was Lloyd George's greatest error that he did not recognize, at least in practical terms, that Welsh social values were undergoing profound changes by the turn of the century for, as we have been told, he remained an Old Liberal in Wales whilst adopting the attitudes of the New Liberalism in England, 'a sectarian in the

---

[33] K. O. Morgan, op. cit. 223–31.

[34] See, in particular, the enlightened speech of the first Welshman to hold office as president of the N.U.T., Tom John, of Llwynypia, Rhondda, at the annual conference held at Llandudno in Apr. 1905. *The Welsh Leader*, 27 Apr., 4 May, 1905.

King George V, the General Strike, and the 1931 Crisis

H. HEARDER

'THERE are good grounds for supposing that George V was the first sovereign who fully accepted the principles of constitutional monarchy in the modern sense of the term. . . .'[1] The conclusion reached by Professor Chrimes in the course of his consideration of the role of the British Crown in modern times provides a useful and fitting starting-point for this study. One of the principles accepted by George V, but never completely by his predecessors, was that of neutrality as between political parties. That Queen Victoria was anything but politically neutral has often been noticed by historians, and has recently been illustrated very emphatically by Mr. Frank Hardie.[2] Edward VII, too, was undeniably partisan, though a far weaker influence than his mother had been. Only with George V does anything approaching complete neutrality emerge. Whoever was in office could always count on George V's confidence and moral support. One consistent feature in the fall of every government during his reign is revealed by his diary—a diary which was obviously not written to be published, nor even to be read by anyone else: each time a prime minister had to leave office, for whatever reason, the king always sincerely regretted his departure. That the same monarch should advise such different men as Asquith, Lloyd George, Baldwin, and Ramsay MacDonald to remain in office if they could possibly manage to do so is something of a tribute to that monarch's political neutrality and to the easy relations he developed with his prime ministers.

It is the purpose of this essay to examine the king's political attitude at two moments of crisis in his reign. At the first moment of crisis—that caused by the General Strike of 1926—a government was firmly in office, and, although threatened by the crisis in the country, did not in the event face a cabinet crisis, but survived the General Strike intact. In such a situation the monarch's role is inevitably, in modern times, simply that of an impartial adviser of his ministers, but in 1926 the advice given by the king, and usually accepted by his government, is not without interest. The monarch's role, however, becomes of greater constitutional importance when a government actually falls from office, especially if it falls from office not as a result of a general election, but because of the illness or death of a prime

[1] S. B. Chrimes, *English Constitutional History*, O.U.P., 1967 edition, 134.
[2] Frank Hardie, *The Political Influence of the British Monarchy, 1868–1952*, London, 1970.

one and a social reformer in the other'.[35] It may be that he had been acting very much in accordance with a variation of a well-known definition of politics to which he was attracted. Politics was not only the art of the possible: it was 'the art of taking and being taken in'.[36]

[35] *Lloyd George Family Letters*, 8.
[36] N.L.W. MS. 20448A (Lloyd George MS. 2089), f. 24.

minister, or because of an unforeseen crisis with which the existing government cannot cope. In such unusual circumstances the monarch's action becomes momentarily of great significance, and in 1931, with the impending collapse of the Labour Government, George V found himself in just such a position. But if his role in the 1931 crisis is intrinsically more important than his role in the 1926 crisis, the latter is equally deserving of treatment here because it has received far less attention in the past. The main authority, Sir Harold Nicolson, in his fine study, *King George V. His Life and Reign*,[3] lavished some forty pages on the House of Lords crisis of 1910/11, some thirty pages on the Irish crisis of 1913/14, another forty pages on the 1931 crisis, but disposed of the General Strike in less than ten pages. The apparently exhaustive use made by Nicolson of the Royal Archives at Windsor has had the unfortunate effect of discouraging subsequent writers from returning to the archives themselves. The political scientist, Reginald Bassett, for example, provided an hour-by-hour account of the 1931 crisis,[4] yet did not think it necessary to go to Windsor himself, but instead depended heavily on Nicolson. Of the two accounts of the General Strike, by Julian Symons, and, more recently, by Christopher Farman, neither uses the Royal Archives.[5] Yet there are papers in the Royal Archives which Nicolson did not use, and which throw some fresh light on both crises, and in the case of the General Strike it can perhaps be shown that a slightly misleading impression was given by Nicolson of the sentiments which decided the king's outlook.

It is a paradox in the history of the British monarchy in the twentieth century that of the two monarchs who were to do most to give the institution its modern stable character—George V and George VI—neither was trained to be king, because both were second sons. As a youth George V had survived the excessive sentimentality of his mother, the Princess of Wales, later Queen Alexandra, who still referred to him as 'my darling Georgie boy' when he was twenty-eight years old. During his career in the navy he had preserved his honesty, good nature, and modesty. If he was not trained to be king, he was at least given an education in the subtleties of the English constitution, by J. R. Tanner, a historian from St. John's, Cambridge, who in 1894 was a regular visitor at Sandringham. It was Tanner who persuaded the future George V, then Duke of York, to read Bagehot's *English Constitution*, from which the Duke took careful and systematic notes, which are preserved in the Windsor archives. Bagehot's great work had been published in 1867. Queen Victoria disapproved of it, and considered Bagehot a radical, perhaps because of the faint suggestion of disrespect with which Bagehot opened his chapter on the monarchy: 'The use of the Queen, in a dignified capacity, is incalculable.' And if he goes on to say 'Without her in England, the present English Government would fail and pass away', he yet makes the famous reference, two sentences later, to the Queen and Prince of

[3] First published by Constable in 1952. References here are to the paperback edition, published by Pan in 1967.   [4] *Nineteen Thirty-one*, London, 1958.

[5] Julian Symons, *The General Strike*, London, 1957; Christopher Farman, *The General Strike. May 1926*, London, 1972. (Since this was written an interesting short account has been given by Mrs. M. Morris, *The British General Strike, 1926*, Historical Association, London, 1973.)

Wales as 'a retired widow and an unemployed youth'.[6] The Duke of York, with his rich sense of humour, probably relished Bagehot's tone. He listed six of Bagehot's points under the heading 'The value of the Crown in its *dignified* capacity'. His list is a good summary. The only point of importance which it omits is Bagehot's insistence that to perform its function effectively the Crown must have no association with any political party, yet it was precisely in this respect that the future George V was to excel his predecessors in the correctness of his behaviour. He went on to summarize three of Bagehot's points under the heading 'The value of the Crown in its *business* capacity'. Under the first of these, 'In the *formation* of Ministries', the Duke noted that the monarch's 'influence' could be 'exercised' 'especially in choosing between the Statesmen who have a claim to lead party'. In fact Bagehot is inclined to be less definite and more ambiguous than the Duke's note suggests. Under the second point, 'During the *continuance* of Ministries', the Duke accurately repeated Bagehot's famous dictum that the Crown has three rights, 'the right to be consulted, the right to encourage, the right to warn', but finally under the third point, 'At the *break up* of a Ministry', the Duke merely paraphrased Bagehot by adding in brackets '(but this can be treated best in connection with the House of Lords)'.

When he became king, George V remembered that 'during the continuance of ministries' he had 'the right to be consulted, the right to encourage, the right to warn'. As well as being consulted informally by his prime ministers, he received formal reports from the cabinet, although he did not himself write regularly to members of the cabinet, as Queen Victoria had done. His influence was exerted in practice through conversations with the prime minister, or in letters from his private secretary to members of the government. He always expressed his opinion bluntly, though he always realized that the responsibility for policy was entirely that of the political government. In one sense his role was like that of a permanent civil servant, or a member of the diplomatic service. His long experience over the years gave him a knowledge and understanding of public affairs that a political minister might lack. Like a permanent under-secretary or an ambassador overseas he was at liberty to give full advice to the government, but he could not object if they chose to ignore his advice.

In 1924 George V experienced something novel in British political history—the formation of a Labour Government. In view of his background and the social circle within which he moved it did not seem likely that he would have an easy relationship with Ramsay MacDonald and his colleagues. George V's respect for the neutrality of the Crown was now to be sharply tested. He was helped by the distinction he had already made in his own mind between 'socialism' and the British Labour movement. He associated 'socialism' with the beliefs of the men who had murdered his cousin, the Czar Nicholas II. But the government formed in 1924 he regarded, rightly, as having little to do with 'socialism'. He quickly acquired strong confidence in Ramsay MacDonald, and a position of neutrality between the Labour and Conservative

----

[6] O.U.P., 1928 edition, 30.

parties throughout the 1920s became second nature to him. In 1926, however, the king was faced with a national crisis which was not a party dispute, and in which MacDonald and the Labour Party played a somewhat negative role. In what became a struggle between the trade unions and Baldwin's Conservative Government the extent to which the Crown could, or should, remain neutral was far less clear. The king's subjects were divided by a clash of loyalties. In the sense that most, if not all, ethical questions can be resolved into ones of conflicting loyalties, the issue between the strikers and the government was a peculiarly painful and basic one. The only two newspapers which were printed during the strike echoed the simple conflict of loyalties. On 12 May the *British Gazette*, which Winston Churchill was editing for the government, included a quotation from Tennyson, entitled 'The Soul of England':

> A nation yet, the rulers and the ruled—
> Some sense of duty, something of a faith.
> Some reverence for the laws ourselves have made,
> Some patient force to change them when we will,
> Some civic manhood, firm against the crowd.

The same number of the *British Gazette* contained a message from the prime minister, which read:

> Every man who does his duty by the country and remains at work or returns to work during the present crisis will be protected by the State from loss of trade union benefits, superannuation allowances, or pension . . .'

The T.U.C.'s *British Worker* had already published on 10 May some 'Meditations of a Trade Unionist on reading Mr. Baldwin's Latest Guarantees to Strike-Breakers':

> So you will guarantee that all I'd lose
> In Union benefits should be made up.
> And you MIGHT keep your promise, though the woes
> Of them that gave up everything to fight
> And now are starving with their wives and kids
> Make one a bit suspicious:
> Still, you MIGHT!
>
> Also you've promised you'd protect my skin
> And save my bones and make it safe for me
> To walk about and work and earn my keep.
> I'm not afraid for that. I know my mates;
> They're decent, quiet chaps, not hooligans.
> They wouldn't try to murder me,
> Not they!
>
> But could you make them treat me as a pal,
> Or shield me from their cold, contemptuous eyes?

> Could you restore the pride of comradeship?
> Could you call back my ruined self-respect,
> Give me protection from my bitter shame,
> From self contempt that drives out happiness?
>
> Such guarantees are not in mortal power.
> I'm sticking to my mates:
> That's my reply.

To juxtapose these two pieces of blank verse—one by the greatest poet laureate of Victorian England, and the other by some anonymous versifier of 1926—is strangely illuminating. To the reader nearly half a century later there is a striking similarity of sentiment in the two passages, a similarity which does not depend only on the distinctly Tennysonian beat in the *British Worker*'s piece. The clash between them is not one likely to lead to revolution. Both reflect the spirit of 'decent, quiet chaps' intent upon the defence of 'the laws ourselves have made'. The clash is one of loyalties to traditions and social groups, loyalties which have more to do with self-respect than self-interest. In such a confrontation the position of the monarch was more complicated than was that of a member of the cabinet, of the middle class, or of a trade union. Clearly he had a responsibility to help the government defend the law and the constitution. But he felt equally clearly that the strikers were also his subjects and their well-being was his concern. Sir Harold Nicolson, in the account already referred to, stressed George V's desire that the strikers should not be pushed too far, and thus depicted him as, to a certain extent, mitigating the tough line pursued by the Baldwin government. Subsequent writers, using the material supplied by Nicolson, have put across the same interpretation in a more emphatic manner. There are, however, two or three pieces of evidence in the Royal Archives which were ignored or played down by Nicolson and which show that the king was in one or two respects as eager as—or, if anything, more eager than—Baldwin was, to ensure that the strikers and their pickets kept strictly within the law.

The General Strike of 1926 lasted from May 4 to May 12. The first independent, specific reaction from the King came on 5 May, in the shape of a letter from his private secretary, Lord Stamfordham, to one of the prime minister's private secretaries, Sir Ronald Waterhouse, a letter not mentioned by Nicolson:

The King wishes me to bring to the notice of the Prime Minister a press statement to the effect that there are in the docks ships containing perishable cargoes and the unlading of which is being prevented by pickets. If this is the case, would it not be possible to introduce emergency legislation to prevent the so-called peaceful picketing and so enable unlading to be carried out by non-Union Labour: and at the same time relieve the police of the additional work imposed upon them in dealing with picket trouble.[7]

---

[7] Royal Archives GV B 2052/9. I would like to acknowledge the gracious permission of Her Majesty the Queen to quote from papers in the Royal Archives.

Replying for Baldwin on 7 May, Waterhouse gently implied that Stamfordham's letter had virtually recommended an amendment of the Trades Disputes Act of 1906, an amendment which 'many Conservative M.P.s' 'would deem desirable', but which 'would be highly controversial' and so 'inopportune'.[8] On that same day Stamfordham had sent Waterhouse a further blast, pressing for a strong policy against the strikers:

> The King is somewhat concerned to find from the official reports that the people who are ready and desirous of assisting the Government in the maintenance of law and order are suffering considerably from intimidation from the strikers and from other evil disposed parties, with the result that transport, which is the mainspring of the Government arrangements, is threatened. . . .
>
> Until Martial Law be proclaimed and the safety of the country passes into the hands of the Military, the Civil Government is answerable for the preservation of law and order; and as in the former eventuality one Military Authority would be in command, so in the latter it seems to the King that, in order to secure the promptest and most successful effects, one Executive Officer should be responsible for all Police control . . .[9]

The imposition of martial law was evidently being anticipated more readily at Buckingham Palace than at Downing Street, though it should be added that the king's concern was rather one of positive sympathy for the volunteer strike-breakers than of personal hostility towards the strikers. While Nicolson did not refer specifically to either of these letters from the Palace, he summarized them by saying: 'While urging the Government to take all possible steps to protect from violence or intimidation all those who volunteered to assist in the maintenance of essential services, the King was opposed to anything that might drive the strikers to desperation.'[10] Nicolson then went on to recount the inclusion by Churchill on 8 May in the *British Gazette* of an announcement apparently inciting the armed forces not to be too soft in the performance of their duties during the strike, and the king's protest to the War Office about the announcement. Nicolson followed this account with a discussion of the Baldwin government's proposal to freeze trade union funds, a proposal to which the king was to react in a significant, and probably decisive, way. The cabinet decided to introduce a Bill on 11 May to amend the law 'with respect to illegal strikes' and to forbid the use of trade-union money on a strike 'which is intended to intimidate or coerce the Government or the community'. Pending the introduction of the Bill an Order in Council was to be issued to prevent banks from paying out cash 'to any person acting in opposition to the National interest'. Such an Order in Council would clearly be difficult to enforce, or, if enforced, provocative in the extreme. The whole institution of monarchy may well appear to have been justified when the king, surveying the situation from the point of view of the country as a whole, and assessing the probability of revolution, decided to protest at the cabinet's decision. In Nicolson's words 'the Cabinet decided to introduce no provocative

---

[8] RA GV B 2052/11.   [9] RA GV B 2052/12.   [10] Nicolson, op. cit. 540.

legislation unless it became essential to do so; milder counsels prevailed'. As a brief summary of what happened Nicolson's account is certainly valid, but it is perhaps worth utilizing the original memorandum by Stamfordham to reconstruct the precise details:

The cabinet met on 8 May, and decided to introduce the Bill on Tuesday, 11 May, and to circulate its terms on Monday, 10 May. They feared, however, that before the Bill could be passed 'the Trade Union might be able to get large sums of money sent to them from Moscow'. To avoid this the King was asked to hold an Emergency Council on Sunday, 9 May, to issue an Order 'to prevent Banks paying out Foreign Money credited to anyone acting in opposition to the National interest'. At the Council the King told

both the Home Secretary and the Attorney General that he was not at all sure that the Government would be acting wisely in adopting either the measures authorized by the Order in Council or those to be obtained by the Bill to be introduced on the 11th . . . Any attempt to get hold of or control the Trades Union Funds might cause exasperation and provoke reprisals. If money were not forthcoming to buy food, there might be looting of shops, even of banks. The King laid stress also upon the inevitable uproar which the introduction of such a Bill would create in the House of Commons. . . .

In the afternoon of Monday, 10th May, private information reached the King that the Cabinet as a whole was by no means satisfied as to the proposed legislation: that there was a danger of the Prime Minister's being rushed by some of his hot-headed colleagues into legislation which might have disastrous effects . . .

Baldwin apparently reassured Stamfordham that a further cabinet meeting would be held, and that anyhow the decision reached on Sunday, 9 May, had been merely 'to prevent the banks paying out Foreign Monies and that this Order and the proposed legislation were two entirely separate matters'. On 10 May a further cabinet meeting was consequently held, as the result of which the king was obliged to hold a further Council on Tuesday, 11 May, 'the object being to strengthen the powers given by the Order in Council of Sunday, 9th, in so far as that the banks will be ordered to furnish such information as may be required by the Government with regard to payments of Foreign Money'.[11] This was clearly a far cry from what had originally been intended. The Order which resulted was comparatively innocuous, and—in spite of Baldwin's disarming remarks to Stamfordham—was a pale shadow of the cabinet's original plan. That the original plan had been nipped in the bud was fairly evidently the king's doing, yet while he did not want the government needlessly to provoke the strikers, he was eager to have men whom he considered to be subversive rounded up. On that same Tuesday, 11 May, he read a report from the War Office which contained eight numbered points. The first five points contained details about 'interference with transport', distribution of communist pamphlets,

11 RA GV B 2052/24.

observation kept on 'N.C.O.s and men suspected of communist leanings', and so on. The next three points were:

6. Mr. Bromley [of the Associated Society of Locomotive Engineers and Firemen] said at Canning Town that the T.U.C. would call out its second line of defence tonight, thus adding one or two millions to the number of strikers.

7. Communists are reported to be endeavouring to find out the strength of guards at various depots and of the police and their reserves in the London district.

8 The Workers Defence Corps are reported to have set up a Central Advisory Committee . . .

Against these three points the king wrote in the margin, in his usual red ink: 'Could these not be arrested?'[12] Stamfordham forwarded the king's question to the War Office, but received a reply from the Home Secretary, Sir William Joynson-Hicks, who explained that Bromley was merely calling the men out on strike, that, however, the whole question of subversive activity was being considered, and the Communists were being watched.[13] The image created by Nicolson and his following of a monarch who always wished to modify the insensitive and dangerous policy of the Conservative Government is thus only half of the picture. The other half of the picture is of a king who was constantly on the alert to prevent the government, through timidity or slackness, from failing in its duty to suppress what the king saw as genuinely revolutionary elements. As a postscript to the king's bearing during the strike, the adoption of his attitude on one final point is worth noting. The miners, who continued on strike after the General Strike had failed, received about £1,800,000 from charitable grants, but more than half of this—about a million pounds—came from Russian trade unions. Baldwin's government, under pressure from its right-wing back-benchers, protested to the Russian government about this. George V objected that it was unreasonable to protest against help given to hungry families. If the king felt profound concern for the preservation of the constitution, and a strong desire to prevent revolution or civil war, he felt, then, also a sense of compassion for that considerable number of his subjects whose comparative poverty was encouraging them to resist the legally established authorities.

The General Strike was an example of a crisis occurring 'during the *continuance of a ministry*', in Bagehot's phrase, and the king's function was thus limited to the traditional one of 'being consulted, encouraging and warning'. That George V performed this function conscientiously and effectively is illustrated by what has already been said. The 1931 crisis was an example of one 'at the *break-up* of a ministry', again to use Bagehot's words, and in such a crisis the monarch has inevitably a more active and responsible function to perform.

On 23 August 1931 Ramsay MacDonald, the prime minister, told the king that the financial crisis demanded immediate economies, especially in unemployment pensions, which he feared important members of the cabinet, including Arthur

---

[12] RA GV B 2052/29.   [13] RA GV B 2052/34.

Henderson, the foreign secretary, would not accept, and that his Labour Government as a whole might therefore have to resign. The pronouncement placed the king in one of the two or three gravest predicaments of his life. The first six months of 1931 had been especially tragic for him. He had himself barely recovered from an acute illness. In January both his sister, the Princess Royal, and Sir Charles Cust, perhaps his closest friend, had died. On 31 March Lord Stamfordham, who had been his private secretary and trusted adviser throughout his reign, had died also. Although Stamfordham was replaced by Sir Clive Wigram, who had been assistant private secretary for very nearly as long, the king was moved to comment in his diary that Stamfordham's 'loss is irreparable'. In a sense a monarch is always in a position of solitude; in 1931 his solitude was more intense than usual. In one respect, however, the king did not feel alone: he had great respect and affection for his prime minister. The close personal understanding between George V and MacDonald is certainly part of the explanation of the outcome of the crisis. As soon as the National Government was formed and the immediate crisis thus passed, the king was to write to MacDonald from Balmoral:

After the momentous times through which we have been passing, I should like to assure you how much I appreciate and admire the courage with which you have put aside all personal and party interest in order to stand by the country in this grave national crisis. By this proof of strength of character and devotion to duty, your name will always hold an honoured place among British Statesmen . . .

I am happy to feel that I have been able to return to my Highland home without changing my Prime Minister, in whom I have full confidence.

To this typed draft the king added in his own hand:

The Queen and I trust you may be able to pay us a short visit here before the H of Cs meets and that you will very soon be able to get away and have some rest.[14]

George V's admiration for MacDonald is perhaps surprising in view of the complete contrast between the two men in temperament and character. The stiff and formal manner of the prime minister concealed a complex and vulnerable personality, while the king immediately articulated all his reactions, irritations, and worries, and was wholly without guile or deceit. Few men in history can have made a greater variety of impressions on others than MacDonald. If to the king he was a reliable man, he was, of course, the exact opposite to his former colleagues of the Labour Government. But the most devastating characterization of MacDonald comes not from the Labour leaders who believed he had betrayed them, but from the chairman of the Conservative Party, J. C. C. Davidson, who wrote of MacDonald:

He was a very treacherous man; he couldn't resist putting his knife into the back of the man in front of him. He was very jealous, very feminine . . .[15]

[14] RA GV K 2330 (1)/19.
[15] Robert Rhodes James, *Memoirs of a Conservative. J. C. C. Davidson's Memoirs and Papers 1910–37*, London, 1969, 372.

The king on the other hand seems to have made exactly the same impression—that of a wholly honest, straightforward, and uncomplicated person—on all alike, from the most powerful emperors to men—like George Lansbury or J. H. Thomas—who came from the most humble backgrounds. His confidence in MacDonald was not then based on any similarity of personality, but perhaps primarily on the fact that both men felt themselves to be outside the rough and tumble of politics, the king for obvious and wholly creditable reasons, the prime minister from a sense of vanity and an exaggerated belief in his own destiny. In his very first speech to the new parliament in 1929 MacDonald had expressed the hope that parliament could think of itself 'more as a Council of State and less as arrayed regiments facing each other in battle', and even before the idea of a National Government had been whispered, MacDonald had come to think of himself as a national, rather than a party, leader. The king was well placed to understand and to sympathize with MacDonald's outlook, and in August 1931 he certainly needed someone in whom to trust.

The position in which the king was placed on 23 August was without precedent. the normal reasons for which a prime minister resigns—his party's loss of a general election, or his own age or ill health—were not operative. MacDonald was warning the king that he might have to resign because of difference of opinion within the cabinet on the question of what steps should be taken to deal with a very acute financial crisis. Since sterling might collapse within days, or even hours, dissolution of the House was unthinkable. Of the two or three other courses open to the king none was obviously the right one, none was without danger, nor would any be free from criticism from some quarter. Even the extent to which the monarch should follow the advice of the existing prime minister, when the latter had evidently lost the confidence of many in his cabinet, was debatable. To follow the exact steps of the crisis during the two or three relevant days illustrates the complexity of the situation and the weight of responsibility so suddenly and untypically laid upon the monarch. The crisis was sudden in the sense that, although the crash on Wall Street had occurred in 1929, its significance for Europe had become apparent only in May 1931 with the collapse of the Credit Anstalt in Vienna. George V had heard of the seriousness of the financial situation only on 11 July, when Sir Clive Wigram had written to him, saying: 'We are sitting on the top of a volcano, and the curious thing is that the Press and the City have not really understood the critical situation. The Governor of the Bank of England is very pessimistic and depressed.'[16]

George V left Sandringham for Balmoral on the night of 21 August, when the government crisis was breaking. He arrived at Balmoral on the morning of 22 August only to hear by telegram of the gravity of the situation and to leave for London again that evening. He arrived at Euston soon after 8 a.m. on Sunday, 23 August, at Buckingham Palace at 8.15 a.m., and received MacDonald there at 10.30 a.m. At this vital interview MacDonald explained the desperate efforts which the government was making to obtain credit from American and French banks, but

[16] Nicolson, op. cit. 577.

expressed the opinion that the credit would not be forthcoming unless economies were announced on a scale, and of a nature, which Henderson and other influential members of the cabinet would refuse to accept. The Labour Government would thus have to resign. In view of the acute possibility of such a development the king and prime minister agreed that the leaders of the Conservative and Liberal Oppositions, Stanley Baldwin and Sir Herbert Samuel, should be consulted. Such is the account given by Nicolson, and generally accepted, of the interview. But for once Nicolson used the Royal Archives inadequately, as a memorandum by Wigram adds significant details concerning his activities on behalf of the king during the two hours following the arrival of the King's train at Euston and the interview with MacDonald at the Palace. Wigram had spoken on the telephone to Geoffrey Dawson, editor of *The Times*, who recorded the conversation, though in a brief and self-effacing manner.[17] From Wigram's unpublished account it is clear that this telephone conversation was by no means trivial or insignificant. Dawson

said that if only the Prime Minister could be 'binged-up', he is the best person to bring the Country through this crisis, but he must have the courage of his own opinions. Dawson said that he had been in touch with all Parties, and this was no time for a change of Government. He agreed that it would be everything if the King could see Mr. Baldwin and Sir Herbert Samuel and impress on them how necessary it is for the three Parties to co-operate to save the situation . . I was able to tell the King the gist of my conversation with Dawson before the Prime Minister arrived at 10.30 a.m.[18]

It is probable, then, that the king and Wigram had already, before the interview on the morning of 23 August, decided that it would be better for MacDonald to remain in office with some kind of unspecified help from Baldwin and Samuel, though help which probably did not yet extend in their minds to the formation of a National Government. They had, anyhow, decided that Baldwin and Samuel should be consulted, and with this suggestion MacDonald readily complied. Soon after MacDonald's departure from the Palace efforts were made to summon Baldwin and Samuel. Baldwin could not at first be located. According to Nicolson 'he had strayed off into the streets'. He had in fact gone for a chat with Geoffrey Dawson, who no doubt told him that the Palace had just been in touch with him on the telephone. Samuel was thus the first opposition leader to see the king, and it was from Samuel that the words 'National Government' were evidently first uttered. Samuel told the king that the best solution would be for the Labour Government to make the necessary economies, but that, if this proved impossible, the next best thing would be a National Government under MacDonald. The king was later to tell Wigram that he found Samuel's arguments clearer and more convincing than those of either MacDonald or Baldwin. J. C. C. Davidson was probably right in concluding that the precise idea of a National Government reached the King first through Samuel,

[17] John Evelyn Wrench, *Geoffrey Dawson and Our Times*, London, 1955, 291.
[18] RA GV K 2330 (2)/1.

of whom Davidson made another of his trenchant assessments, saying that 'he had a very clever brain that enabled him to be really dishonest without appearing to be so'.[19]

Baldwin was finally located, and arrived at the Palace at 3 p.m. Like Samuel, he declared that the best solution would be for a Labour Government to pass the economies, but when—apparently—asked point-blank by the king if, should it be necessary, he would agree to serve in a National Government under MacDonald, Baldwin said that he would. After a heated meeting of the Labour cabinet MacDonald returned to the Palace for a further interview with the king in the late evening of that same Sunday, 23 August. The interview lasted for only twenty minutes, but the part played by the king was significant. Nicolson has printed Wigram's account:

> The Prime Minister looked scared and unbalanced. He told the King that all was up and that at the Cabinet 11 had voted for accepting the terms of the Bankers and 8 against . . . In these circumstances the Prime Minister had no alternative than to tender the resignation of the Cabinet.
>
> The King impressed on the Prime Minister that he was the only man to lead the country through this crisis and hoped he would reconsider the situation . . .[20]

On this occasion MacDonald was swayed by the King's advice at least to the extent of agreeing to withhold his resignation until the two men could meet the Conservative and Liberal leaders on the Monday morning. But MacDonald did not wait until the morning. Instead he met Samuel, Baldwin, Neville Chamberlain, and the three Governors of the Bank of England very late on the Sunday night—about midnight. At this meeting it was Chamberlain who pressed the idea of a coalition government led by MacDonald, an idea about which Baldwin was always lukewarm. Baldwin's line had always been that he had broken up one coalition government—that of Lloyd George in 1922—and he was not eager to create another one. The initiative for pressing for the formation of the National Government seems in fact to have been taken by neither of the principal actors in the drama—MacDonald and Baldwin—but rather by the secondary figures, Samuel and Chamberlain. The king's position was very close to that of MacDonald: neither man had actually proposed the idea, but both were pleased with the proposal when it was made. The king was not only pleased, but positively enthusiastic about it, and by the morning of 24 August, was quite clear in his own mind on the necessity for a National Government.

The meeting at the Palace on the Monday morning, attended by MacDonald, Baldwin, and Samuel was in a very real sense chaired by the king. To begin with, in Wigram's words he 'impressed upon' the three men 'that before they left the Palace some communiqué must be issued which would no longer keep the country and the world in suspense'. When MacDonald reacted to this by saying 'that he had the resignation of his Cabinet in his pocket', 'the King replied that he trusted there was no question of the Prime Minister's resignation: the leaders of the three Parties must get together and come to some arrangement'. He then became more specific,

[19] R. R. James, op. cit. 373.   [20] Nicolson, op. cit. 596.

saying that he 'hoped that the Prime Minister, with the colleagues who remained faithful to him, would help in the formation of a National Government . . .' After thirty-five minutes the king left the three politicians alone for over an hour, but only 'to settle the details of the communiqué'. In a sense the National Government had become accepted policy before the king left the room.

At the time the phrase 'National Government' had a specific significance which it was to lose in the months and years ahead. Although Chamberlain had spoken at the late night meeting on 23 August of a 'coalition government' the other political leaders were clear that there was a distinction. Coalition governments had been formed in the past as the result of formal agreements between parliamentary political parties to deal with some prolonged crisis, like a war. The 'National Government' of 1931, on the other hand, was to be a cabinet of individuals working closely together to overcome a very short, sharp, financial crisis. Political parties were not to be merged into each other, nor to forget their separate identities, and the next election was not to be fought by a coalition party with a 'coupon'. That the formation of a National Government was a conspiracy between bankers and the Conservative Party leaders to destroy the Labour Party is thus a gross over-simplification. The bankers had merely behaved like bankers, without conscious political motives. Baldwin, like Dawson of *The Times*, probably believed that the Labour Party would be more severely damaged by remaining in office and introducing economies, than by giving way to a National Government. Only Chamberlain, and perhaps Samuel, may have had some sense of the extent to which the Labour Party could be crippled by the action which was in the event taken. Certainly there is no reason to suppose that the king ever considered the future of the Labour Party—or, for that matter, of the Conservative or Liberal Parties—one way or the other.

That the king played an important role in the formation of the National Government, and that in the last resort he threw his whole weight behind the idea, has been tacitly implied by the two writers, Harold Nicolson and Reginald Bassett, who have written in greatest depth on the subject. It has been emphatically asserted by writers far to the left, like Raymond Postgate,[21] and by writers far to the right, like John Buchan.[22] But two further questions must be asked. Did the King act constitutionally? And, even if he did, did he act wisely within the constitution? To these questions a great variety of answers have been given. Perhaps the hardest verdict was that of Harold Laski, who believed that the National Government was 'born of a Palace Revolution' and MacDonald was 'the King's nominee'. But Bassett has shown that Laski had no idea of the details of the king's part in the crisis, and other writers, even when they suggest that the king's policy was mistaken, yet agree that it was constitutional. Thus Herbert Morrison believed that the king was the victim of 'bad advice' in assuming that the bulk of the Labour Party would support a National Government under MacDonald. The king, Morrison argued, should have checked by consulting Labour privy councillors, but he was nevertheless within the bounds

[21] In *George Lansbury*, London, 1951.   [22] In *The King's Grace*, London, 1935.

of the constitution. Sir Ivor Jennings, in his *Cabinet Government*, declared the king's action 'quite constitutional', though he could not say the same of MacDonald's. Charles Mowat, in his surprisingly detailed account in *Britain between the Wars*, concluded that 'the King's intervention was both constitutional and decisive'. John Mackintosh, in *The British Cabinet* refers to the convention that the monarch 'should seek to establish the strongest government possible in the circumstances', but surely goes too far when he subsequently concludes that George V 'had no other choice open to him'. Graeme Moodie, in an article in *Political Studies* in 1957, argued that the correct constitutional line for the king would have been to ask Baldwin to form a government, using whatever support he could get. H. R. G. Greaves, in *The British Constitution*, argued, rather differently, that if the king had asked Arthur Henderson to form a government from the Parliamentary Labour Party, which was still, of course, the largest in the House, he could not have been charged with acting unconstitutionally. Both Moodie and Greaves, however, are too exclusive in their arguments. Either of their retrospective recommendations may well have been within constitutional law, but the policy which was, historically, taken by the king was no less constitutional for that reason. All the arguments of politicians, political scientists, and historians taken together lead towards one general conclusion—that a number of options was open to the king, who thus was given, by a freak situation, greater responsibility than usually falls to a British monarch in modern times. Given the advice he received, he took the line most likely to establish a stable government which could overcome the immediate crisis.

The two crises of 1926 and 1931 well illustrate the role of the Crown in the reign of George V. A simple and almost boyish sense of fair play prevented the king from being partisan as between social groups or political parties. But his neutrality was an active thing: on the rare occasions when it was necessary for him to make a decision or to exert an influence he was not afraid to do so. On such occasions he behaved correctly and conscientiously, consulting trusted advisers—the prime minister, leader or leaders of the opposition, and his own private secretary—but his action in the end had a spontaneous and ingenuous character which owed nothing to anyone but himself. If this achievement in finally raising the Crown above struggles of party or class was one of character rather than of intelligence, it was not the less important on that account.

The Principal Writings of S. B. Chrimes

(*to* 1973)

Compiled by NORA TEMPLE

BOOKS

English Constitutional Ideas in the Fifteenth Century, Cambridge, Cambridge University Press, 1936, pp. xx, 415, rep. New York, American Scholar Publications, 1965.

Kingship and Law in the Middle Ages (Studies by Fritz Kern, translated from the German, with an introduction), Oxford, Blackwell (Studies in Mediaeval History, no. 4, ed. G. Barraclough), 1939, pp. xxxi, 214, rep. New York, Barnes and Noble, 1968, Harper Torchbook, 1970.

Sir John Fortescue's *De Laudibus Legum Anglie* (edited and translated, with an introduction and notes), Cambridge, Cambridge University Press (Cambridge Studies in English Legal History, gen. ed. H. D. Hazeltine), 1942, pp. cxiv, 235.

English Constitutional History, London, Oxford University Press (Home University Library), 1948, pp. 201, second revised edn. 1953, pp. 201 (reprinted by Maruzen, Tokyo, 1962), third revised edn. 1965, pp. 202, fourth revised edn. (Opus 16, O.U.P. Paperbacks University Series), 1967, pp. 148.

The General Election in Glasgow, February 1950 (general editor and contributor—see below), Glasgow, Jackson, 1950, pp. xi, 189.

An Introduction to the Administrative History of Mediaeval England, Oxford, Blackwell (Studies in Mediaeval History, vol. 7), 1952, pp. xv, 277, second revised edn. 1959, pp. xv, 285 (simultaneous American edn. New York, Barnes and Noble), third revised edn. 1966, pp. xv, 285 (simultaneous American edn. New York, Barnes and Noble).

Select Documents of English Constitutional History, 1307–1485 (ed., with A. L. Brown), London, A. & C. Black, 1961, pp. xxiv, 398 (simultaneous American edn. New York, Barnes and Noble).

Lancastrians, Yorkists, and Henry VII, London, Macmillan, 1964, pp. xiv, 190, second revised edn. 1967, pp. xv, 190.

Fifteenth century England, 1399–1509: studies in politics and society (ed., with C. D. Ross, and R. A. Griffiths), Manchester, Manchester University Press, 1972, pp. 192 (simultaneous American edn. New York, Barnes and Noble).

Henry VII, London, Eyre Methuen, 1972, pp. xv, 373 (simultaneous American edn. Berkeley, University of California Press).

CONTRIBUTIONS TO VOLUMES

'Glasgow University General Election Survey, February 1950' and 'Conclusion and Commentary' in *The General Election in Glasgow, February 1950*, ed. S. B. Chrimes, Glasgow, Jackson, 1950, pp. 1–6, 178–89.

'Introductory Essay' in *A History of English Law* by Sir William Holdsworth (seventh revised edn., ed. by A. L. Goodhart and H. G. Hanbury), London, Methuen, vol. i, 1956, pp. 1–77.

'Henry VI', 'The King's Council', and 'The Government of Henry VII' in *History of the English Speaking Peoples*, London, Purnell for B.P.C. Publishing Ltd., 1970, vol. 2, pp. 866–70, 875–8, 1019–22.

'The Reign of Henry VII' in *Fifteenth Century England, 1399–1509: Studies in Politics and Society* (ed. by S. B. Chrimes, C. D. Ross, and R. A. Griffiths), Manchester, Manchester University Press, 1972, pp. 67–85.

ARTICLES AND LECTURES

'John, first duke of Bedford; his work and policy in England, 1389–1435' (summary of M.A. thesis), *Bulletin of the Institute of Historical Research*, vol. vii, no. 20, 1929, pp. 110–13.

'The Pretensions of the Duke of Gloucester in 1422', *English Historical Review*, vol. xlv, 1930, pp. 101–3.

'Studies in constitutional ideas in England during the fifteenth century', *Abstracts of Dissertations Approved, University of Cambridge, 1931–32*, Cambridge, Cambridge University Press, 1933, pp. 66–7.

'The Liability of Lords for Payment of Knights of the Shire', *English Historical Review*, vol. xlix, 1934, pp. 306–8.

' "House of Lords" and "House of Commons" in the Fifteenth Century', ibid., pp. 494–7.

'Sir John Fortescue and his Theory of Dominion' (The Alexander Prize Essay), *Transactions of the Royal Historical Society*, fourth series, vol. xvii, 1934, pp. 117–47.

'Some Letters of John of Lancaster as Warden of the East Marches towards Scotland', *Speculum* (Journal of the Mediaeval Academy of America), vol. xiv, 1939, pp. 1–27.

'Some Proposals for Constitutional Reform', *The New English Review*, vol. 14, no. 2, 1947, pp. 130–8.

'The Gregor Papers: Some Unpublished Correspondence of Francis Gregor, Esquire, 1729–37', *Notes and Queries*, vol. cxcii, 1947, pp. 2–6, 29–33, 50–3.

'The Constitutional Ideas of Dr. John Cowell', *English Historical Review*, vol. lxiv, 1949, pp. 461–87.

'The Evolution of Parties and the Party System before 1600', *Parliamentary Affairs* (Hansard Society), vol. v, 1951, pp. 1–12.

'Some reflections upon the study of history'. An inaugural lecture delivered at University College, Cardiff, 2 March 1954. Cardiff, University of Wales Press, 1954, pp. 27.

'Richard II's Questions to the Judges, 1387', *The Law Quarterly Review*, vol. 72, 1956, pp. 365–90.

'The Fifteenth Century' (review article), *History*, vol. xlviii, no. 162, 1963, pp. 18–27.

'The Landing Place of Henry of Richmond, 1485', *The Welsh History Review*, vol. 2, no. 2, 1964, pp. 173–80.

'Recent Contributions to the study of the Administrative History of Mediaeval England' (review article), *Annali della Fondazione italiana per la storia amministrativa* (Milan), vol. i, pt. ii, 1964, pp. 431–6.

'Sir Roland de Veleville', *The Welsh History Review*, vol. 3, no. 3, 1967, pp. 287–9.

King Edward I's Policy for Wales. A public lecture delivered in the National Museum of Wales, 18 June 1969. Cardiff, National Museum of Wales, 1969, pp. 18.

BIBLIOGRAPHIES

'The Later Middle Ages, 1200–1500', *Annual Bulletin of Historical Literature*, no. xxxiii, Publications of the Year 1947, The Historical Association, 1948, pp. 16–20.

'The Later Middle Ages, 1200–1500', ibid., no. xxxiv, Publications of the Year 1948, The Historical Association, 1949, pp. 19–22.

'The Later Middle Ages 1200–1500', ibid., no. xxxv, Publications of the Year 1949, The Historical Association, 1950, pp. 19–22.

A Select Bibliography of English Constitutional History (with I. A. Roots), London, Routledge and Kegan Paul for The Historical Association, Helps for Students of History, no. 58, 1958, pp. 39.